D0705421

Student Atlas of Anthropology

John L. Allen
University of Wyoming

Audrey C. Shalinsky
University of Wyoming

The McGraw-Hill Companies

Book Team
Vice-President & Publisher *Jeffrey L. Hahn*
Managing Editor *Theodore Knight*
Director of Production *Brenda S. Filley*
Developmental Editor *Ava Suntoke*
Designer *Charles Vitelli*
Typesetting *Supervisor* *Juliana Arbo*
Cartography *Carto-Graphics*

We would like to thank Digital Wisdom Incorporated for allowing us to use their Mountain High Maps cartography software. This software was used to create maps 105, 106, 108–117.

Cover: © Animals Animals Enterprise, Inc./Roger de la Harpe

The credit section for this book begins on page 177 and is considered an extension of the copyright page.

Student atlas of anthropology John L. Allen and Audrey C. Shalinsky, editors. Guilford, CT: McGraw-Hill/Dushkin, © 2004

First edition

192 pp. :ill., maps; cm.

I. Anthropology—atlases. II. Ethnology—atlases. II. Archeology—atlases. IV. Environment—atlases. 1. Allen, John. L. ed. 2. Shalinsky, Audrey C. ed.

0-07-288985-3

301

ISBN 0-07-288985-3 ISSN: 1544-2004

Printed in the United States of America

123456789QPDQPD54

About the Authors

John L. Allen is professor and chair of the Department of Geography at the University of Wyoming and emeritus professor of geography at the University of Connecticut, where he taught from 1967 to 2000. He received his bachelor's degree in 1963 and his M.A. in 1964 from the University of Wyoming, and in 1969 his Ph.D. from Clark University. His special areas of interest are perceptions of the environment and the impact of human societies on environmental systems. Dr. Allen is the author and editor of many books and articles as well as several other student atlases, including the best-selling *Student Atlas of World Politics.*

Audrey C. Shalinsky is professor and chair of the Department of Anthropology at the University of Wyoming. She has taught there since 1980. She received her bachelor's degree in 1973 from the University of Chicago and her M.A. and Ph.D. from Harvard University in 1975 and 1979 respectively. A sociocultural anthropologist, Dr. Shalinsky has conducted research in Afghanistan and among Afghan refugees in Pakistan. Her areas of special interest are gender, ethnicity, and the anthropology of religion in the Middle East and South Asia. She has also conducted fieldwork in the United States.

Acknowledgments

This atlas would not have been possible without the help and advice of colleagues from the Anthropology Department at the University of Wyoming. From formulating ideas to discovering data and discussing construction, they were instrumental in the creation of this volume.

Archaeology: Robert Kelly, Marcell Kornfeld, Mary Lou Larson, Charles Reher

Biological Anthropology: James Ahern, George Gill, Rick Weathermon

Cultural Anthropology: Michael Harkin, Lin Poyer, Sarah Strauss

Linguistic Anthropology: Pamela Innes

We also gratefully acknowledge the assistance of University of Wyoming Professor Emerita Anne Slater, staff members Kathy Fowler and Lynda Payne, and graduate assistant Dena Sedar.

A Note to the Student

Congratulations! You have decided to enroll in an anthropology course at your college or university. You may not know too much about anthropology right now, but you will learn information and concepts that will help you understand the world and your place in it. Anthropology is one of the fields that studies human beings. As the American Anthropological Association, the premier national association for anthropology, stated in 2002, the year of its one-hundredth anniversary, "Only anthropology seeks to understand the whole panorama–in geographic space and evolutionary time–of human existence." In other words, anthropology seeks to ask questions and find answers about humanity in the broadest possible sense. Anthropologists recognize humans as biological creatures who have developed through millions of years of evolution. Anthropologists understand humans as communicators who have a genetic capacity to speak and express this biological endowment in thousands of languages worldwide. Anthropologists view humans as carriers of culture, learned patterns of behaviors, practices, and ideas that enable people to survive and make sense of the world. Anthropologists study the human past and present all around the world.

You may be using this atlas to accompany a course in one or more specific types of anthropology. In the United States, anthropology has traditionally been divided into these four basic areas:

Biological or physical anthropology–the study of human biological evolution and variation

Archaeology–the study of past cultures from the artifacts that remain

Linguistic anthropology–the study of language diversity in its cultural context

Cultural Anthropology–the study of the wide variety of lifeways in the world today

Your atlas contains maps that will supplement your study in all these types of anthropology. Some anthropologists today also consider a fifth type, applied anthropology, to be a basic part of anthropology. Applied anthropology is anthropology that is purposefully set the task of solving important problems. Anthropologists who identify unknown skeletal remains for law enforcement agencies, anthropologists who make sure new oil pipelines do not disturb archaeological sites, and anthropologists who help Native American communities develop educational materials in order to preserve indigenous languages and cultures are all doing types of applied anthropology. Your teacher may tell you about the type of anthropology she or he does. Your teacher is probably an expert on a part of the world in addition to a certain type of anthropology. A typical anthropology department in an American university might have experts on modern South Asian cultures, new hominid fossil discoveries in East Africa, Native American languages spoken in Oklahoma, and the ancient civilizations high in the Andes Mountains of South America.

Some of you will use this atlas because you are taking a course in general anthropology and you will be studying all the types of anthropology: biological, cultural, linguistic, and archaeological. This atlas is designed to accompany a textbook in general anthropology or what is frequently referred to as four-field anthropology. Four-field anthropology classes provide a general overview of anthropology. They frequently follow chronological order beginning with the human evolutionary past; then taking modern humans from their basic adaptation as foragers to urban civilization; and concluding with an examination of linguistic and cultural diversity today. The atlas follows this basic organization of a four-field anthropology class.

This atlas is divided into seven sections. The information provided below describes each section, its organization and features, and how it may be used. Your instructor also will guide you to the sections that she or he finds most significant for your particular course.

I. World Patterns: The Environmental Dimensions of Anthropology

This part tells you about the world in which we live. It is the foundation for all the other sections. Basic political, ecological, and climatic information orients you to world geographical features. You may return to this section again and again to remind yourself of the global context for the specific problems you learn about in your course. For example, if you are studying foraging people, hunters and gatherers, in prehistory or today, you might like to see if there are any common features in the areas where they have lived. If you are studying migration in the aftermath of natural disasters or regional conflicts today, you might wish to check the extent to which environmental zones, political boundaries, and cultural areas coincide using the maps in this section along with those in Sections V, VI, or VII.

II. Physical Anthropology

This section on physical or biological anthropology provides maps on three basic topics: primates and their evolution; hominids (including humans) and their evolution; and modern biological variation among humans. These maps will provide you with information about the biological foundation of our species. You will be able to think about exciting fossil discoveries dating back millions of years as well as contemporary human biological variation. There are many biological differences between people as a result of adaptive responses to past or present environments. Using this section, you will be able to compare and contrast the geographical distributions of human biological diversity.

III. Archaeology

This section on archaeology provides maps on the prehistory of the "Old World": Africa, Asia, and Europe; and the "New World": North, Central, and South America. The time period covered runs from the first emergence of modern humans over 100,000 years ago to the era of European expansion, about 500 years ago. The maps provide you with information about the development of agriculture and urban civilization and even tell you about the diverse places where ancient artistic traditions flourished. In addition, there are maps about the prehistory of different regions of what is now the United States. You may learn something about the archaeology of the place where you live!

IV. Linguistic Anthropology

This section provides information about human languages spoken around the world today. Just as many animal and plant species are disappearing, so too are many languages. Linguistic anthropologists are trying to find ways to preserve the language diversity of our species as many world languages increasingly displace native languages. In addition to information about this important subject, the section provides a map on parts of the world where languages in contact provide the context for the creation of new languages. The section is also useful for the archaeological study of the Americas. One current controversial topic in archaeology concerns how people came to the "New World." The languages of Native Americans, their distribution and relationship to each other provide information about this topic.

V. Cultural Anthropology

This section provides information about human cultures with an emphasis on the contemporary world. Information about population characteristics, how people make a living, religion, family structure, and political systems are provided. You will be able to work within a broad comparative framework in examining contemporary human cultures. You may think about the different ways people obtain food and fuel from their environment, the different family structures that each enable people to raise their children, and the different ways people have organized themselves politically. You may also use this section to help you think about modern conflicts of the last hundred years and their consequences.

VI. The Changing World: Environment and Culture

This section will help you consider how much the world today is changing. You can examine whether all the world's cultures can survive given the many environmental problems we see on these maps. What difficulties might pastoralists, animal herding people, in Africa and Asia confront in the twenty-first century? What might happen to traditional agricultural people? These are some important questions that this section addresses.

VII. World Regions

This section provides you with land features and political units in different parts of the world. Your anthropology course may include specific case studies of one or more of the world's cultures. This section will help you to put your case study in regional context. For example, if you are studying a culture in Native North America, you will find that the North American map section includes the location of Indian reservations today. If you are studying the Yanomami people of the Amazon rain forest, the map of the physical features in South America will be important to your study.

Using this atlas along with your anthropology textbook, other readings, and your instructor's lecture materials should help you get the most out of your anthropology course. As we continue to move into the twenty-first century and consider humanity's future, it is also important to remember and examine where we as human beings are today and from where we have come. Have fun learning about all the people past and present who have been part of our world.

Audrey C. Shalinsky

Introduction: How to Read an Atlas

An atlas is a book containing maps, which are "models" of the real world. By the term *model* we mean exactly what you think a model is: a representation of reality that is generalized, usually considerably smaller than the original, and with certain features emphasized, depending on the purpose of the model. A model of a car does not contain all of the parts of the original but it may contain enough parts that it is recognizable as a car and can be used to study principles of automotive design or maintenance. A car model designed for racing, on the other hand, may contain fewer parts but would have the mobility of a real automobile. Car models come in a wide variety of types containing almost anything you can think of relative to automobiles that doesn't require the presence of a full-size car. Since anthropologists deal with the real world and its peoples, virtually all of the printed or published studies in the discipline require models. Unlike a mechanic in an automotive shop, we can't roll our study subjects and their natural settings into the shop, take them apart, and put them back together. We must use models. In other words, we must generalize our subject, and one of the ways we do that is by using maps. Some maps are designed to show specific physical geographic phenomena, such as the topography of the world's surface; others are intended to portray the distribution of human characteristics across the earth's surface–such as the relative rates of population growth for the world's countries or the distribution of religions. Still other maps may be used to show the relationship between the natural environment and human characteristics: a map of the relationship between human height and weight and the geographic distribution of temperature would be an example. Each of these types of maps is found in this atlas. Learning to read and interpret them requires you to understand certain things about maps: how they are made using what are called *projections*; how the level of mathematical proportion of the map, or what is called *scale*, affects what you see; and how we use *generalization* techniques such as symbols and simplification where it would be impossible to draw a small version of the real world feature the map is intended to portray.

Map Projections

Perhaps the most basic problem in *cartography*, the art and science of map-making, is the fact that the subject of maps, the earth's surface, is what is called by mathematicians a *nondevelopable surface*. Since the world is a sphere (or nearly so–it is actually slightly flattened at the poles and bulges a tiny bit at the equator), it is impossible to flatten out the world or any part of its curved surface without producing some kind of distortion. This *near sphere* is represented by a geographic grid, a coordinate system of lines of latitude or *parallels* that run east and west and are used to measure distance north and south on the globe, and lines of longitude or *meridians* that run north and south and are used to measure distance east and west. All the lines of longitude are half circles of equal length and they all converge at the poles. These meridians are numbered from 0 degrees (Prime or Greenwich Meridian) east and west to 180 degrees. The

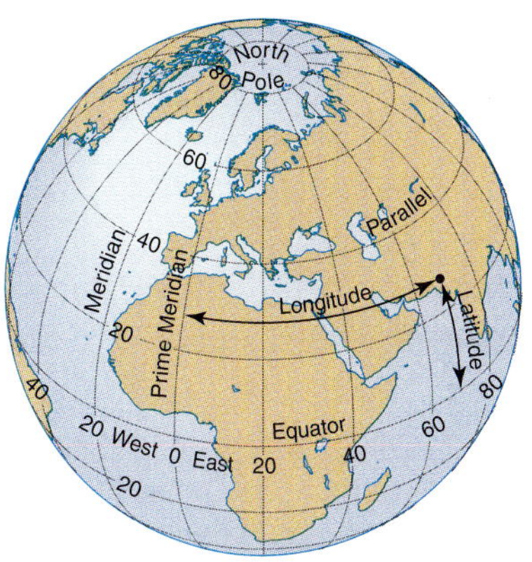
North Pole
80
60
40
20
Meridian
Prime Meridian
Parallel
Longitude
Latitude
Equator
20 West 0 East 20
40
60
80
40
20

The Coordinate System

meridian of 0 degrees and the meridian of 180 degrees are halves of the same "great circle" or line representing a plane that bisects the globe into two equal hemispheres. All lines of longitude are halves of great circles. All the lines of latitude are complete circles that are parallel to one another and are spaced equidistant on the meridians. The circumference of these circles lessens as you move from the equator. Parallels of latitude are numbered from 0 degrees at the equator, and they run north and south to 90 degrees at the North and South poles. The only line of latitude that is a great circle is the equator, which equally divides the world into a northern and southern hemisphere. In the real world, all these grid lines of latitude and longitude intersect at right angles. The problem for cartographers is to convert this spherical or curved grid into a geometrical shape that is "developable"; that is, it can be flattened (such as a cylinder or cone) or is already flat (a plane). The solution to this problem is the *map projection*: a geometric or mathematical conversion process that translates the sphere to a flat surface. It is important to remember that all projections distort the geographic grid and continental outlines in characteristic ways. The only representation of the world that does not distort either shape or area is a globe. You can see why we must use projections: can you imagine an atlas that you would have to carry back and forth across campus that would be made up entirely of globes?

It is also important to remember that different projections have been designed for different purposes. The map at the top of page viii is a Mercator projection, named after the famous Dutch cartographer, Gerhardus Mercator, who designed the projection in 1567 as a navigation aid. Mercator's projection has the unique property of all straight lines on the map being lines of constant compass direction in the real world. To lay out a course across the ocean, a navigator could simply draw a straight line between a European port city and one in North America and then keep his sailing ship "on course" by sailing along the line of constant compass direction ("Mr. Fletcher, set a course of 47 degrees south by west."). Unfortunately, Mercator's projection, still useful four and a half centuries after its invention for navigational purposes, has been used for purposes that were not originally intended. If you look at the

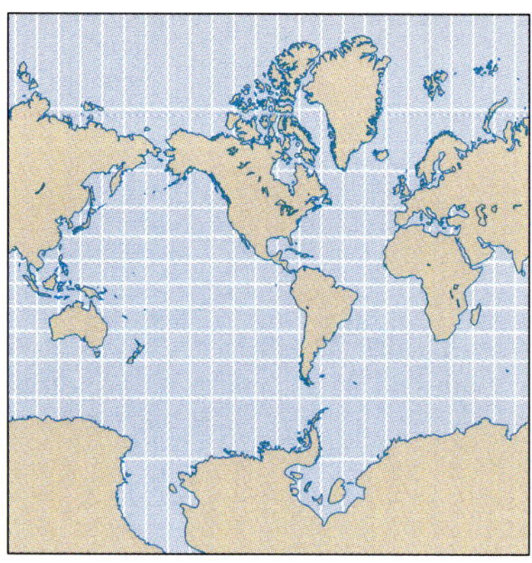

The Mercator Projection

map above, you will note that regions in the higher latitudes (closer to the poles) are increased in area while mid-latitude and low-latitude regions are reduced in area. It is this distorting property of the Mercator projection that makes Greenland on the map appear to be larger than South America, when it is actually less than one-seventh the size! Partly because the tidy rectangular grid of the Mercator projection fits into the way that Europeans and Americans tend to think about space or area, the projection has often been used inappropriately to show, for example, the countries of the world–leaving generations of school children confused about the real sizes of Canada when compared to Brazil and many other areal discrepancies.

In order to make a map that shows regions more accurately in relation to their actual area of the earth's surface, other kinds of projection techniques than those used by Mercator need to be used. Unfortunately, many of these projections distort the shapes of countries so badly that the maps end up being, quite simply put, funny looking. An example of this kind of map is the recently developed Peters projection shown below. The areas on this map are true in proportion but the shapes of continents are distorted.

Often, the solution to the problem of true shape versus true area is resolved by using a compromise projection that shows neither shape nor area in truly proportional representation but gives such a close approximation of each that the world "looks right" and, in fact, the visual impression is much closer to reality. These maps, such as the Robinson projection shown in the next column, are often the choice for atlases like this one. But even this projection can present views of the world that may be biased or culturally inappropriate. The

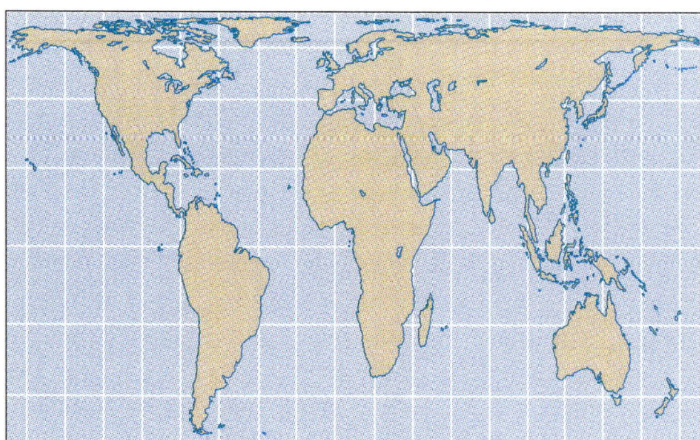

The Peters Projection

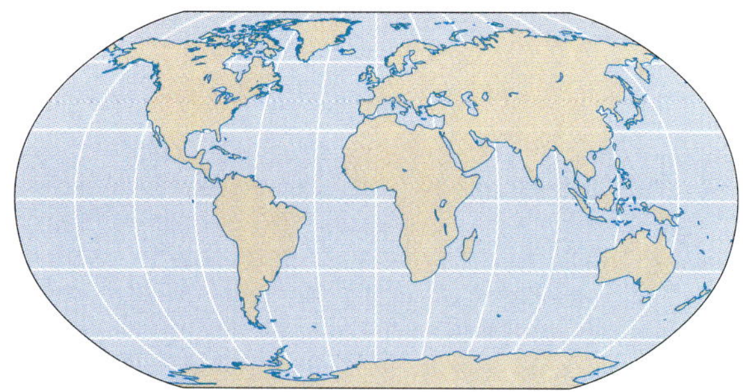

The Robinson Projection
Centered on 0 Degrees Longitude

Robinson projection at the top of the page is "centered" on the Greenwich Standard or Prime Meridian of 0 degrees longitude.

This works nicely for a map that intends to show the continental areas of the world. But suppose that the primary purpose of the map would be to show the Pacific Ocean basin. On the map above the Pacific is split into eastern and western portions. What would the map look like if the projection were centered on 180 degrees of longitude rather than 0 degrees? For an answer see the map below.

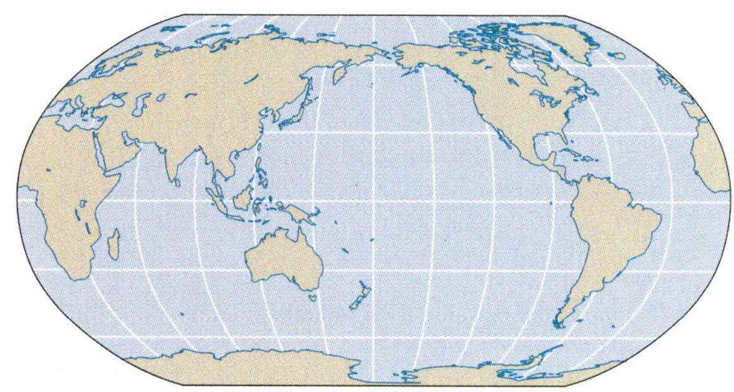

The Robinson Projection Centered on 180 Degrees

See how changing the central point of the projection changes your view of the world? The conventional mapping system for global maps is to use Greenwich Prime Meridian as the center of the map. This allows all continents to be shown without the splitting that would occur if, for example, the central meridian of the map ran through the center of North America. Where a map's central meridian occurs is often a matter of cultural perspective and historical convention. Since so many of our world maps were first drawn in Europe, it was natural that those maps be "Eurocentric." Chinese maps tended to be drawn with China in the center for the same reasons–most people tend to see their own regions as the most important and therefore "central" to maps.

Map Scale and Generalization

Learning about different projections and how they can distort our view of the world is not the only task faced by students interested in understanding how to use an atlas. You also must understand something about the factor of *scale*. Since maps are models of the real world, it follows that they are not the same size as the real world or any portion of it. Every map, then, is subject to generalization, which is another way of saying that maps are drawn to certain scales. The term *scale* refers to the mathematical quality of

Map 1 Small-Scale Map of the United States

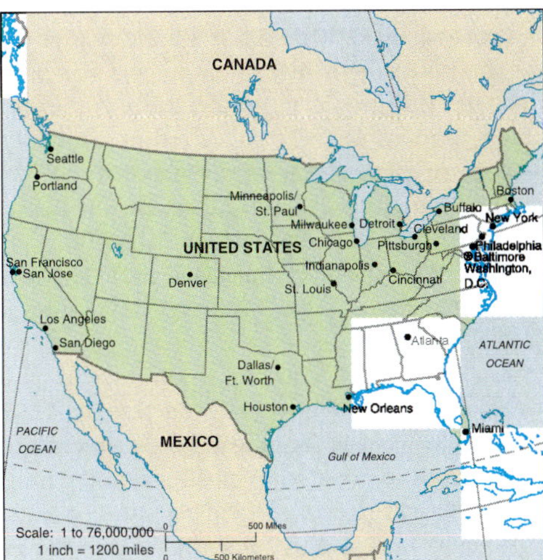
CANADA
Seattle
Portland
San Francisco
San Jose
Minneapolis/
St. Paul
Milwaukee
Detroit
Buffalo
Boston
New York
Cleveland
Chicago
Pittsburgh
Philadelphia
Baltimore
Washington, D.C.
UNITED STATES
Denver
Indianapolis
Cincinnati
St. Louis
Los Angeles
San Diego
Atlanta
ATLANTIC OCEAN
Dallas/
Ft. Worth
Houston
New Orleans
PACIFIC OCEAN
MEXICO
Gulf of Mexico
Miami
Scale: 1 to 76,000,000
1 inch = 1200 miles

Map 2 Map of the Northeast

Scale: 1 to 17,500,000
1 inch = 277 miles
CANADA
MAINE
VERMONT
NEW HAMPSHIRE
NEW YORK
Lake Ontario
Manchester
Lowell
Boston
Syracuse
Rochester
Springfield
Worcester
MASS.
Providence
Buffalo
Hartford
RHODE ISLAND
Waterbury
New Haven
CONNECTICUT
Bridgeport
Stamford
Lake Erie
Erie
PENNSYLVANIA
Newark
Jersey City
New York
Allentown
Altoona
NEW JERSEY
ATLANTIC OCEAN
Pittsburgh
Philadelphia
Baltimore

Map 3 Map of Southeastern New England

NEW HAMPSHIRE
Manchester
Exeter
Hampton
Nashua
Lawrence
Lowell
Haverhill
Newburyport
Fitchburg
Leominster
Gloucester
Salem
Lynn
Worcester
Framingham
Waltham
Medford
Malden
Somerville
Cambridge
Brookline
Boston
Quincy
Weymouth
ATLANTIC OCEAN
MASSACHUSETTS
Brockton
Provincetown
Woonsocket
Attleboro
Taunton
Plymouth
Cape Cod Bay
Providence
Pawtucket
Cranston
Warwick
West Warwick
Fall River
New Bedford
Newport
Barnstable
Falmouth
Norwich
RHODE ISLAND
New London
Nantucket
Montauk
Scale: 1 to 7,000,000
1 inch = 108 miles

Map 4 Large-Scale Map of Boston, MA

CAMBRIDGE
NORTH END
CHARLES RIVER
BEACON HILL
BOSTON
BOSTON COMMON
PUBLIC GARDENS
BACK BAY
CHINATOWN
FORT POINT CHANNEL
SOUTH BOSTON
SOUTH END
Scale: 1 to 95,000
1 inch = 1.5 miles

proportional representation, and is expressed as a ratio between an area of the real world or the distance between places on the real world and the same area or distance on the map. The most important thing to keep in mind about scale, and the reason why knowing map scale is important to being able to correctly read a map, is the relationship between proportional representation and generalization. A map that fills a page but shows the whole world is much more highly generalized than a map that fills a page but shows a single city. On the world map, the city may appear as a dot. On the city map, streets and other features may be clearly seen. We call the first map, the world map, a *small-scale map* because the proportional representation is a small number. A page size map showing the whole world may be drawn at a scale of 1:150,000,000. That is a very small number indeed, hence the term *small-scale map* even though the area shown is large. Conversely, the second map, a city map, may be drawn at a scale of 1:250,000. That is still a very small number, but it is a great deal larger than 1:150,000,000! And so we would refer to the city map as a *large-scale map*, even though it shows only a small area. On our world map, geographical features are generalized greatly and many features can't even be shown at all. On the city map, much less generalization occurs–we can show specific features that we couldn't on the world map–but generalization still takes place. The general rule is that the smaller the map scale, the greater the degree of generalization; the larger the map scale, the less the degree of generalization. But the only map that would not generalize would be a map at a scale of 1:1. And that map wouldn't be very handy to use. Examine the relationship between scale and generalization in the four maps above.

A review of the four maps above should give you some indication of how cartographers generalize on maps. You may have noticed that the first map, that of the United States, is much simpler than the other three and that the level of *simplification* decreases with each map. When a cartographer simplifies map data, information that is not important for the purposes of the map are just left off. Another type of generalization is *classification*. Map 1 above shows cities that have a population of over 1 million people. Map 2 shows cities of several different sizes and a different symbol is used for each size classification or category. Many of the thematic maps used in this atlas rely on classification to show data. A thematic map showing population growth rates (see Map 50) will use different colors to show growth rates in different classification levels or what are sometimes called *class intervals*. Classification is necessary because it is impossible to find enough symbols or colors to represent precise values.

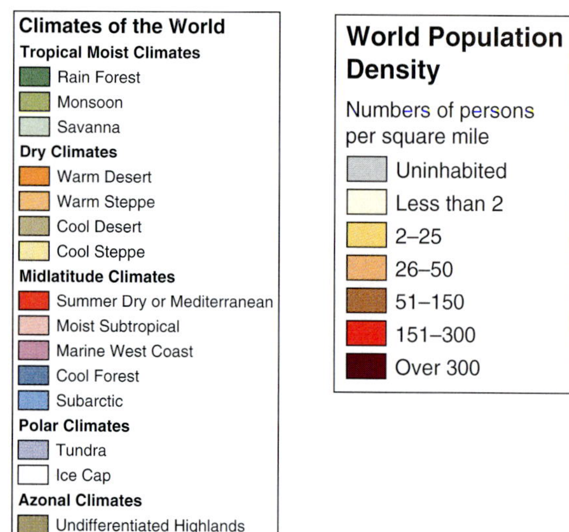
Climates of the World
Tropical Moist Climates
Rain Forest
Monsoon
Savanna
Dry Climates
Warm Desert
Warm Steppe
Cool Desert
Cool Steppe
Midlatitude Climates
Summer Dry or Mediterranean
Moist Subtropical
Marine West Coast
Cool Forest
Subarctic
Polar Climates
Tundra
Ice Cap
Azonal Climates
Undifferentiated Highlands
World Population Density
Numbers of persons per square mile
Uninhabited
Less than 2
2–25
26–50
51–150
151–300
Over 300

Map Legends from Maps 6 and 47

Cartographers show the values of classification levels or class intervals in important sections of maps called *legends*, as on the previous page, that make it possible for the reader of the map to interpret the patterns shown.

A third technique of generalization is *symbolization* and we have already noted several different kinds of symbols: those used to represent cities on the preceding maps, or the colors used to indicate population growth levels on Map 52. Some map symbols are quantitative in nature; others are qualitative. But all symbols are intended to do the same thing: generalize a wide range of very complex data into a form that is readable on a map.

And you thought all you had to do to read an atlas was look at the maps! You've now learned that it is a bit more involved than that. As you read and study this atlas, keep in mind the principles of projection and scale and generalization (including simplification, classification, and symbolization) and you'll do just fine. Good luck and enjoy your study of anthropology through the world of maps as well as maps of the world!

Table of Contents

A Note to the Student v

Introduction: How to Read an Atlas vii

Part I World Patterns: The Environmental Dimensions of Anthropology 1

Map 1 World Countries 2
Map 2 World Physical Features 4
Map 3a World Average Annual Precipitation 6
Map 3b World Variation in Annual Precipitation 7
Map 4a World Temperature Regions 8
Map 4b World Average January Temperature 9
Map 4c World Average July Temperature 9
Map 5 World Ecological Regions 10
Map 6 World Climate Regions 12
Map 7 World Vegetation Types 13
Map 8 World Soil Orders 14
Map 9 World Topography 15
Map 10 World Natural Hazards 16

Part II Physical Anthropology 17

Map 11 Major Primate Groups 18
Map 12 African Apes 19
Map 13 The Evolution of Primates 20
Map 14 Early Hominids: Origins and Diffusion 22
Map 15 Later Old World Hominids 23
Map 16 The Origins and Distribution of *Homo Sapiens* 24
Map 17 Human Variations: Blood Types 26
Map 18 Biocultural Evolution: The Sickle-Cell Trait 27
Map 19 Human Variations: Cranial Capacity 28
Map 20 Human Variations: Body Mass Index 30
Map 21 Human Variations: Skin Color 31

Part III Archaeology 33

Map 22 Major Old World Archaeological Sites of the Paleolithic 34
Map 23 Ancient Forms of Art and Architecture 36
Map 24 Early Neolithic Sites and the Spread of Agriculture 38
Map 25 Megalithic Sites of Europe 40
Map 26 Ancient Civilizations of the Old World 42
Map 27 Major Sites of Ancient Egypt and Mesopotamia 43
Map 28 Ancient Trade Systems of the Old World 44
Map 29 Peopling of the New World I 46
Map 30 Peopling of the New World II 47
Map 31 Ancient Civilizations of Mesoamerica and South America 48
Map 32 Ancient Trade Systems of the New World 49
Map 33 Culture Regions of the New World 50
Map 34 Mound Builder Sites of Eastern North America 51
Map 35 Great Houses, Roadway Systems, and Ruins of the Southwest 52
Map 36 Native American–European Trade: Early Contact Period in North America 53

Part IV Linguistic Anthropology 55

Map 37 World Languages 56
Map 38 Linguistic Diversity 57
Map 39 Modern Languages: Common versus Rare 58
Map 40 The Spread of Indo-European Languages 60
Map 41 Invented Languages: Pidgins, Jargons, and Creoles 62
Map 42 Language Families of Eurasia, A.D. 1500 64
Map 43 Language Families of Africa 65
Map 44a Language Families of the New World: North America 66
Map 44b Language Families of the New World: South America 67
Map 45 Native New World Languages: Interpretations 68

Part V Cultural Anthropology 69

Section A Demographics 69
Map 46 Past Population Distributions and Densities 70
Map 47 World Population Density 72
Map 48 World Migrations 73
Map 49 World Urban Populations 74
Map 50 Population Growth Rates 75
Map 51 Total Fertility Rates 76
Map 52 Infant Mortality Rates 77
Map 53 Average Life Expectancy at Birth 78
Map 54 Population by Age Group 79

Section B Economy 81
Map 55 World Land Use, A.D. 1500 82
Map 56 World Land Use, A.D. 2000 84
Map 57 World Transportation Patterns 86
Map 58 Rich and Poor Countries: Gross National Income 87
Map 59 Economic Growth GDP Change Per Capita 88
Map 60 Total Labor Force 89
Map 61 Female Labor Force 90
Map 62 Employment by Sector 91
Map 63 Agricultural Production Per Capita 92
Map 64 Exports of Primary Products 93
Map 65 Dependence on Trade 94
Map 66 Per Capita Income 95
Map 67 Purchasing Power Parity 96
Map 68 Energy Production Per Capita 97
Map 69 Energy Consumption Per Capita 98
Map 70 World Daily Per Capita Food Supply 99

Section C Human Society 101
Map 71 World Religions 102
Map 72 Household and Family Structures 104
Map 73 Kinship Structures 106
Map 74 Child Malnutrition 108
Map 75 Primary School Enrollment 109
Map 76 Illiteracy Rate 110
Map 77 Female/Male Inequality in Education and Employment 111
Map 78 The Quality of Life: The Human Development Index 112

Section D Political Systems 113
Map 79 Political Systems 114
Map 80 Sovereign States: Duration of Independence 115
Map 81 The Emergence of the State 116
Map 82 Organized States and Chiefdoms, A.D. 1500 118
Map 83 European Colonialism, 1500-2000 120
Map 84 The Middle East: Territorial Changes, 1918-Present 122
Map 85 Africa: Colonialism to Independence, 1910-2000 123
Map 86 Asia: Colonialism to Independence, 1930-2000 124
Map 87 Global Distribution of Minority Groups 125
Map 88 World Refugee Population 126
Map 89 Post-Cold War International Alliances 127
Map 90 Nations with Nuclear Weapons 128
Map 91 Military Expenditures as a Percentage of Gross National Product 129
Map 92 Size of Armed Forces 130

Part VI The Changing World: Environment and Culture 131

Map 93 Global Air Pollution: Sources and Wind Currents 132
Map 94 Major Polluters and Common Pollutants 133
Map 95 Global Carbon Dioxide Emissions 134
Map 96 Pollution of the Oceans 135
Map 97 Cropland Per Capita: Changes, 1987-1997 136
Map 98 Annual Change in Forest Cover, 1990-1997 137
Map 99 Global Hotspots of Biodiversity 138
Map 100 The Loss of Biodiversity: Globally Threatened Animal Species 139
Map 101 The Loss of Biodiversity: Globally Threatened Plant Species 140
Map 102 The Risks of Desertification 141
Map 103 Global Soil Degradation 142
Map 104 The Degree of Human Disturbance 143

Part VII World Regions 145

Map 105 North America: Physical Features 146
Map 106 North America: Political Divisions 147
Map 107a Indian Reservations, United States 148
Map 107b Indian Reserves, Canada 149
Map 108 South America: Physical Features 150
Map 109 South America: Political Divisions 151
Map 110 Europe: Physical Features 152
Map 111 Europe: Political Divisions 153
Map 112 Asia: Physical Features 154
Map 113 Asia: Political Divisions 155
Map 114 Africa: Physical Features 156
Map 115 Africa: Political Divisions 157
Map 116 Australia and Oceania: Physical Features 158
Map 117 Australia and Oceania: Political Divisions 159

Part VIII Geographic Index 161

Part I

World Patterns: The Environmental Dimensions of Anthropology

Map 1 World Countries
Map 2 World Physical Features
Map 3a World Average Annual Precipitation
Map 3b World Variation in Annual Precipitation
Map 4a World Temperature Regions
Map 4b World Average January Temperature
Map 4c World Average July Temperature
Map 5 World Ecological Regions
Map 6 World Climate Regions
Map 7 World Vegetation Types
Map 8 World Soil Orders
Map 9 World Topography
Map 10 World Natural Hazards

Map 1 World Countries

The international system includes political units called "nation-states" or countries as the most important component. The boundaries of countries are the primary source of political division in the world, and for many people nationalism is the strongest source of political and even personal identity. A country's boundaries are an important indicator of cultural, linguistic, economic, and other geographic divisions, and normally they serve as the base level for which most global statistics are available. The political boundaries of nation-states may change. Three hundred years ago, there were different nation-states than there are today. Anthropologists study the formation of all types of political units including bands, tribes, chiefdoms, and states.

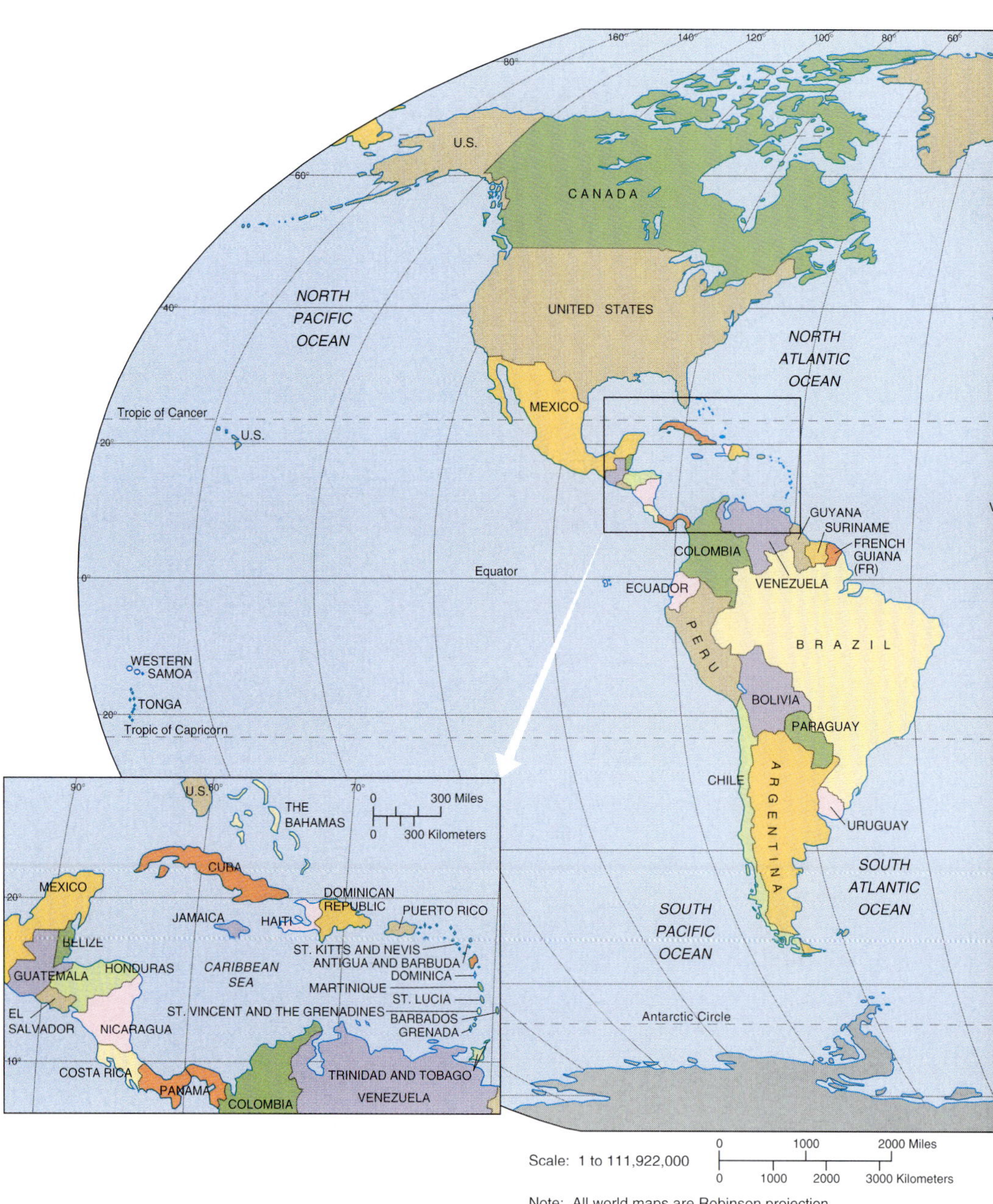

U.S.
CANADA
UNITED STATES
NORTH PACIFIC OCEAN
NORTH ATLANTIC OCEAN
MEXICO
Tropic of Cancer
U.S.
GUYANA
SURINAME
FRENCH GUIANA (FR)
COLOMBIA
VENEZUELA
Equator
ECUADOR
PERU
BRAZIL
WESTERN SAMOA
TONGA
BOLIVIA
PARAGUAY
Tropic of Capricorn
CHILE
ARGENTINA
URUGUAY
SOUTH ATLANTIC OCEAN
SOUTH PACIFIC OCEAN
Antarctic Circle
U.S.
THE BAHAMAS
0 300 Miles
0 300 Kilometers
CUBA
MEXICO
DOMINICAN REPUBLIC
JAMAICA
HAITI
PUERTO RICO
BELIZE
ST. KITTS AND NEVIS
ANTIGUA AND BARBUDA
GUATEMALA
HONDURAS
CARIBBEAN SEA
DOMINICA
MARTINIQUE
ST. LUCIA
EL SALVADOR
ST. VINCENT AND THE GRENADINES
BARBADOS
GRENADA
NICARAGUA
COSTA RICA
PANAMA
TRINIDAD AND TOBAGO
COLOMBIA
VENEZUELA
Scale: 1 to 111,922,000
0 1000 2000 Miles
0 1000 2000 3000 Kilometers
Note: All world maps are Robinson projection.

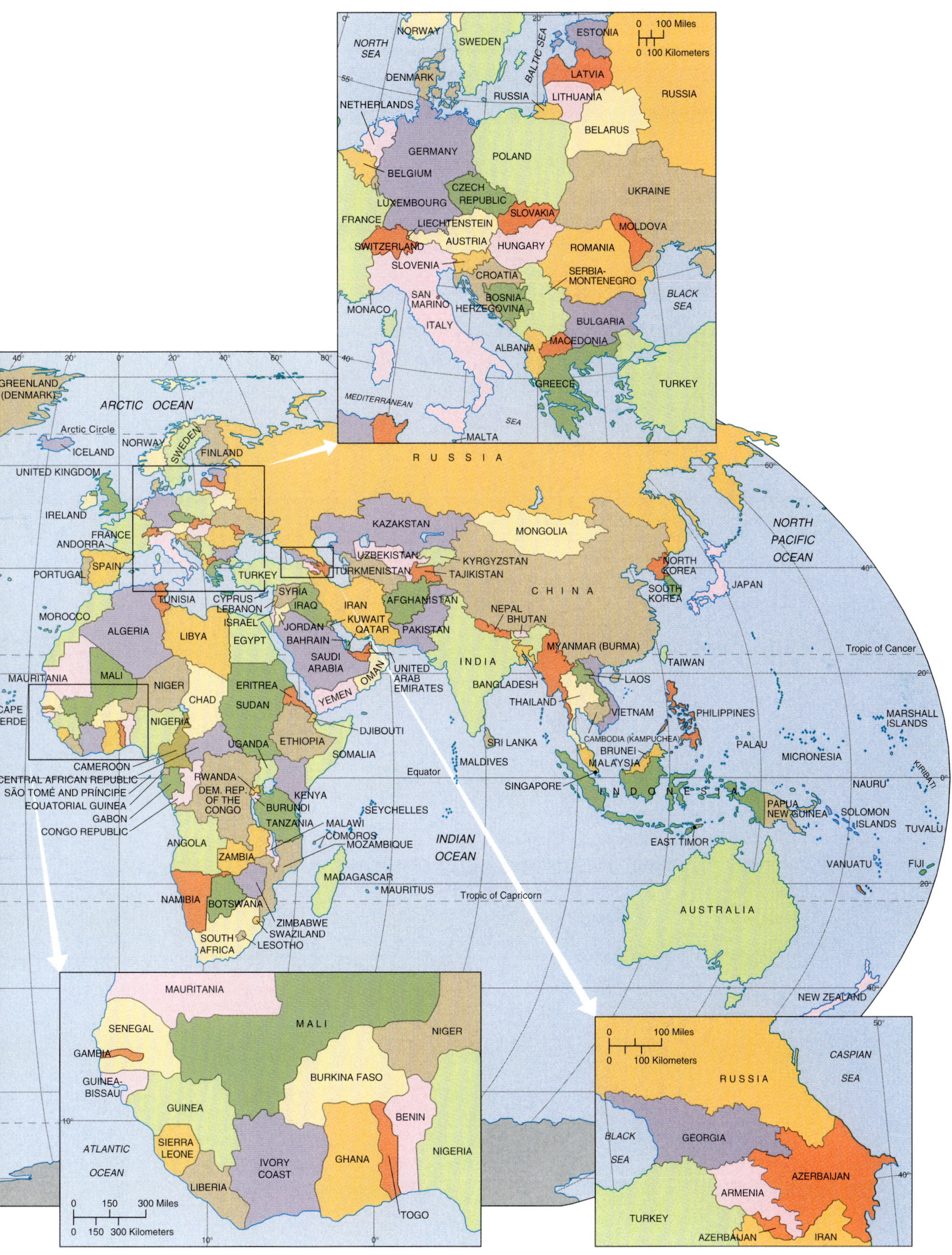

NORTH SEA
NORWAY
SWEDEN
BALTIC SEA
ESTONIA
0 100 Miles
0 100 Kilometers
LATVIA
DENMARK
RUSSIA
LITHUANIA
NETHERLANDS
BELARUS
GERMANY
POLAND
BELGIUM
CZECH REPUBLIC
UKRAINE
LUXEMBOURG
SLOVAKIA
FRANCE
LIECHTENSTEIN
MOLDOVA
SWITZERLAND
AUSTRIA
HUNGARY
ROMANIA
SLOVENIA
CROATIA
SERBIA-MONTENEGRO
SAN MARINO
BOSNIA-HERZEGOVINA
BLACK SEA
MONACO
ITALY
BULGARIA
ALBANIA
MACEDONIA
GREECE
TURKEY
MEDITERRANEAN SEA
MALTA
GREENLAND (DENMARK)
ARCTIC OCEAN
Arctic Circle
ICELAND
FINLAND
UNITED KINGDOM
R U S S I A
IRELAND
KAZAKSTAN
MONGOLIA
NORTH PACIFIC OCEAN
ANDORRA
SPAIN
PORTUGAL
UZBEKISTAN
KYRGYZSTAN
TURKMENISTAN
TAJIKISTAN
NORTH KOREA
SOUTH KOREA
JAPAN
C H I N A
TUNISIA
CYPRUS
LEBANON
SYRIA
IRAQ
IRAN
AFGHANISTAN
MOROCCO
ISRAEL
JORDAN
KUWAIT
NEPAL
BHUTAN
ALGERIA
LIBYA
EGYPT
BAHRAIN
QATAR
PAKISTAN
SAUDI ARABIA
MYANMAR (BURMA)
Tropic of Cancer
I N D I A
TAIWAN
MAURITANIA
MALI
NIGER
UNITED ARAB EMIRATES
LAOS
OMAN
BANGLADESH
ERITREA
YEMEN
CAPE VERDE
CHAD
SUDAN
THAILAND
VIETNAM
PHILIPPINES
MARSHALL ISLANDS
NIGERIA
DJIBOUTI
CAMBODIA (KAMPUCHEA)
ETHIOPIA
SRI LANKA
UGANDA
BRUNEI
PALAU
SOMALIA
MALAYSIA
MICRONESIA
CAMEROON
MALDIVES
KIRIBATI
CENTRAL AFRICAN REPUBLIC
Equator
RWANDA
SINGAPORE
NAURU
SÃO TOMÉ AND PRÍNCIPE
DEM. REP. OF THE CONGO
I N D O N E S I A
KENYA
EQUATORIAL GUINEA
SEYCHELLES
PAPUA NEW GUINEA
SOLOMON ISLANDS
GABON
BURUNDI
TANZANIA
MALAWI
CONGO REPUBLIC
COMOROS
TUVALU
INDIAN OCEAN
ANGOLA
MOZAMBIQUE
EAST TIMOR
ZAMBIA
VANUATU
FIJI
MADAGASCAR
MAURITIUS
Tropic of Capricorn
NAMIBIA
BOTSWANA
A U S T R A L I A
ZIMBABWE
SWAZILAND
SOUTH AFRICA
LESOTHO
NEW ZEALAND
MAURITANIA
M A L I
SENEGAL
NIGER
GAMBIA
GUINEA-BISSAU
BURKINA FASO
GUINEA
BENIN
ATLANTIC OCEAN
SIERRA LEONE
IVORY COAST
GHANA
NIGERIA
LIBERIA
0 150 300 Miles
0 150 300 Kilometers
TOGO
0 100 Miles
0 100 Kilometers
R U S S I A
CASPIAN SEA
BLACK SEA
GEORGIA
AZERBAIJAN
ARMENIA
TURKEY
AZERBAIJAN
IRAN

Map 2 World Physical Features

Sometimes human cultures do not coincide with the boundaries of nation-states. Cultural systems, however, often do adapt to features of the environment. In particular, ways of procuring food and other forms of energy, necessary for the survival of human groups, are linked to environmental conditions.

ARCTIC OCEAN
CANADA BASIN
12,468 ft.
BANKS I.
QUEEN ELIZABETH ISLANDS
GREENLAND
Gunnbjørn Fjeld 12,139 ft.
CHUKCHI SEA
Pt. Barrow
BEAUFORT SEA
VICTORIA ISLAND
7,008 ft.
Baffin Bay
BAFFIN ISLAND
Davis Strait
BROOKS RANGE
Bering Strait
BERING SEA
Yukon R.
Mt. McKinley 20,320 ft.
Great Bear Lake
NORTH AMERICA
Mt. Logan 19,551 ft.
Great Slave Lake
Hudson Bay
988 ft.
LABRADOR SEA
Gulf of Alaska
ALEUTIAN ISLANDS
26,576 ft.
ALEUTIAN TRENCH
Mt. Fairweather 15,300 ft.
Mt. Waddington 13,163 ft.
Mt. Robson 12,972 ft.
Mt. Columbia 12,294 ft.
NORTHERN LOWLAND
LAURENTIAN PLATEAU
L. Winnipeg
Strait of Belle Isle
REYKJANES RIDGE
NEWFOUNDLAND
17,248 ft.
Mt. Rainier 14,410 ft.
Borah Pk. 12,662 ft.
GREAT PLAINS
Granite Pk. 12,799 ft.
Columbia R.
Gannett Pk. 13,804 ft.
Cloud Pk. 13,167 ft.
The Great Lakes
St. Lawrence R.
Cape Sable
Cape Cod
20,700 ft.
NORTH ATLANTIC OCEAN
Kings Pk. 13,528 ft.
Uncompahgre Pk. 14,309 ft.
Grays Pk. 14,270 ft.
Boundary Pk. 13,140 ft.
Blanca Pk. 14,345 ft.
Mt. Whitney 14,494 ft.
Colorado R.
Wheeler Pk. 13,161 ft.
Mt. Elbert 14,433 ft.
ROCKY MTS.
GREAT CENTRAL LOWLAND
Ohio R.
Mississippi R.
APPALACHIAN MTS.
Cape Hatteras
AZORES
MADEIRA
20,664 ft.
NORTH PACIFIC OCEAN
Humphreys Pk. 12,633 ft.
Rio Grande
BERMUDA
Pico de Teide 12,188 ft.
CANARY ISLANDS
MIDWAY IS.
5,758 ft.
SIERRA MADRE
Gulf of Mexico
13,199 ft.
17,921 ft.
22,950 ft.
NORTH AMERICAN BASIN
CAPE VERDE PLAIN
HAWAIIAN RIDGE
HAWAIIAN ISLANDS
Mauna Kea 13,796 ft.
Tropic of Cancer
Cabo San Lucas
Pico de Orizaba 18,406 ft.
WEST INDIES
25,218 ft.
CAPE VERDE ISLANDS
3,468 ft.
15,778 ft.
18,767 ft.
Tajumulco (Vol.) 13,845 ft.
CARIBBEAN SEA
17,783 ft.
MID-ATLANTIC RIDGE
23,925 ft.
Cape Verde
Chirripo (Vol.) 12,530 ft.
Pico Bolivar 16,427 ft.
COCOS RIDGE
Nevado de Huila 18,865 ft.
LLANOS
GUIANA HIGHLANDS
13,783 ft.
Chimborazo 20,702 ft.
Rio Negro
Amazon
Equator
GALAPAGOS ISLANDS
AMAZON BASIN
SELVAS
21,448 ft.
PHOENIX ISLANDS
17,996 ft.
15,877 ft.
ANDES MOUNTAINS
SOUTH AMERICA
BRAZILIAN HIGHLANDS
CAMPOS
Nevado Huascaran 22,133 ft.
WESTERN SAMOA
TUAMOTU
NAZCA RIDGE
PLATEAU OF MATO GROSSO
TONGA IS.
TONGA
SOCIETY IS.
ARCHIPELAGO
ATACAMA
26,465 ft.
TRENCH
Tropic of Capricorn
35,704 ft.
1,079 ft.
Rio Paraguay
Paraná
18,879 ft.
KERMADEC
33,292 ft.
KERMADEC IS.
TRENCH
Nevado Ojos del Salado 22,615 ft.
GREAT CENTRAL LOWLAND
RIO GRANDE RISE
SOUTHWEST PACIFIC BASIN
PACIFIC
EAST PACIFIC RISE
Cerro Aconcagua 22,831 ft.
PAMPA
Rio de la Plata
SOUTH PACIFIC OCEAN
16,963 ft.
17,278 ft.
SOUTH ATLANTIC OCEAN
CHATHAM ISLANDS
13,049 ft.
CHONOS ARCH.
15,998 ft.
20,382 ft.
Strait of Magellan
FALKLAND ISLANDS
SOUTH GEORGIA
PACIFIC-ANTARCTIC RIDGE
Cape Horn
Drake Passage
SOUTH SANDWICH TRENCH
BELLINGSHAUSEN PLAIN
17,192 ft.
1,641 ft.
Antarctic Circle
WEDDELL
ANTARCTIC PENINSULA
15,847 ft.
WEDDELL SEA
ROSS SEA
Vinson Massif 16,066 ft.

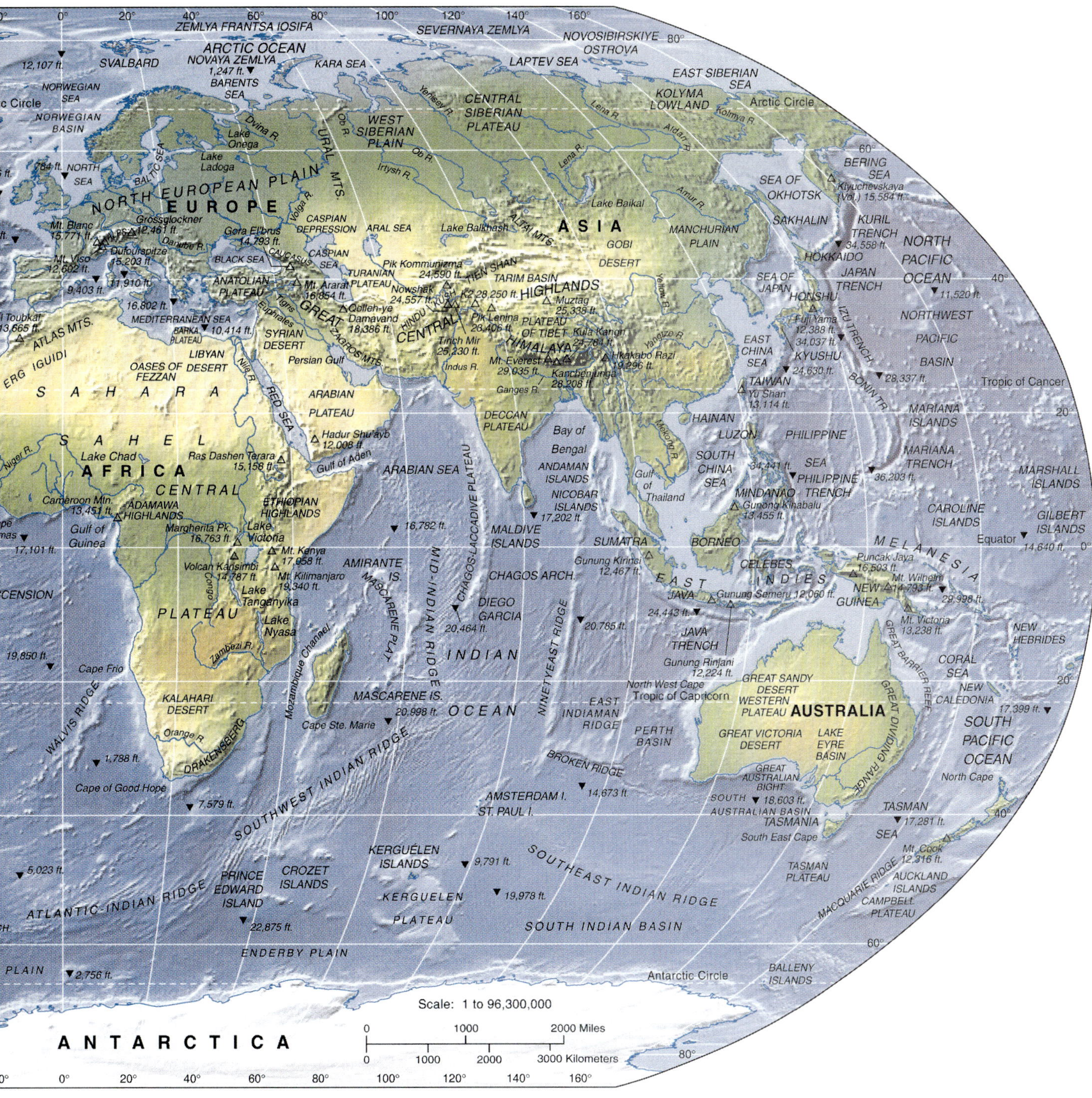
ZEMLYA FRANTSA IOSIFA
SEVERNAYA ZEMLYA
NOVOSIBIRSKIYE OSTROVA
ARCTIC OCEAN
SVALBARD
NOVAYA ZEMLYA
1,247 ft.
KARA SEA
LAPTEV SEA
EAST SIBERIAN SEA
BARENTS SEA
NORWEGIAN SEA
NORWEGIAN BASIN
Arctic Circle
CENTRAL SIBERIAN PLATEAU
KOLYMA LOWLAND
WEST SIBERIAN PLAIN
URAL MTS.
Lake Onega
Lake Ladoga
Dvina R.
Ob R.
Yenisey R.
Lena R.
Kolyma R.
Aldan R.
Irtysh R.
BERING SEA
NORTH SEA
BALTIC SEA
NORTH EUROPEAN PLAIN
EUROPE
Volga R.
SEA OF OKHOTSK
Klyuchevskaya (Vol.) 15,584 ft.
Lake Baikal
ASIA
Amur R.
SAKHALIN
KURIL TRENCH
34,558 ft.
NORTH PACIFIC OCEAN
Mt. Blanc 15,771 ft.
Grossglockner 12,461 ft.
ALPS
Danube R.
Dufourspitze 15,203 ft.
Mt. Viso 12,602 ft.
CASPIAN DEPRESSION
ARAL SEA
Lake Balkhash
ALTAI MTS.
MANCHURIAN PLAIN
GOBI DESERT
HOKKAIDO
JAPAN TRENCH
Gora El'brus 18,510 ft.
CAUCASUS
BLACK SEA
CASPIAN SEA
Pik Kommunizma 24,590 ft.
TIEN SHAN
TARIM BASIN
TURANIAN PLATEAU
SEA OF JAPAN
HONSHU
ANATOLIAN PLATEAU
Mt. Ararat 16,854 ft.
Nowshak 24,557 ft.
K2 28,250 ft.
HIGHLANDS
Muztag 25,338 ft.
11,520 ft.
MEDITERRANEAN SEA
Qolleh-ye Damavand 18,386 ft.
HINDU KUSH
Pik Lenina 23,406 ft.
PLATEAU OF TIBET
Kula Kangri 24,784 ft.
Fuji Yama 12,388 ft.
34,037 ft.
IZU TRENCH
NORTHWEST PACIFIC BASIN
ATLAS MTS.
BARKA PLATEAU
10,414 ft.
SYRIAN DESERT
CENTRAL
Tirich Mir 25,230 ft.
HIMALAYA
Hkakabo Razi 19,296 ft.
EAST CHINA SEA
KYUSHU
LIBYAN DESERT
GREAT ZAGROS MTS.
Persian Gulf
Indus R.
Mt. Everest 29,035 ft.
Kanchenjunga 28,208 ft.
24,630 ft.
28,337 ft.
Tropic of Cancer
ERG IGUIDI
OASES OF FEZZAN
Nile R.
TAIWAN
Yu Shan 13,114 ft.
BONIN TR.
SAHARA
ARABIAN PLATEAU
RED SEA
Ganges R.
MARIANA ISLANDS
DECCAN PLATEAU
Bay of Bengal
HAINAN
LUZON
PHILIPPINE SEA
Hadur Shu'ayb 12,008 ft.
SAHEL
Lake Chad
Niger R.
Ras Dashen Terara 15,158 ft.
Gulf of Aden
ARABIAN SEA
Mekong R.
SOUTH CHINA SEA
34,441 ft.
PHILIPPINE TRENCH
36,203 ft.
MARIANA TRENCH
MARSHALL ISLANDS
AFRICA
ANDAMAN ISLANDS
NICOBAR ISLANDS
Gulf of Thailand
CENTRAL
ETHIOPIAN HIGHLANDS
Cameroon Mtn. 13,451 ft.
ADAMAWA HIGHLANDS
17,202 ft.
MINDANAO
Gunong Kinabalu 13,455 ft.
CAROLINE ISLANDS
GILBERT ISLANDS
Gulf of Guinea
Margherita Pk. 16,763 ft.
Lake Victoria
16,782 ft.
MALDIVE ISLANDS
SUMATRA
BORNEO
MELANESIA
Puncak Jaya 16,503 ft.
Equator
14,640 ft.
17,101 ft.
Mt. Kenya 17,058 ft.
AMIRANTE IS.
CHAGOS-LACCADIVE PLATEAU
Gunung Kirinci 12,467 ft.
CELEBES
EAST INDIES
Mt. Wilhelm 14,793 ft.
Volcan Karisimbi 14,787 ft.
Congo
Mt. Kilimanjaro 19,340 ft.
MID-INDIAN RIDGE
CHAGOS ARCH.
JAVA
Gunung Semeru 12,060 ft.
NEW GUINEA
29,988 ft.
Lake Tanganyika
MASCARENE PLAT.
DIEGO GARCIA
24,443 ft.
PLATEAU
Lake Nyasa
20,464 ft.
20,785 ft.
JAVA TRENCH
Mt. Victoria 13,238 ft.
NEW HEBRIDES
19,850 ft.
Zambezi R.
Mozambique Channel
INDIAN
NINETYEAST RIDGE
Gunung Rinjani 12,224 ft.
CORAL SEA
Cape Frio
WALVIS RIDGE
KALAHARI DESERT
MASCARENE IS.
20,998 ft.
OCEAN
EAST INDIAMAN RIDGE
North West Cape
Tropic of Capricorn
GREAT SANDY DESERT
WESTERN PLATEAU
AUSTRALIA
GREAT BARRIER REEF
NEW CALEDONIA
17,399 ft.
Orange R.
Cape Ste. Marie
PERTH BASIN
GREAT VICTORIA DESERT
LAKE EYRE BASIN
GREAT DIVIDING RANGE
SOUTH PACIFIC OCEAN
1,788 ft.
DRAKENSBERG
BROKEN RIDGE
GREAT AUSTRALIAN BIGHT
North Cape
Cape of Good Hope
SOUTHWEST INDIAN RIDGE
AMSTERDAM I.
ST. PAUL I.
14,673 ft.
SOUTH AUSTRALIAN BASIN
18,603 ft.
TASMAN SEA
7,579 ft.
TASMANIA
South East Cape
17,281 ft.
Mt. Cook 12,316 ft.
5,023 ft.
KERGUELEN ISLANDS
9,791 ft.
SOUTHEAST INDIAN RIDGE
TASMAN PLATEAU
AUCKLAND ISLANDS
PRINCE EDWARD ISLAND
CROZET ISLANDS
KERGUELEN PLATEAU
19,978 ft.
MACQUARIE RIDGE
CAMPBELL PLATEAU
ATLANTIC-INDIAN RIDGE
22,875 ft.
SOUTH INDIAN BASIN
ENDERBY PLAIN
PLAIN
2,756 ft.
Antarctic Circle
BALLENY ISLANDS
ANTARCTICA
Scale: 1 to 96,300,000
0
1000
2000 Miles
0
1000
2000
3000 Kilometers
0°
20°
40°
60°
80°
100°
120°
140°
160°

Map 3a World Average Annual Precipitation

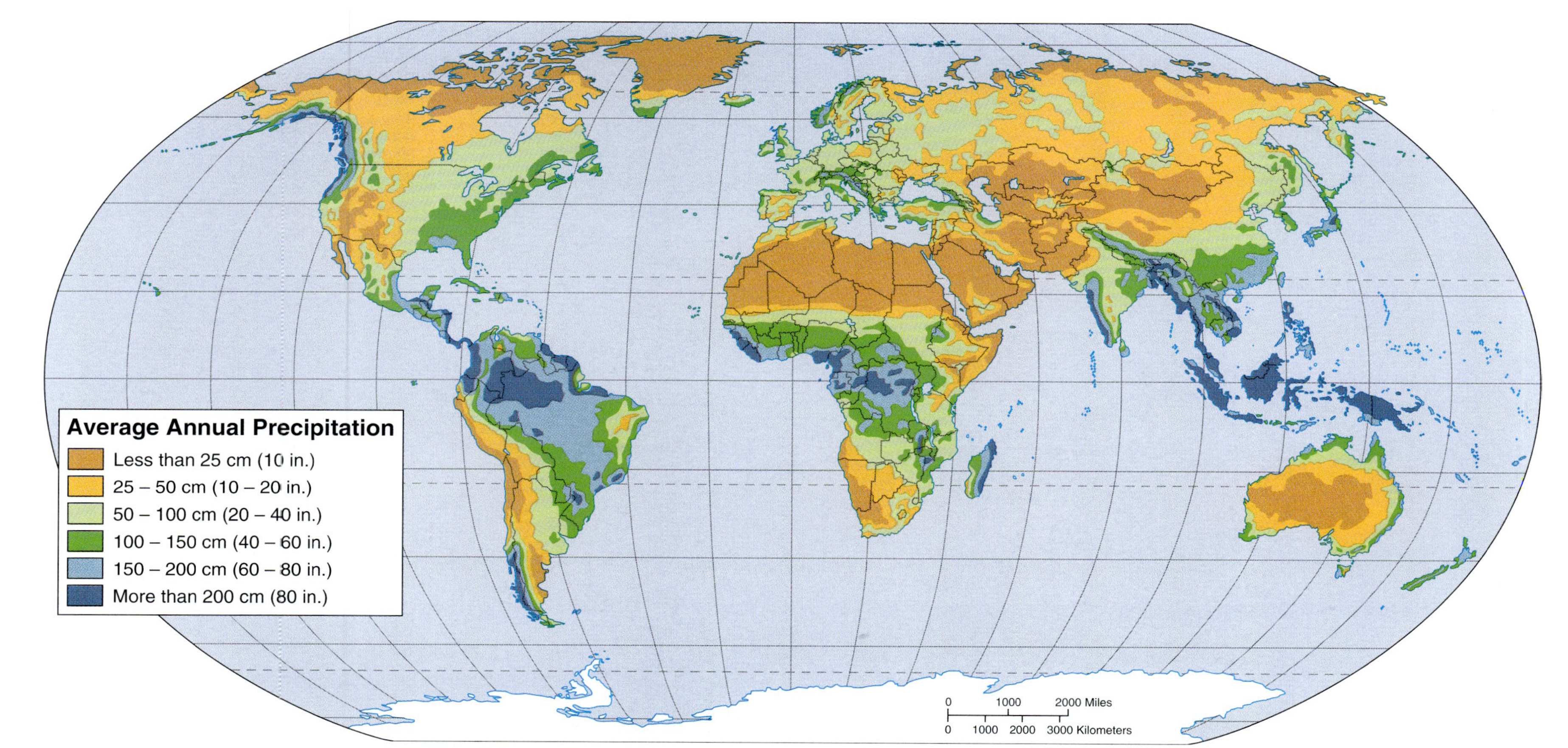
Average Annual Precipitation
Less than 25 cm (10 in.)
25 – 50 cm (10 – 20 in.)
50 – 100 cm (20 – 40 in.)
100 – 150 cm (40 – 60 in.)
150 – 200 cm (60 – 80 in.)
More than 200 cm (80 in.)
0 1000 2000 Miles
0 1000 2000 3000 Kilometers

The two most important physical geographic variables are precipitation and temperature, the essential elements of weather and climate. Precipitation is a conditioner of both soil type and vegetation. More than any other single environmental element, it influences where people do or do not live. Water is the most precious resource available to humans, and water availability is largely a function of precipitation. Water availability is also a function of several precipitation variables that do not appear on this map: the seasonal distribution of precipitation (is precipitation or drought concentrated in a particular season?), the ratio between precipitation and temperature (how much of the water that comes to the earth in the form of precipitation is lost through mechanisms such as evaporation and transpiration that are a function of temperature?), and the annual variability of precipitation (how much do annual precipitation totals for a place or region tend to vary from the "normal" or average precipitation?). In order to obtain a complete understanding of precipitation, these variables should be examined along with the more general data presented on this map. The pattern of subsistence for a human group depends on precipitation. For example, foraging, the use of wild plant and animal resources, or pastoralism, animal herding, exist in regions today that do not have enough rainfall to sustain agriculture.

Map 3b World Variation in Annual Precipitation

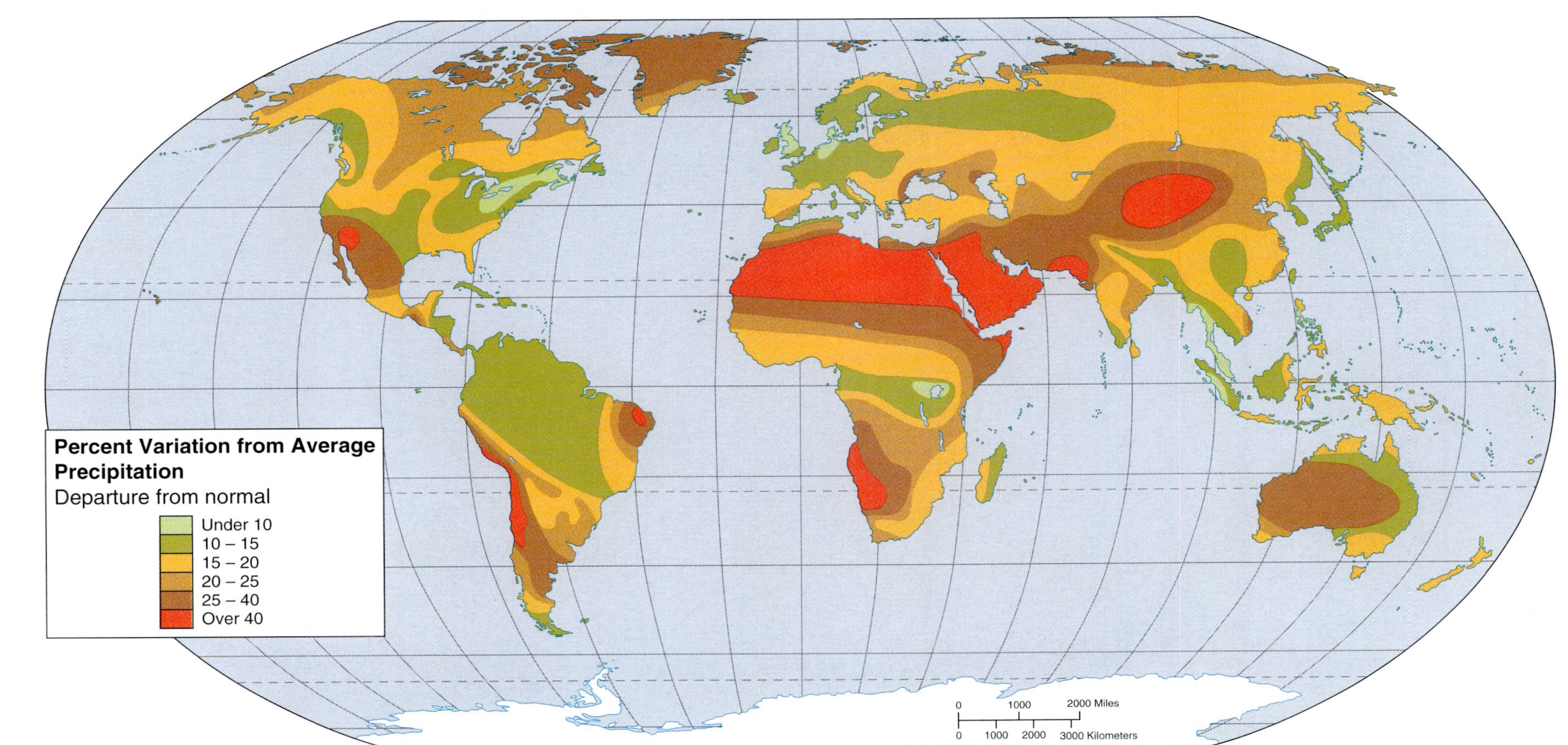

Percent Variation from Average Precipitation
Departure from normal
Under 10
10 – 15
15 – 20
20 – 25
25 – 40
Over 40
0 1000 2000 Miles
0 1000 2000 3000 Kilometers

While annual precipitation totals and seasonal distribution of precipitation are important variables, the variability of precipitation from one year to the next may be even more critical. You will note from the map that there is a general spatial correlation between the world's drylands and the amount of annual variation in precipitation. Generally, the drier the climate, the more likely it is that there will be considerable differences in rainfall and/or snowfall from one year to the next. We might determine that the average precipitation of the mid-Sahara is 2″ per year. What this really means is that a particular location in the Sahara during one year might receive .5″, during the next year 3.5″, and during a third year 2″. If you add these together and divide by the number of years, the average precipitation is 2″ per year. The significance of this is that much of the world's crucial agricultural output of cereals (grains) comes from dryland climates (the great plains of the United States, the pampas of Argentina, the steppes of Ukraine and Russia, for example), and variations in annual rainfall totals can have significant impacts on levels of grain production and therefore important consequences for both economic and political processes.

Map 4a Temperature Regions

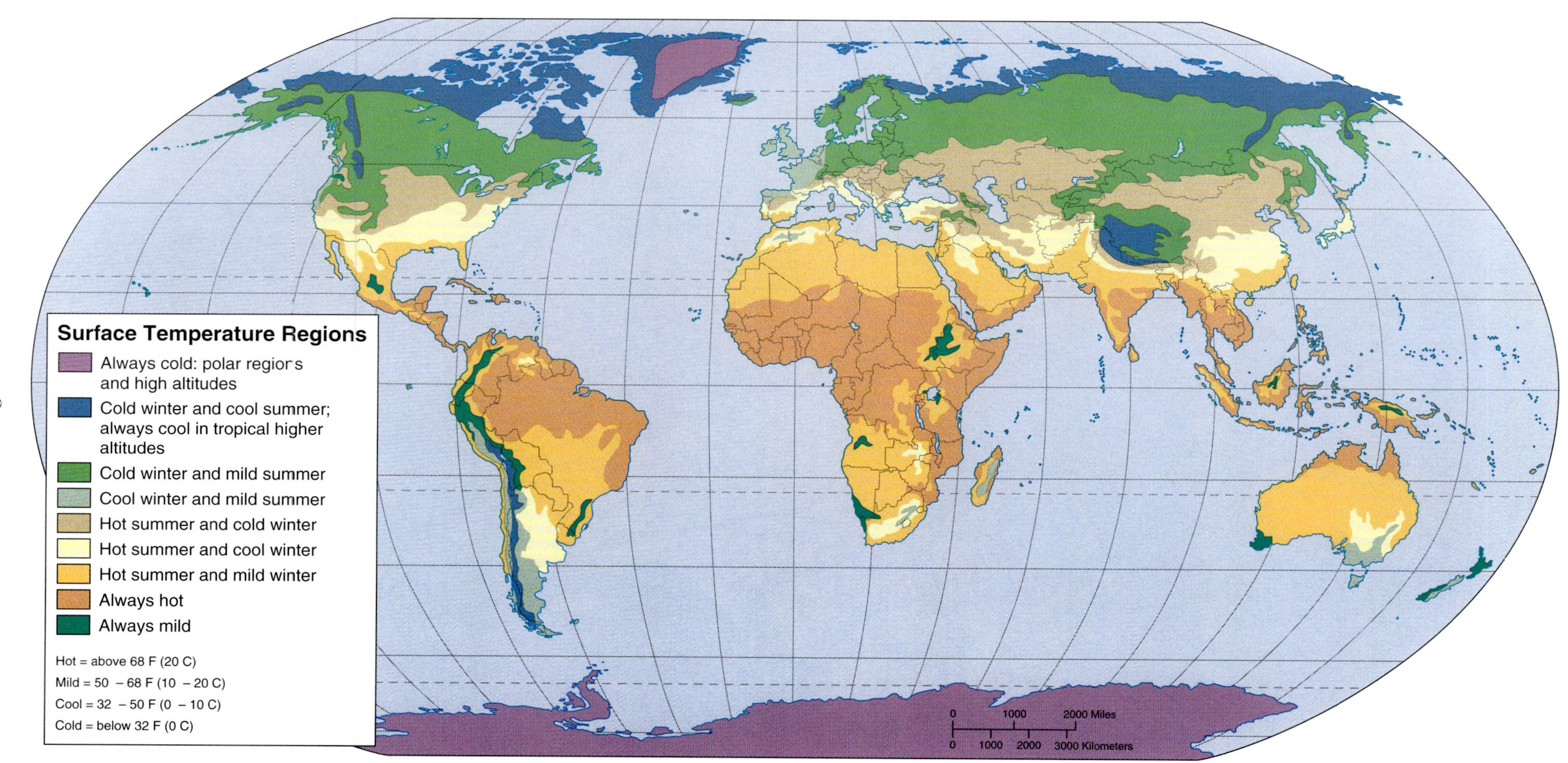

Surface Temperature Regions
Always cold: polar regions and high altitudes
Cold winter and cool summer; always cool in tropical higher altitudes
Cold winter and mild summer
Cool winter and mild summer
Hot summer and cold winter
Hot summer and cool winter
Hot summer and mild winter
Always hot
Always mild
Hot = above 68 F (20 C)
Mild = 50 – 68 F (10 – 20 C)
Cool = 32 – 50 F (0 – 10 C)
Cold = below 32 F (0 C)
0 1000 2000 Miles
0 1000 2000 3000 Kilometers

Along with precipitation, temperature is one of the two most important environmental variables, defining the climate conditions so essential for the distribution of human populations and human activities such as agriculture. The seasonal rhythm of temperature, including such measures as the average annual temperature range (difference between the average temperature of the warmest month and that of the coldest month), is an additional variable not shown on the map but, like the seasonality of precipitation, should be a part of any comprehensive study of climate. Human groups adapt to climatic conditions like temperature through such mechanisms as clothing and shelter.

Map 4b World Average January Temperature

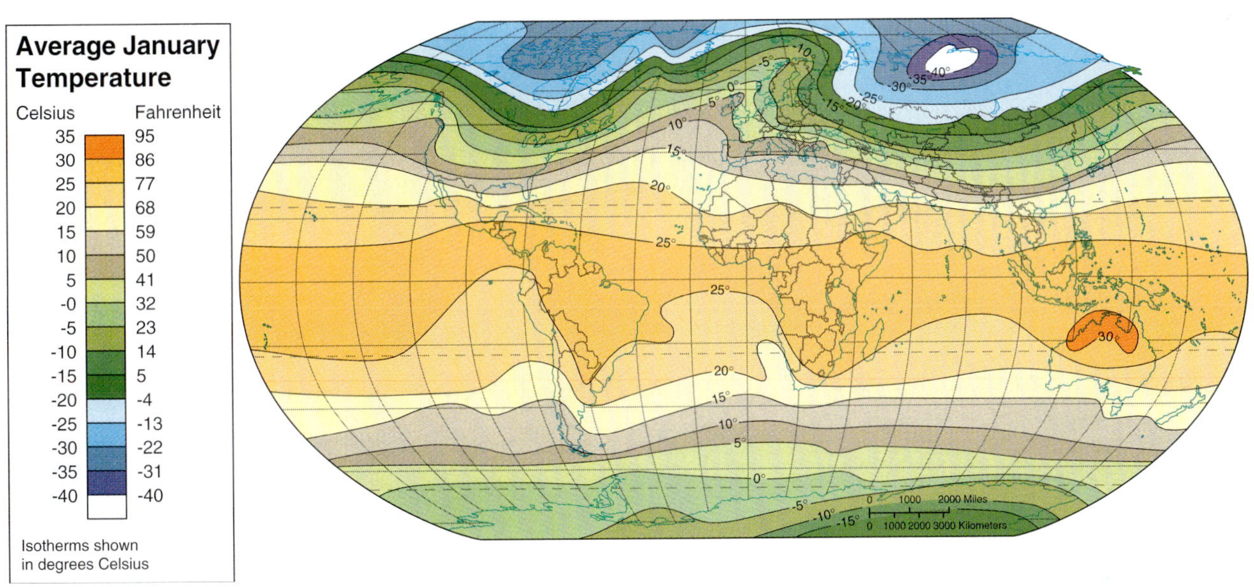

Average January Temperature
Celsius
Fahrenheit
35 95
30 86
25 77
20 68
15 59
10 50
5 41
-0 32
-5 23
-10 14
-15 5
-20 -4
-25 -13
-30 -22
-35 -31
-40 -40
Isotherms shown in degrees Celsius
0 1000 2000 Miles
0 1000 2000 3000 Kilometers

Map 4c World Average July Temperature

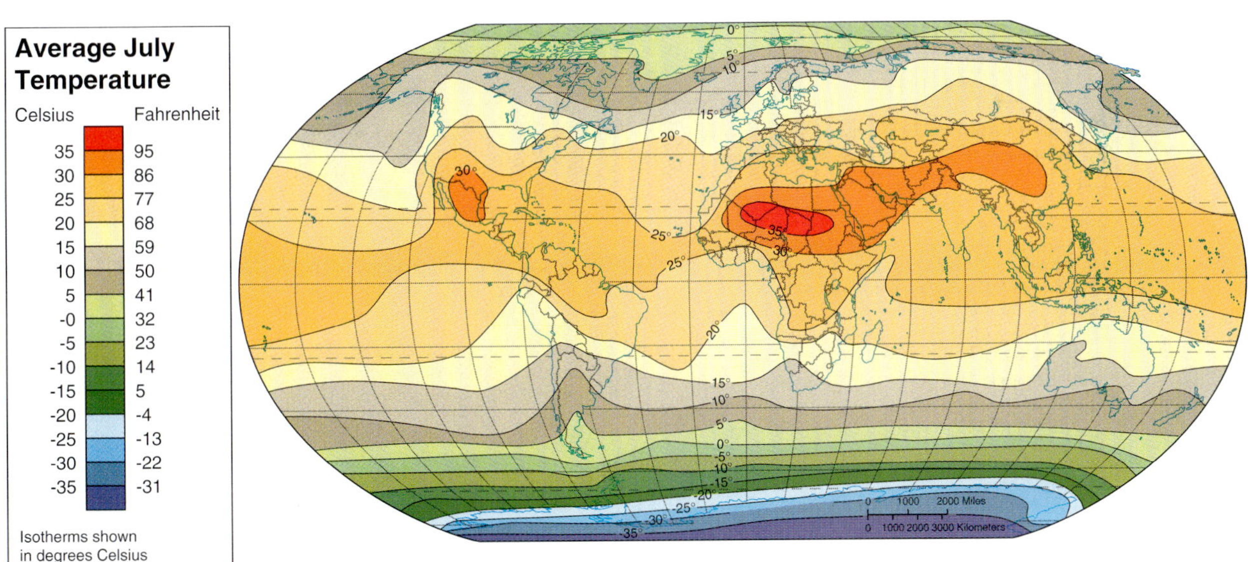

Average July Temperature
Celsius
Fahrenheit
35 95
30 86
25 77
20 68
15 59
10 50
5 41
-0 32
-5 23
-10 14
-15 5
-20 -4
-25 -13
-30 -22
-35 -31
Isotherms shown in degrees Celsius
0 1000 2000 Miles
0 1000 2000 3000 Kilometers

Where moisture availability tends to mark the seasons in the tropics and subtropics, in the mid-latitudes, seasons are marked by temperature. Temperature is determined by latitudinal transition, by altitude or elevation above sea level, and by location of a place relative to the world's landmasses and oceans. The most important of these controls is latitude, and temperatures generally become lower with increasing latitude. Proximity to water, however, tends to moderate temperature extremes, and "maritime" climates influenced by the oceans will be warmer in the winter and cooler in the summer than continental climates in the same general latitude. Maritime climates will also show smaller temperature ranges, the difference between January and July temperatures, while climates of the continental interiors, far from the moderating influences of the oceans, will tend to have greater temperature ranges. In the Northern Hemisphere, where there are both large landmasses and oceans, the range is great. But in the Southern Hemisphere, dominated by water and, hence, by the more moderate maritime air masses, the temperature range is comparatively small. Significant temperature departures from the "normal" produced by latitude may also be the result of elevation. With exceptions, lower temperatures produced by topography are difficult to see on maps of this scale.

Map 5 World Ecological Regions

Ecological regions are distinctive areas within which unique sets of organisms and environments are found. We call the study of the relationships between organisms and their environmental surroundings "ecology." Within each of the ecological regions portrayed on the map, a particular combination of vegetation, wildlife, soil, water, climate, and terrain defines that region's habitability, or ability to support life, including human life. Culture is a way in which humans adapt to their environmental conditions. Culture is also the way in which humans transform their environment. The field or approach in the social sciences known as "cultural ecology" studies human-environment interactions and interrelationships.

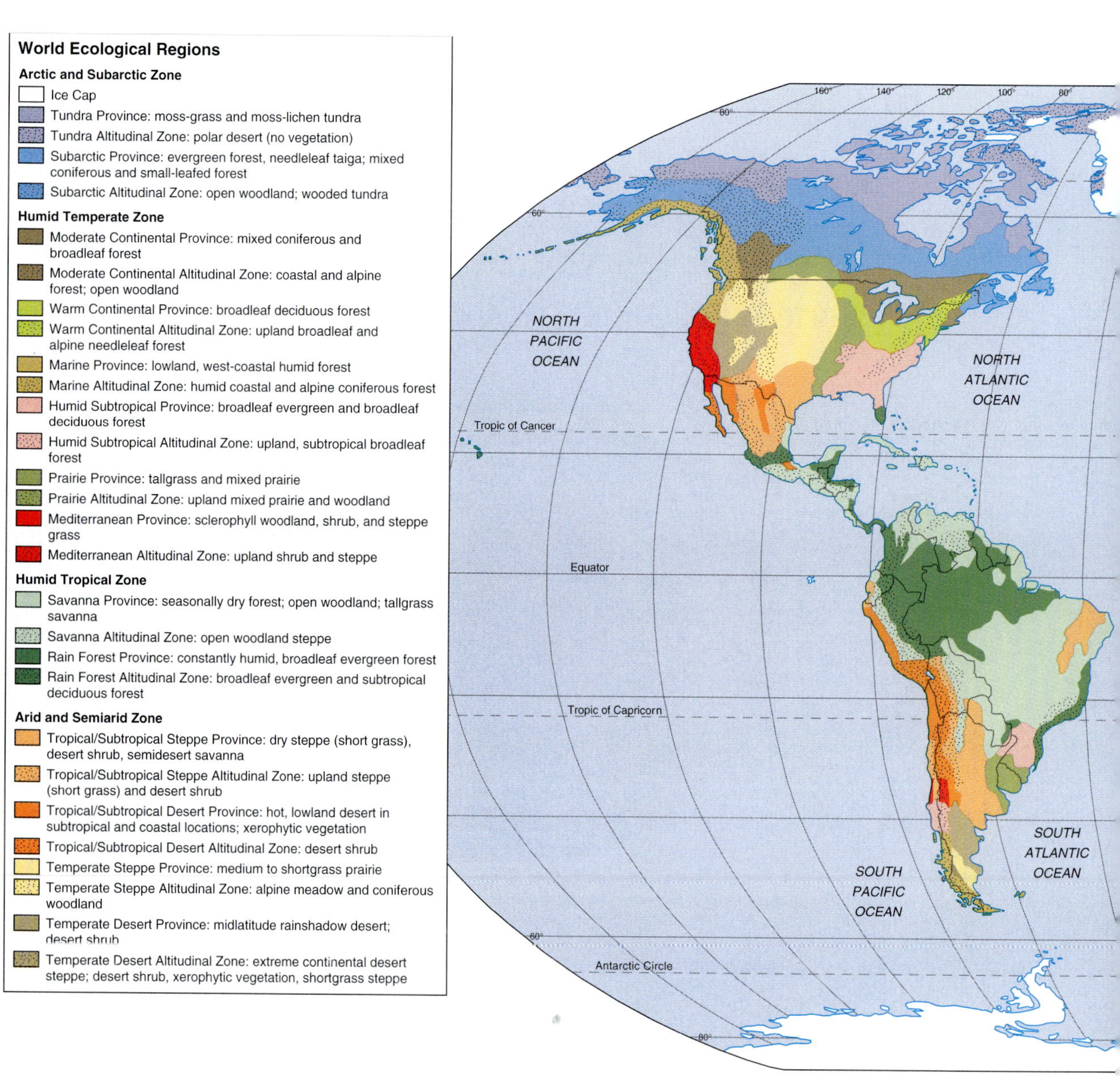

World Ecological Regions
Arctic and Subarctic Zone
Ice Cap
Tundra Province: moss-grass and moss-lichen tundra
Tundra Altitudinal Zone: polar desert (no vegetation)
Subarctic Province: evergreen forest, needleleaf taiga; mixed coniferous and small-leafed forest
Subarctic Altitudinal Zone: open woodland; wooded tundra
Humid Temperate Zone
Moderate Continental Province: mixed coniferous and broadleaf forest
Moderate Continental Altitudinal Zone: coastal and alpine forest; open woodland
Warm Continental Province: broadleaf deciduous forest
Warm Continental Altitudinal Zone: upland broadleaf and alpine needleleaf forest
Marine Province: lowland, west-coastal humid forest
Marine Altitudinal Zone: humid coastal and alpine coniferous forest
Humid Subtropical Province: broadleaf evergreen and broadleaf deciduous forest
Humid Subtropical Altitudinal Zone: upland, subtropical broadleaf forest
Prairie Province: tallgrass and mixed prairie
Prairie Altitudinal Zone: upland mixed prairie and woodland
Mediterranean Province: sclerophyll woodland, shrub, and steppe grass
Mediterranean Altitudinal Zone: upland shrub and steppe
Humid Tropical Zone
Savanna Province: seasonally dry forest; open woodland; tallgrass savanna
Savanna Altitudinal Zone: open woodland steppe
Rain Forest Province: constantly humid, broadleaf evergreen forest
Rain Forest Altitudinal Zone: broadleaf evergreen and subtropical deciduous forest
Arid and Semiarid Zone
Tropical/Subtropical Steppe Province: dry steppe (short grass), desert shrub, semidesert savanna
Tropical/Subtropical Steppe Altitudinal Zone: upland steppe (short grass) and desert shrub
Tropical/Subtropical Desert Province: hot, lowland desert in subtropical and coastal locations; xerophytic vegetation
Tropical/Subtropical Desert Altitudinal Zone: desert shrub
Temperate Steppe Province: medium to shortgrass prairie
Temperate Steppe Altitudinal Zone: alpine meadow and coniferous woodland
Temperate Desert Province: midlatitude rainshadow desert; desert shrub
Temperate Desert Altitudinal Zone: extreme continental desert steppe; desert shrub, xerophytic vegetation, shortgrass steppe
160°
140°
120°
100°
80°
80°
60°
NORTH PACIFIC OCEAN
NORTH ATLANTIC OCEAN
Tropic of Cancer
Equator
Tropic of Capricorn
SOUTH PACIFIC OCEAN
SOUTH ATLANTIC OCEAN
60°
Antarctic Circle
80°

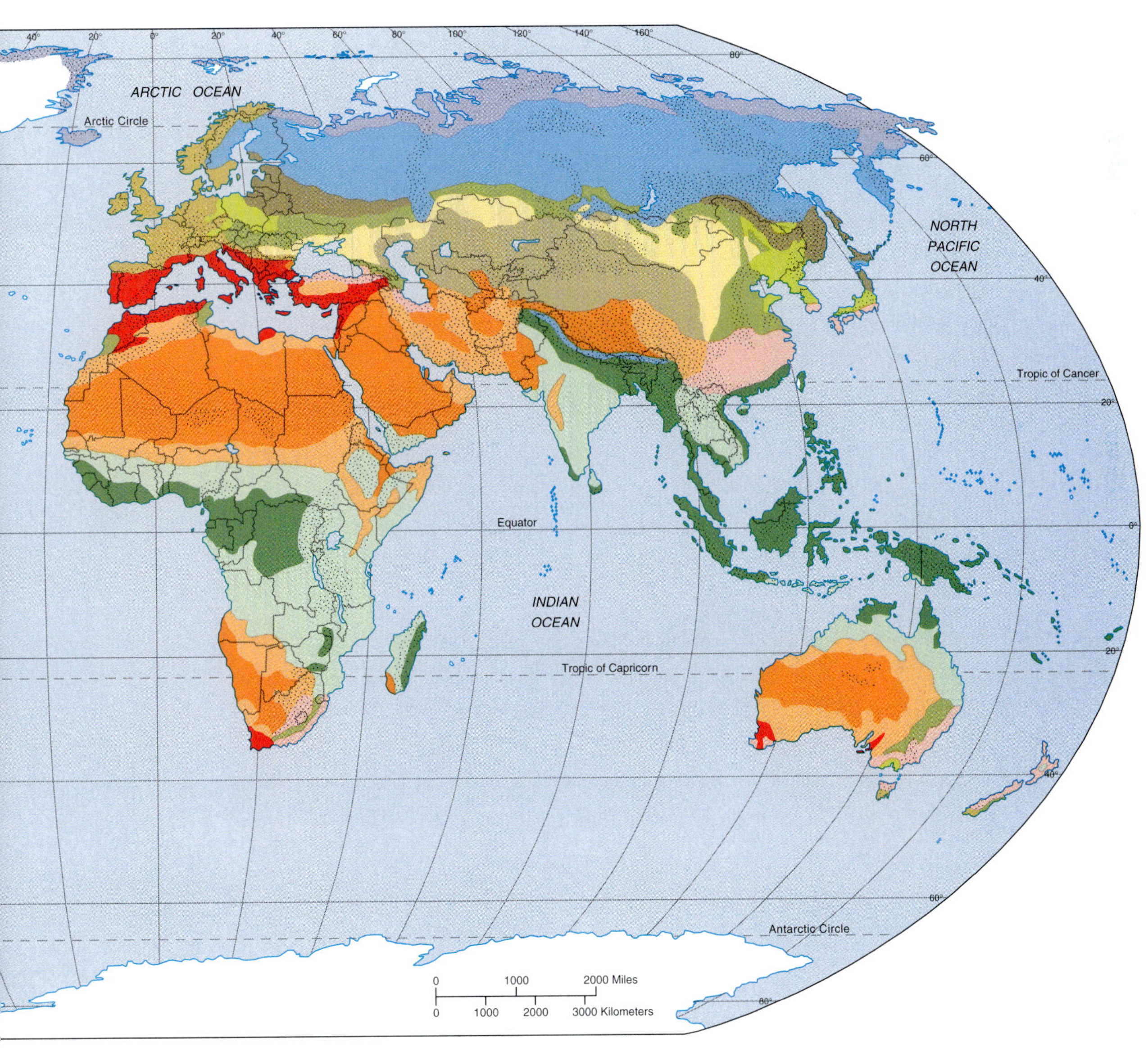
ARCTIC OCEAN
Arctic Circle
NORTH
PACIFIC
OCEAN
Tropic of Cancer
Equator
INDIAN
OCEAN
Tropic of Capricorn
Antarctic Circle
0
1000
2000 Miles
0
1000
2000
3000 Kilometers

Map 6 World Climate Regions

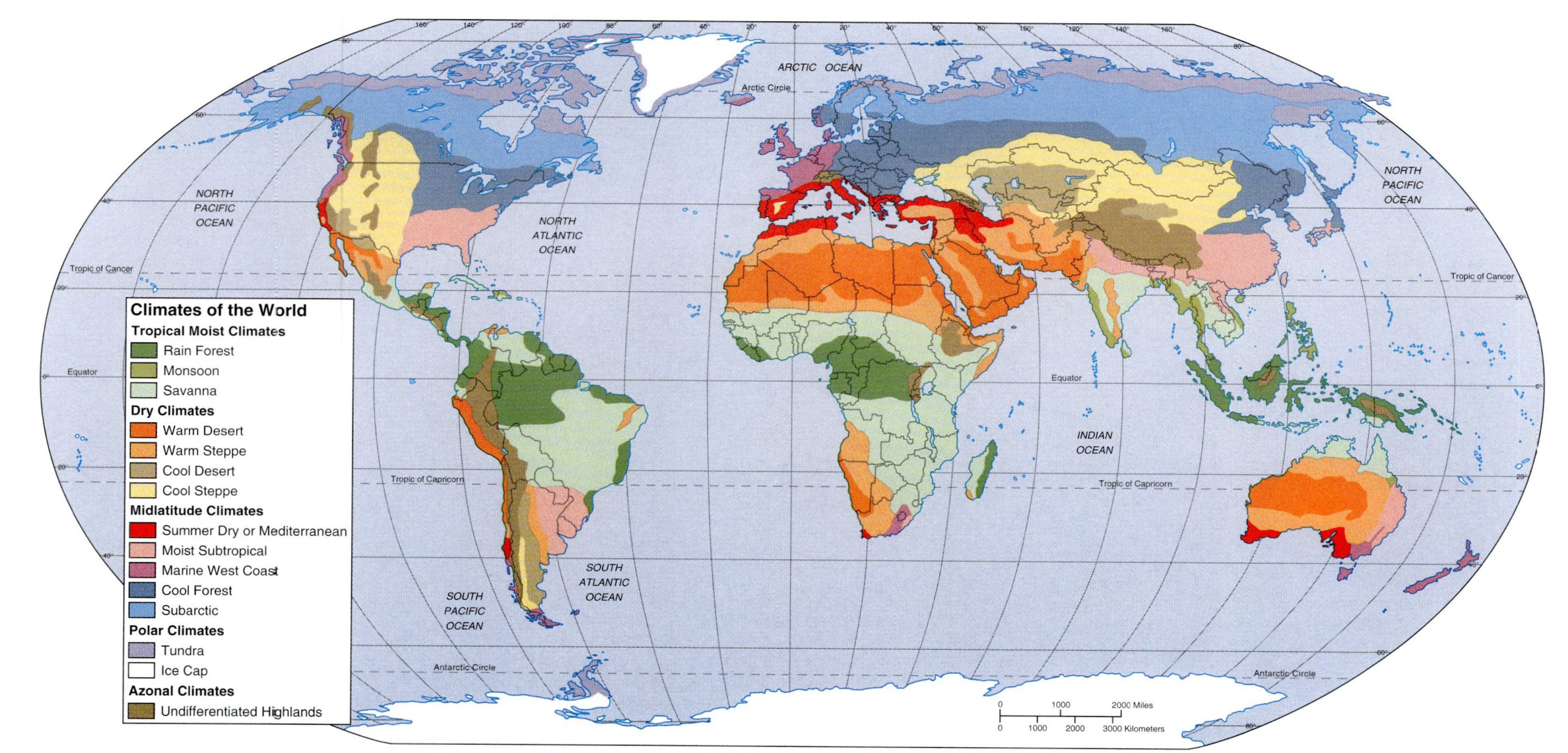
Climates of the World
Tropical Moist Climates
Rain Forest
Monsoon
Savanna
Dry Climates
Warm Desert
Warm Steppe
Cool Desert
Cool Steppe
Midlatitude Climates
Summer Dry or Mediterranean
Moist Subtropical
Marine West Coast
Cool Forest
Subarctic
Polar Climates
Tundra
Ice Cap
Azonal Climates
Undifferentiated Highlands
ARCTIC OCEAN
Arctic Circle
NORTH PACIFIC OCEAN
NORTH ATLANTIC OCEAN
SOUTH PACIFIC OCEAN
SOUTH ATLANTIC OCEAN
INDIAN OCEAN
Tropic of Cancer
Equator
Tropic of Capricorn
Antarctic Circle
0 1000 2000 Miles
0 1000 2000 3000 Kilometers

Of the world's many patterns of physical geography, climate or the long-term average of weather conditions such as temperature and precipitation is the most important. It is climate that conditions the distribution of natural vegetation and the types of soils that exist in an area. Climate also influences the availability of our most crucial resource: water. Climate is a basic determinant of the distribution of human populations as well. Subsistence patterns or ways human groups make a living, whether they are foragers, horticulturists, pastoralists, or intensive agriculturalists, are obviously heavily influenced by climate.

Map 7 World Vegetation Types

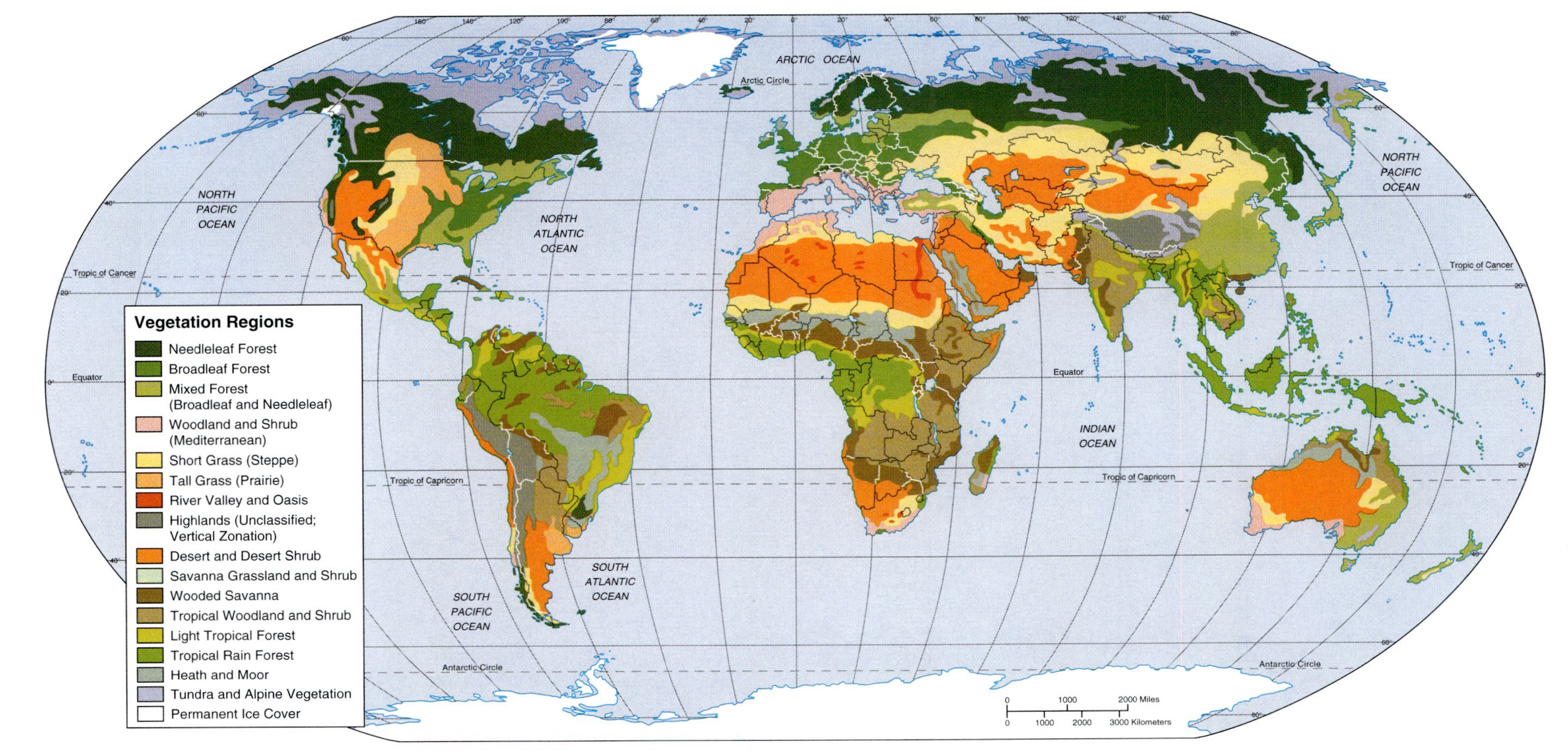
Vegetation Regions
Needleleaf Forest
Broadleaf Forest
Mixed Forest (Broadleaf and Needleleaf)
Woodland and Shrub (Mediterranean)
Short Grass (Steppe)
Tall Grass (Prairie)
River Valley and Oasis
Highlands (Unclassified; Vertical Zonation)
Desert and Desert Shrub
Savanna Grassland and Shrub
Wooded Savanna
Tropical Woodland and Shrub
Light Tropical Forest
Tropical Rain Forest
Heath and Moor
Tundra and Alpine Vegetation
Permanent Ice Cover
ARCTIC OCEAN
Arctic Circle
NORTH PACIFIC OCEAN
NORTH ATLANTIC OCEAN
SOUTH PACIFIC OCEAN
SOUTH ATLANTIC OCEAN
INDIAN OCEAN
NORTH PACIFIC OCEAN
Tropic of Cancer
Equator
Tropic of Capricorn
Antarctic Circle
0 1000 2000 Miles
0 1000 2000 3000 Kilometers

Vegetation is the most visible consequence of the distribution of temperature and precipitation. The global pattern of vegetative types or "habitat classes" and the global pattern of climate are closely related and make up one of the great global spatial correlations. But not all vegetation types are the consequence of temperature and precipitation or other climatic variables. Many types of vegetation in many areas of the world are the consequence of human activities, particularly the grazing of domesticated livestock, burning, and forest clearance. This map shows the pattern of natural or "potential" vegetation, or vegetation as it might be expected to exist without significant human influences, rather than the actual vegetation that results from a combination of environmental and human factors.

Map 8 World Soil Orders

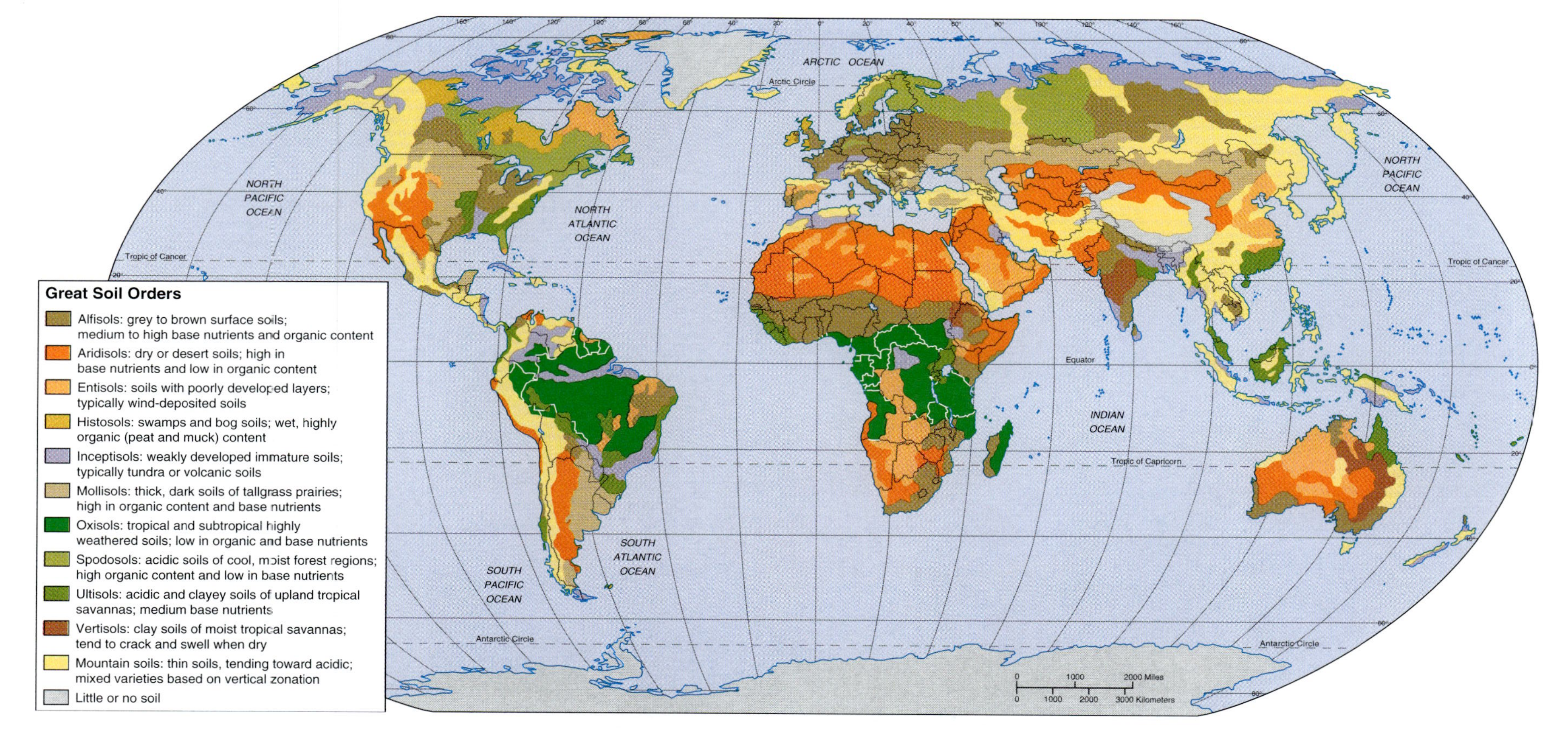

Great Soil Orders
Alfisols: grey to brown surface soils; medium to high base nutrients and organic content
Aridisols: dry or desert soils; high in base nutrients and low in organic content
Entisols: soils with poorly developed layers; typically wind-deposited soils
Histosols: swamps and bog soils; wet, highly organic (peat and muck) content
Inceptisols: weakly developed immature soils; typically tundra or volcanic soils
Mollisols: thick, dark soils of tallgrass prairies; high in organic content and base nutrients
Oxisols: tropical and subtropical highly weathered soils; low in organic and base nutrients
Spodosols: acidic soils of cool, moist forest regions; high organic content and low in base nutrients
Ultisols: acidic and clayey soils of upland tropical savannas; medium base nutrients
Vertisols: clay soils of moist tropical savannas; tend to crack and swell when dry
Mountain soils: thin soils, tending toward acidic; mixed varieties based on vertical zonation
Little or no soil
ARCTIC OCEAN
Arctic Circle
NORTH PACIFIC OCEAN
NORTH ATLANTIC OCEAN
NORTH PACIFIC OCEAN
Tropic of Cancer
Tropic of Cancer
Equator
INDIAN OCEAN
Tropic of Capricorn
SOUTH ATLANTIC OCEAN
SOUTH PACIFIC OCEAN
Antarctic Circle
Antarctic Circle
0 1000 2000 Miles
0 1000 2000 3000 Kilometers

The characteristics of soil are one of the three primary physical geographic factors, along with climate and vegetation, which determine the habitability of regions for humans. In particular, soils influence the kinds of agricultural uses to which land is put. Since soils support the plants that are the primary producers of all food in the terrestrial food chain, their characteristics are crucial to the health and stability of ecosystems. Two types of soil are shown on this map: zonal soils, the characteristics of which are based on climatic patterns; and azonal soils, such as alluvial (water-deposited) or aeolian (wind-deposited) soils, the characteristics of which are derived from forces other than climate. Many of the azonal soils, however, particularly those dependent upon drainage conditions, appear over areas too small to be readily shown on a map of this scale. Thus, almost none of the world's swamp or bog soils appear on this map.

Map 9 World Topography

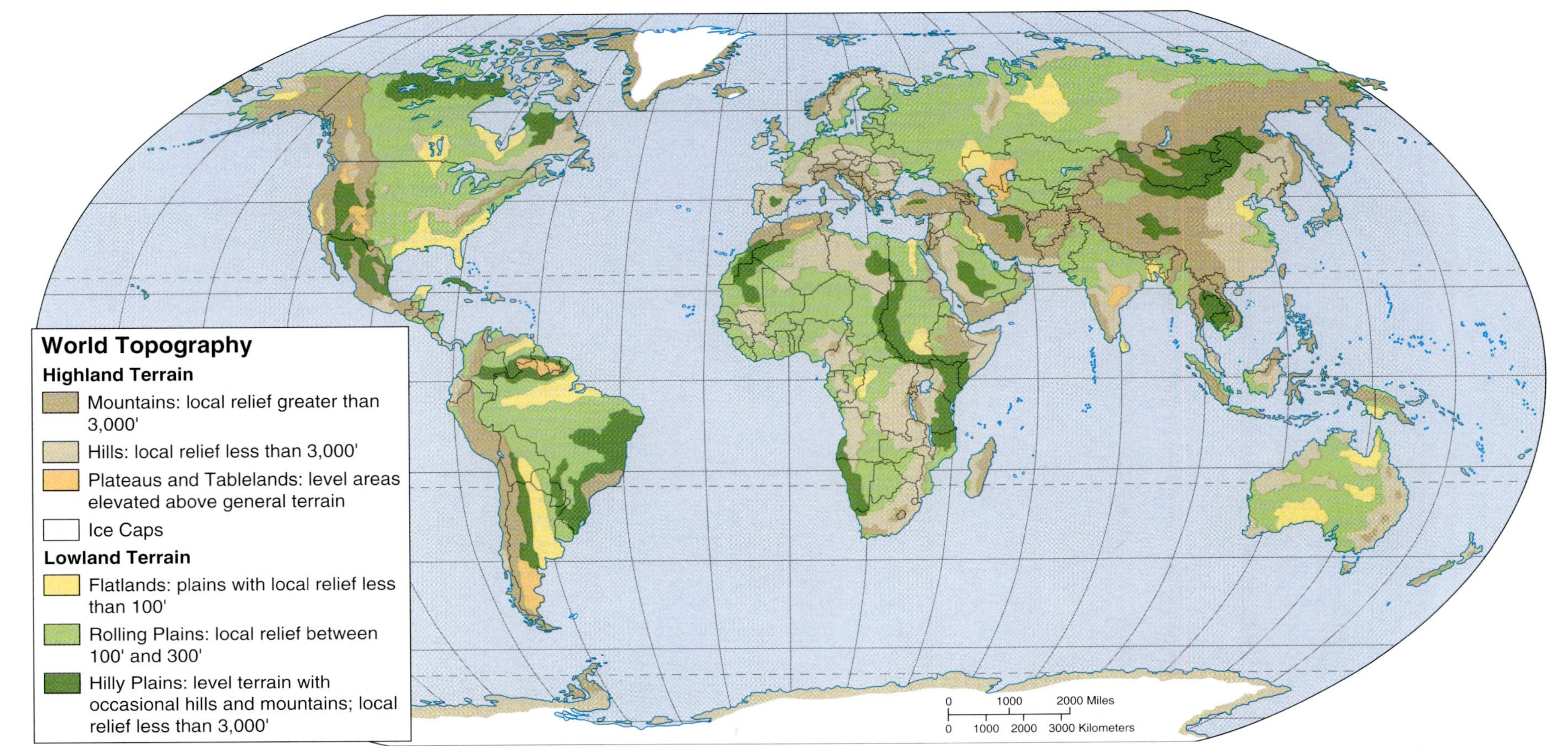
World Topography
Highland Terrain
Mountains: local relief greater than 3,000'
Hills: local relief less than 3,000'
Plateaus and Tablelands: level areas elevated above general terrain
Ice Caps
Lowland Terrain
Flatlands: plains with local relief less than 100'
Rolling Plains: local relief between 100' and 300'
Hilly Plains: level terrain with occasional hills and mountains; local relief less than 3,000'
0 1000 2000 Miles
0 1000 2000 3000 Kilometers

Topography or terrain, also called "landforms," is second only to climate as a conditioner of human activity, particularly agriculture but also the location of cities and industry. A comparison of this map of mountains, valleys, plains, plateaus, and other features of the earth's surface with a map of land use (Map 58) shows that most of the world's productive agricultural zones are located in lowland and relatively level regions. Where large regions of agricultural productivity are found, we also tend to find urban concentrations and, with cities, we find industry. There is also a good spatial correlation between the map of topography and the map showing the distribution and density of the human population (Map 47). Normally the world's major landforms are the result of extremely gradual primary geologic activity such as the long-term movement of crustal plates. This activity occurs over hundreds of millions of years. Also important is the more rapid (but still slow by human standards) geomorphological or erosional activity of water, wind, glacial ice, and waves, tides, and currents. Some landforms may be produced by abrupt or "cataclysmic" events such as a major volcanic eruption or a meteor strike, but such events are relatively rare and their effects are usually too minor to show up on a map of this scale.

Map 10 World Natural Hazards

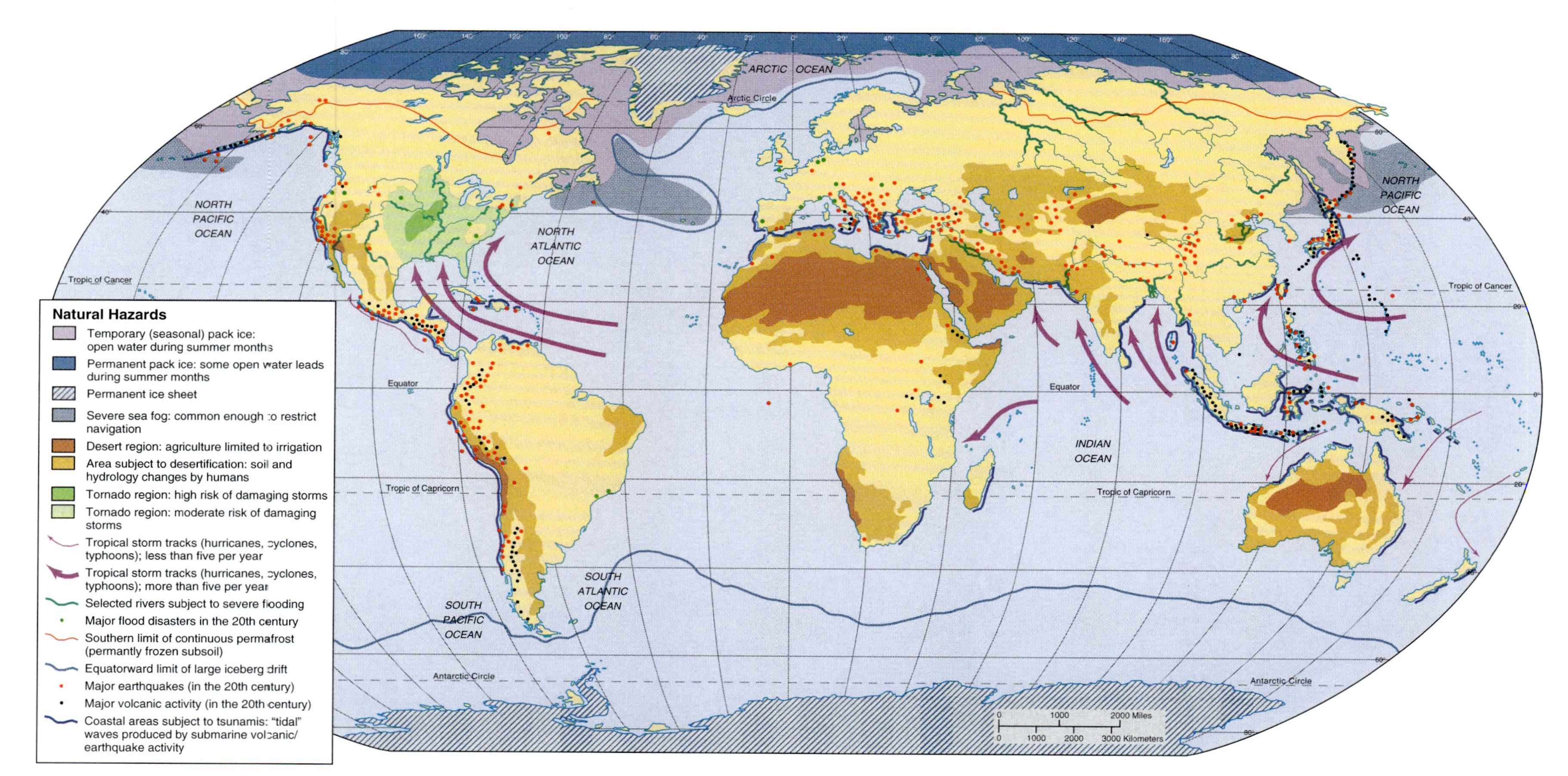
ARCTIC OCEAN
Arctic Circle
NORTH PACIFIC OCEAN
NORTH ATLANTIC OCEAN
NORTH PACIFIC OCEAN
Tropic of Cancer
Equator
INDIAN OCEAN
Tropic of Capricorn
SOUTH PACIFIC OCEAN
SOUTH ATLANTIC OCEAN
Antarctic Circle
0 1000 2000 Miles
0 1000 2000 3000 Kilometers
Natural Hazards
Temporary (seasonal) pack ice: open water during summer months
Permanent pack ice: some open water leads during summer months
Permanent ice sheet
Severe sea fog: common enough to restrict navigation
Desert region: agriculture limited to irrigation
Area subject to desertification: soil and hydrology changes by humans
Tornado region: high risk of damaging storms
Tornado region: moderate risk of damaging storms
Tropical storm tracks (hurricanes, cyclones, typhoons); less than five per year
Tropical storm tracks (hurricanes, cyclones, typhoons); more than five per year
Selected rivers subject to severe flooding
Major flood disasters in the 20th century
Southern limit of continuous permafrost (permantly frozen subsoil)
Equatorward limit of large iceberg drift
Major earthquakes (in the 20th century)
Major volcanic activity (in the 20th century)
Coastal areas subject to tsunamis: "tidal" waves produced by submarine volcanic/ earthquake activity

Unlike other elements of physical geography, most natural hazards are unpredictable. There are certain regions, however, where the *probability* of the occurrence of a particular natural hazard is high. This map shows regions affected by major natural hazards at rates that are higher than the global norm. The presence of persistent natural hazards may influence the types of modifications that people make in the environment and certainly influence the styles of housing and other cultural features. Natural hazards may also undermine the utility of an area for economic purposes, and some scholars suggest that regions of environmental instability may be regions of political instability as well.

Part II

Physical Anthropology

Map 11 Major Primate Groups
Map 12 African Apes
Map 13 The Evolution of Primates
Map 14 Early Hominids: Origins and Diffusion
Map 15 Later Old World Hominids
Map 16 The Origins and Distribution of *Homo Sapiens*
Map 17 Human Variations: Blood Types
Map 18 Biocultural Evolution: The Sickle-Cell Trait
Map 19 Human Variations: Cranial Capacity
Map 20 Human Variations: Body Mass Index
Map 21 Human Variations: Skin Color

Map 11 Major Primate Groups

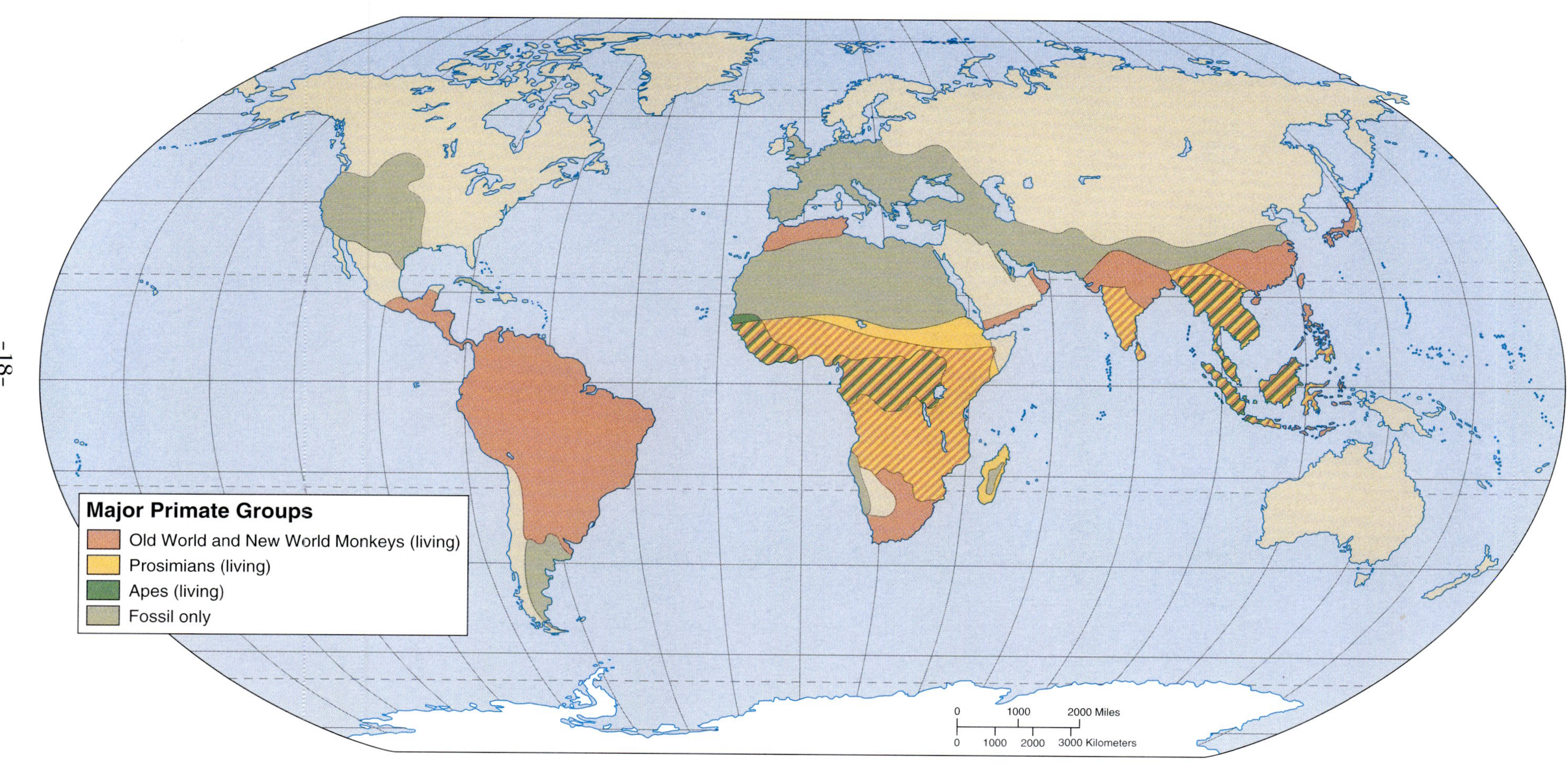

Major Primate Groups
Old World and New World Monkeys (living)
Prosimians (living)
Apes (living)
Fossil only
0 1000 2000 Miles
0 1000 2000 3000 Kilometers

Primates are a zoological order ranging from lemurs to monkeys to apes to humans. With the exception of humans, today primates are found mostly in tropical areas. They used to have a wider distribution, as indicated by places where fossils of ancestral forms have been found.

Map 12 African Apes

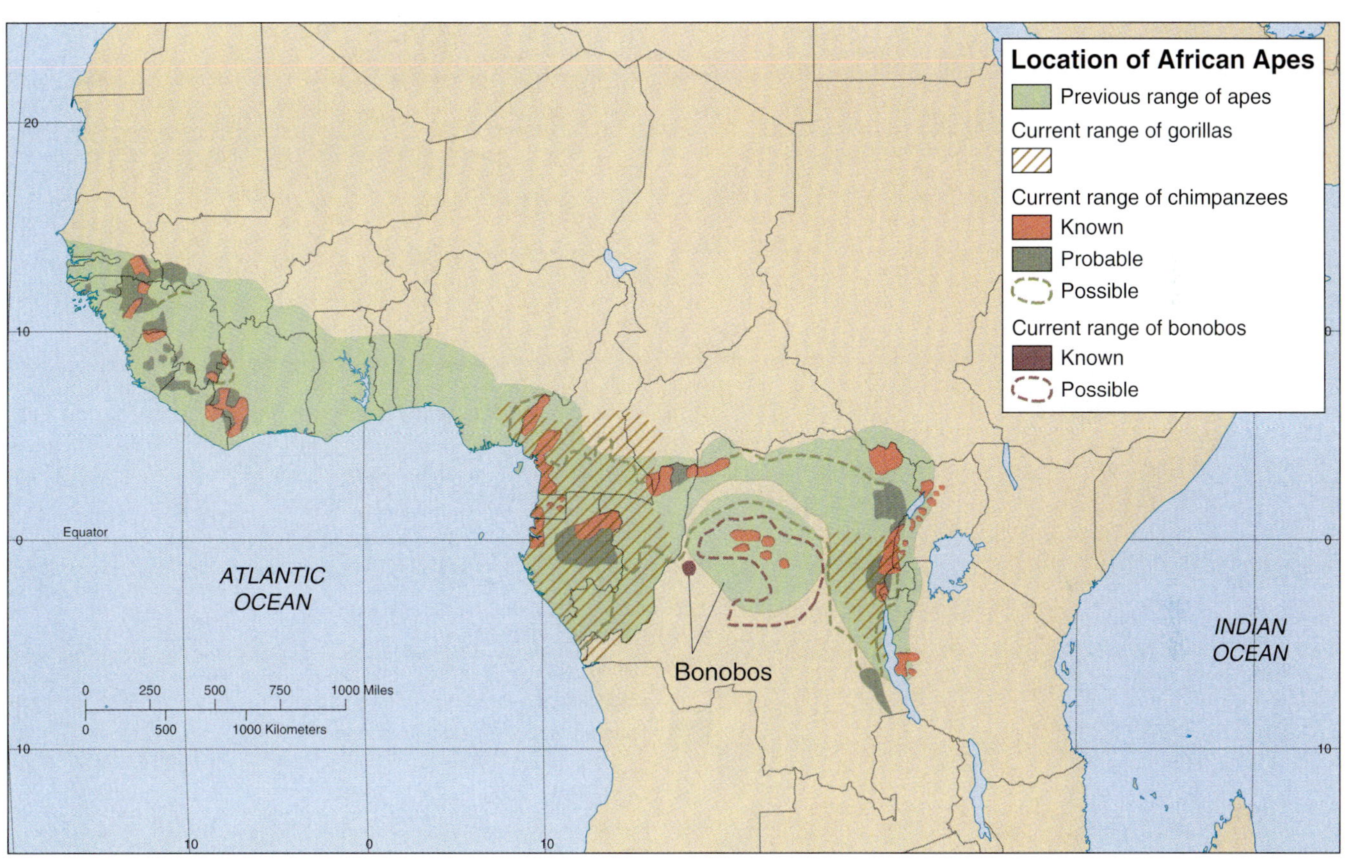

Location of African Apes
Previous range of apes
Current range of gorillas
Current range of chimpanzees
Known
Probable
Possible
Current range of bonobos
Known
Possible
ATLANTIC OCEAN
INDIAN OCEAN
Bonobos
Equator
0
250
500
750
1000 Miles
0
500
1000 Kilometers
20
10
0
10
10
0
10

Humans' closest primate relatives are the Great Apes. Gorillas and chimpanzees are the main groups of African apes. The largest of the Great Apes, gorillas, are primarily peaceful vegetarians despite their fierce image in popular movies such as *King Kong*. Closest to humans genetically, chimpanzees (*Pan troglodytes*) are tool-using social apes. Primatologists such as Jane Goodall have noted that chimpanzees maintain close bonds with their mothers and siblings throughout their lives. Bonobos (*Pan paniscus*) are closely related to common chimps, although scientists consider them a different species. While there may be only as few as 10,000 remaining, bonobos attract much scientific attention because of their egalitarian lifeways and bonding mechanisms. The territories of all the Great Apes are shrinking rapidly, endangering their survival.

Map 13 The Evolution of Primates

Scientists trace modern primates back to ancestral forms, just as they do humans. Prosimians, a lower form of primates such as today's lemurs and tarsiers, evolved earliest, almost 60 million years ago, in the Americas. Fossil sites with the ancestors of New World monkeys date back between 23 and 37 million years. Old World monkeys and apes evolved at about the same time, but Old World monkeys spread into many parts of the Old World only in the last 5 million years.

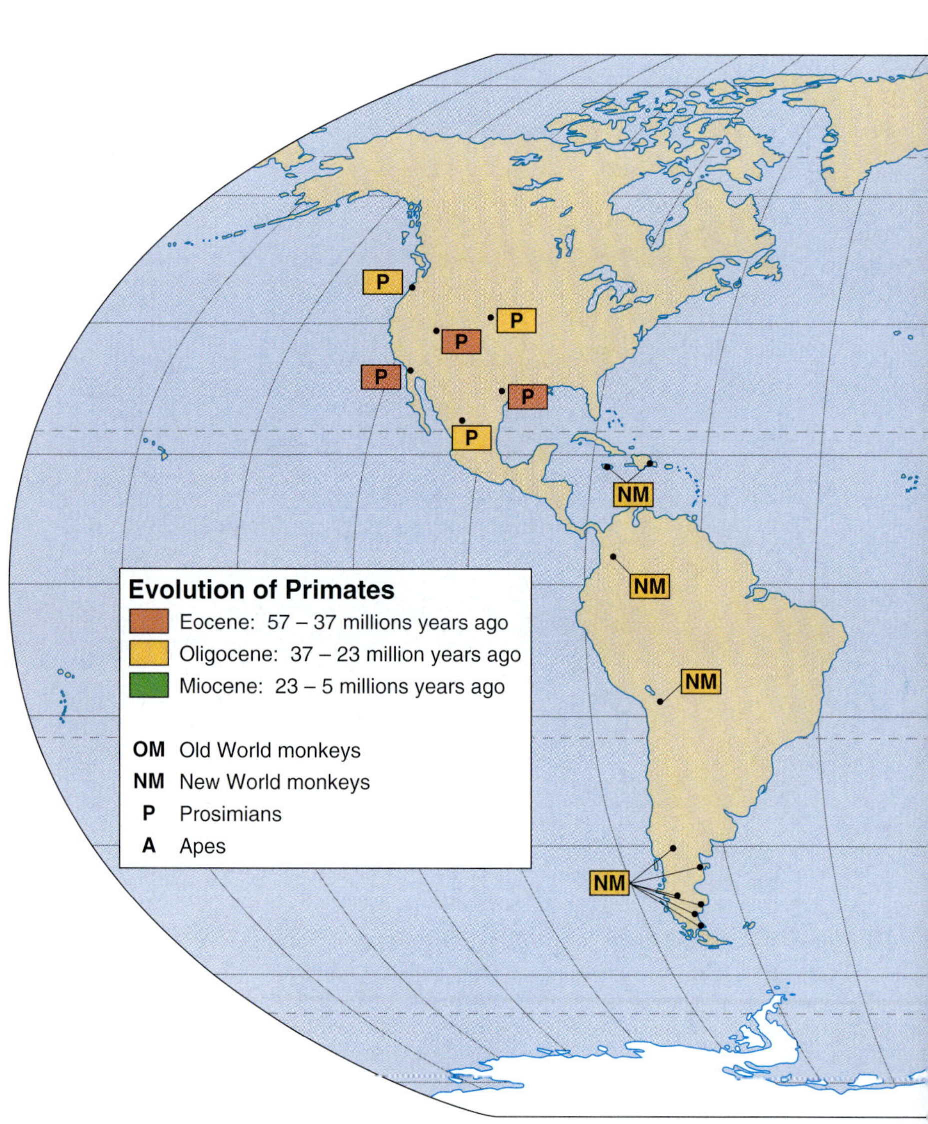

P
P
P
P
P
P
NM
NM
NM
NM
Evolution of Primates
Eocene: 57 – 37 millions years ago
Oligocene: 37 – 23 million years ago
Miocene: 23 – 5 millions years ago
OM Old World monkeys
NM New World monkeys
P Prosimians
A Apes

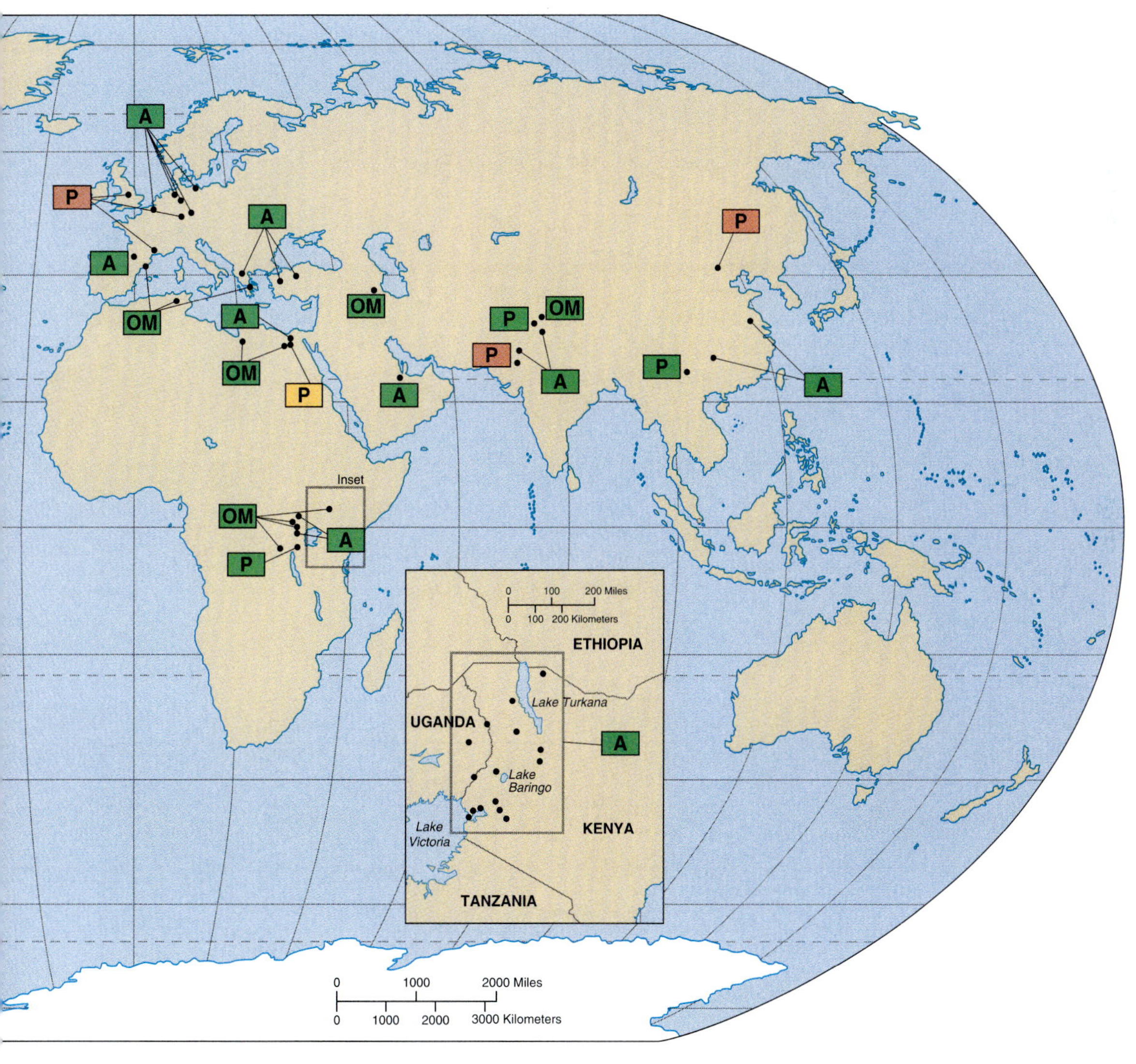
A
P
A
A
OM
A
OM
OM
P
A
P
OM
P
A
P
P
A
P
Inset
OM
A
P
0 100 200 Miles
0 100 200 Kilometers
ETHIOPIA
Lake Turkana
UGANDA
A
Lake Baringo
KENYA
Lake Victoria
TANZANIA
0 1000 2000 Miles
0 1000 2000 3000 Kilometers

Map 14 Early Hominids: Origins and Diffusion

The ancestors of modern humans first evolved in Africa. There are many sites dating to the late Miocene (5 million years ago) when the lines leading to modern humans and chimps may first have separated. Scientists agree that in the Pliocene (5–1.8 million years ago), we have sites with the fossil remains of human ancestors, *Homo*. The Pleistocene Era (1.8 million–10,000 years ago) is the period when humans spread all over the world. Scholars do not always agree on the evolutionary connections between the different fossils, as indicated in the question marks and broken lines on the time line.

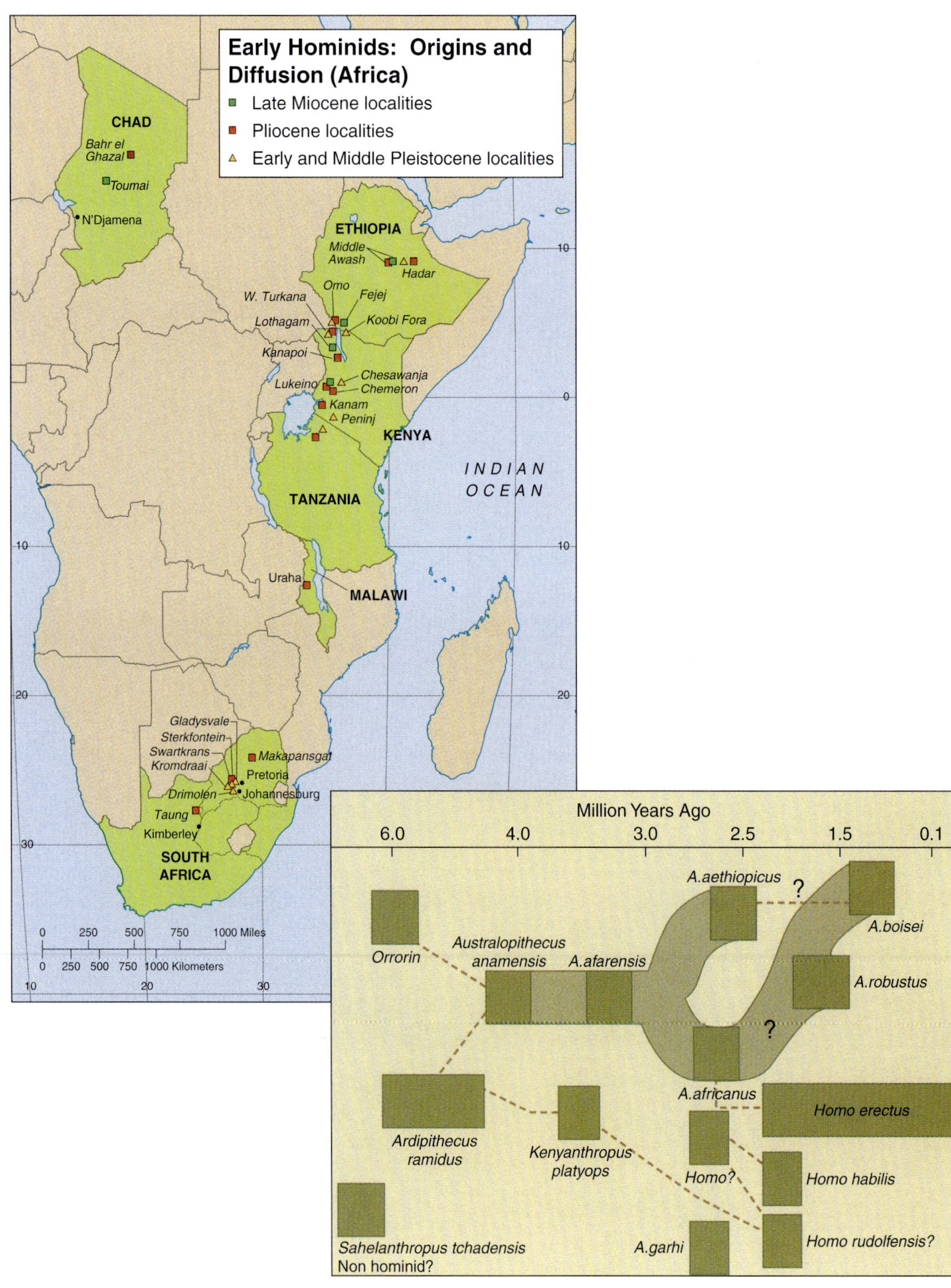

Early Hominids: Origins and Diffusion (Africa)
Late Miocene localities
Pliocene localities
Early and Middle Pleistocene localities
CHAD
Bahr el Ghazal
Toumai
N'Djamena
ETHIOPIA
Middle Awash
Hadar
Omo
Fejej
W. Turkana
Lothagam
Koobi Fora
Kanapoi
Chesawanja
Chemeron
Lukeino
Kanam
Peninj
KENYA
INDIAN OCEAN
TANZANIA
Uraha
MALAWI
Gladysvale
Sterkfontein
Swartkrans
Kromdraai
Makapansgat
Pretoria
Drimolen
Johannesburg
Taung
Kimberley
SOUTH AFRICA
0 250 500 750 1000 Miles
0 250 500 750 1000 Kilometers
Million Years Ago
6.0
4.0
3.0
2.5
1.5
0.1
A.aethiopicus
?
A.boisei
Orrorin
Australopithecus anamensis
A.afarensis
A.robustus
?
A.africanus
Homo erectus
Ardipithecus ramidus
Kenyanthropus platyops
Homo?
Homo habilis
Homo rudolfensis?
Sahelanthropus tchadensis
Non hominid?
A.garhi

Map 15 Later Old World Hominids

Boxgrove
St. Acheul
Soleilhac
Terra Amata
Ceprano
Gran Dolina
Torralba/ Ambrona
Ternifine
Salé
Thomas Quarry
Sidi Abderahman
BALTIC SEA
Dmanisi
BLACK SEA
CASPIAN SEA
MEDITERRANEAN SEA
Ubeidiya
ARAL SEA
Lake Balkash
Lake Baikal
Persian Gulf
RED SEA
Zhoukoudian
Lantian
Hexian
Yunxian
Tangshan Cave
Longgupo
Bose Basin
Bouri
Konso-Gardula
Nariokotome
Olorgesailie
Olduvai
Kalambo Falls
INDIAN OCEAN
ATLANTIC OCEAN
Sangiran
Modjokerto
Sambungmachan

Later Old World Hominids
1.5 million to 250,000 years ago

- • *Homo erectus* and *homo ergaster* fossil finds
- ▲ *Homo erectus* and *homo ergaster* archaeological sites (without hominid bones)

0 500 1000 1500 Miles
0 500 1000 1500 Kilometers

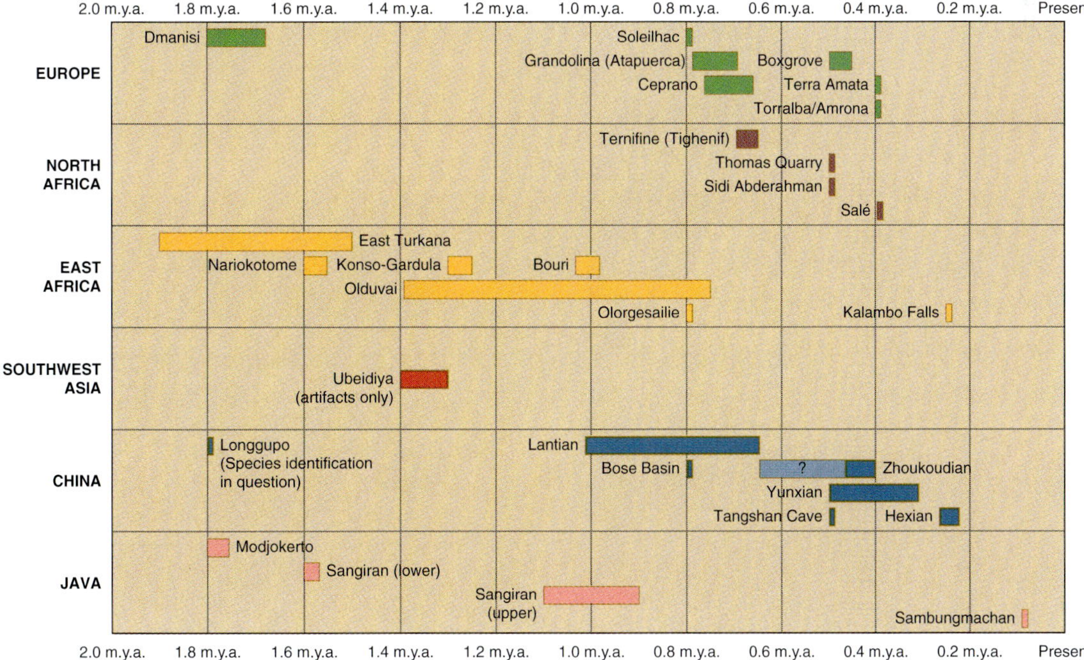

2.0 m.y.a.
1.8 m.y.a.
1.6 m.y.a.
1.4 m.y.a.
1.2 m.y.a.
1.0 m.y.a.
0.8 m.y.a.
0.6 m.y.a.
0.4 m.y.a.
0.2 m.y.a.
Present
EUROPE
Dmanisi
Soleilhac
Grandolina (Atapuerca)
Boxgrove
Ceprano
Terra Amata
Torralba/Amrona
NORTH AFRICA
Ternifine (Tighenif)
Thomas Quarry
Sidi Abderahman
Salé
EAST AFRICA
East Turkana
Nariokotome
Konso-Gardula
Bouri
Olduvai
Olorgesailie
Kalambo Falls
SOUTHWEST ASIA
Ubeidiya (artifacts only)
CHINA
Longgupo (Species identification in question)
Lantian
Bose Basin
?
Zhoukoudian
Yunxian
Tangshan Cave
Hexian
JAVA
Modjokerto
Sangiran (lower)
Sangiran (upper)
Sambungmachan

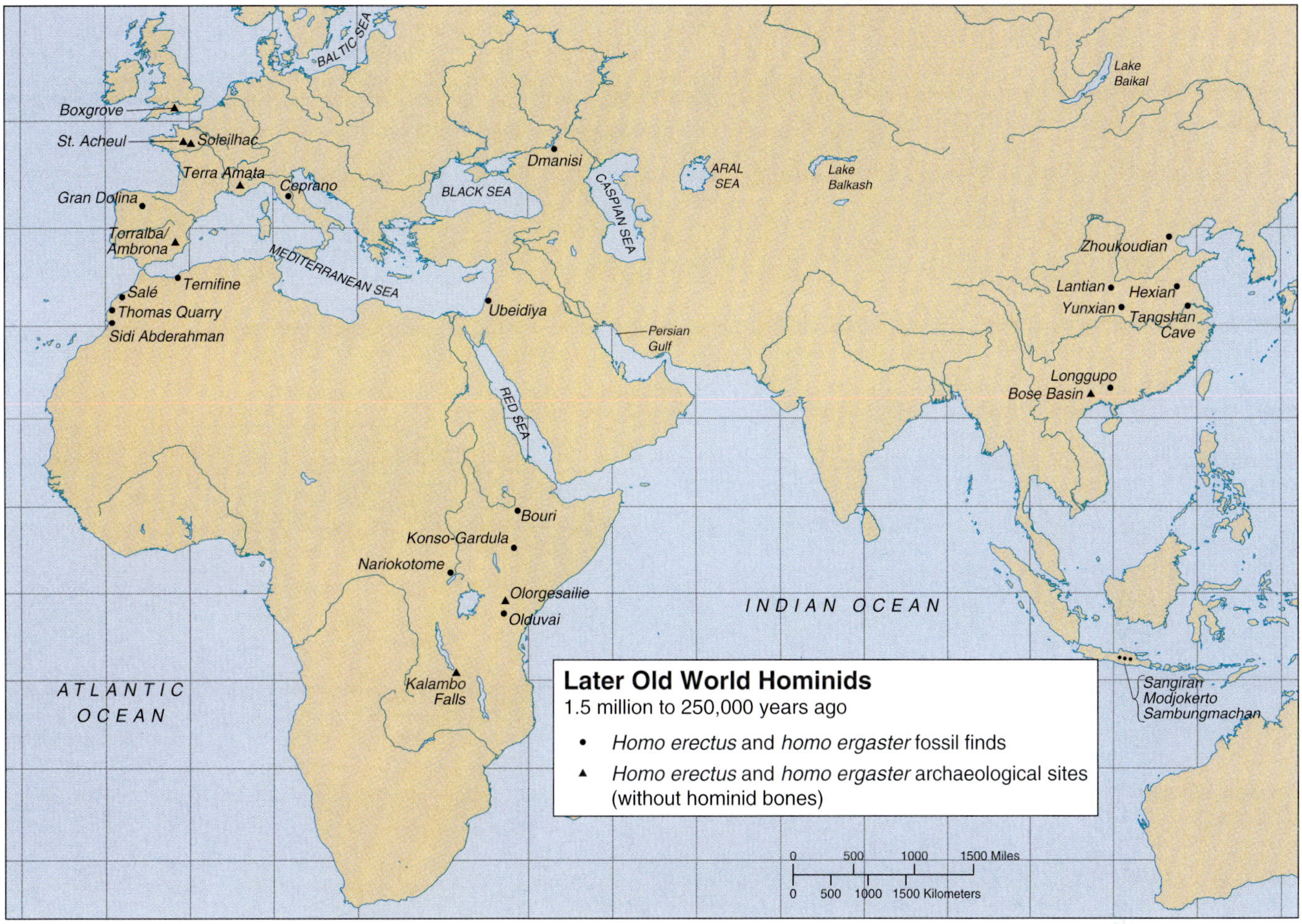

The map shows some important *Homo erectus* and *Homo ergaster* fossil sites, ranging from about 1.5 million to 250,000 years ago. The sites cluster in certain parts of the Old World, which may indicate that paleoanthropologists have searched more intensively in those locales. Associated with chopper tool or hand-axe cultures, these ancient hominids had an average brain size of about 1,000 cubic centimeters. Modern humans have an average brain size of 1,200–1,400 cubic centimeters. See also Map 14 and Map 19.

Map 16 The Origins and Distribution of *Homo Sapiens*

Archaic forms of *Homo sapiens* spread around the world. Modern humans appeared earliest in Africa and migrated into the rest of the Old World between 100,000 and 30,000 years ago. Whether these early modern humans interbred with archaic *Homo sapiens,* including Neandertals, outside of Africa is still debated. Sometime between 9,000 and 25,000 years ago, humans colonized the New World.

Settled
c. 35,000 B.C.E.
First settled
c. 45,000 B.C.E.
c.100,000 –
90,000 B.C.E.
Omo
Migration of *Homo sapiens*
began from here c. 130,000 B.C.E.?
Settled
c. 100,000 – 90,000 B.C.E.
0
1000
2000 Miles
0
1000
2000
3000 Kilomet

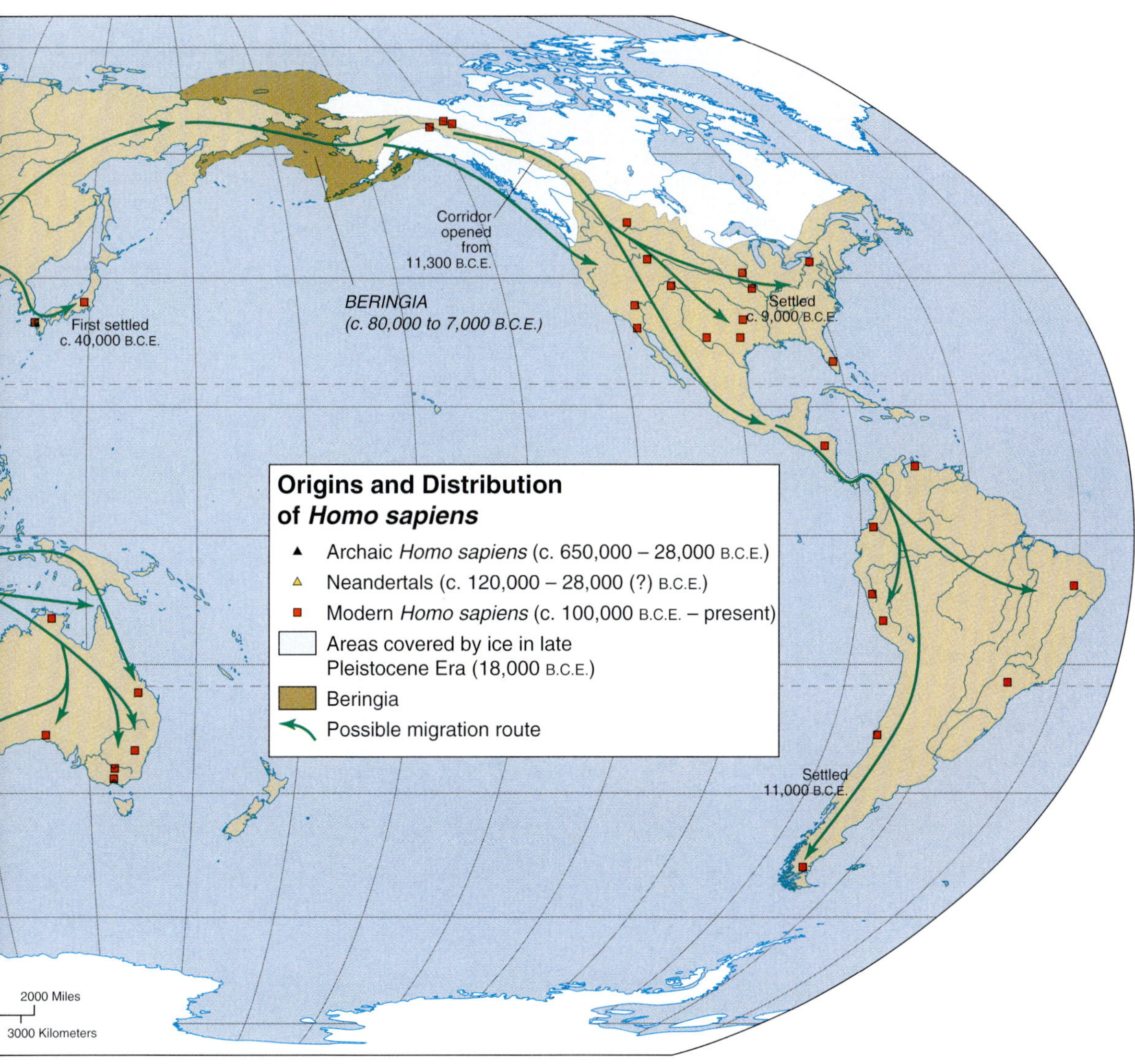
Origins and Distribution of *Homo sapiens*
Archaic *Homo sapiens* (c. 650,000 – 28,000 B.C.E.)
Neandertals (c. 120,000 – 28,000 (?) B.C.E.)
Modern *Homo sapiens* (c. 100,000 B.C.E. – present)
Areas covered by ice in late Pleistocene Era (18,000 B.C.E.)
Beringia
Possible migration route
BERINGIA
(c. 80,000 to 7,000 B.C.E.)
Corridor opened from 11,300 B.C.E.
First settled c. 40,000 B.C.E.
Settled c. 9,000 B.C.E.
Settled 11,000 B.C.E.
2000 Miles
3000 Kilometers

Map 17 Human Variations: Blood Types

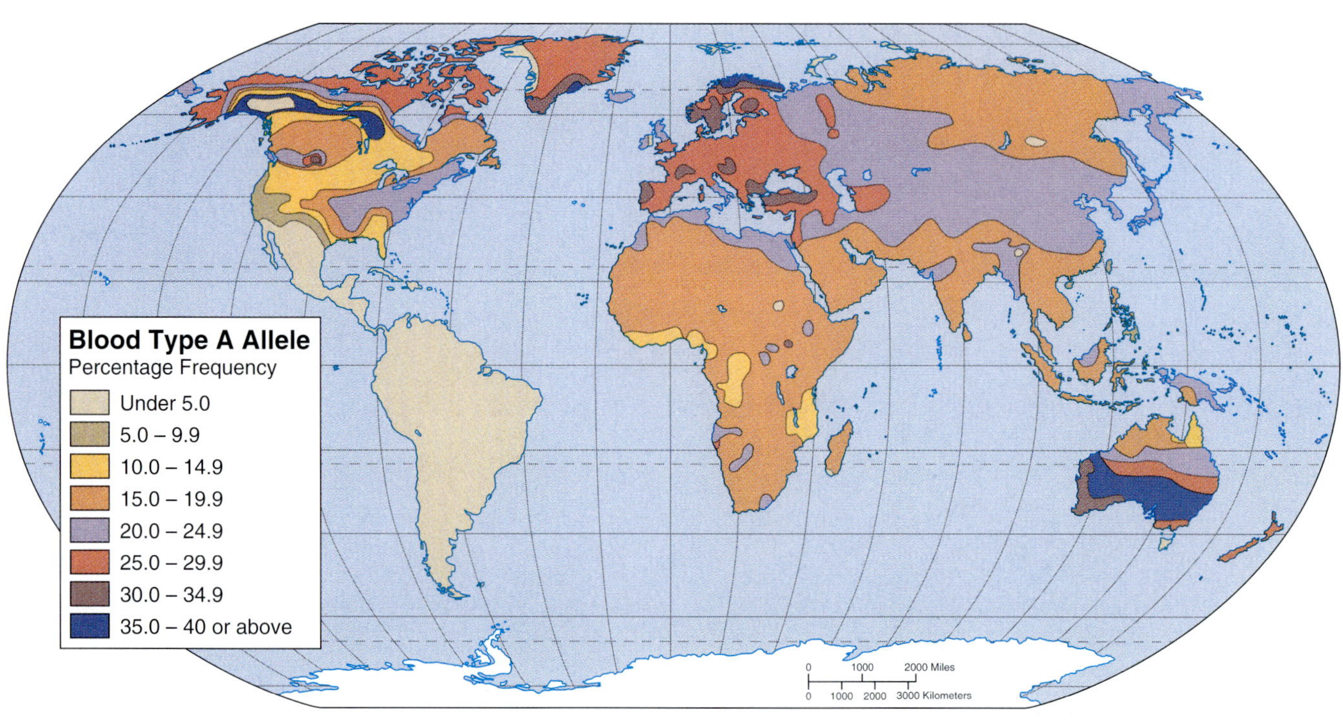
Blood Type A Allele
Percentage Frequency
Under 5.0
5.0 – 9.9
10.0 – 14.9
15.0 – 19.9
20.0 – 24.9
25.0 – 29.9
30.0 – 34.9
35.0 – 40 or above
0 1000 2000 Miles
0 1000 2000 3000 Kilometers

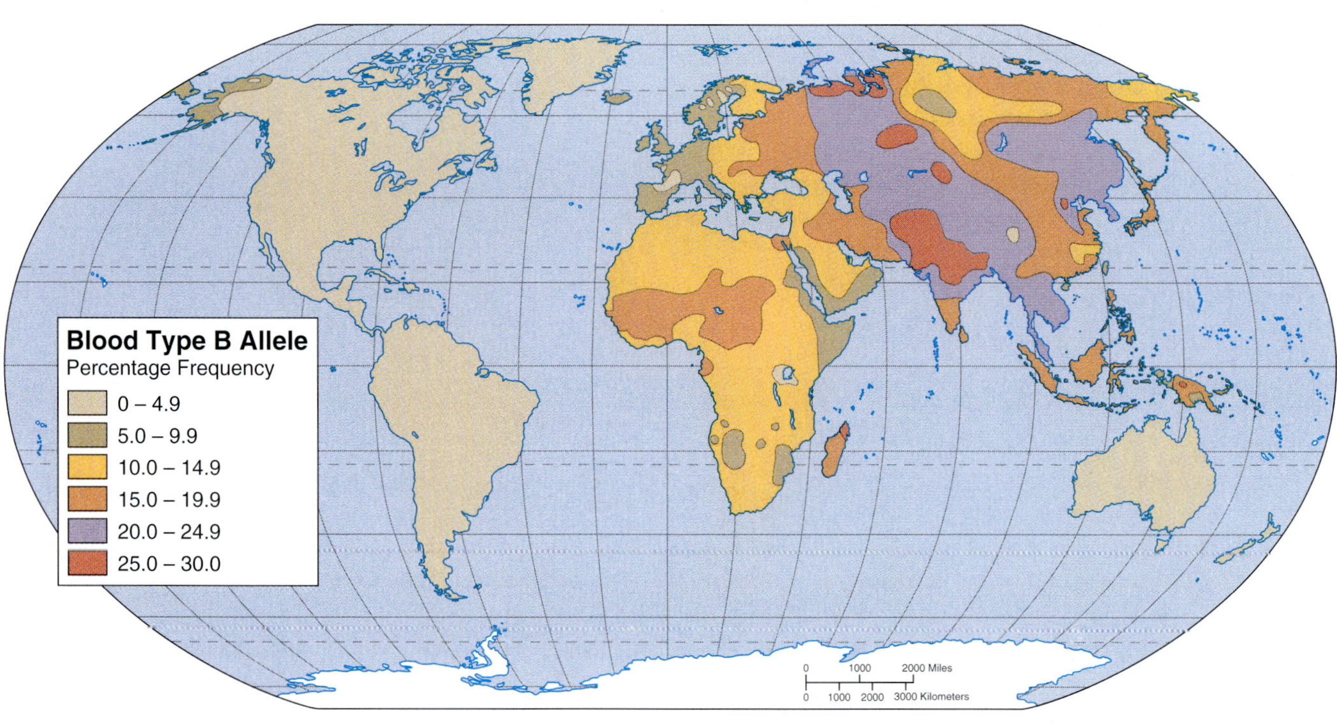
Blood Type B Allele
Percentage Frequency
0 – 4.9
5.0 – 9.9
10.0 – 14.9
15.0 – 19.9
20.0 – 24.9
25.0 – 30.0
0 1000 2000 Miles
0 1000 2000 3000 Kilometers

Blood groups are one way to classify humans. People may have type O, A, B, or AB blood. A person with type O blood, the most common type, does not have either A or B alleles (alleles are gene variants). A person with an A allele but not a B will have type A blood. A person with type B blood has the B allele but not the A. A small percentage of people have both A and B alleles and thus have type AB blood. The maps show the distribution of A and B alleles in the world. In places where there are high frequencies of both A and B alleles, we would expect to find all the different blood types. In places where there are low frequencies of A and B alleles, we would expect many people to have type O blood.

Map 18 Biocultural Evolution: The Sickle-Cell Trait

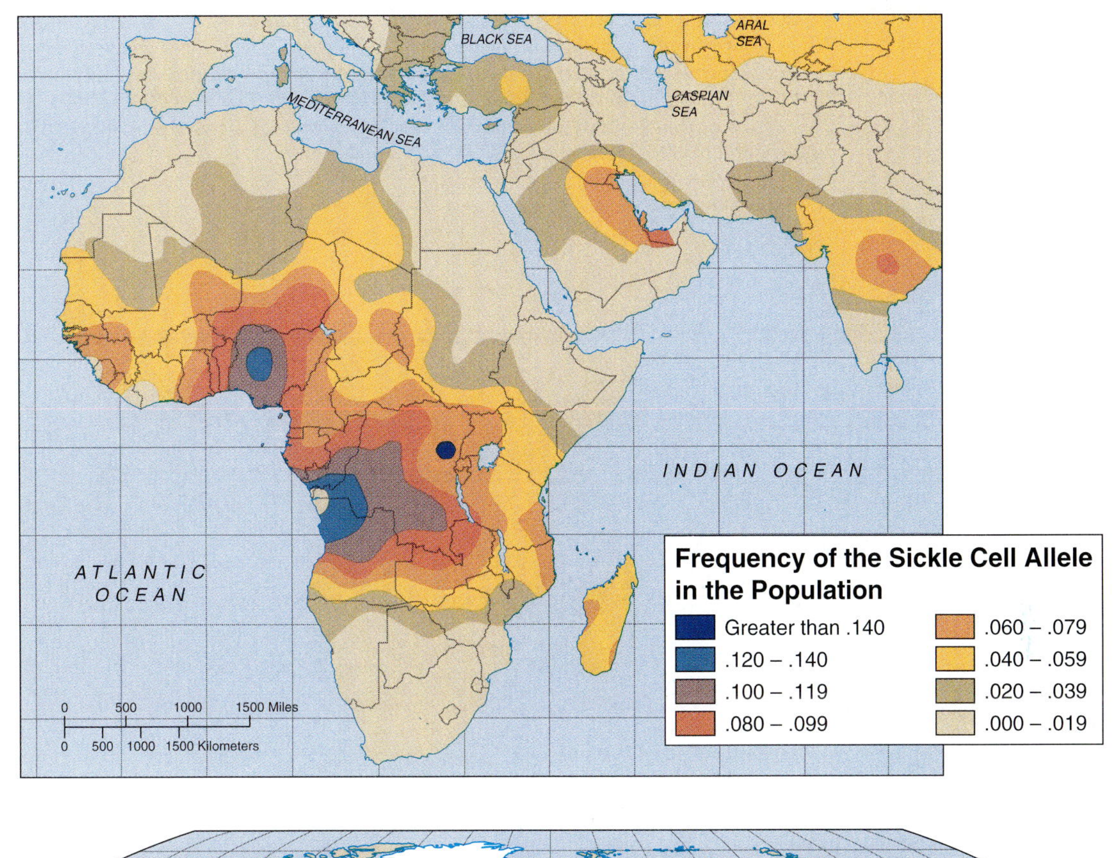

BLACK SEA
ARAL SEA
CASPIAN SEA
MEDITERRANEAN SEA
INDIAN OCEAN
ATLANTIC OCEAN
Frequency of the Sickle Cell Allele in the Population
Greater than .140
.120 – .140
.100 – .119
.080 – .099
.060 – .079
.040 – .059
.020 – .039
.000 – .019
0 500 1000 1500 Miles
0 500 1000 1500 Kilometers

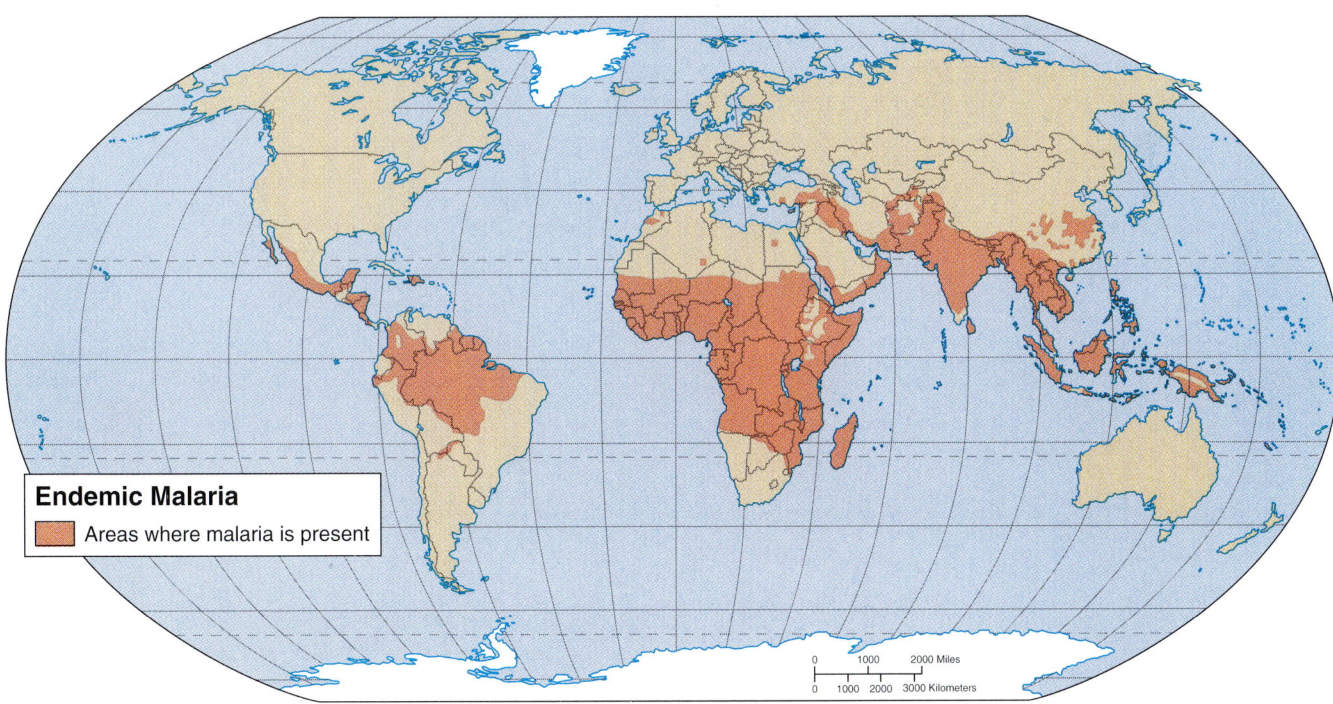

Endemic Malaria
Areas where malaria is present
0 1000 2000 Miles
0 1000 2000 3000 Kilometers

The sickle-cell trait in humans illustrates biocultural evolution. The cultural component arose as malaria became a significant danger to humans with the development of slash-and-burn agriculture (horticulture), which can create many stagnant pools of water, ideal mosquito habitats in certain climates. Biologically, the sickle-cell trait, an example of balanced polymorphism, was an adaptive response to the humanly transformed horticultural environment. The sickle cell is a variant type of the human red blood cell that is resistant to the mosquito-borne parasites that cause malaria. In malarial areas, individuals who lack the sickle-cell trait are more susceptible to malaria, an often fatal disease. The homozygous recessive condition (both alleles are sickle cell) leads to sickle-cell disease, symptoms of which are anemia, pain, susceptibility to stroke or infections, leg ulcers, bone damage, jaundice, and delayed growth. It may be fatal. The heterozygous condition (one allele for sickle cell and one normal) is beneficial and enhances survival in malarial areas. Thus, there is a reproductive advantage for those heterozygous individuals.

Map 19 Human Variations: Cranial Capacity

Some biological anthropologists believe that temperature is the most important factor in shaping human head form variation, including variation in cranial capacity (a rough reflection of brain size). Tall, round heads with high cranial capacity are well suited to maintaining heat, while long, low heads with smaller cranial capacity are well suited to losing heat (Beals et al., 1984). Differing cranial capacity in modern humans is not related to intelligence.

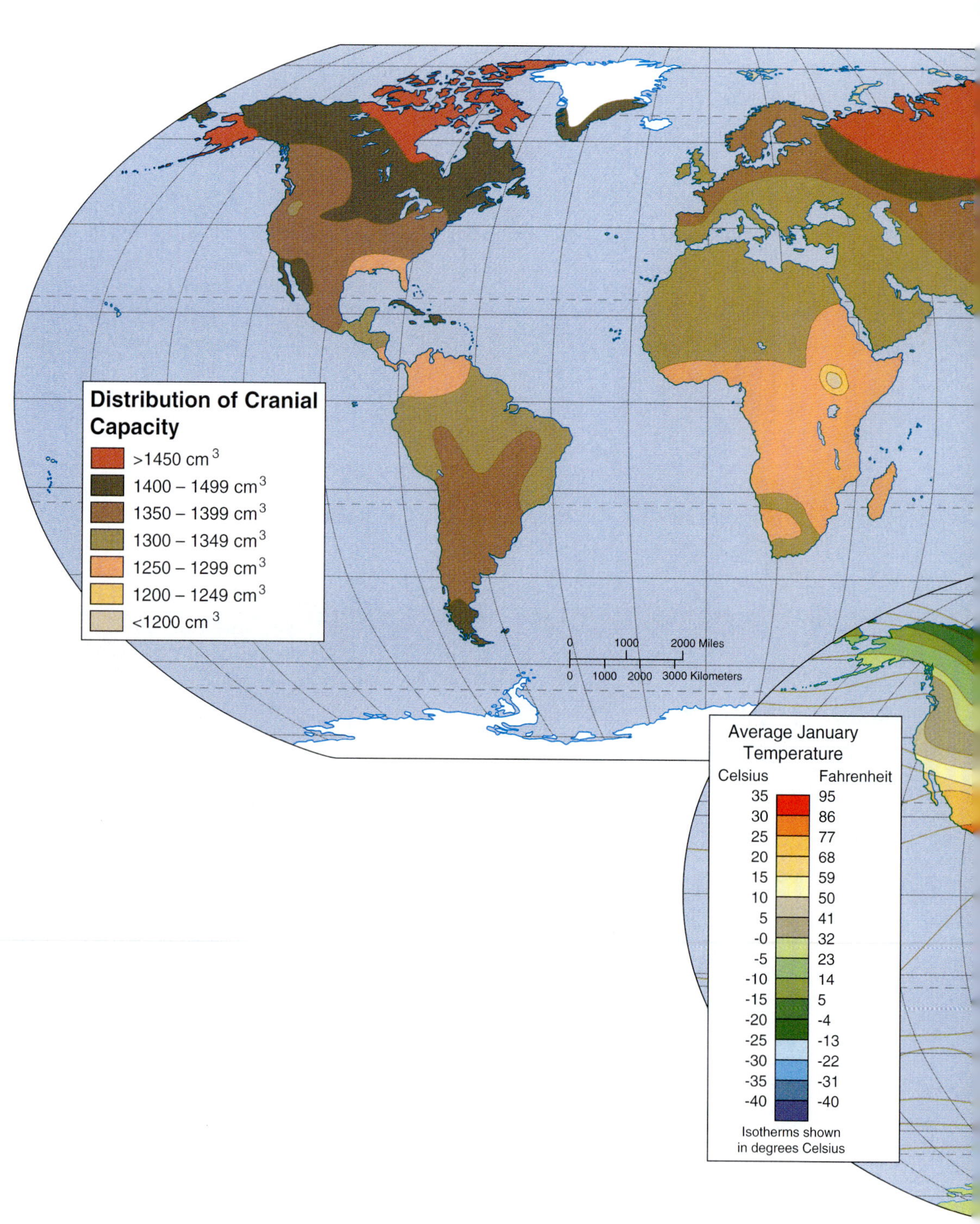

Distribution of Cranial Capacity
>1450 cm³
1400 – 1499 cm³
1350 – 1399 cm³
1300 – 1349 cm³
1250 – 1299 cm³
1200 – 1249 cm³
<1200 cm³
0 1000 2000 Miles
0 1000 2000 3000 Kilometers
Average January Temperature
Celsius Fahrenheit
35 95
30 86
25 77
20 68
15 59
10 50
5 41
-0 32
-5 23
-10 14
-15 5
-20 -4
-25 -13
-30 -22
-35 -31
-40 -40
Isotherms shown in degrees Celsius

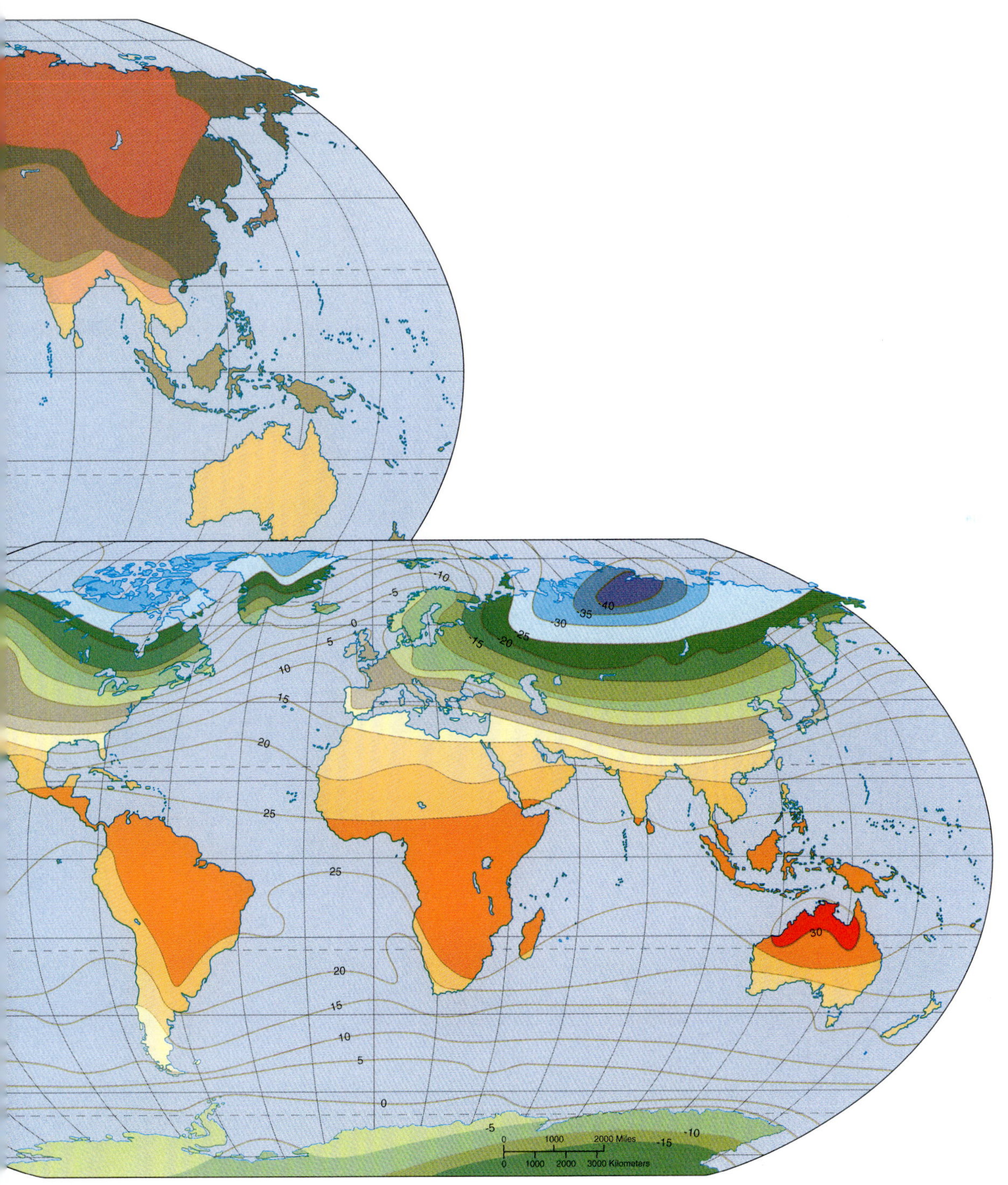
-10
-5
0
5
10
15
20
25
25
20
15
10
5
0
-5
-15
-20
-25
-30
-35
-40
30
-10
-15
0 1000 2000 Miles
0 1000 2000 3000 Kilometers

Map 20 Human Variations: Body Mass Index

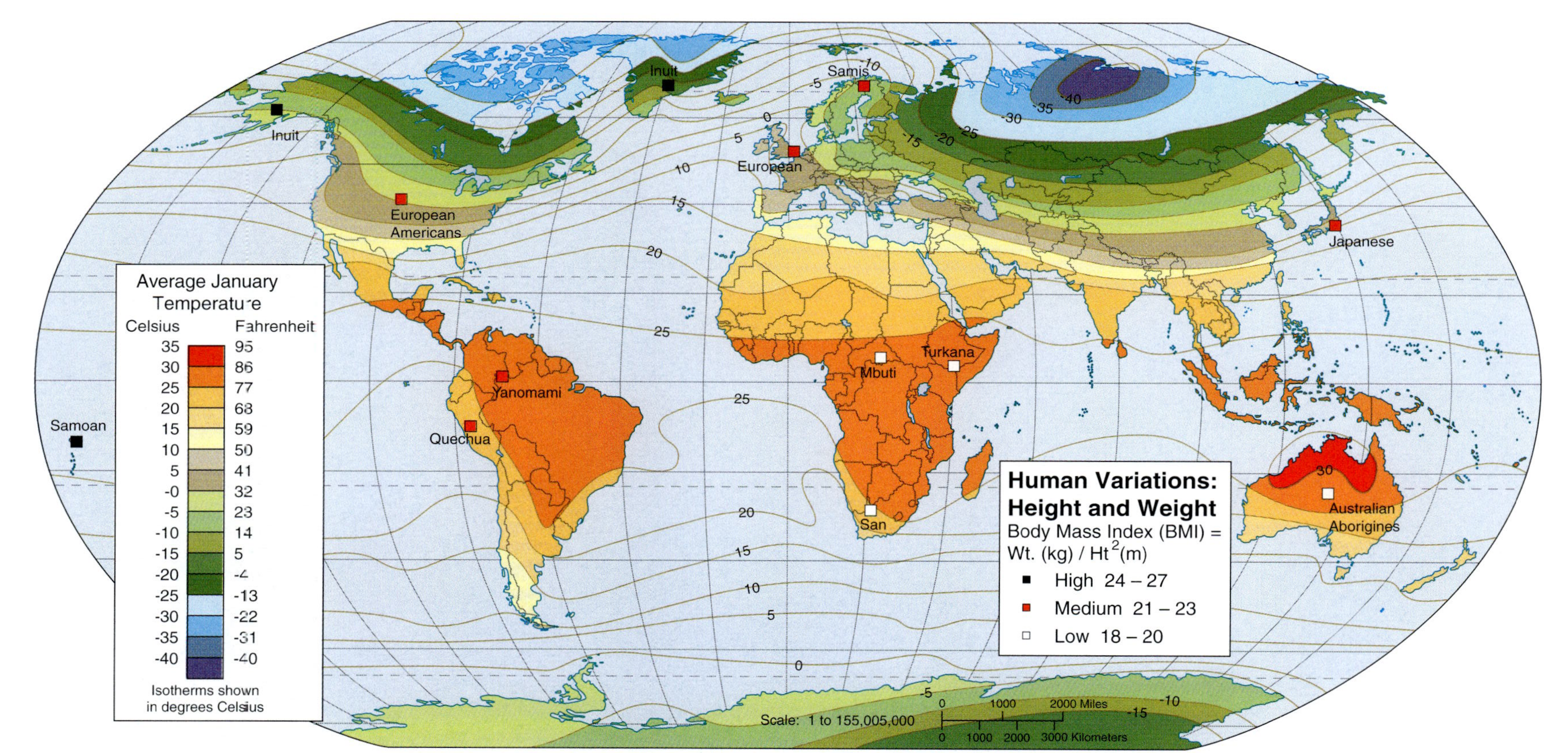

Human Variations: Height and Weight
Body Mass Index (BMI) = Wt. (kg) / Ht^2(m)
High 24 – 27
Medium 21 – 23
Low 18 – 20
Average January Temperature
Celsius
Fahrenheit
35 95
30 86
25 77
20 68
15 59
10 50
5 41
-0 32
-5 23
-10 14
-15 5
-20 -4
-25 -13
-30 -22
-35 -31
-40 -40
Isotherms shown in degrees Celsius
Inuit
Inuit
Samis
European
European Americans
Japanese
Yanomami
Quechua
Samoan
Mbuti
Turkana
San
Australian Aborigines
Scale: 1 to 155,005,000
0 1000 2000 Miles
0 1000 2000 3000 Kilometers

Body Mass Index (BMI), a ratio of height to weight, is determined by a mathematical formula. Most humans have a BMI between 18 and 30. Human groups adapt to their environments biologically and culturally, but biological adaptation is a much slower process. Some human groups who have been in the same environment for thousands of years have bodies that have adapted biologically to conserve heat or promote cooling.

Map 21 Human Variations: Skin Color

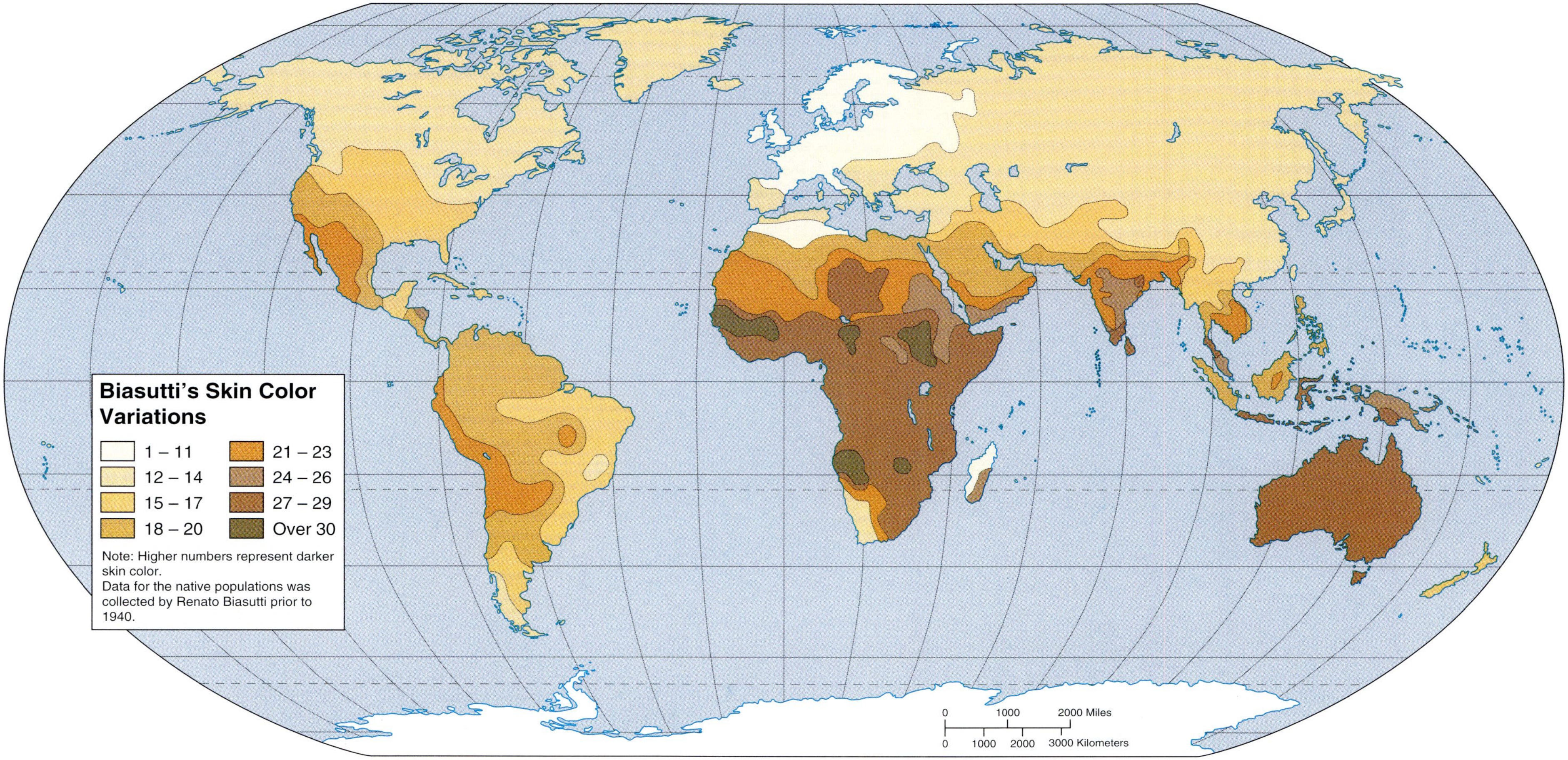

Biasutti's Skin Color Variations
1 – 11
12 – 14
15 – 17
18 – 20
21 – 23
24 – 26
27 – 29
Over 30
Note: Higher numbers represent darker skin color.
Data for the native populations was collected by Renato Biasutti prior to 1940.
0 1000 2000 Miles
0 1000 2000 3000 Kilometers

Human skin color varies. The pigmentation is caused by the presence of melanin in the skin, which protects the skin from damage due to ultraviolet radiation. In areas with much UV radiation, people biologically adapted to their environments by increased melanin production.

Part III

Archaeology

Map 22 Major Old World Archaeological Sites of the Paleolithic
Map 23 Ancient Forms of Art and Architecture
Map 24 Early Neolithic Sites and the Spread of Agriculture
Map 25 Megalithic Sites of Europe
Map 26 Ancient Civilizations of the Old World
Map 27 Major Sites of Ancient Egypt and Mesopotamia
Map 28 Ancient Trade Systems of the Old World
Map 29 Peopling of the New World I
Map 30 Peopling of the New World II
Map 31 Ancient Civilizations of Mesoamerica and South America
Map 32 Ancient Trade Systems of the New World
Map 33 Culture Regions of the New World
Map 34 Mound Builder Sites of Eastern North America
Map 35 Great Houses, Roadway Systems, and Ruins of the Southwest
Map 36 Native American–European Trade: Early Contact Period in North America

Map 22 Major Old World Archaeological Sites of the Paleolithic

The Paleolithic or Old Stone Age begins in the Old World with the first tool-making people in Africa, some 2.6 million years ago. Eventually, archaic types of humans spread throughout the Old World. The Paleolithic ends after anatomically modern humans spread throughout the Old World developing complex cultures and artistic traditions. At the end

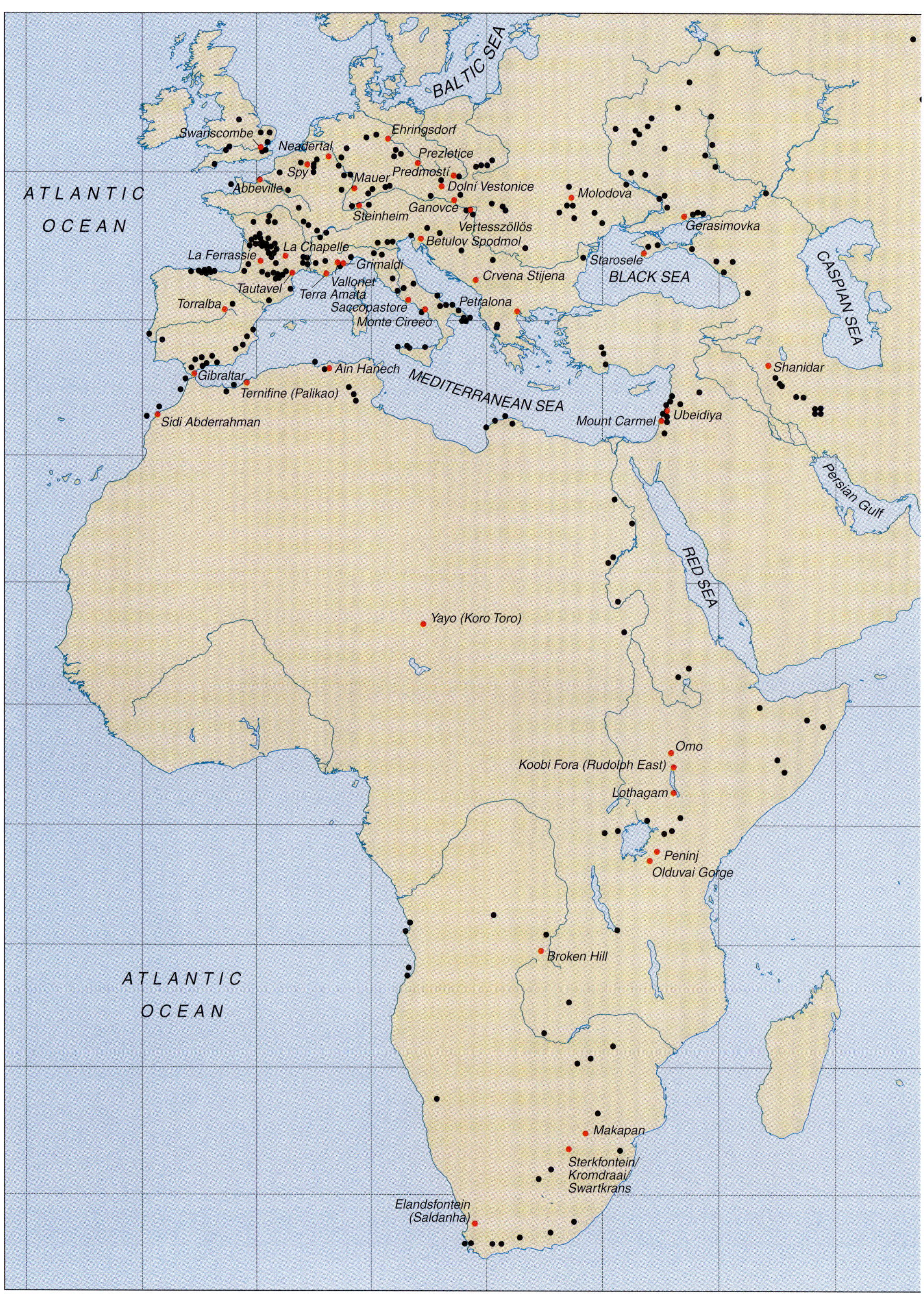
BALTIC SEA
ATLANTIC OCEAN
Swanscombe
Neadertal
Ehringsdorf
Prezletice
Spy
Mauer
Predmostí
Abbeville
Dolní Vestonice
Molodova
Ganovce
Steinheim
Vertesszöllös
Gerasimovka
CASPIAN SEA
La Chapelle
La Ferrassie
Betulov Spodmol
Grimaldi
Starosele
BLACK SEA
Vallonet
Tautavel
Terra Amata
Crvena Stijena
Torralba
Saccopastore
Petralona
Monte Cireeo
Shanidar
Ain Hanech
Gibraltar
MEDITERRANEAN SEA
Ternifine (Palikao)
Mount Carmel
Ubeidiya
Sidi Abderrahman
Persian Gulf
RED SEA
Yayo (Koro Toro)
Omo
Koobi Fora (Rudolph East)
Lothagam
Peninj
Olduvai Gorge
Broken Hill
ATLANTIC OCEAN
Makapan
Sterkfontein/
Kromdraai/
Swartkrans
Elandsfontein
(Saldanha)

of the Ice Age, about 15,000 years ago, new adaptations to a changed environment became necessary. The Mesolithic or Middle Stone Age brought more intensive foraging and greater sedentism to some parts of the Old World. See also Maps 14 and 15.

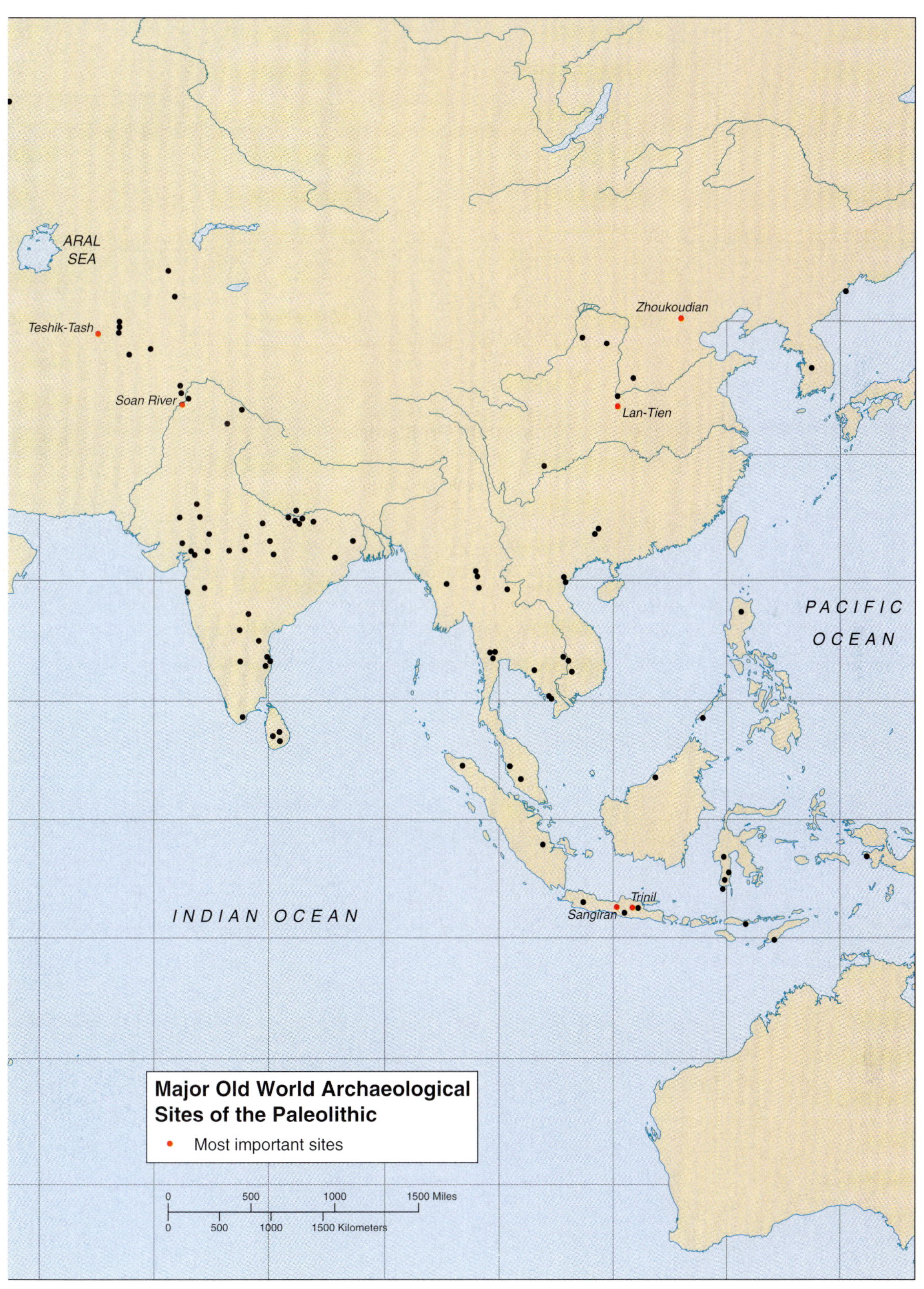

ARAL SEA
Teshik-Tash
Soan River
Zhoukoudian
Lan-Tien
PACIFIC OCEAN
INDIAN OCEAN
Trinil
Sangiran
Major Old World Archaeological Sites of the Paleolithic
Most important sites
0
500
1000
1500 Miles
0
500
1000
1500 Kilometers

Map 23 Ancient Forms of Art and Architecture

Since prehistoric times, humans have created art—carvings, paintings, sculpture, and more. Creativity is a universal human characteristic. The map shows different kinds of art and architecture. Megaliths are architectural stone forms constructed in the landscape (see Map 25). Petroglyphs are carvings on the surface of rocks; sometimes these are pecked in. Pictographs are paintings on canyon walls often made with red or yellow ochre or colored clays. The insert map to the left shows selected petroglyph and/or pictograph sites in the western United States. The carvings or paintings depict animals, peo-

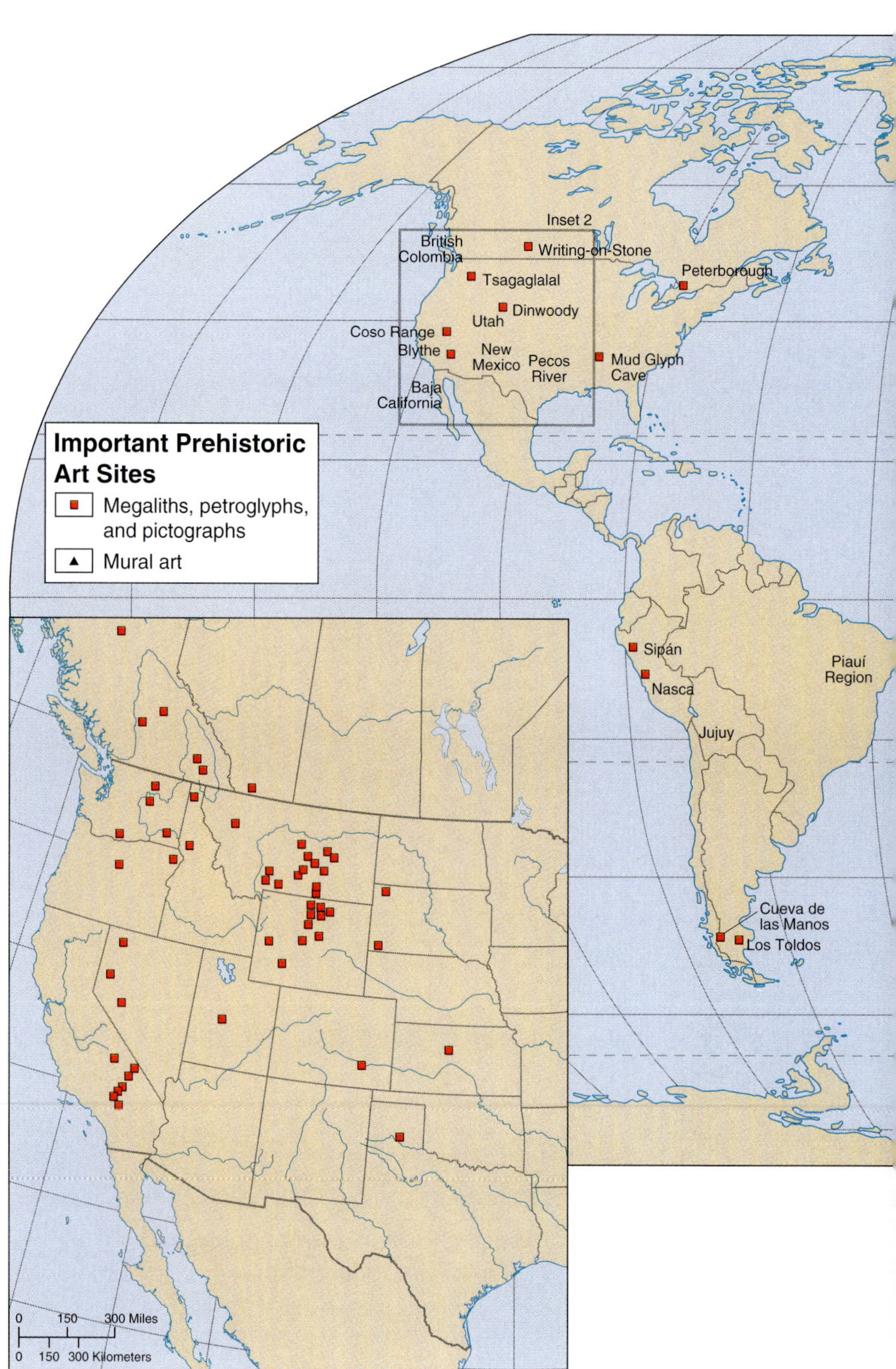

Important Prehistoric Art Sites
Megaliths, petroglyphs, and pictographs
Mural art
Inset 2
British Colombia
Writing-on-Stone
Tsagaglalal
Peterborough
Dinwoody
Utah
Coso Range
Blythe
New Mexico
Pecos River
Mud Glyph Cave
Baja California
Sipán
Nasca
Jujuy
Piauí Region
Cueva de las Manos
Los Toldos
0 150 300 Miles
0 150 300 Kilometers

ple, and objects sacred to the people who made them. The insert map in the center indicates numerous cave-painting sites in France and Spain, many of which contain murals of animals such as bison, horses, and deer. Although the cave paintings of Europe and the rock art of the western United States are widely separated in geography and time period, they are similar in that both types of artistic creations may be part of the religious practices of their respective societies.

Alta
Lake Onega
Sungir
Kapova
Ignatiev
Orkney
New Grange
Bohuslän
Uffington
Gouy
Gönnersdorf
Mayenne Sciences
Dolní Věstonice
Inset
Los Casares
La Hoz
Butmir
Mazouco
El Reguerillo
Escoural
La Pileta
Las Palomas
Nerja
Ardales
Romanelh
Levanzo
Malta
Jebel
Bes Seba
Berekhat Ram
Tassili
5 sites
3 sites
Fezzan
Libya
8 sites
4 sites
Libyan-Nubian Desert
Chad
Yenisei
Inner Mongolia
Altai
Helan Mts.
Huashan
Bhimbetka
Khok Phanom Di
Victoria River District
Kakadu/ Arnhem Land
Kimberly
Queensland
Spear Hill
Carnarvon Gorge
Mt. Gambier/Glenisia
Sydney
Tasmania
Brandberg
Cederberg
Drakensberg
0 1000 2000 Miles
0 1000 2000 3000 Kilometers
0 50 100 Miles
0 50 100 Kilometers
Angles-sur-l'Anglin
Teyjat
Montgaudier
Roc de Sers
Rouffignac
Fourneau du Diable
Le Poisson
Le Gabillou
Combarelles
Cap Blanc
Pair-non-Pair
Lascaux
Bara-Bahau
Laussel
St. Cirq
Bernifal
La Mouthe
Cougnac
Font de Gaume
Pech-Merle
La Magdeleine
Ebbou
Candamo
Altamira
Pindal
Cullalvera
Tito Bustillo
Herrerías
Ekain
Istruits
Brassempouy
La Baume-Latrone
Chufin
Castillo
Santimamiñe
Altxerri
Lespugue
Les Trois Frères
L'Aldène
Labastide
Le Mas-d'Azil
Bédeihac
Niaux
Gargas
Ganties-Montepsan
Le Tuc d'Audoubert

Map 24 Early Neolithic Sites and the Spread of Agriculture

The Neolithic, or New Stone Age, refers to the period of early farming settlements when people who had been foragers shifted to agriculture. This pattern of subsistence was based on the domestication of plants and animals. Through domestication, people transformed plants and animals from their wild state to a form more useful to humans. The Neolithic began in the Fertile Crescent area of the Middle East over 10,000 years ago. It spread to the Levant and Mediterranean, finally reaching Britain and Scandinavia around 5,000 years ago.

0
250
500 Miles
0
250
500 Kilometers
NORTH SEA
Dog
Goose
ATLANTIC OCEAN
Elbe R.
Rhine R.
Marne R.
Seine R.
Loire R.
Danube R.
Rhône R.
Po R.
Ebro R.
Douro R.
Tagus R.
Guadalquivir R.
ADRIATIC
8,000
MEDITERRANEAN
Southwest Asia Domestication
Barley
Beans
Beets
Camel (Bactrian)
Carrots
Cattle
Dog
Duck
Fruits (seed and stone)
Goat
Grapes
Hemp
Horse
Melons
Oats
Oil seeds
Onions
Rye
Sheep
Wheat
Mediterranean Domestication
Barley
Cattle
Celery
Dates
Garlic
Goat
Grapes
Lentils
Lettuce
Olives

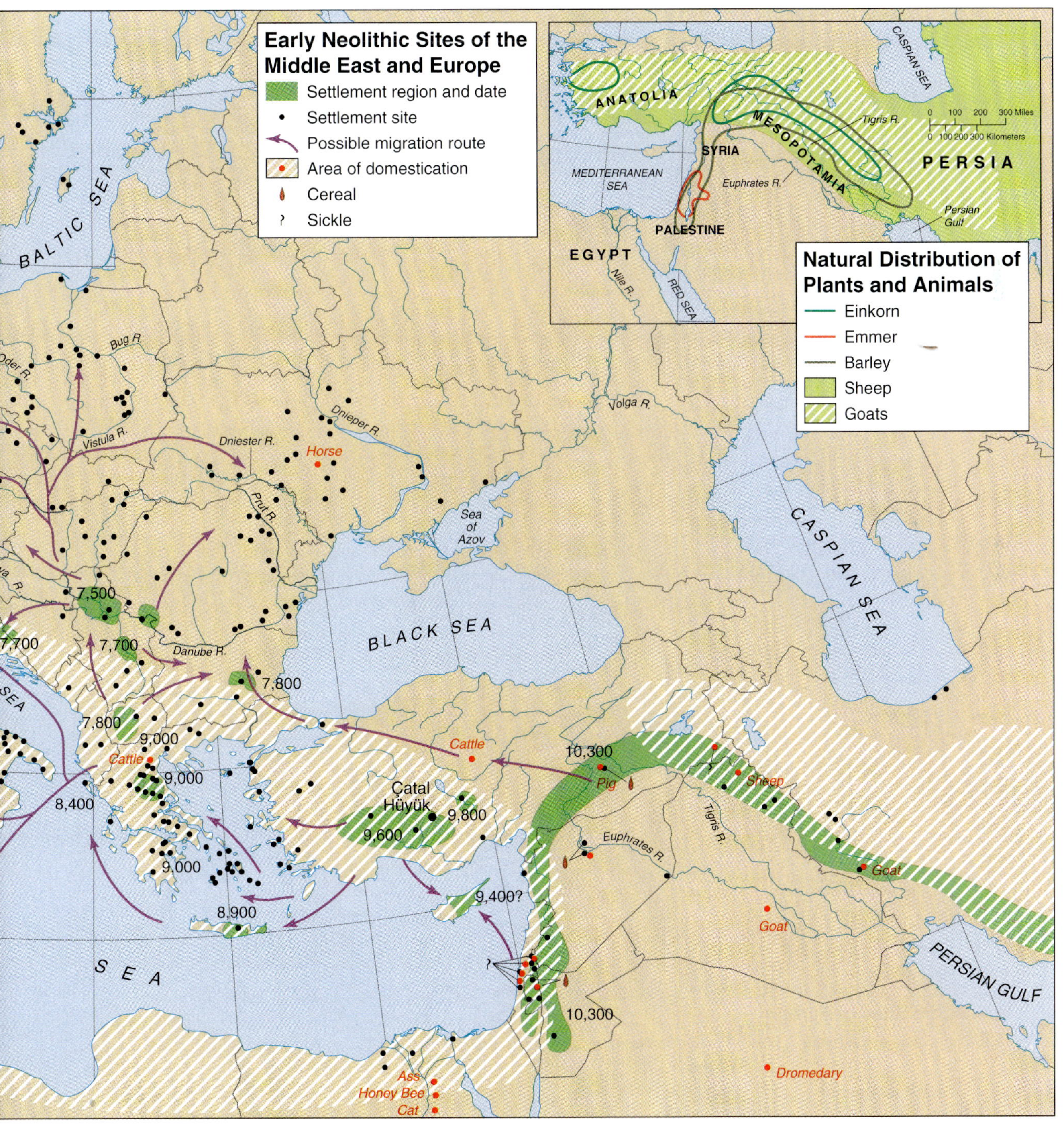

Early Neolithic Sites of the Middle East and Europe
Settlement region and date
Settlement site
Possible migration route
Area of domestication
Cereal
Sickle
Natural Distribution of Plants and Animals
Einkorn
Emmer
Barley
Sheep
Goats
ANATOLIA
MESOPOTAMIA
SYRIA
PALESTINE
PERSIA
EGYPT
MEDITERRANEAN SEA
CASPIAN SEA
RED SEA
Persian Gulf
BALTIC SEA
BLACK SEA
Sea of Azov
PERSIAN GULF
Horse
Cattle
Pig
Sheep
Goat
Ass
Honey Bee
Cat
Dromedary
Çatal Hüyük
7,500
7,700
7,800
9,000
8,400
9,600
9,800
9,400?
8,900
10,300

Map 25 Megalithic Sites of Europe

From 5,600 to 4,500 years ago, the early farming peoples of Europe constructed megalithic (stone slab) tombs as communal burial places. Eventually a different ritual orientation developed, perhaps involving astronomical and seasonal events, with stone circles or

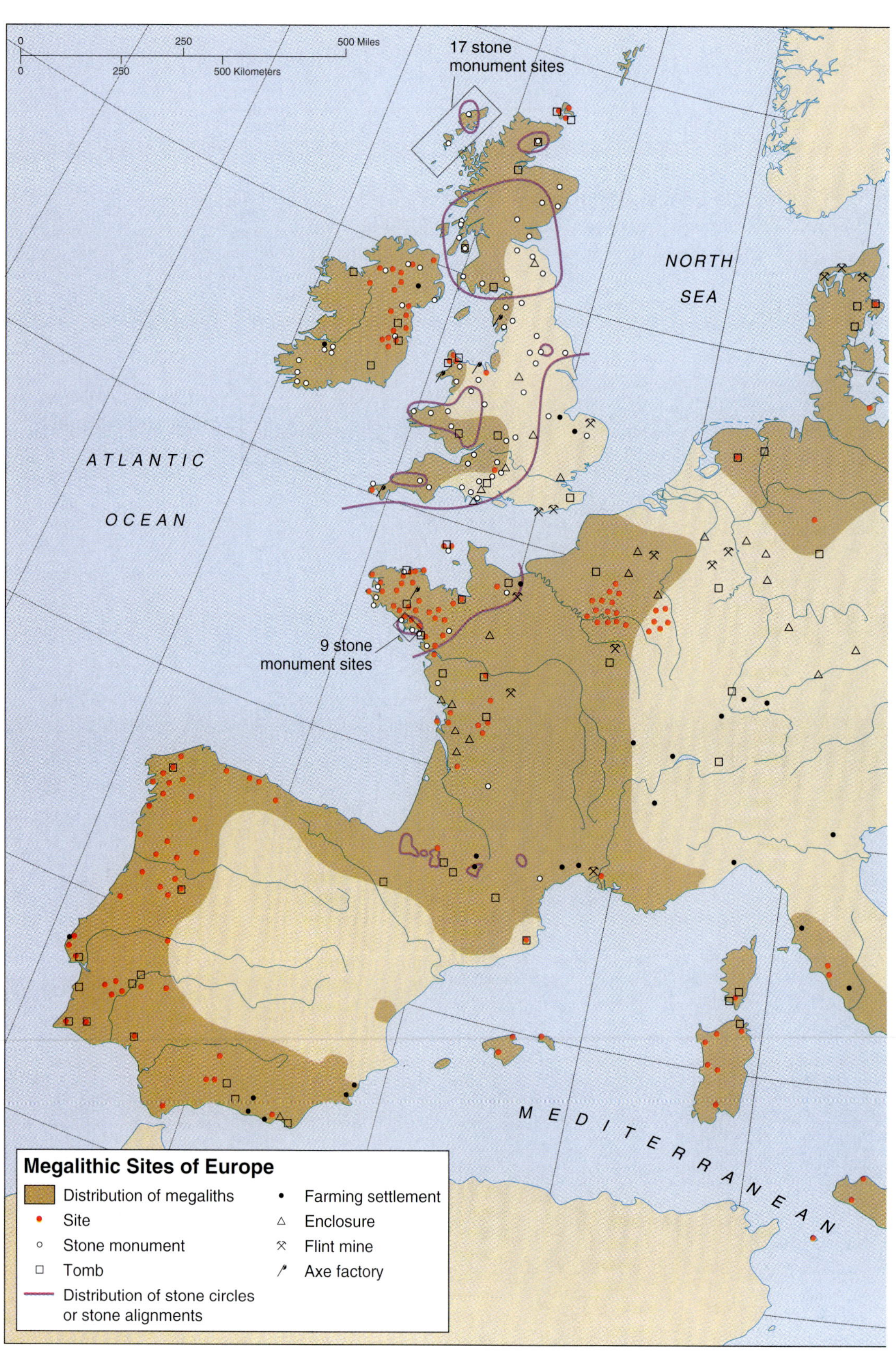

0
250
500 Miles
0
250
500 Kilometers
17 stone
monument sites
NORTH
SEA
ATLANTIC
OCEAN
9 stone
monument sites
MEDITERRANEAN
Megalithic Sites of Europe
Distribution of megaliths
Site
Stone monument
Tomb
Distribution of stone circles
or stone alignments
Farming settlement
Enclosure
Flint mine
Axe factory

rows of standing stones. Along with henges (circular enclosures) and menhirs (single standing stones), several traditions of ritual monuments flourished 5,200–3,500 years ago.

BALTIC SEA
ADRIATIC SEA
BLACK SEA
SEA

Map 26 Ancient Civilizations of the Old World

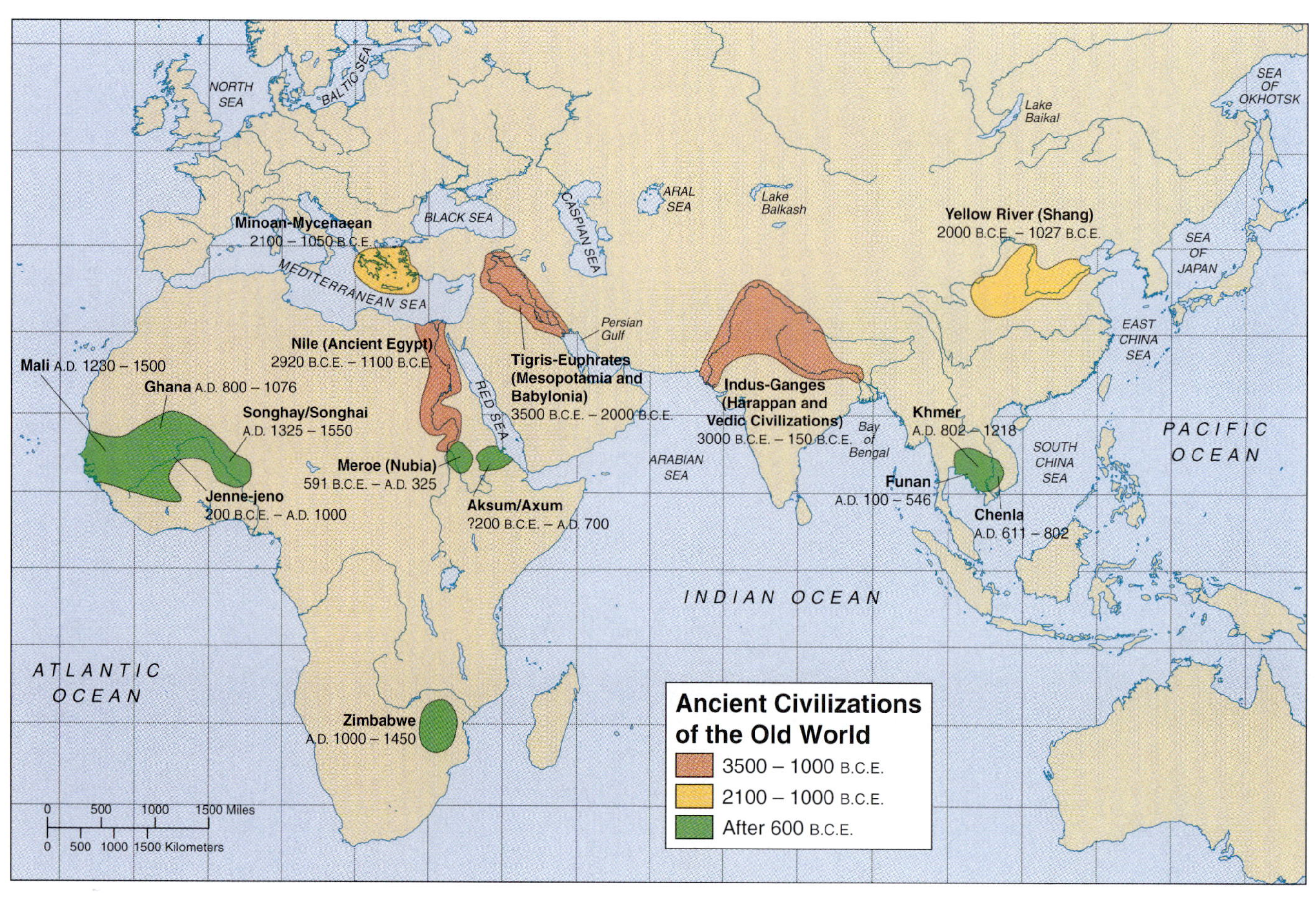
NORTH SEA
BALTIC SEA
Lake Baikal
SEA OF OKHOTSK
ARAL SEA
Lake Balkash
CASPIAN SEA
BLACK SEA
Minoan-Mycenaean
2100 – 1050 B.C.E.
MEDITERRANEAN SEA
Yellow River (Shang)
2000 B.C.E. – 1027 B.C.E.
SEA OF JAPAN
Persian Gulf
EAST CHINA SEA
Nile (Ancient Egypt)
2920 B.C.E. – 1100 B.C.E.
Mali A.D. 1230 – 1500
Ghana A.D. 800 – 1076
Tigris-Euphrates (Mesopotamia and Babylonia)
3500 B.C.E. – 2000 B.C.E.
RED SEA
Indus-Ganges (Harappan and Vedic Civilizations)
3000 B.C.E. – 150 B.C.E.
Songhay/Songhai
A.D. 1325 – 1550
Khmer
A.D. 802 – 1218
PACIFIC OCEAN
Bay of Bengal
SOUTH CHINA SEA
ARABIAN SEA
Meroe (Nubia)
591 B.C.E. – A.D. 325
Funan
A.D. 100 – 546
Jenne-jeno
200 B.C.E. – A.D. 1000
Aksum/Axum
?200 B.C.E. – A.D. 700
Chenla
A.D. 611 – 802
INDIAN OCEAN
ATLANTIC OCEAN
Zimbabwe
A.D. 1000 – 1450
Ancient Civilizations of the Old World
3500 – 1000 B.C.E.
2100 – 1000 B.C.E.
After 600 B.C.E.
0 500 1000 1500 Miles
0 500 1000 1500 Kilometers

Archaic states developed in many parts of the Old World. States are organized in hierarchical socioeconomic units, headed by a centralized government led by an elite. States include a full-time bureaucracy and specialized subsystems for such activities ar military action, taxation, and social control.

Map 27 Major Sites of Ancient Egypt and Mesopotamia

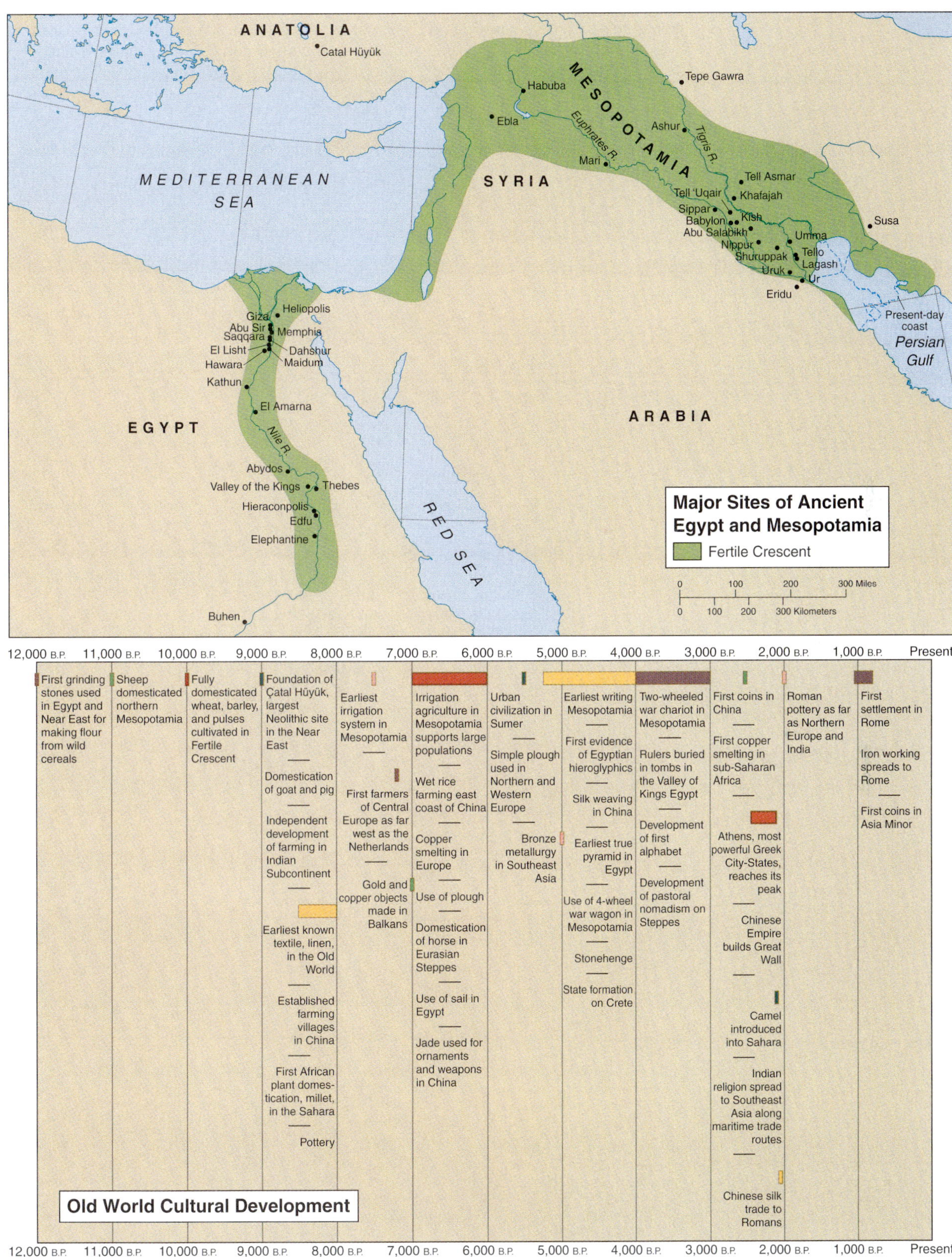

ANATOLIA
Catal Hüyük
MESOPOTAMIA
Tepe Gawra
Habuba
Ebla
Ashur
Euphrates R.
Tigris R.
Mari
SYRIA
MEDITERRANEAN SEA
Tell Asmar
Khafajah
Tell 'Uqair
Sippar
Babylon
Kish
Abu Salabikh
Nippur
Umma
Shuruppak
Tello
Lagash
Uruk
Ur
Eridu
Susa
Present-day coast
Persian Gulf
Heliopolis
Giza
Abu Sir
Saqqara
Memphis
El Lisht
Dahshur
Hawara
Maidum
Kathun
El Amarna
EGYPT
Nile R.
ARABIA
Abydos
Valley of the Kings
Thebes
Hieraconpolis
Edfu
Elephantine
RED SEA
Buhen
Major Sites of Ancient Egypt and Mesopotamia
Fertile Crescent
0 100 200 300 Miles
0 100 200 300 Kilometers
12,000 B.P. 11,000 B.P. 10,000 B.P. 9,000 B.P. 8,000 B.P. 7,000 B.P. 6,000 B.P. 5,000 B.P. 4,000 B.P. 3,000 B.P. 2,000 B.P. 1,000 B.P. Present
First grinding stones used in Egypt and Near East for making flour from wild cereals
Sheep domesticated northern Mesopotamia
Fully domesticated wheat, barley, and pulses cultivated in Fertile Crescent
Foundation of Çatal Hüyük, largest Neolithic site in the Near East
Domestication of goat and pig
Independent development of farming in Indian Subcontinent
Earliest known textile, linen, in the Old World
Established farming villages in China
First African plant domestication, millet, in the Sahara
Pottery
Earliest irrigation system in Mesopotamia
First farmers of Central Europe as far west as the Netherlands
Gold and copper objects made in Balkans
Irrigation agriculture in Mesopotamia supports large populations
Wet rice farming east coast of China
Copper smelting in Europe
Use of plough
Domestication of horse in Eurasian Steppes
Use of sail in Egypt
Jade used for ornaments and weapons in China
Urban civilization in Sumer
Simple plough used in Northern and Western Europe
Bronze metallurgy in Southeast Asia
Earliest writing Mesopotamia
First evidence of Egyptian hieroglyphics
Silk weaving in China
Earliest true pyramid in Egypt
Use of 4-wheel war wagon in Mesopotamia
Stonehenge
State formation on Crete
Two-wheeled war chariot in Mesopotamia
Rulers buried in tombs in the Valley of Kings Egypt
Development of first alphabet
Development of pastoral nomadism on Steppes
First coins in China
First copper smelting in sub-Saharan Africa
Athens, most powerful Greek City-States, reaches its peak
Chinese Empire builds Great Wall
Camel introduced into Sahara
Indian religion spread to Southeast Asia along maritime trade routes
Chinese silk trade to Romans
Roman pottery as far as Northern Europe and India
First settlement in Rome
Iron working spreads to Rome
First coins in Asia Minor
Old World Cultural Development

Egypt and Mesopotamia were the first centers of civilization in the Old World. By 7,000 years ago, farming based on cereal agriculture and cattle had developed along the Nile River. Within 2,000 years, small kingdoms and villages became consolidated into a great state led by a king (pharaoh) who was viewed as both father and god. Elites had power through the control of agricultural surplus and labor. The first great flowering of Egyptian civilization was in the Old Kingdom period of 4,680–3,134 years ago, when the great pyramid tombs were built. Originating with farming villages, Mesopotamia developed cities, irrigation agriculture, and writing. Mesopotamian civilization dates to 5,500 years ago and displays craft specialization, growth of centralized religious and secular control, and an expansion in trade.

Map 28 Ancient Trade Systems of the Old World

Some archaeologists have linked the origins and evolution of complex societies to technological innovation and increasing trade in raw materials and luxury products. Trade involves two elements: commodities and people doing the exchange. People develop trading networks when they need goods and services that are not available within their local area. For-

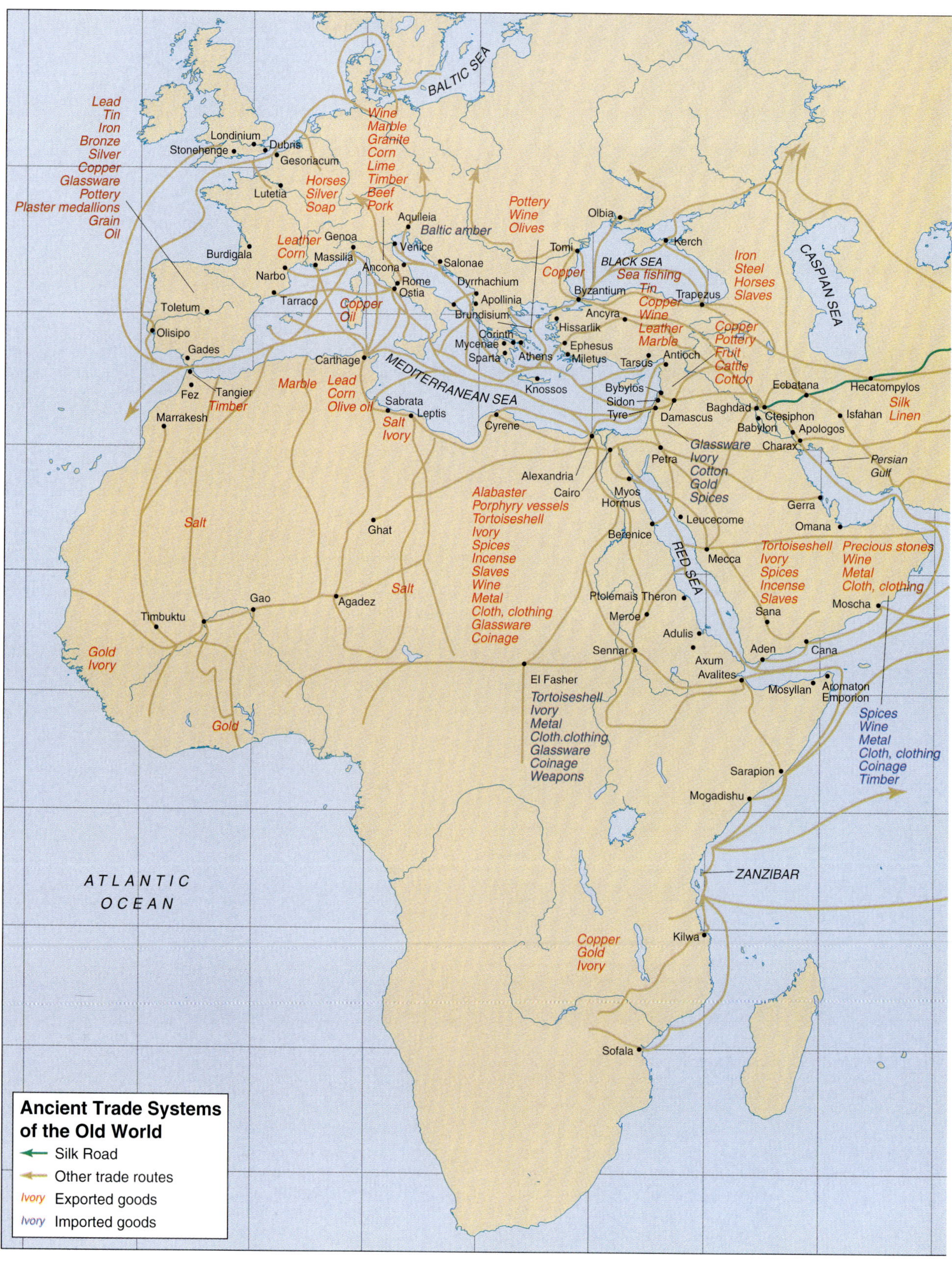

BALTIC SEA
Lead
Tin
Iron
Bronze
Silver
Copper
Glassware
Pottery
Plaster medallions
Grain
Oil
Londinium
Stonehenge
Dubris
Gesoriacum
Lutetia
Wine
Marble
Granite
Corn
Lime
Timber
Beef
Pork
Horses
Silver
Soap
Aquileia
Baltic amber
Pottery
Wine
Olives
Olbia
Burdigala
Leather
Corn
Genoa
Venice
Massilia
Narbo
Ancona
Salonae
Rome
Ostia
Tarraco
Copper
Oil
Dyrrhachium
Apollinia
Brundisium
Tomi
Kerch
BLACK SEA
Sea fishing
Copper
Byzantium
Tin
Copper
Wine
Leather
Marble
Trapezus
Iron
Steel
Horses
Slaves
CASPIAN SEA
Toletum
Olisipo
Gades
Ancyra
Hissarlik
Corinth
Mycenae
Sparta
Athens
Ephesus
Miletus
Tarsus
Antioch
Copper
Pottery
Fruit
Cattle
Cotton
Carthage
MEDITERRANEAN SEA
Fez
Tangier
Timber
Marrakesh
Marble
Lead
Corn
Olive oil
Sabrata
Leptis
Salt
Ivory
Cyrene
Knossos
Byblos
Sidon
Tyre
Damascus
Baghdad
Ctesiphon
Babylon
Apologos
Ecbatana
Hecatompylos
Isfahan
Silk
Linen
Charax
Persian Gulf
Petra
Glassware
Ivory
Cotton
Gold
Spices
Alexandria
Cairo
Myos Hormus
Alabaster
Porphyry vessels
Tortoiseshell
Ivory
Spices
Incense
Slaves
Wine
Metal
Cloth, clothing
Glassware
Coinage
Salt
Ghat
Gerra
Omana
Leucecome
Berenice
RED SEA
Mecca
Tortoiseshell
Ivory
Spices
Incense
Slaves
Precious stones
Wine
Metal
Cloth, clothing
Salt
Agadez
Gao
Timbuktu
Ptolemais Theron
Meroe
Sana
Moscha
Adulis
Axum
Aden
Cana
Sennar
Avalites
Mosyllan
Aromaton Emporion
Gold
Ivory
Gold
El Fasher
Tortoiseshell
Ivory
Metal
Cloth.clothing
Glassware
Coinage
Weapons
Spices
Wine
Metal
Cloth, clothing
Coinage
Timber
Sarapion
Mogadishu
ATLANTIC OCEAN
ZANZIBAR
Kilwa
Copper
Gold
Ivory
Sofala
Ancient Trade Systems of the Old World
Silk Road
Other trade routes
Ivory Exported goods
Ivory Imported goods

mal trade based on regulated commerce and currency is closely linked to the development of state-level societies. Trade facilitated the development of complex transportation systems over land and water and fostered the spread of innovations in the Old World such as the alphabet and metallurgy. Religions diffused along trade routes as did diseases.

Lake Baikal
Lake Balkash
ARAL SEA
Kuldja
Turfan
Aksu
Anxi
Samarkand
Kashgar
Dunhuang
Bactra
Yarkand
Merv
Khotan
Wuwei
Luoyang
Kaifeng
Herat
Begram
Taxila
Chang'an
Kandahar
Incense
Wine
Metal
Cloth, clothing
Glassware
Coinage
Ivory
Furniture Inlay
Tortoiseshell
Spices
Incense
Precious stones
Cloth, clothing
Timber
Sugar
Mathura
Chengdu
Silk
Clothing
Han mirrors
Laquerware
Spices
Drugs
Porcelain
Hangzhou
Hankou
Ningbo
Fuzhou
Quanzhou
Barbaricon
Pataliputra
Nalanda
Kunming
Tamluk
Nanhai (Guangzhou)
Cattigara
Barygaza
Mandagora
PACIFIC OCEAN
Amaravati
Masulipatam
Thaton
Gold
Ivory
Furniture Inlay
Tortoiseshell
Spices
Incense
Precious stones
Cloth, clothing
Poduca
Muziris
Colchi
Oc Eo
Trang
Cinnamon
Precious stones
Ivory
Spices
Incense
Wine
Metal
Cloth, clothing
Glassware
Coinage
Malacca
INDIAN OCEAN
Spices
Camphor
0 500 1000 1500 Miles
0 500 1000 1500 Kilometers

Map 29 Peopling of the New World I

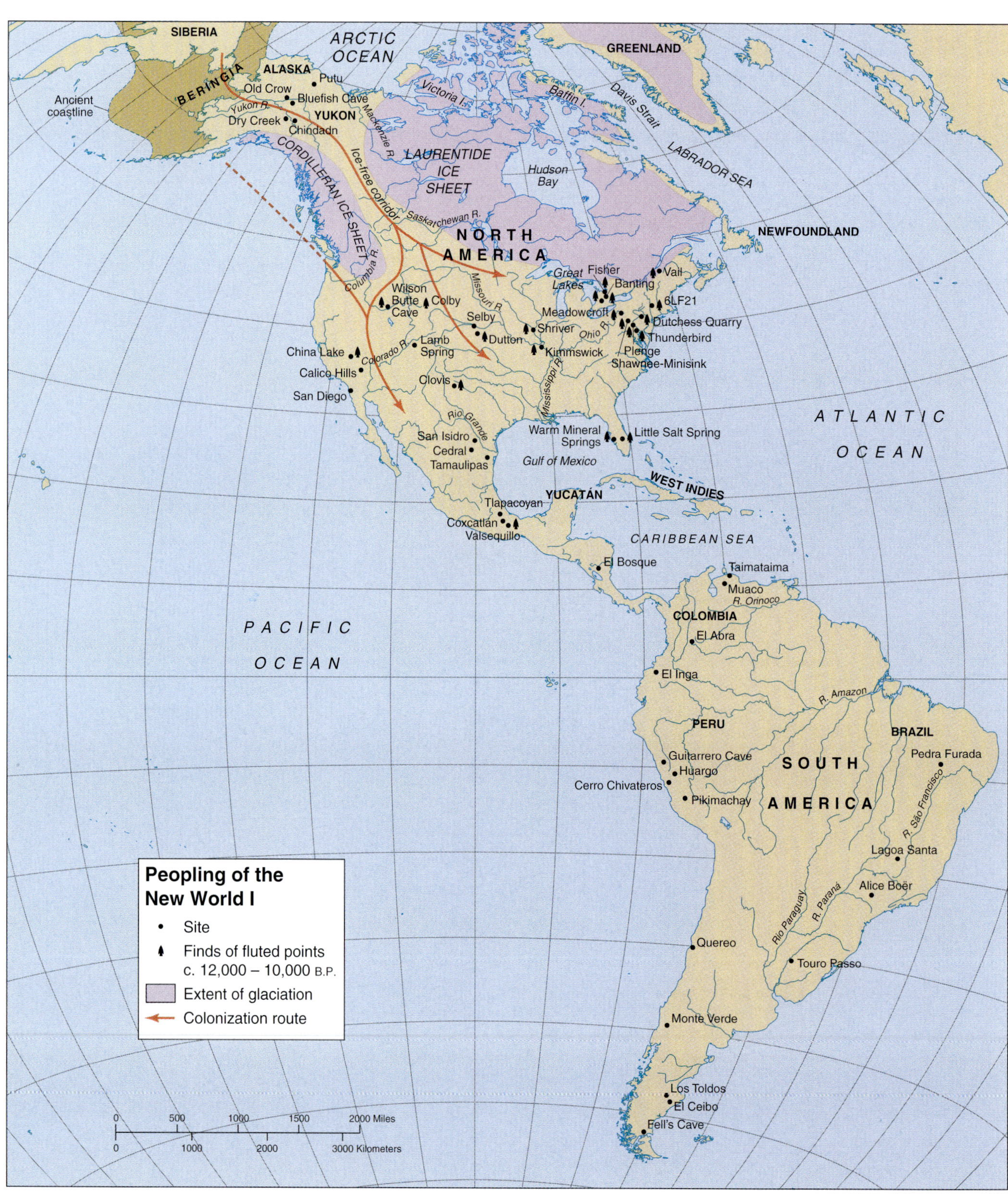

SIBERIA
ARCTIC OCEAN
GREENLAND
ALASKA
BERINGIA
Ancient coastline
Putu
Old Crow
Bluefish Cave
Yukon R.
YUKON
Dry Creek
Chindadn
Victoria I.
Baffin I.
Davis Strait
Mackenzie R.
LAURENTIDE ICE SHEET
Hudson Bay
LABRADOR SEA
CORDILLERAN ICE SHEET
Ice-free corridor
Saskatchewan R.
NEWFOUNDLAND
NORTH AMERICA
Columbia R.
Great Lakes
Fisher
Banting
Vail
6LF21
Wilson Butte Cave
Colby
Missouri R.
Selby
Meadowcroft
Dutchess Quarry
Shriver
Ohio R.
Thunderbird
Dutton
Lamb Spring
Colorado R.
Kimmswick
Plenge
China Lake
Shawnee-Minisink
Calico Hills
Clovis
Mississippi R.
San Diego
ATLANTIC OCEAN
Rio Grande
Warm Mineral Springs
Little Salt Spring
San Isidro
Cedral
Tamaulipas
Gulf of Mexico
WEST INDIES
YUCATÁN
Tlapacoyan
Coxcatlán
Valsequillo
CARIBBEAN SEA
El Bosque
Taimataima
Muaco
R. Orinoco
PACIFIC OCEAN
COLOMBIA
El Abra
El Inga
R. Amazon
PERU
BRAZIL
Pedra Furada
Guitarrero Cave
Huargo
SOUTH AMERICA
Cerro Chivateros
Pikimachay
R. São Francisco
Lagoa Santa
Alice Boër
Rio Paraguay
R. Paraná
Quereo
Touro Passo
Monte Verde
Los Toldos
El Ceibo
Fell's Cave
0 500 1000 1500 2000 Miles
0 1000 2000 3000 Kilometers
Peopling of the New World I
Site
Finds of fluted points c. 12,000 – 10,000 B.P.
Extent of glaciation
Colonization route

This map shows migrations across Beringia into northwestern North America. The people who came into the Americas are often referred to as Paleoindians, from the word *paleo*, meaning "old." Often tool types name the cultural sequences of the Paleoindians. For example, the Clovis peoples (10,000–11,000+ years ago) are known for their lanceolate points from 1 to 5 inches long with fluting (lengthwise channels) on both sides. Clovis peoples hunted now-extinct animals such as mammoths and archaic forms of bison.

Map 30 Peopling of the New World II

ARCTIC OCEAN
PACIFIC OCEAN
ATLANTIC OCEAN
LABRADOR SEA
Hudson Bay
Gulf of Mexico
CARIBBEAN SEA
NORTH AMERICA
SOUTH AMERICA
Yukon R.
Mackenzie R.
Saskatchewan R.
Columbia R.
Missouri R.
Great Lakes
Ohio R.
Colorado R.
Mississippi R.
Rio Grande
R. Orinoco
R. Amazon
R. São Francisco
Rio Paraguay
R. Paraná
Peopling of the New World II
Areas inhabited until recent times by farming cultures
Areas of independent Arctic influence
Areas of early food domestication and monumental ceremonial centers
Areas inhabited by hunting-and-gathering groups that received cultural influences from other regions
Probable routes followed by early and late hunting tribes from Inner Asia and Ice-Age Beringia
Probable paths for the diffusion of cultural, mythic and ritual forms
Suggested arrival of Asian influences c. 3000 B.P.
ARCTIC OCEAN
CHUKCHI SEA
Pt. Hope
Ipiutak
INUIT
PALEO-INDIANS
ALASKA
SIBERIA
NA-DENE
HUNTERS
Cape Denbigh
BERING SEA
ALEUTS
ALEUTIAN ISLANDS
ANAGULA ISLAND
Beringia
Estimated maximum land-bridge area
0 500 Miles
0 500 Kilometers
0 500 1000 1500 2000 Miles
0 1000 2000 3000 Kilometers

The map shows migrations into the Americas indicating possible routes into Mesoamerica and South America. A problem for archaeologists who study the New World is that some archaeological sites in South America seem to date from earlier periods than sites in North America. Archaeologists ask, Did people come through Beringia and move rapidly down coastal regions? Could some dates be wrong? Have earlier sites in North America not yet been found because they lie beneath the ocean? The last prehistoric migration into North America (perhaps around 1,500 years ago) was Inuit peoples moving into the Arctic region.

Map 31 Ancient Civilizations of Mesoamerica and South America

Rio Grande
Setaria
Pumpkin
Common bean
Bottle gourd
Gulf of Mexico
TOLTEC
TEOTIHUACÁN
OLMEC
Valley of Mexico
MAYA
Cucurbit (squash)
Maize
Cotton
Chilli pepper
Bottle gourd
Tepary bean
Amaranth
AZTEC
Valley of Oaxaca
Bottle gourd
Maize
Pumpkin
CARIBBEAN SEA
ATLANTIC OCEAN
R.Orinoco
Maize
Maize
Guinea pig
Maize
R. Amazon
PACIFIC OCEAN

Lima bean
Dog
Llama
Llama
Llama
SOUTH AMERICA
Cucurbit (squash)
Bottle gourd
INKA
Ulluco
Sweet potato
Potato
Lima bean
Maize
Quinoa
Bottle gourd
Llama
Guinea pig
R. Paraguay
R. Paraná
ATLANTIC OCEAN
Ancient Civilizations and Sites of Mesoamerica and South America
Teotihuacán
Toltec
Aztec
Olmec
Maya
Inka
Early agricultural settlement
Oldest dated pottery
Early plant domestication
Early animal domestication
Growth of teosinte (wild ancestor of maize)
Habitat of wild llama
Maize Early domesticated plants
Llama Early domesticated animals
0 500 1000 Miles
0 500 1000 Kilometers

Complex calendars, ceremonial centers, and elaborate architecture epitomize the urban civilizations of Mesoamerica, including the Olmec, Maya, Toltec, and Aztec. The origins of urban civilizations in Mesoamerica date back to village farming communities that flourished about 4,000 years ago. The Spanish under Hernán Cortés conquered the Aztec Empire in 1519–1521. Long-distance roadways, intricate tapestry weavings, and metallurgy are among the features of Andean civilizations, which include the Moche, Chimú, Nazca, and Inka. The Inka Empire, which at its zenith extended over as many as 6 million people, was conquered by the Spanish under Francisco Pizarro in 1532–1534.

Map 32 Ancient Trade Systems of the New World

Ancient Trade Systems of the New World
Hopewell
Teotihuacán
Toltec
Aztec
Olmec
Maya
Inka
Trade center
Early agricultural site
Trade routes
Chert Traded items
0 500 1000 Miles
0 500 1000 Kilometers
NORTH AMERICA
ATLANTIC OCEAN
PACIFIC OCEAN
Gulf of Mexico
CARIBBEAN SEA
Saskatchewan R.
Fraser R.
Columbia R.
Missouri R.
Mississippi R.
Ohio R.
Colorado R.
Rio Grande
R. Orinoco
R. Amazon
HOPEWELL
TOLTEC
OLMEC
MAYA
INKA
Fish grease
Shells
Hides
Exotic raw materials
Flint
Obsidian
Obsidian
Chert
Turquoise
Copper bells
Shells
Copper
Silver
Chert
Bauxite
Flint
Fluorspar
Flint
Galena
Copper
Galena
Shells
Galena
Mica
Chlorite
Mica
Quartz crystal
Conch shell
Conch shell
Alligator teeth
Shark teeth
Turtle shell
Shells
Turquoise
Slaves
Chaco Canyon
Hopi
Rio Grande Pueblos
Casa Grandes
Zape
Chalchihuites
La Quemaja
Tula
Teotihuacán
Tenochtitlan
Cholula
Inset area
Inset area
Items traded by Maya
Copal incense
Bark paper
Metalwork
Cacao
Obsidian
Jade
Feathers
Slaves
Marine products and shells
Salt
0 250 500 Miles
0 250 500 Kilometers
Schroeder
Chalchihuites
White jade
Blue green stones
Flint
Haematite
La Quemada
Amapa
Las Flores
El Tajín
Teotihuacán
Tlaxcala
Cempoala
Apatzingán
Xochicalco
Cholula
Cerro de las Mesas
Champotón
Chichén Itzá
Cosimel
Xelha
Coba
Dzibilchaltún
Mayapán
Tulum
Turquoise
Cacao
Tres Zapotes
Lime
Matacapan
Potonchan
Becan
Tayasal
Tikal
Altun Ha
Moho Cay
Items traded by Olmec
Basalt
Magnetite
Serpentine
Jade
Monte Albán
Chiapa de Corzo
Yaxhá
Nebaj
Utatlán
Zaculeu
Tajamulco
El Chayal
Copan
Kaminaljuyú
Cotzumalhuapa
Excuintla
Conch
Thorny oyster shells
Metalwork imported from Central America
Center of Aztec foreign trade
Trade routes
Trade center
Jade Traded items
Quito
Tumbes
Tomebamba
Cosibamba
Cajamarca
Feathers
Hallucinogens
Chan Chan
Coastal area
Cotton
Marine shells
Huanuco Pampa
Pumpu
Tarma-Tambo
Jauja
Highland area
Root crops
Wool
Paramonga
Ancón
Lurin
Inkawasi
Tambo Colorado
Ica
Vilcashuamán
Limatambo
Pucará
Machu Pichu
Pisac
Ollantaytambo
Cuzco
Raqhi
Ayavin
Hatuncolla
Chucuito
Chuquiabo
Cotopachi
Cochabamba
R. Amazon
PACIFIC OCEAN
0 500 Miles
0 500 Kilometers
Inka road
Major Inka center
Minor Inka center
Wool Traded items

Trade is an important source of power in urban civilizations. It fosters the integration of local communities and the state. Tribute and trade were often combined, as, for example, in the Aztec Empire, which relied on a professional merchant class. In Andean civilization, trade was important in linking coastal and highland cultures. Even in nonstate societies, cultures are not isolated; long-distance trading networks were important in aboriginal North America and tropical South America too. See Maps 34 and 35 for some cultural developments in aboriginal North America that may have been fostered by long-distance trade from Mesoamerica.

Map 33 Culture Regions of the New World

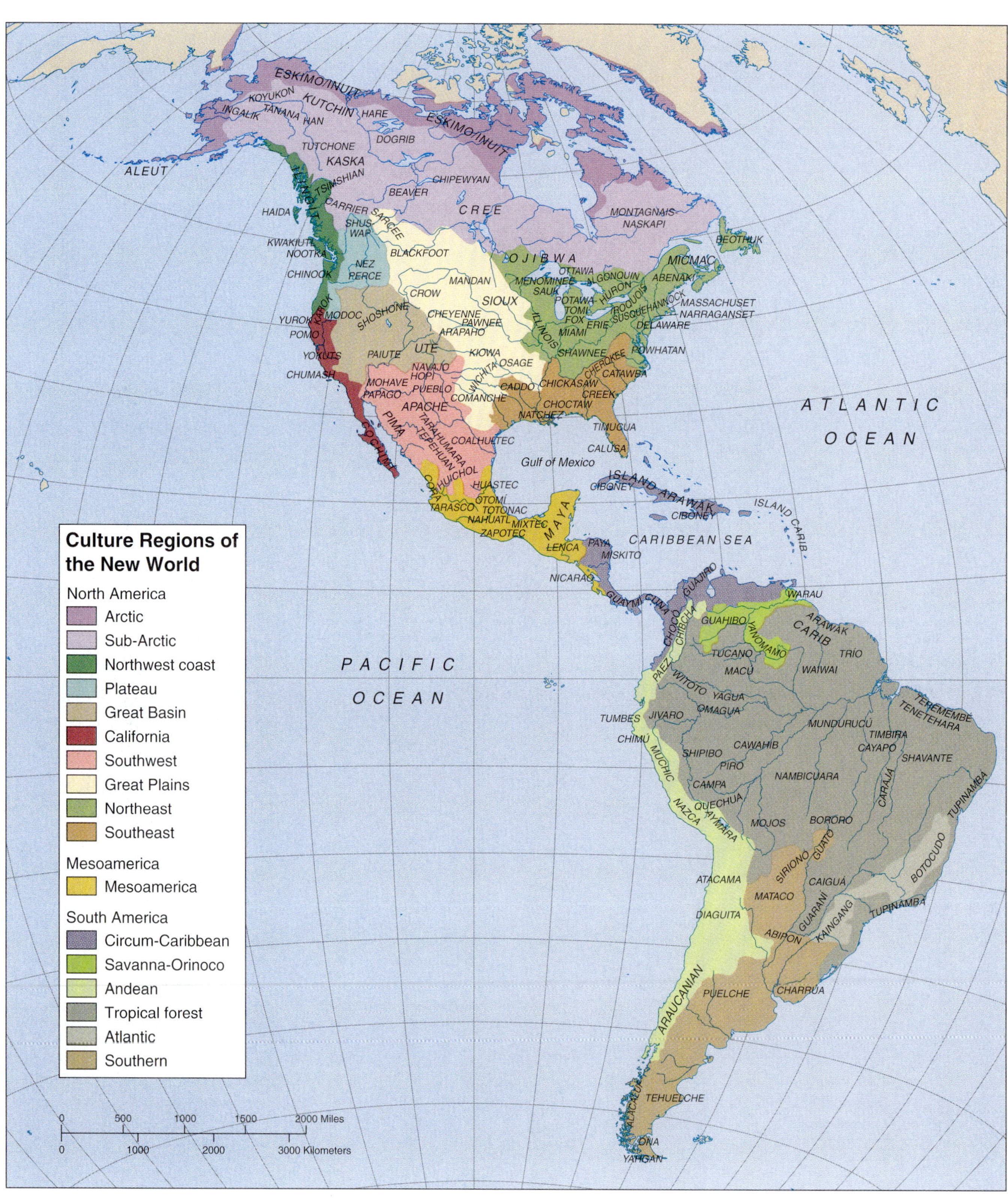
Culture Regions of the New World
North America
Arctic
Sub-Arctic
Northwest coast
Plateau
Great Basin
California
Southwest
Great Plains
Northeast
Southeast
Mesoamerica
Mesoamerica
South America
Circum-Caribbean
Savanna-Orinoco
Andean
Tropical forest
Atlantic
Southern
0 500 1000 1500 2000 Miles
0 1000 2000 3000 Kilometers
ATLANTIC OCEAN
PACIFIC OCEAN
Gulf of Mexico
CARIBBEAN SEA
ESKIMO/INUIT
KOYUKON
KUTCHIN
INGALIK
TANANA
HAN
HARE
ESKIMO/INUIT
DOGRIB
TUTCHONE
KASKA
ALEUT
TSIMSHIAN
TLINGIT
BEAVER
CHIPEWYAN
HAIDA
CARRIER
SARCEE
SHUSWAP
CREE
MONTAGNAIS-NASKAPI
BEOTHUK
KWAKIUTL
NOOTKA
BLACKFOOT
OJIBWA
MICMAC
CHINOOK
NEZ PERCE
OTTAWA
ALGONQUIN
ABENAKI
MANDAN
MENOMINEE
SAUK
HURON
CROW
SIOUX
POTAWATOMI
IROQUOIS
SUSQUEHANNOCK
MASSACHUSET
NARRAGANSET
YUROK
KAROK
MODOC
SHOSHONE
CHEYENNE
PAWNEE
ARAPAHO
FOX
ERIE
DELAWARE
POMO
MIAMI
ILLINOIS
UTE
PAIUTE
KIOWA
SHAWNEE
POWHATAN
YOKUTS
NAVAJO
OSAGE
CHEROKEE
CATAWBA
CHUMASH
HOPI
WICHITA
MOHAVE
PUEBLO
CADDO
CHICKASAW
PAPAGO
COMANCHE
CREEK
APACHE
CHOCTAW
NATCHEZ
PIMA
TARAHUMARA
TEPEHUAN
TIMUCUA
COCHIMI
COAHUILTEC
CALUSA
CORA
HUICHOL
HUASTEC
ISLAND ARAWAK
CIBONEY
OTOMÍ
TARASCO
TOTONAC
NAHUATL
MIXTEC
ZAPOTEC
MAYA
CIBONEY
ISLAND CARIB
LENCA
PAYA
MISKITO
NICARAO
GUAYMI
CUNA
GUAJIRO
CHOCO
CHIBCHA
WARAU
GUAHIBO
YANOMAMO
ARAWAK
CARIB
TUCANO
TRIO
MACU
WAIWAI
PAEZ
WITOTO
YAGUA
OMAGUA
TEREMEMBE
TENETEHARA
TUMBES
JIVARO
MUNDURUCÚ
CHIMÚ
TIMBIRA
CAYAPO
SHIPIBO
CAWAHIB
SHAVANTE
MUCHIC
PIRO
NAMBICUARA
CAMPA
CARAJA
TUPINAMBA
NAZCA
QUECHUA
AYMARA
MOJOS
BORORO
SIRIONO
GUATO
BOTOCUDO
ATACAMA
CAIGUÁ
MATACO
GUARANÍ
KAINGANG
TUPINAMBA
DIAGUITA
ABIPON
CHARRUA
PUELCHE
ARAUCANIAN
TEHUELCHE
ALACALUF
ONA
YAHGAN

The culture regions of the New World roughly correspond to ecological zones. Societies in the same region were often similar in subsistence pattern, the way the group obtained food and fuel from the environment.

Map 34 Mound Builder Sites of Eastern North America

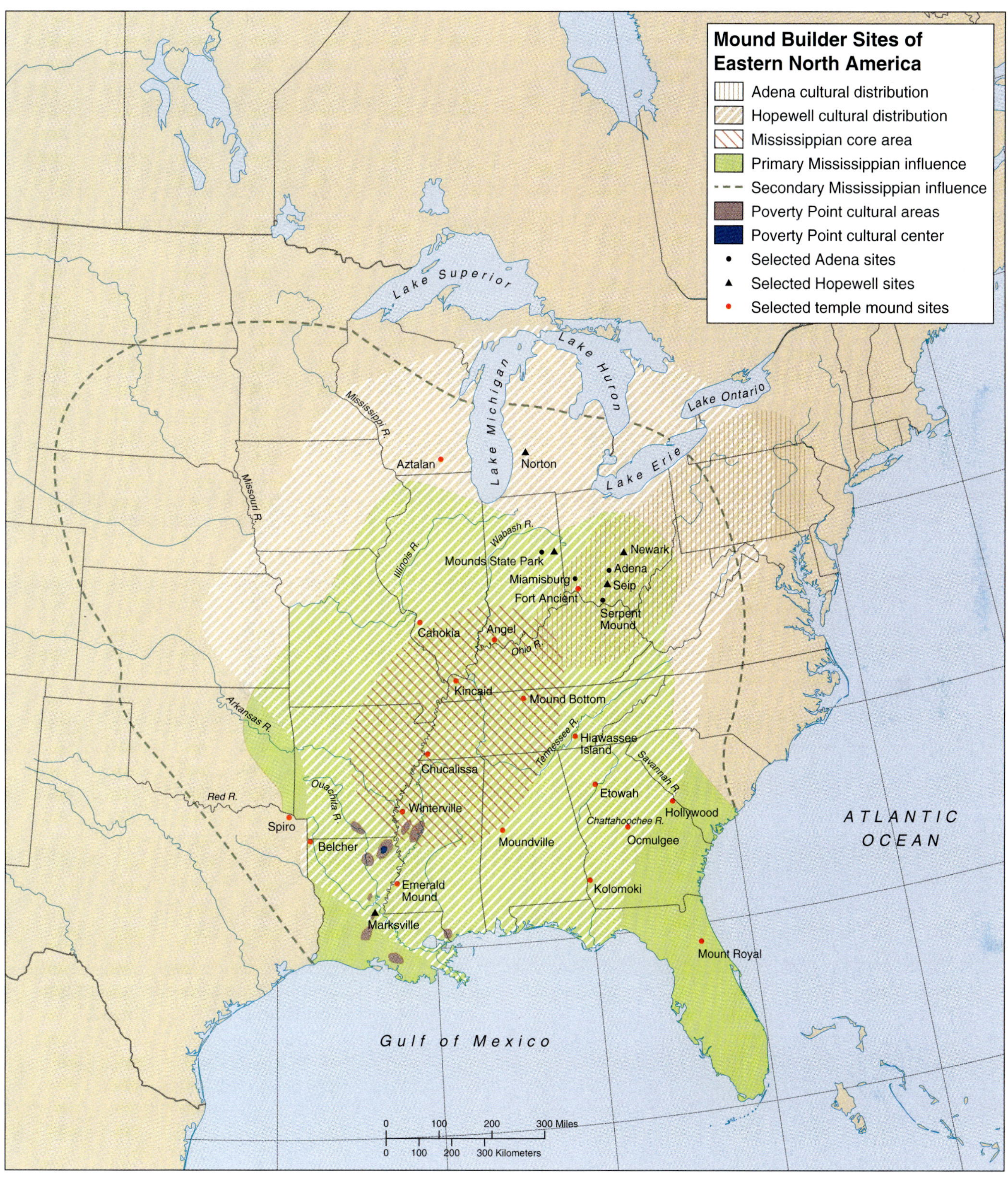

Mound Builder Sites of Eastern North America
Adena cultural distribution
Hopewell cultural distribution
Mississippian core area
Primary Mississippian influence
Secondary Mississippian influence
Poverty Point cultural areas
Poverty Point cultural center
Selected Adena sites
Selected Hopewell sites
Selected temple mound sites
Lake Superior
Lake Michigan
Lake Huron
Lake Ontario
Lake Erie
Mississippi R.
Missouri R.
Illinois R.
Wabash R.
Ohio R.
Tennessee R.
Arkansas R.
Red R.
Ouachita R.
Savannah R.
Chattahoochee R.
Aztalan
Norton
Newark
Mounds State Park
Adena
Miamisburg
Seip
Fort Ancient
Serpent Mound
Cahokia
Angel
Kincaid
Mound Bottom
Hiawassee Island
Chucalissa
Etowah
Hollywood
Winterville
Spiro
Belcher
Moundville
Ocmulgee
Emerald Mound
Kolomoki
Marksville
Mount Royal
ATLANTIC OCEAN
Gulf of Mexico
0 100 200 300 Miles
0 100 200 300 Kilometers

Different social and cultural patterns developed in North America as compared to Mesoamerica and South America. Although pre-contact North America lacked ancient states, the Mound Builder cultures did develop complex social and political organizations, distinctive artistic traditions, social stratification, and large earthworks for burials and temples. Some of the later Mound Builder centers, such as at Cahokia, supported large populations based on the cultivation of corn, beans, and squash; as many as 30,000 people may have lived there. The Mound Builders traded over great distances—archaeologists have found obsidian from northwest Wyoming in Mound Builder sites.

Map 35 Great Houses, Roadway Systems, and Ruins of the Southwest

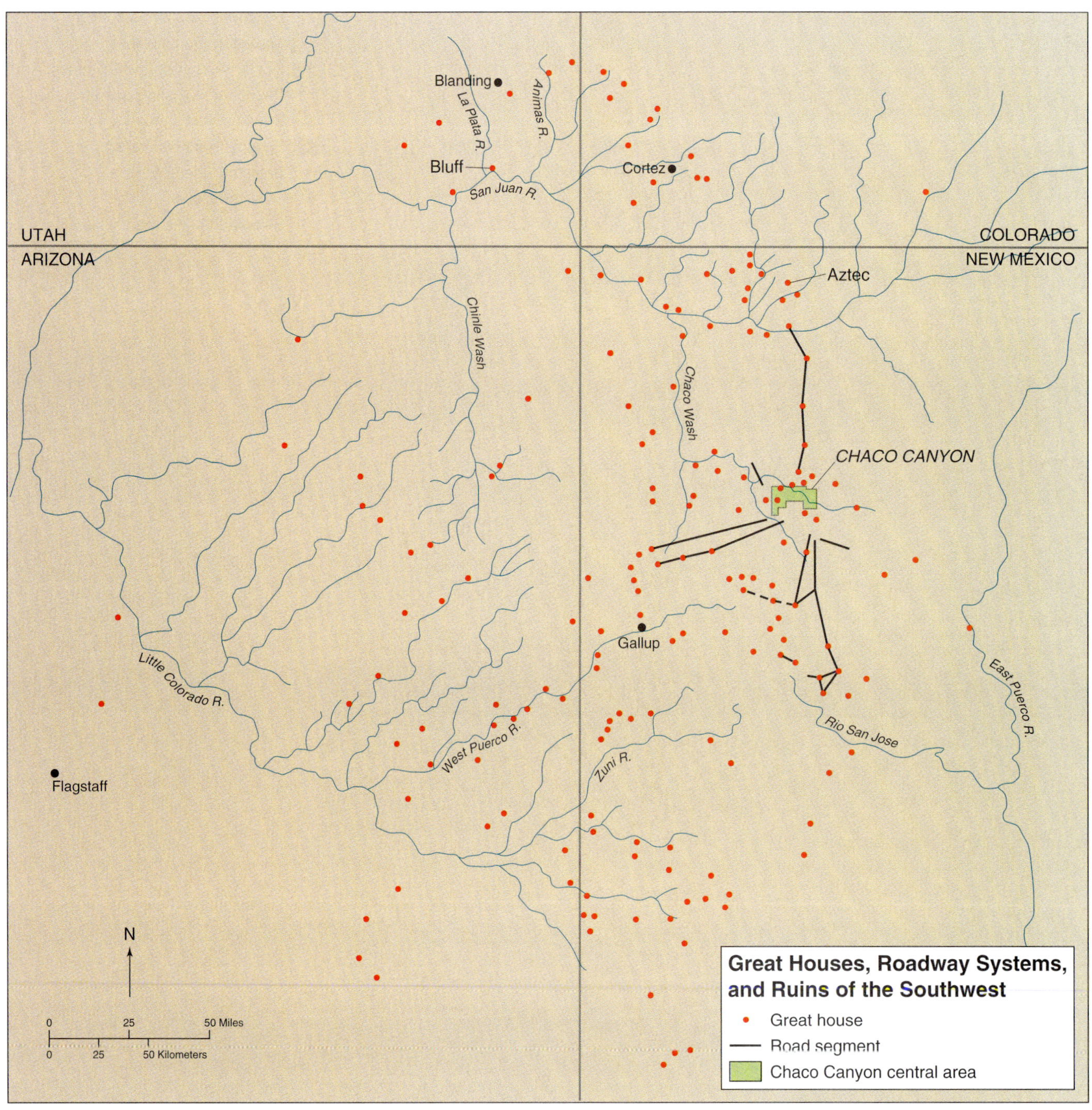

Blanding
La Plata R.
Animas R.
Bluff
San Juan R.
Cortez
UTAH
ARIZONA
COLORADO
NEW MEXICO
Aztec
Chinle Wash
Chaco Wash
CHACO CANYON
Gallup
Little Colorado R.
West Puerco R.
Zuni R.
Rio San Jose
East Puerco R.
Flagstaff
N
0
25
50 Miles
0
25
50 Kilometers
Great Houses, Roadway Systems, and Ruins of the Southwest
Great house
Road segment
Chaco Canyon central area

Unlike Mesoamerica and South America, ancient North America lacked archaic state-level societies. The Anasazi people of the Southwest, however, developed a complex society based on maize cultivation. Villages were linked for social, political, and ceremonial purposes through an intricate road system. The Anasazi culture flourished from 2,100 to 700 years ago. Their modern descendants are the Pueblo Indians.

Map 36 Native American–European Trade: Early Contact Period in North America

RUSSIA
ALASKA
CANADA
BERING SEA
0 250 Miles
0 250 Kilometers
SACREE
PLAINS CREE
1750
1730
BLOOD
BLACKFEET
1770
PLAINS OJIBWAY
ASSINIBOINE
1730
1710 PIEGAN
1720
GROS VENTRE
PALOUSE
NEZ PERCE
CAYUSE
1750
CROW
HIDATSA
MANDAN
1730
ARIKARA
1770
SIOUX
CHEYENNE
1775
1690–1700
SHOSHONE
PONCA
SIOUX
CALIFORNIA TRIBES
1720–1725
OMAHA
IOWAY
PAWNEE
1770
ARAPAHO
ILLINOIS
UTE
OTOE
KAW
MISSOURIA
1724
OSAGE
1659
NAVAJO
RIO GRANDE PUEBLOS
WESTERN PUEBLOS
1719
KIOWA
QUAPAW
KIOWA-APACHE
1600
APACHE
WICHITA
APACHE
KICHAI
1690
CADDO
COMANCHE
TAWAKONI
TONKAWA
ATLANTIC OCEAN
PACIFIC OCEAN
1690
Gulf of Mexico
0 100 200 300 Miles
0 100 200 300 Kilometers

Native American–European Trade
Early Contact Period in North America

- Route and approximate date of introduction of the horse

Fur Trading Posts
- French trading posts 1604–1760
- Hudson's Bay Company 1670–1869
- Montreal-based fur trade 1763–1784
- North West Company 1784–1821
- Spain and New Mexico 1598–1821
- Russian trading posts 1784–1867
- American colonies and United States 1686–1834

When different cultures come into contact, traits may diffuse or spread from one to the other. One or both cultures may be transformed by the contact situation. The map shows two types of cultural change based in the contact relationship of Native Americans and Europeans. In the Southwest, plateau, and the Plains, the use of the horse diffused among the Native Americans from Spanish colonizers in Mexico. Some tribes began to hunt the bison herds of the Plains from horseback, allowing increased reliance on this unique resource. In other parts of North America, Europeans were interested in the furs available in North America and sought relationships with Native Americans via trading companies. Some tribes became dependent on trading posts and modified their subsistence patterns with far-reaching consequences, entering the world market as the suppliers of fur to European entrepreneurs.

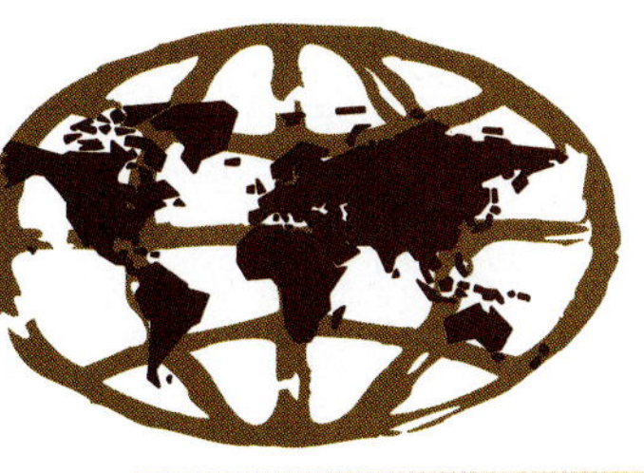

Part IV

Linguistic Anthropology

Map 37 World Languages
Map 38 Linguistic Diversity
Map 39 Modern Languages: Common versus Rare
Map 40 The Spread of Indo-European Languages
Map 41 Invented Languages: Pidgins, Jargons, and Creoles
Map 42 Language Families of Eurasia, A.D. 1500
Map 43 Language Families of Africa
Map 44a Language Families of the New World: North America
Map 44b Language Families of the New World: South America
Map 45 Native New World Languages: Interpretations

Map 37 World Languages

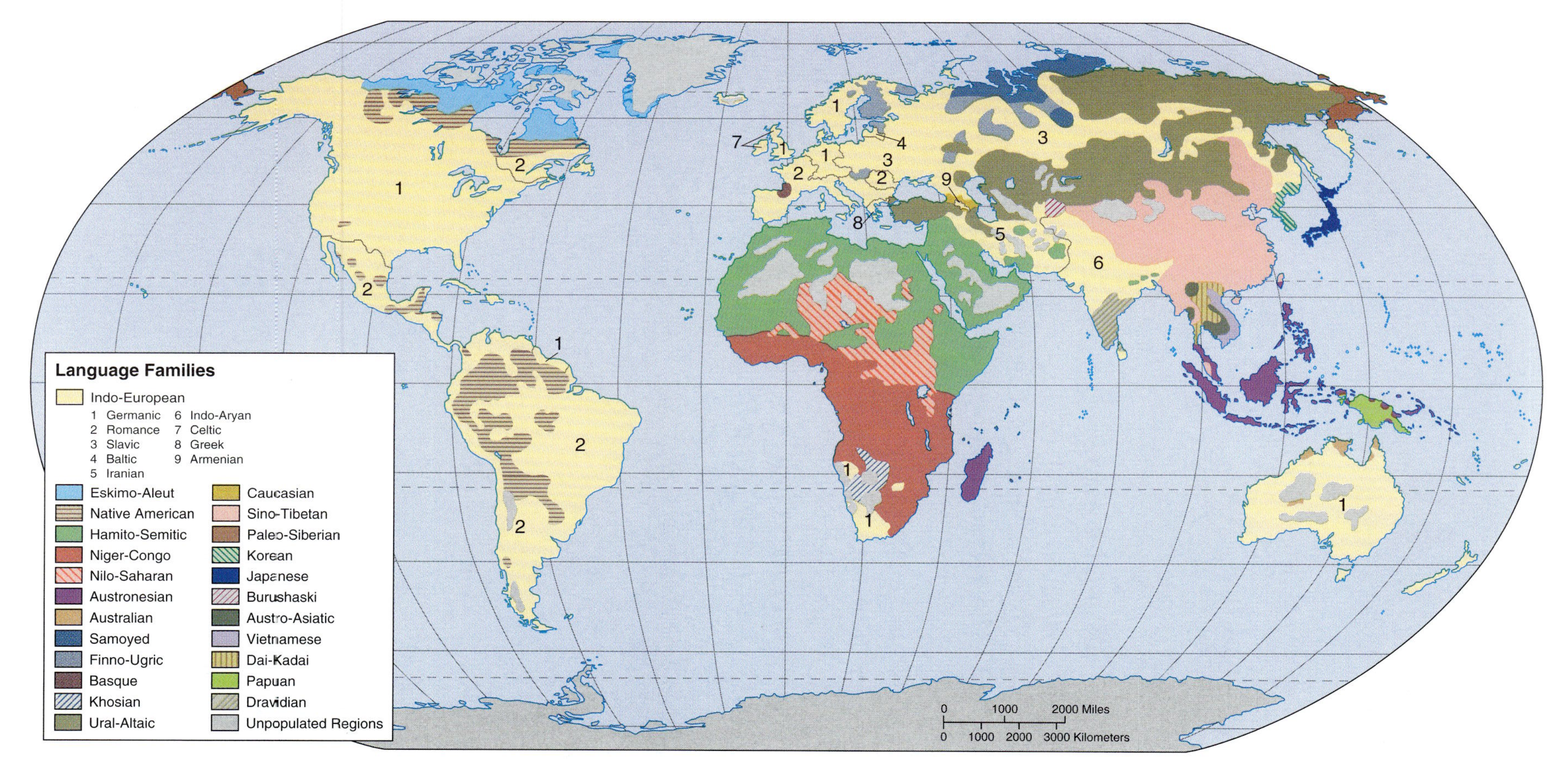

Language Families
Indo-European
1 Germanic
2 Romance
3 Slavic
4 Baltic
5 Iranian
6 Indo-Aryan
7 Celtic
8 Greek
9 Armenian
Eskimo-Aleut
Native American
Hamito-Semitic
Niger-Congo
Nilo-Saharan
Austronesian
Australian
Samoyed
Finno-Ugric
Basque
Khosian
Ural-Altaic
Caucasian
Sino-Tibetan
Paleo-Siberian
Korean
Japenese
Burushaski
Austro-Asiatic
Vietnamese
Dai-Kadai
Papuan
Dravidian
Unpopulated Regions
0 1000 2000 Miles
0 1000 2000 3000 Kilometers

Language, like religion, is an important identifying characteristic of culture. Indeed, it is perhaps the most durable of all those identifying characteristics or *cultural traits:* language, religion, institutions, material technologies, and ways of making a living. After centuries of exposure to other languages or even conquest by speakers of other languages, the speakers of a specific tongue will often retain their own linguistic identity. Language helps us to locate areas of potential conflict, particularly in regions where two or more languages overlap. Many, if not most, of the world's conflict zones are also areas of linguistic diversity. Knowing the distribution of languages helps us to understand some of the reasons behind important current events: for example, linguistic identity differences played an important part in the disintegration of the Soviet Union in the early 1990s; and in areas emerging from recent colonial rule, such as Africa, the participants in conflicts over territory and power are often defined in terms of linguistic groups. Language distributions also help us to comprehend the nature of the human past by providing clues that enable us to chart the course of human migrations, as shown in the distribution of Indo-European, Austronesian, or Hamito-Semitic languages. Finally, because languages have a great deal to do with the way people perceive and understand the world around them, linguistic patterns help to explain the global variations in the ways that people interact.

Map 38 Linguistic Diversity

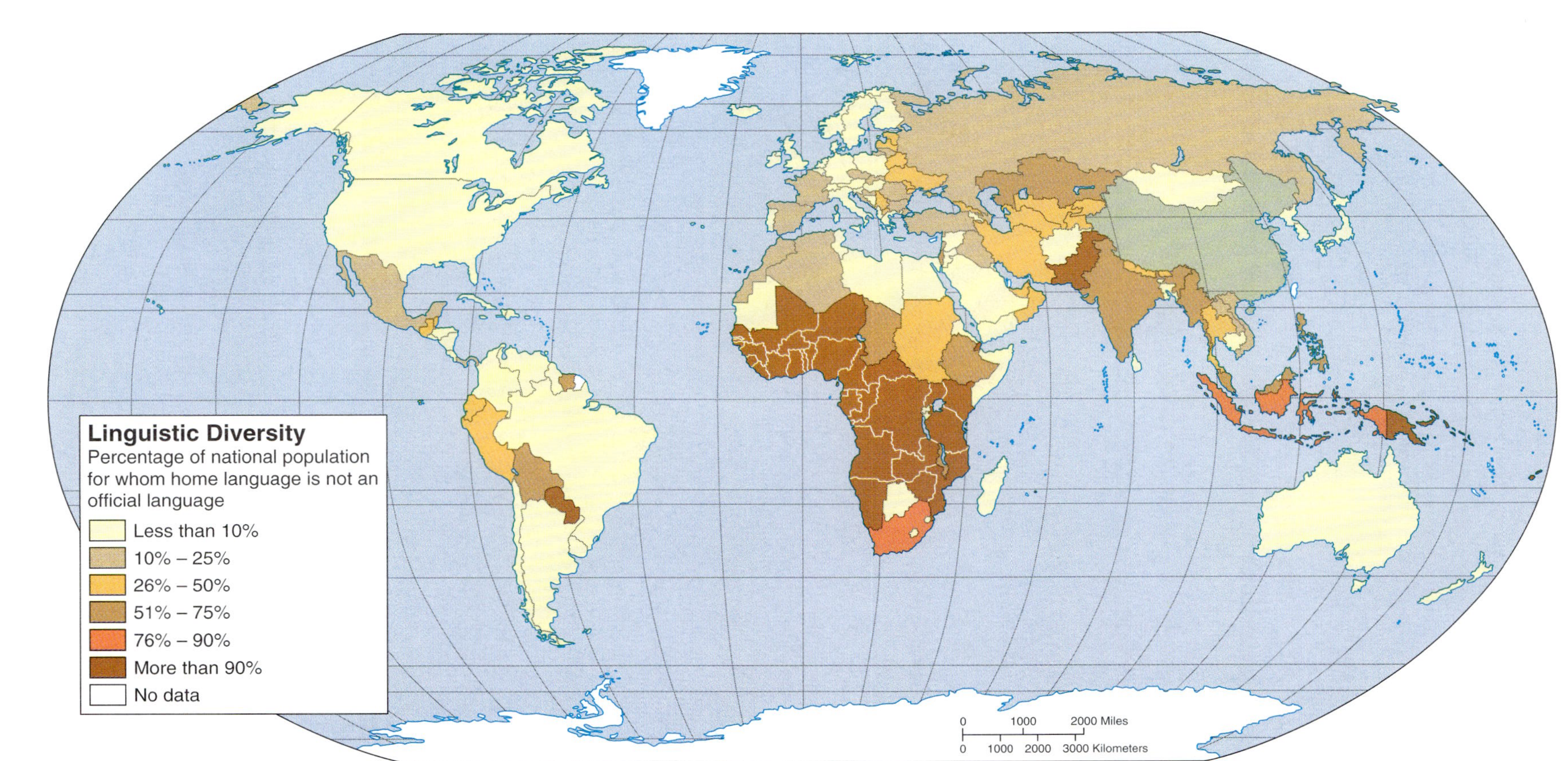

Linguistic Diversity
Percentage of national population for whom home language is not an official language
Less than 10%
10% – 25%
26% – 50%
51% – 75%
76% – 90%
More than 90%
No data
0 1000 2000 Miles
0 1000 2000 3000 Kilometers

Of the world's approximately 6,000 languages, fewer than 100 are official languages, those designated by a country as the language of government, commerce, education, and information. This means that for much of the world's population, the language that is spoken in the home is different from the official language of the country of residence. The world's former colonial areas in Middle and South America, Africa, and South and Southeast Asia stand out on the map as regions in which there is significant disparity between home languages and official languages. To complicate matters further, for most of the world's population, the primary international languages of trade and tourism (French and English) are neither home nor official languages.

Map 39 Modern Languages: Common Versus Rare

There are over 6,000 languages in the world today. Familiar languages like English, French, and Spanish have millions of speakers, as do languages like Arabic, Chinese, and Hindi. The map shows the world's most common languages in their home regions. As people have migrated to other places, so too have their languages. The map also shows some languages spoken by indigenous peoples that are far less common. Still, many tribal languages have hundreds of thousands of speakers and are not in danger of disappearing.

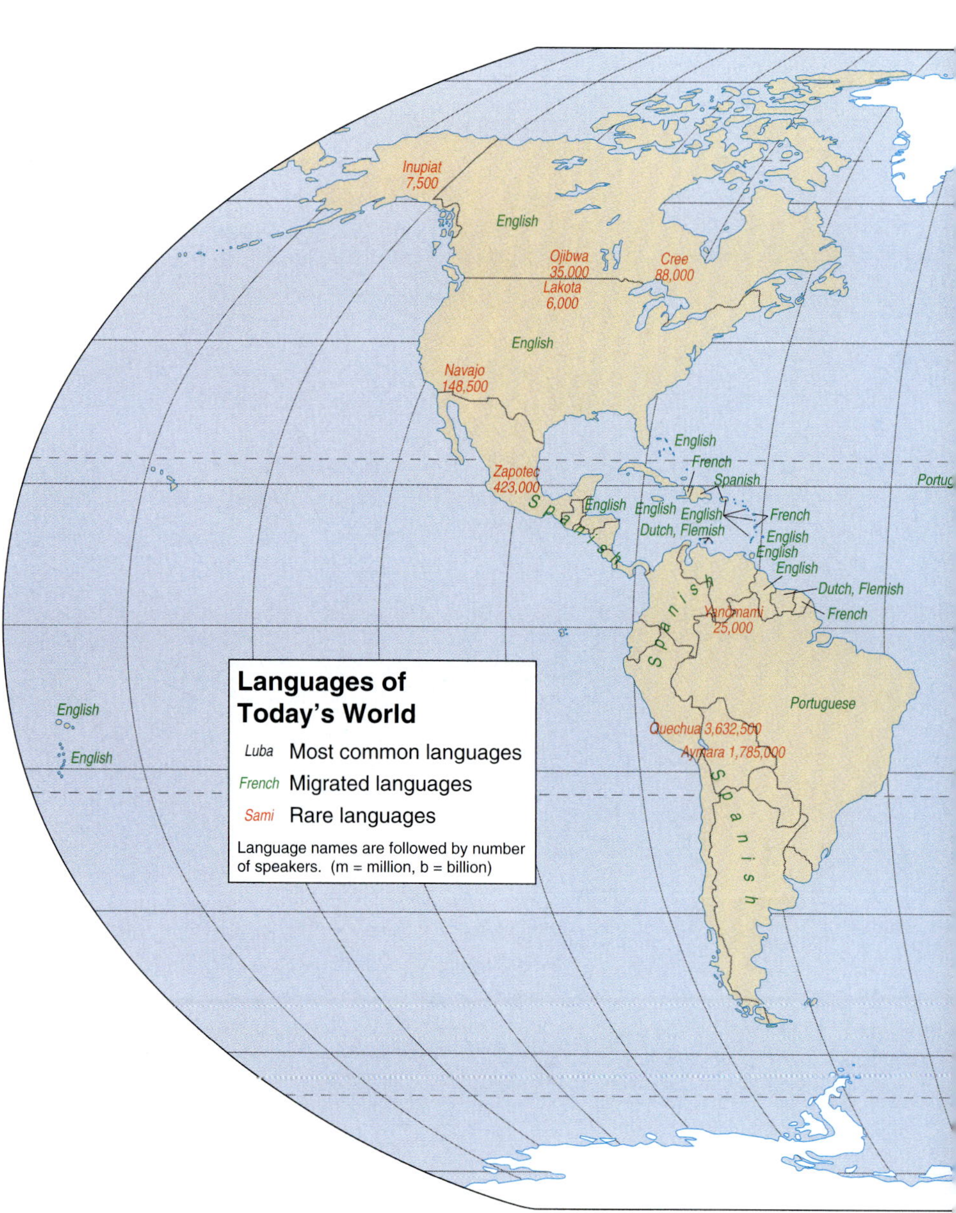

Languages of Today's World
Luba Most common languages
French Migrated languages
Sami Rare languages
Language names are followed by number of speakers. (m = million, b = billion)
Inupiat 7,500
English
Ojibwa 35,000
Lakota 6,000
Cree 88,000
English
Navajo 148,500
Zapotec 423,000
Spanish
English
French
Spanish
English
English
English
Dutch, Flemish
French
English
English
English
Dutch, Flemish
French
Spanish
Yanomami 25,000
Spanish
Portuguese
Quechua 3,632,500
Aymara 1,785,000
Spanish
English
English

Sami 17,000
Tungus 24,000
Chukchi 10,000
Dutch, Flemish 30m
English 1b
German 125m
Polish 47m
Russian 320m
French, Geman
Czech/Slovak 16m
Hungarian 15m
Ukrainian 60m
French 125m
Romanian 27m
Bulgarian 10m
Tatar, Bashkir 10m
Kazakh, Kirghiz 20m
Uzbek, Uyghur 25m
Italian 70m
Portuguese 200m
Spanish 450m
Serbo-Croat 19m
Greek 12m
Wider Turkish 70m
Wu 85m
Xiang 48m
Gan 20m
Hakka 35m
Min-bei 12m
Min-nan 55m
Korean 75m
Japanese 130m
Arabic
English
Kurdish 15m
Persian 40m
Pashto 25m
Arabic
Assamese 11m
Spanish
Panjabi 85m
Nepali 17m
Sindhi 18m
Mandarin 1b
English
Urdu/Hindi 900m
Bhojpuri, Maithili 60m
Gujarati 45m
Marathi 60m
Bengali 250m
Zhuang, Buyi 15m
Cantonese 70m
Berber 12m
Arabic 250m
Burmese 33m
Lao 30m
Dai 45m
Vietnamese 75m
Tagalog 45m
Cebuano 17m
Oriya 33m
Tamil 65m
Malayalam 35m
Telugu 70m
Kannada 45m
Sinhalese 14m
Hausa 40m
Mandinka 13m
Fula 16m
Igbo 19m
Yoruba 25m
Amharic 25m
Somali 10m
Oromo 14m
English
Malay-Indonesian 160m
Portuguese
Kongo 14m
Kikuyu, Kamba 11m
Lingala 15m
Luganda 18m
Rundi, Rwanda 15m
Swahili 60m
French, English
Enga 164,000
Huli 70,000
Melpa 130,000
Wahgi 87,000
Luba 12m
Madura 13m
Jawa 80m
Sunda 30m
Malagasy 13m
Fijian 330,400
French
French
English,
French
English
Aboriginal languages 47,000
Sotho, Tswana 20m
Zulu, Xhosa 30m
English
Maori 60,000
0 1000 2000 Miles
0 1000 2000 3000 Kilometers

Map 40 The Spread of Indo-European Languages

During the Age of Exploration, Europeans began to colonize other parts of the world. The map shows the expansion and dominance of European languages. Compare this map to Map 42, which shows the limits of the Indo-European language family before the Age of Exploration.

Bering
1741
Hudson
Frobisher 157
Champlain
1609
Cartier 1540
Minuet 1626
Raleigh1585
Cook 1779
Castillo
1521
Columbus1500's
Pizarro
1530's
Cook 1771 (Tahiti)
The Spread of Indo-European Languages
English
German
Dutch
French
Spanish
Portuguese
Russian
Cook
1771
Major explorer
In the colonial dominions of the European powers in Asia and Africa, the coloring shows the language of the dominant nation.

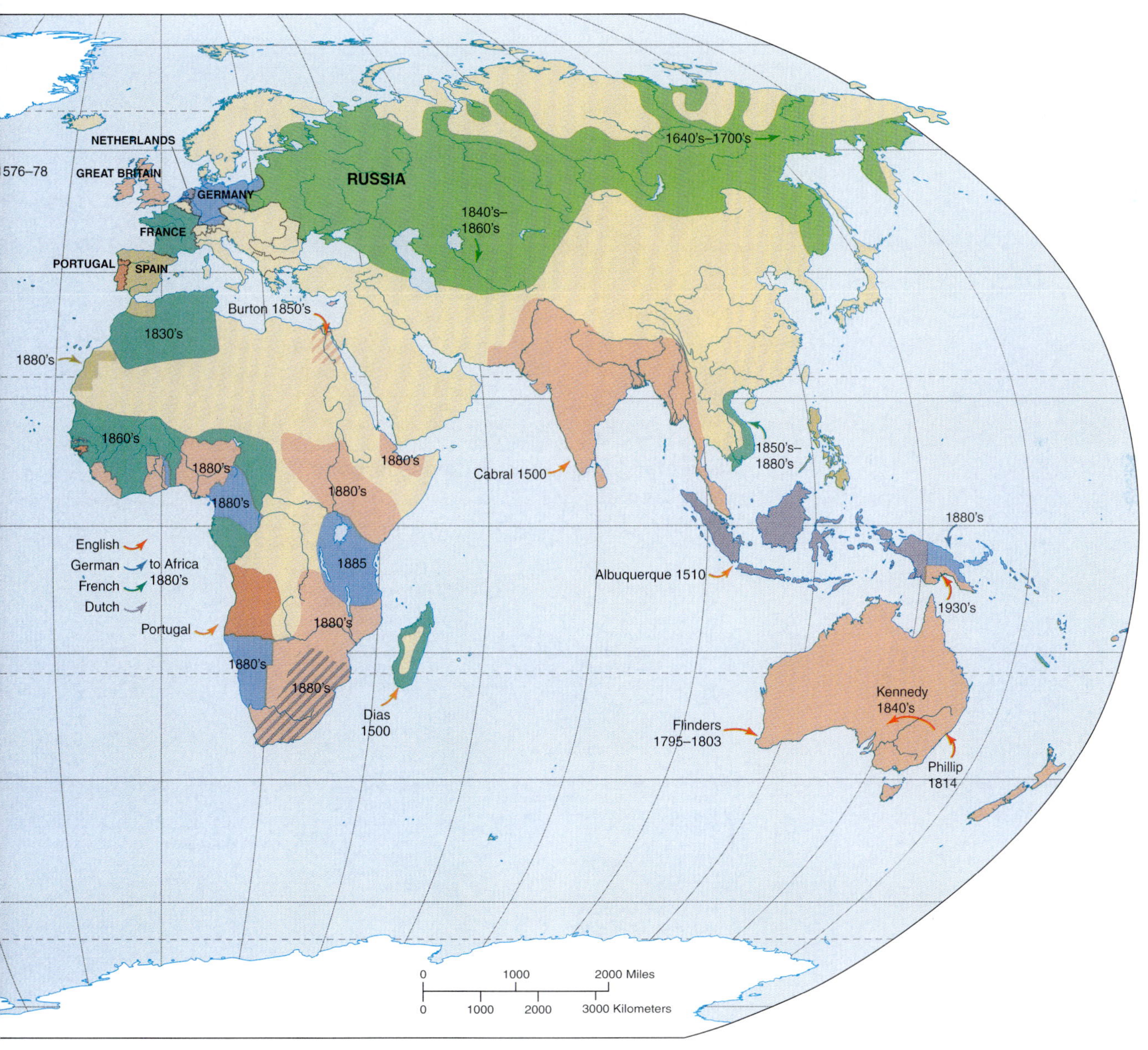

NETHERLANDS
576–78
GREAT BRITAIN
GERMANY
FRANCE
PORTUGAL
SPAIN
RUSSIA
1640's–1700's
1840's–
1860's
Burton 1850's
1830's
1880's
1860's
1880's
1880's
1880's
1880's
Cabral 1500
1850's–
1880's
1880's
English
German
French
Dutch
to Africa
1880's
Portugal
1885
Albuquerque 1510
1930's
1880's
1880's
1880's
Dias
1500
Kennedy
1840's
Flinders
1795–1803
Phillip
1814
0
1000
2000 Miles
0
1000
2000
3000 Kilometers

Map 41 Invented Languages: Pidgins, Jargons, and Creoles

Pidgins are languages that people create when speakers of two different languages have come into contact with each other. They are usually simplified forms that have vocabulary from both languages, which the people use as a second language to be able to talk to members of the other group. Over time, later generations in the area may come to speak this new language as their native tongue. It then is called a creole. Creoles are fully developed grammatical languages. Languages that have developed to meet specialized purposes, such as trade, are known as jargons.

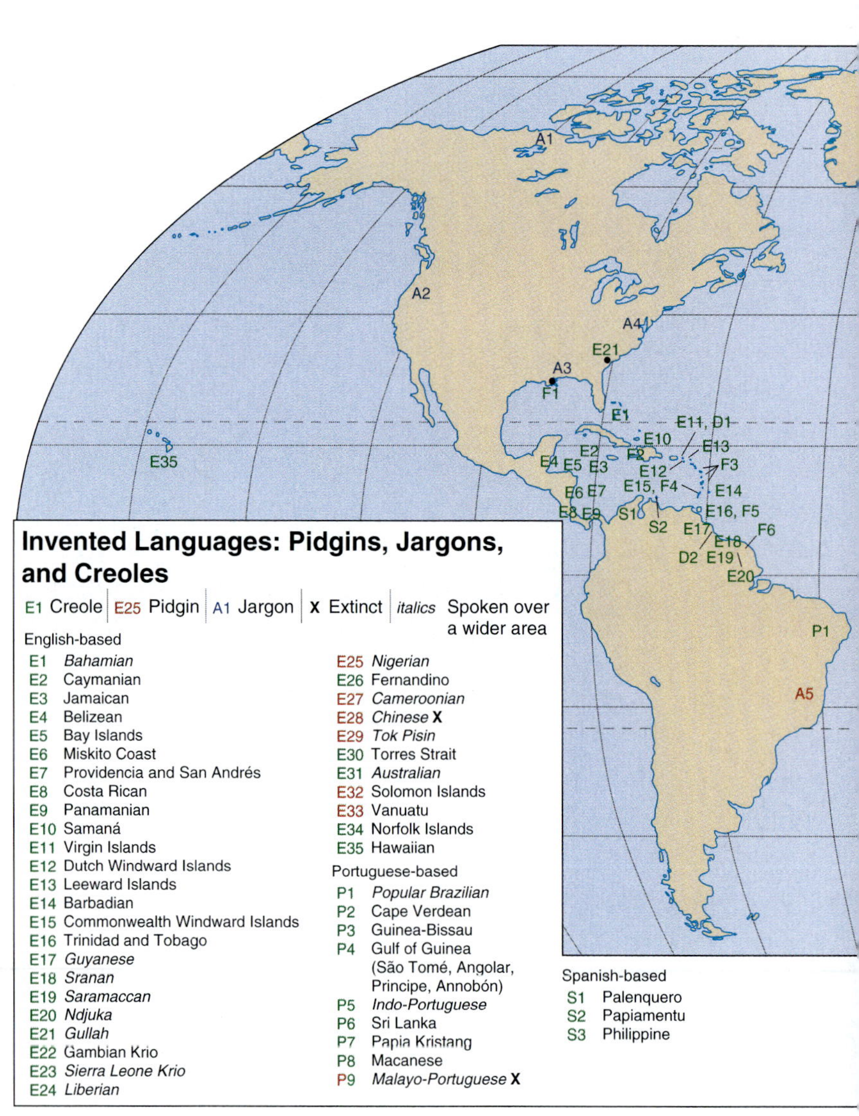

A1
A2
A4
E21
A3
F1
E1
E11, D1
E10
E13
E2
F2
E4 E5 E3
E12
F3
E35
E6 E7
E15, F4
E14
E8 E9
S1
E16, F5
S2
E17
E18
F6
D2 E19
E20
P1
A5
Invented Languages: Pidgins, Jargons, and Creoles
E1 Creole
E25 Pidgin
A1 Jargon
X Extinct
italics Spoken over a wider area
English-based
E1 Bahamian
E2 Caymanian
E3 Jamaican
E4 Belizean
E5 Bay Islands
E6 Miskito Coast
E7 Providencia and San Andrés
E8 Costa Rican
E9 Panamanian
E10 Samaná
E11 Virgin Islands
E12 Dutch Windward Islands
E13 Leeward Islands
E14 Barbadian
E15 Commonwealth Windward Islands
E16 Trinidad and Tobago
E17 Guyanese
E18 Sranan
E19 Saramaccan
E20 Ndjuka
E21 Gullah
E22 Gambian Krio
E23 Sierra Leone Krio
E24 Liberian
E25 Nigerian
E26 Fernandino
E27 Cameroonian
E28 Chinese X
E29 Tok Pisin
E30 Torres Strait
E31 Australian
E32 Solomon Islands
E33 Vanuatu
E34 Norfolk Islands
E35 Hawaiian
Portuguese-based
P1 Popular Brazilian
P2 Cape Verdean
P3 Guinea-Bissau
P4 Gulf of Guinea (São Tomé, Angolar, Principe, Annobón)
P5 Indo-Portuguese
P6 Sri Lanka
P7 Papia Kristang
P8 Macanese
P9 Malayo-Portuguese X
Spanish-based
S1 Palenquero
S2 Papiamentu
S3 Philippine

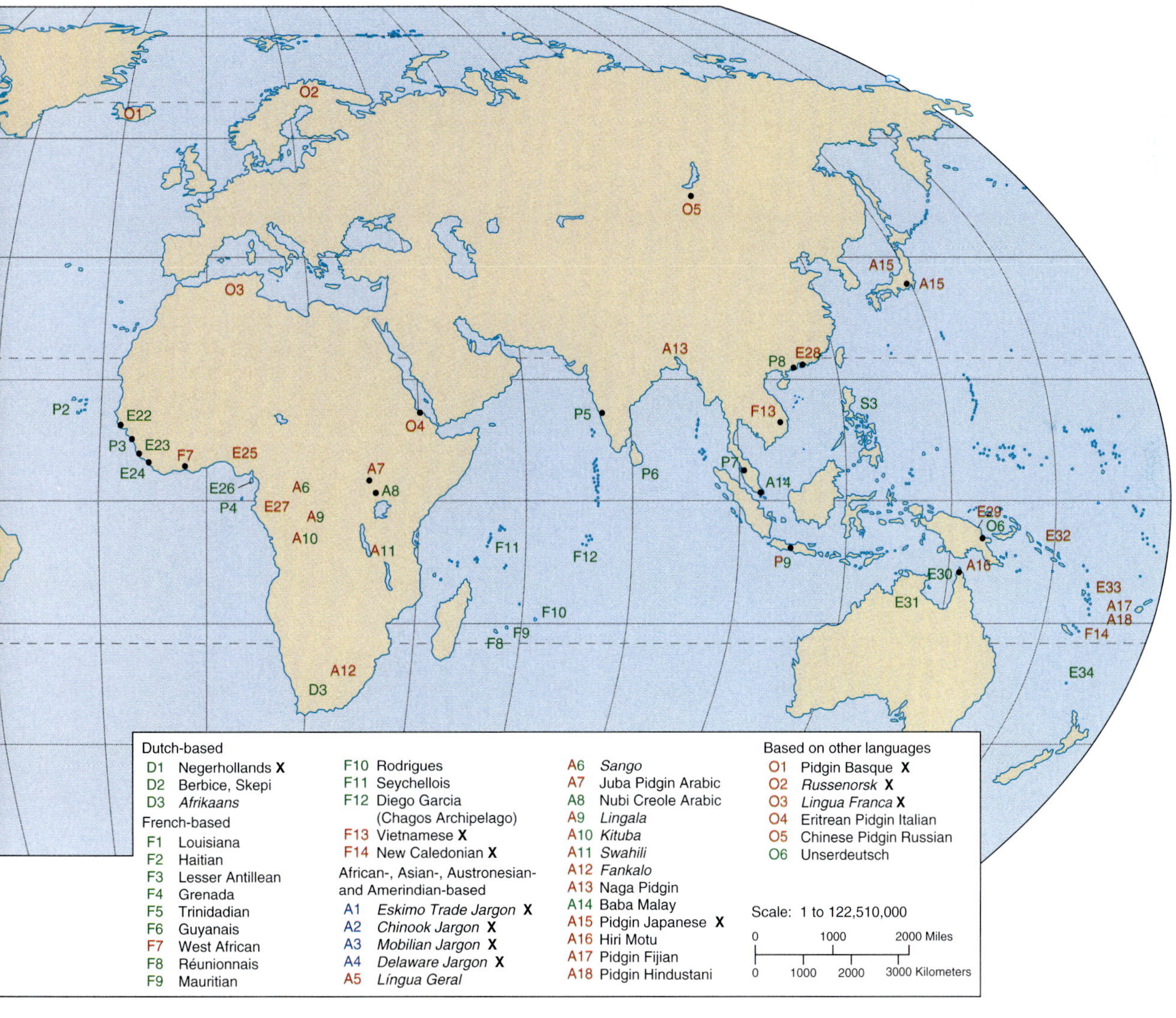
O1
O2
O5
O3
A15
A15
A13
P8
E28
P2
E22
P3
E23
F7
E25
O4
P5
F13
S3
E24
E26
P4
A6
E27
A9
A10
A7
A8
A11
P6
P7
A14
E29
O6
E32
F11
F12
P9
E30
A16
E31
E33
A17
A18
F14
F10
F9
F8
A12
D3
E34
Dutch-based
D1 Negerhollands X
D2 Berbice, Skepi
D3 Afrikaans
French-based
F1 Louisiana
F2 Haitian
F3 Lesser Antillean
F4 Grenada
F5 Trinidadian
F6 Guyanais
F7 West African
F8 Réunionnais
F9 Mauritian
F10 Rodrigues
F11 Seychellois
F12 Diego Garcia (Chagos Archipelago)
F13 Vietnamese X
F14 New Caledonian X
African-, Asian-, Austronesian- and Amerindian-based
A1 Eskimo Trade Jargon X
A2 Chinook Jargon X
A3 Mobilian Jargon X
A4 Delaware Jargon X
A5 Língua Geral
A6 Sango
A7 Juba Pidgin Arabic
A8 Nubi Creole Arabic
A9 Lingala
A10 Kituba
A11 Swahili
A12 Fankalo
A13 Naga Pidgin
A14 Baba Malay
A15 Pidgin Japanese X
A16 Hiri Motu
A17 Pidgin Fijian
A18 Pidgin Hindustani
Based on other languages
O1 Pidgin Basque X
O2 Russenorsk X
O3 Lingua Franca X
O4 Eritrean Pidgin Italian
O5 Chinese Pidgin Russian
O6 Unserdeutsch
Scale: 1 to 122,510,000
0 1000 2000 Miles
0 1000 2000 3000 Kilometers

Map 42 Language Families of Eurasia, A.D.1500

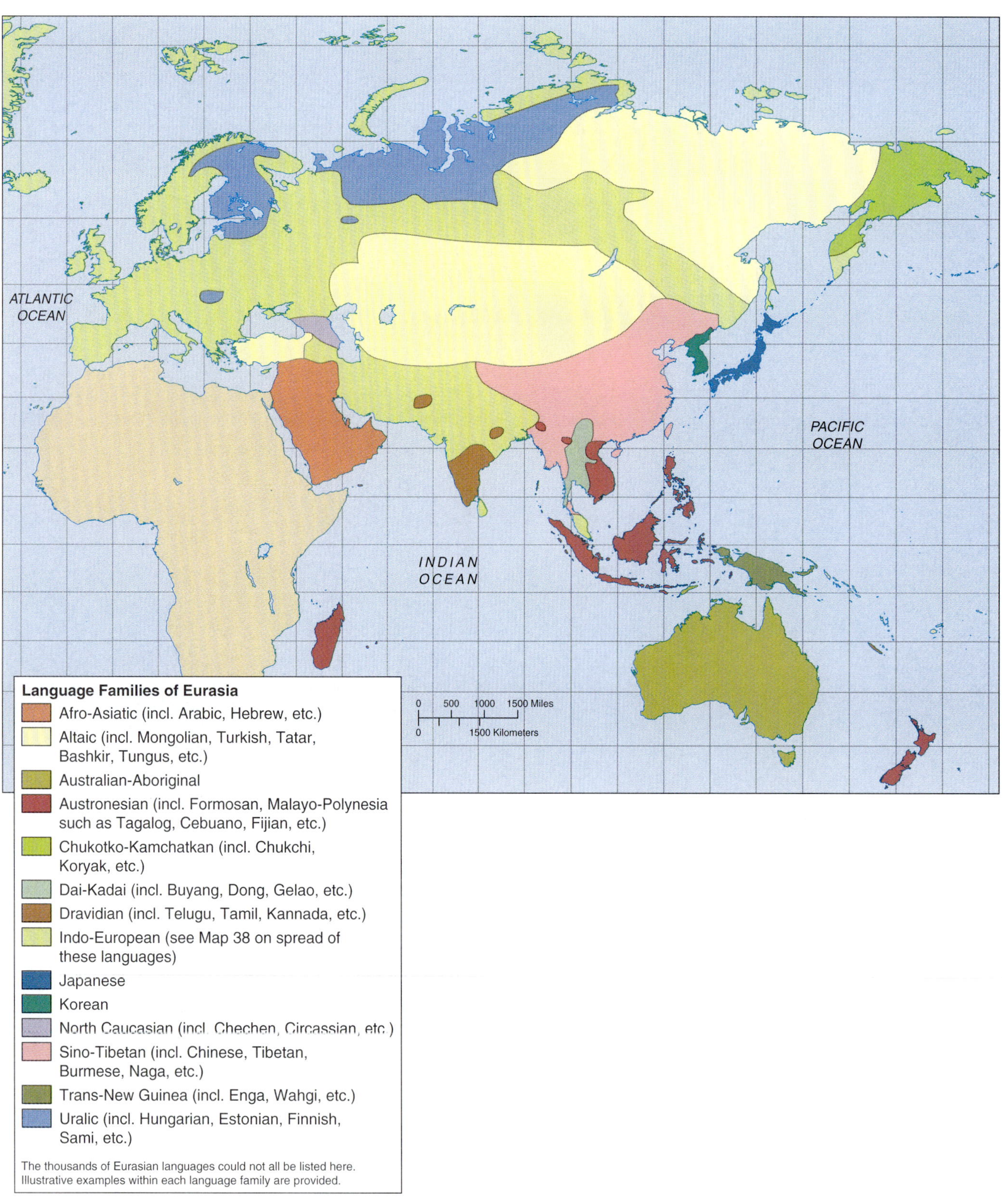
ATLANTIC OCEAN
PACIFIC OCEAN
INDIAN OCEAN
0 500 1000 1500 Miles
0 1500 Kilometers
Language Families of Eurasia
Afro-Asiatic (incl. Arabic, Hebrew, etc.)
Altaic (incl. Mongolian, Turkish, Tatar, Bashkir, Tungus, etc.)
Australian-Aboriginal
Austronesian (incl. Formosan, Malayo-Polynesia such as Tagalog, Cebuano, Fijian, etc.)
Chukotko-Kamchatkan (incl. Chukchi, Koryak, etc.)
Dai-Kadai (incl. Buyang, Dong, Gelao, etc.)
Dravidian (incl. Telugu, Tamil, Kannada, etc.)
Indo-European (see Map 38 on spread of these languages)
Japanese
Korean
North Caucasian (incl. Chechen, Circassian, etc.)
Sino-Tibetan (incl. Chinese, Tibetan, Burmese, Naga, etc.)
Trans-New Guinea (incl. Enga, Wahgi, etc.)
Uralic (incl. Hungarian, Estonian, Finnish, Sami, etc.)
The thousands of Eurasian languages could not all be listed here. Illustrative examples within each language family are provided.

The language families of the world in their premodern locations are indicated here. Language families are groups of related languages with common origins.

Map 43 Language Families of Africa

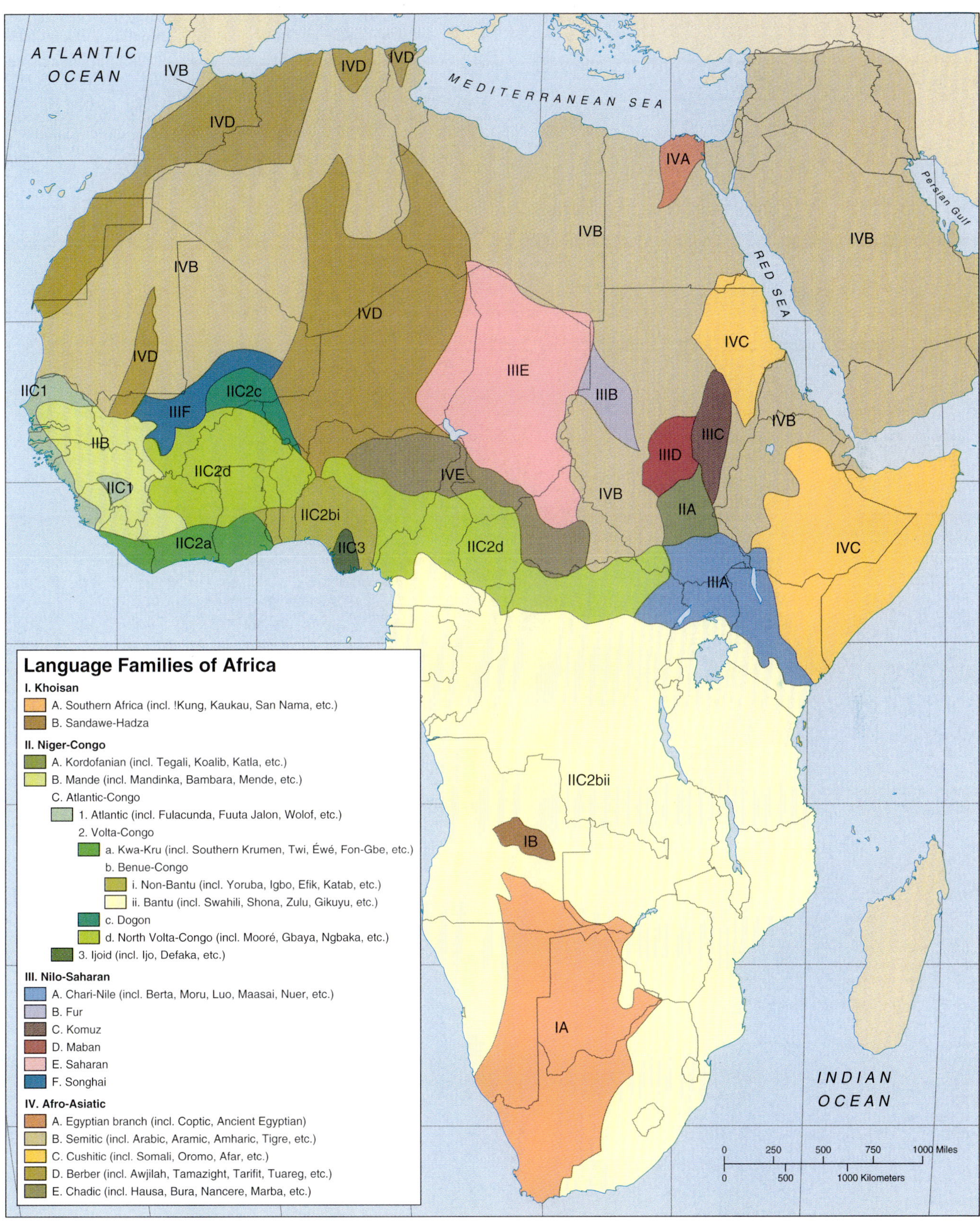

ATLANTIC OCEAN
MEDITERRANEAN SEA
RED SEA
Persian Gulf
INDIAN OCEAN
IVB
IVD
IVA
IVC
IIIE
IIIB
IIIF
IIIC
IIID
IIIA
IIC1
IIC2c
IIB
IIC2d
IVE
IIC2bi
IIA
IIC2a
IIC3
IIC2bii
IB
IA
0 250 500 750 1000 Miles
0 500 1000 Kilometers
Language Families of Africa
I. Khoisan
A. Southern Africa (incl. !Kung, Kaukau, San Nama, etc.)
B. Sandawe-Hadza
II. Niger-Congo
A. Kordofanian (incl. Tegali, Koalib, Katla, etc.)
B. Mande (incl. Mandinka, Bambara, Mende, etc.)
C. Atlantic-Congo
1. Atlantic (incl. Fulacunda, Fuuta Jalon, Wolof, etc.)
2. Volta-Congo
a. Kwa-Kru (incl. Southern Krumen, Twi, Éwé, Fon-Gbe, etc.)
b. Benue-Congo
i. Non-Bantu (incl. Yoruba, Igbo, Efik, Katab, etc.)
ii. Bantu (incl. Swahili, Shona, Zulu, Gikuyu, etc.)
c. Dogon
d. North Volta-Congo (incl. Mooré, Gbaya, Ngbaka, etc.)
3. Ijoid (incl. Ijo, Defaka, etc.)
III. Nilo-Saharan
A. Chari-Nile (incl. Berta, Moru, Luo, Maasai, Nuer, etc.)
B. Fur
C. Komuz
D. Maban
E. Saharan
F. Songhai
IV. Afro-Asiatic
A. Egyptian branch (incl. Coptic, Ancient Egyptian)
B. Semitic (incl. Arabic, Aramic, Amharic, Tigre, etc.)
C. Cushitic (incl. Somali, Oromo, Afar, etc.)
D. Berber (incl. Awjilah, Tamazight, Tarifit, Tuareg, etc.)
E. Chadic (incl. Hausa, Bura, Nancere, Marba, etc.)

Linguistic anthropologists are interested in the historical relationships of languages. Languages diverge over time as people migrate away from each other or as communities lose frequent contact. The languages that have thus diverged derive from a common origin and may be viewed as descendants from an ancestor language. Descendant or related languages are said to belong to a language family. The map shows the most important language families in Africa before European contact, with examples of related languages.

Map 44a Language Families of the New World: North America

Historical relationships among languages are studied by linguistic anthropologists. Languages of common origin are said to belong to the same family. The map shows the language families in North America before European contact, with selected examples of descendant or related languages. Some languages such as Zuni, Tlingit, and Haida are called language isolates because many linguists do not consider them to be related to any other known language.

IB
IA
IIA
IIB1
XXIV
XIX
III
IV
XVI
XV
XVII
IIB2
VA
XVIII
XIII
VIA
VB1
VB2
VIIIB
IX
XIB
VIIIA
XIA
XA
XB
XII
XIV
VIIB
VIIA
IIB3
XX
XXI
XXII
XXIII
Uninhabited
ATLANTIC OCEAN
PACIFIC OCEAN
Gulf of Mexico
CARIBBEAN SEA
0 500 1000 Miles
0 500 1000 Kilometers

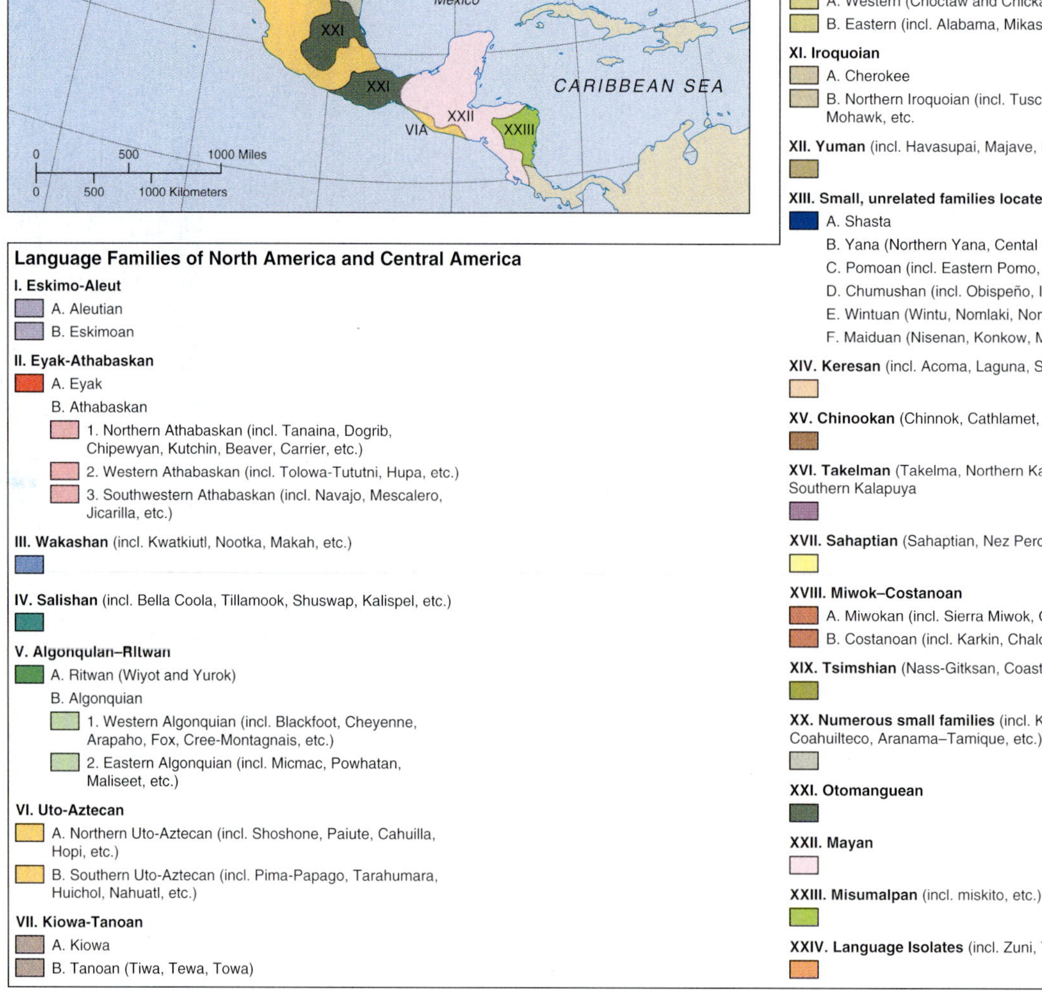

Language Families of North America and Central America

I. Eskimo-Aleut
- A. Aleutian
- B. Eskimoan

II. Eyak-Athabaskan
- A. Eyak
- B. Athabaskan
  1. Northern Athabaskan (incl. Tanaina, Dogrib, Chipewyan, Kutchin, Beaver, Carrier, etc.)
  2. Western Athabaskan (incl. Tolowa-Tututni, Hupa, etc.)
  3. Southwestern Athabaskan (incl. Navajo, Mescalero, Jicarilla, etc.)

III. Wakashan (incl. Kwatkiutl, Nootka, Makah, etc.)

IV. Salishan (incl. Bella Coola, Tillamook, Shuswap, Kalispel, etc.)

V. Algonquian–Ritwan
- A. Ritwan (Wiyot and Yurok)
- B. Algonquian
  1. Western Algonquian (incl. Blackfoot, Cheyenne, Arapaho, Fox, Cree-Montagnais, etc.)
  2. Eastern Algonquian (incl. Micmac, Powhatan, Maliseet, etc.)

VI. Uto-Aztecan
- A. Northern Uto-Aztecan (incl. Shoshone, Paiute, Cahuilla, Hopi, etc.)
- B. Southern Uto-Aztecan (incl. Pima-Papago, Tarahumara, Huichol, Nahuatl, etc.)

VII. Kiowa-Tanoan
- A. Kiowa
- B. Tanoan (Tiwa, Tewa, Towa)

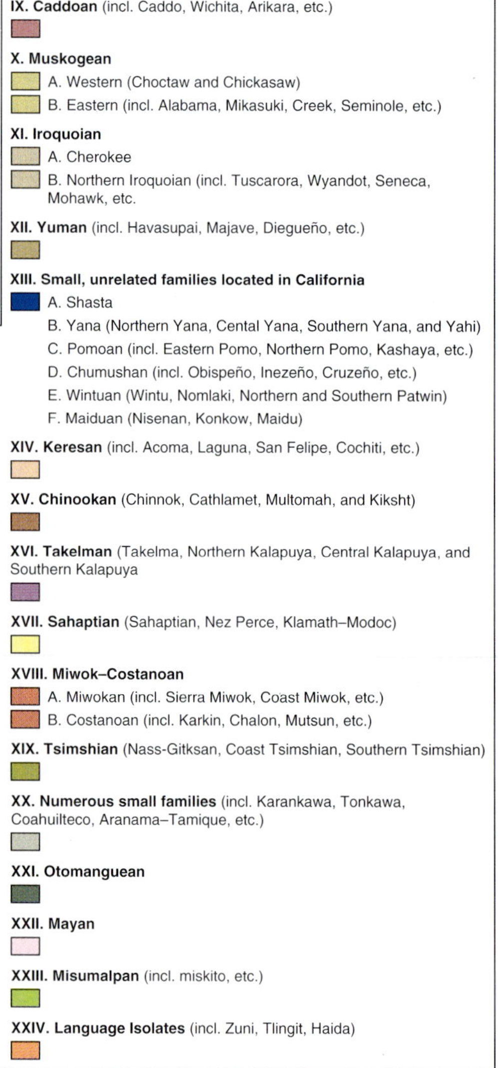

VIII. Siouan
- A.Catawban (Catawba and Woccon)
- B. Mississippi Valley–Plains Siouan (incl. Ofo-Biloxi, Dakota, Omaha, Winnebago, Crow, etc.)

IX. Caddoan (incl. Caddo, Wichita, Arikara, etc.)

X. Muskogean
- A. Western (Choctaw and Chickasaw)
- B. Eastern (incl. Alabama, Mikasuki, Creek, Seminole, etc.)

XI. Iroquoian
- A. Cherokee
- B. Northern Iroquoian (incl. Tuscarora, Wyandot, Seneca, Mohawk, etc.

XII. Yuman (incl. Havasupai, Majave, Diegueño, etc.)

XIII. Small, unrelated families located in California
- A. Shasta
- B. Yana (Northern Yana, Cental Yana, Southern Yana, and Yahi)
- C. Pomoan (incl. Eastern Pomo, Northern Pomo, Kashaya, etc.)
- D. Chumushan (incl. Obispeño, Inezeño, Cruzeño, etc.)
- E. Wintuan (Wintu, Nomlaki, Northern and Southern Patwin)
- F. Maiduan (Nisenan, Konkow, Maidu)

XIV. Keresan (incl. Acoma, Laguna, San Felipe, Cochiti, etc.)

XV. Chinookan (Chinnok, Cathlamet, Multomah, and Kiksht)

XVI. Takelman (Takelma, Northern Kalapuya, Central Kalapuya, and Southern Kalapuya

XVII. Sahaptian (Sahaptian, Nez Perce, Klamath–Modoc)

XVIII. Miwok–Costanoan
- A. Miwokan (incl. Sierra Miwok, Coast Miwok, etc.)
- B. Costanoan (incl. Karkin, Chalon, Mutsun, etc.)

XIX. Tsimshian (Nass-Gitksan, Coast Tsimshian, Southern Tsimshian)

XX. Numerous small families (incl. Karankawa, Tonkawa, Coahuilteco, Aranama–Tamique, etc.)

XXI. Otomanguean

XXII. Mayan

XXIII. Misumalpan (incl. miskito, etc.)

XXIV. Language Isolates (incl. Zuni, Tlingit, Haida)

Map 44b Language Families of the New World: South America

Languages of common origin are grouped together into language families. The map displays the language families of South America before contact with Europeans. Little is known about some parts of South America before the Europeans came. Thus, some areas on the map are listed as unknown affiliation.

CARIBBEAN SEA
ATLANTIC OCEAN
PACIFIC OCEAN
ATLANTIC OCEAN
IB
IB
XX
XIXA
XX
XX
?
?
XIXA1
XX
IA
IIA
?
IIB
XXII
XIXA
XXIII
XXII
IIIA
XIXA2
XIV
?
XVIII
VIA1
?
IIIB
XIXB
XVIII
XXI
XXI
II
?
XIV
XVII
IV
XIII
XIV
VIA2
?
V
XVI
VIB
XIV
XV
VIA1
XIII
IX
?
XII
VIII
XI
XA
XB
0
500
1000 Miles
0
500
1000 Kilometers

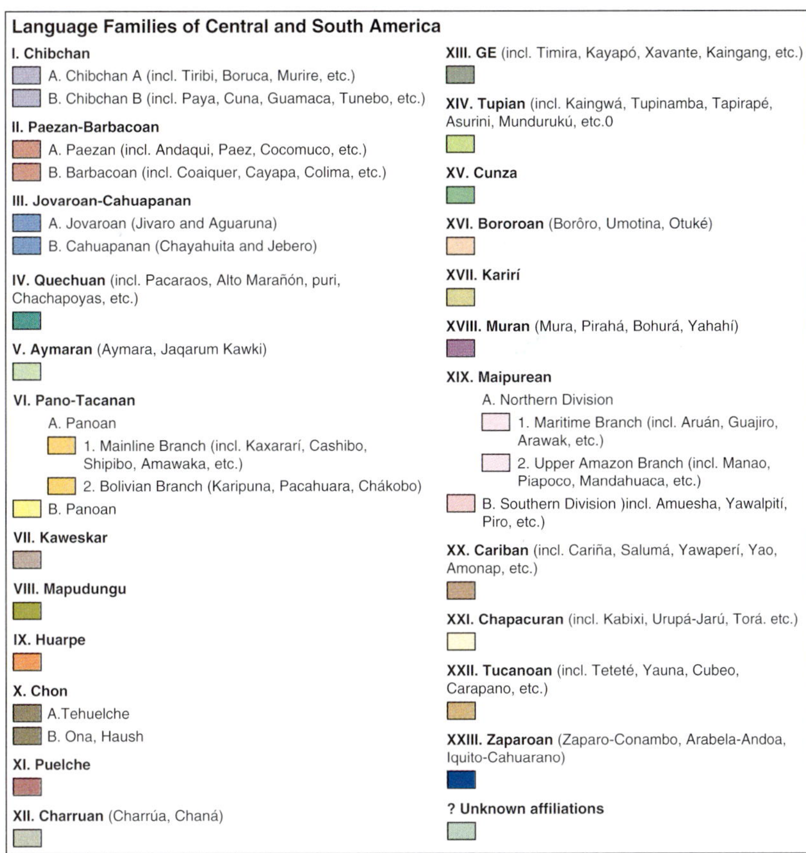
Language Families of Central and South America
I. Chibchan
A. Chibchan A (incl. Tiribi, Boruca, Murire, etc.)
B. Chibchan B (incl. Paya, Cuna, Guamaca, Tunebo, etc.)
II. Paezan-Barbacoan
A. Paezan (incl. Andaqui, Paez, Cocomuco, etc.)
B. Barbacoan (incl. Coaiquer, Cayapa, Colima, etc.)
III. Jovaroan-Cahuapanan
A. Jovaroan (Jivaro and Aguaruna)
B. Cahuapanan (Chayahuita and Jebero)
IV. Quechuan (incl. Pacaraos, Alto Marañón, puri, Chachapoyas, etc.)
V. Aymaran (Aymara, Jaqarum Kawki)
VI. Pano-Tacanan
A. Panoan
1. Mainline Branch (incl. Kaxararí, Cashibo, Shipibo, Amawaka, etc.)
2. Bolivian Branch (Karipuna, Pacahuara, Chákobo)
B. Panoan
VII. Kaweskar
VIII. Mapudungu
IX. Huarpe
X. Chon
A.Tehuelche
B. Ona, Haush
XI. Puelche
XII. Charruan (Charrúa, Chaná)
XIII. GE (incl. Timira, Kayapó, Xavante, Kaingang, etc.)
XIV. Tupian (incl. Kaingwá, Tupinamba, Tapirapé, Asurini, Mundurukú, etc.0
XV. Cunza
XVI. Bororoan (Borôro, Umotina, Otuké)
XVII. Karirí
XVIII. Muran (Mura, Pirahá, Bohurá, Yahahí)
XIX. Maipurean
A. Northern Division
1. Maritime Branch (incl. Aruán, Guajiro, Arawak, etc.)
2. Upper Amazon Branch (incl. Manao, Piapoco, Mandahuaca, etc.)
B. Southern Division)incl. Amuesha, Yawalpití, Piro, etc.)
XX. Cariban (incl. Cariña, Salumá, Yawaperí, Yao, Amonap, etc.)
XXI. Chapacuran (incl. Kabixi, Urupá-Jarú, Torá. etc.)
XXII. Tucanoan (incl. Teteté, Yauna, Cubeo, Carapano, etc.)
XXIII. Zaparoan (Zaparo-Conambo, Arabela-Andoa, Iquito-Cahuarano)
? Unknown affiliations

Map 45 Native New World Languages: Interpretations

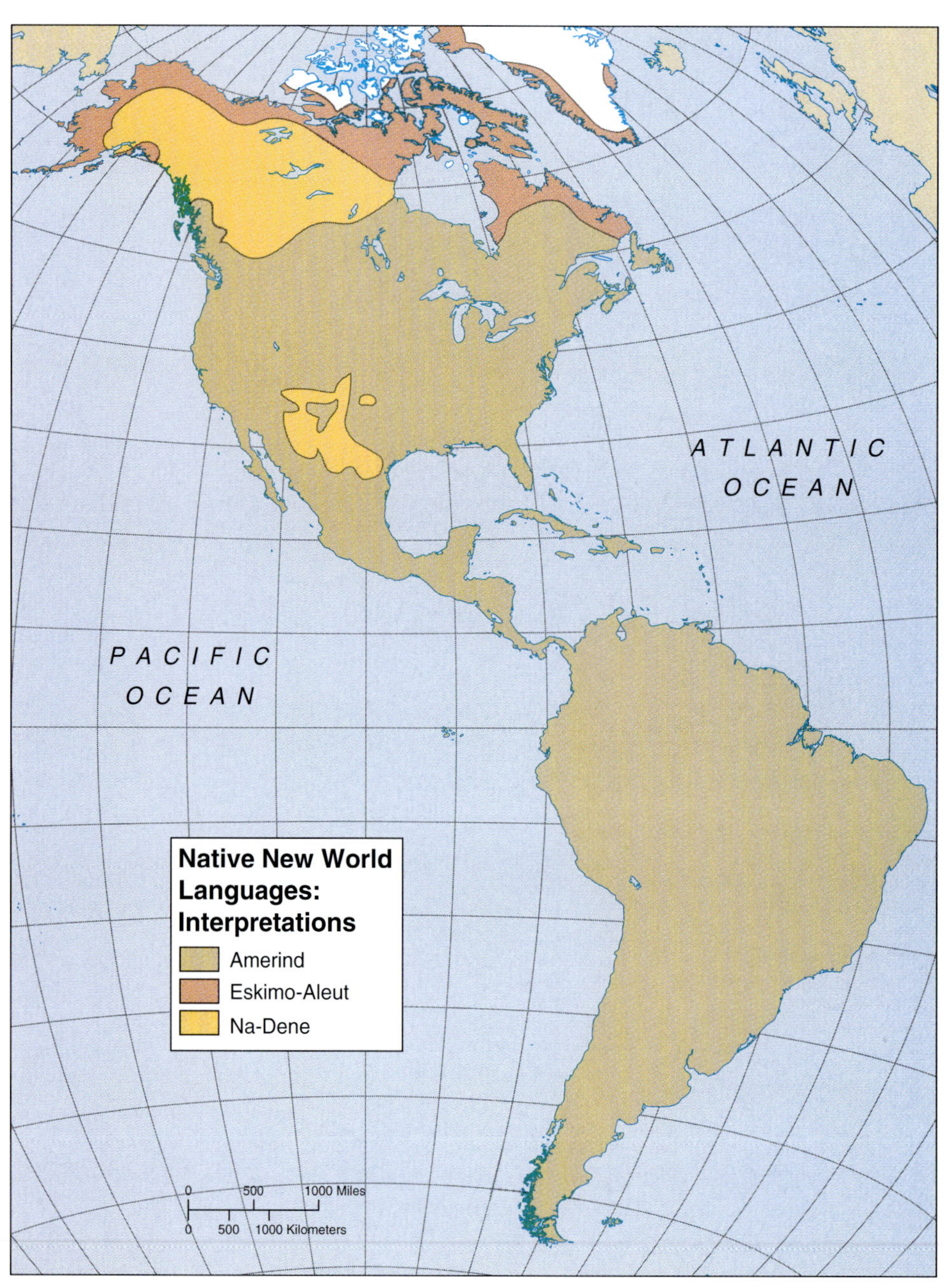

ATLANTIC OCEAN
PACIFIC OCEAN
Native New World Languages: Interpretations
Amerind
Eskimo-Aleut
Na-Dene
0 500 1000 Miles
0 500 1000 Kilometers

Some scholars debate the historical relationships among Native American languages. This debate is relevant to the question of when the Americas were first populated and which different groups and languages were part of this migration. Linguist Joseph Greenberg argues that there were three waves of major migration into the Americas and that there are only three major language families represented in the New World: Amerind, Na-Dene, and Eskimo-Aleut. He believes that most languages in North and South America are distantly related to each other as Amerind languages. Many linguists and linguistic anthropologists find Greenberg's ideas are unsupported by the evidence, and they contend that he has lumped too many languages together without adequate proof. They support other, painstaking research that so far has shown the many language families of the Americas, shown on Maps 44a and 44b.

Part V

Cultural Anthropology

Section A Demographics

Map 46 Past Population Densities
Map 47 World Population Density
Map 48 World Migrations
Map 49 World Urban Populations
Map 50 Population Growth Rates
Map 51 Total Fertility Rate
Map 52 Infant Mortality Rates
Map 53 Average Life Expectancy at Birth
Map 54 Population by Age Group

Section B Economy

Section C Human Society

Section D Political Systems

Map 46 Past Population Distributions and Densities

The map of the world at 100,000 B.P. shows the distributions of hominids who at that time had spread from their probable origin in Africa into parts of the Old World. At 30,000 B.P. few places in the Old World remained uninhabited. All the people then were hunters and gatherers who subsisted on wild foods. The environment probably was not at its carrying capacity for human populations until about 15, 000 B.P.

By 10,000 B.P. hunting and gathering people had spread throughout the world. Plant and animal domestication (farming and pastoralism) had begun in some parts of the Old World

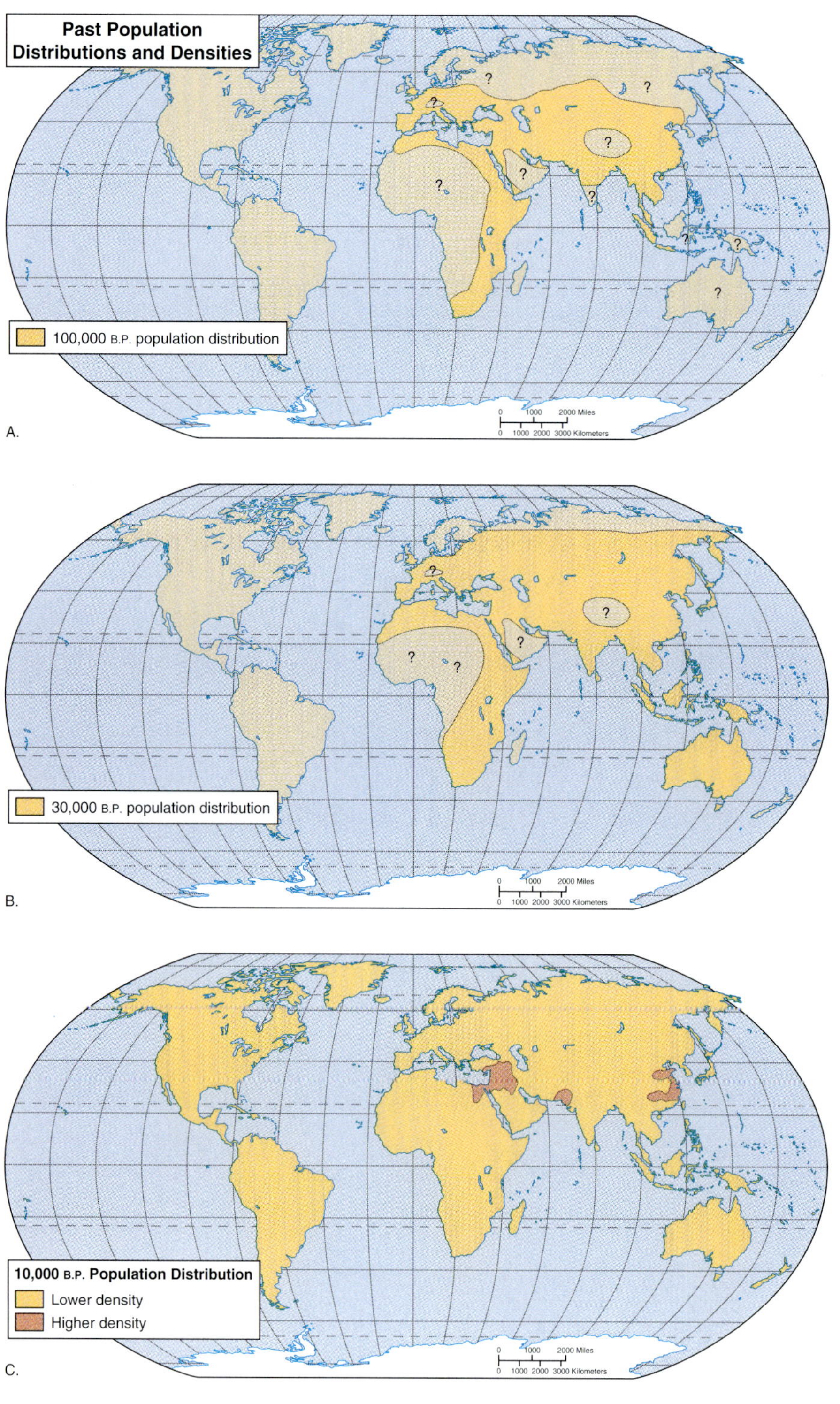

Past Population Distributions and Densities
100,000 B.P. population distribution
A.
30,000 B.P. population distribution
B.
10,000 B.P. Population Distribution
Lower density
Higher density
C.
0 1000 2000 Miles
0 1000 2000 3000 Kilometers

perhaps as a response to behavioral changes necessitated by the population, which now exceeded the environmental carrying capacity. Farming supports higher population densites than hunting and gathering. Urban civilization with cities dependent on their hinterlands had developed by 5000 B.P. The maps of A.D. 1 and A.D. 1500 approximate actual population density on a scale of one dot to every million people. A chart provides total world population figures for different time periods. Compare these maps to the contemporary population density map (Map 47).

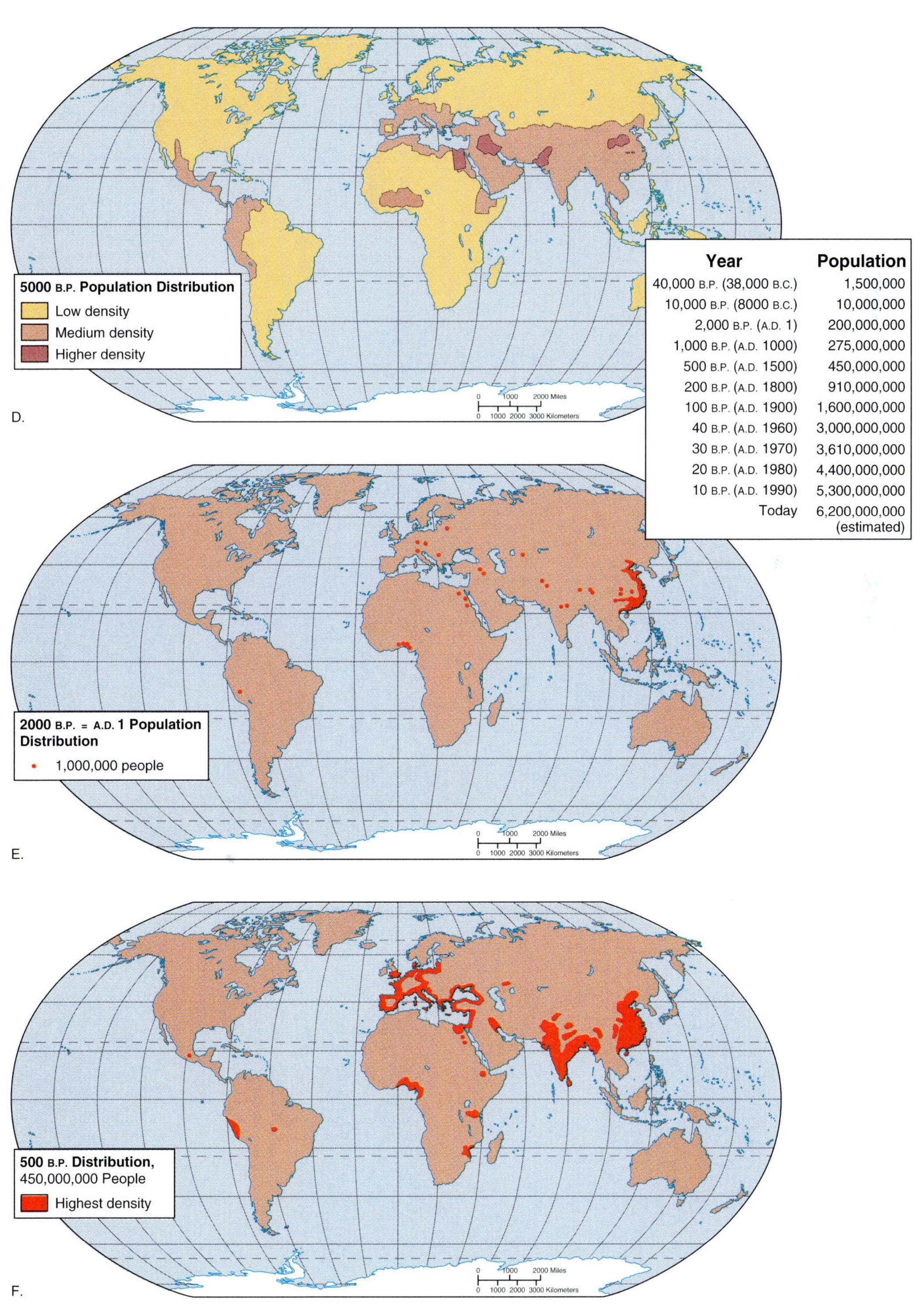

5000 B.P. Population Distribution
Low density
Medium density
Higher density
D.
0 1000 2000 Miles
0 1000 2000 3000 Kilometers
2000 B.P. = A.D. 1 Population Distribution
1,000,000 people
E.
0 1000 2000 Miles
0 1000 2000 3000 Kilometers
500 B.P. Distribution, 450,000,000 People
Highest density
F.
0 1000 2000 Miles
0 1000 2000 3000 Kilometers

Year	Population
40,000 B.P. (38,000 B.C.)	1,500,000
10,000 B.P. (8000 B.C.)	10,000,000
2,000 B.P. (A.D. 1)	200,000,000
1,000 B.P. (A.D. 1000)	275,000,000
500 B.P. (A.D. 1500)	450,000,000
200 B.P. (A.D. 1800)	910,000,000
100 B.P. (A.D. 1900)	1,600,000,000
40 B.P. (A.D. 1960)	3,000,000,000
30 B.P. (A.D. 1970)	3,610,000,000
20 B.P. (A.D. 1980)	4,400,000,000
10 B.P. (A.D. 1990)	5,300,000,000
Today	6,200,000,000 (estimated)

Map 47 World Population Density

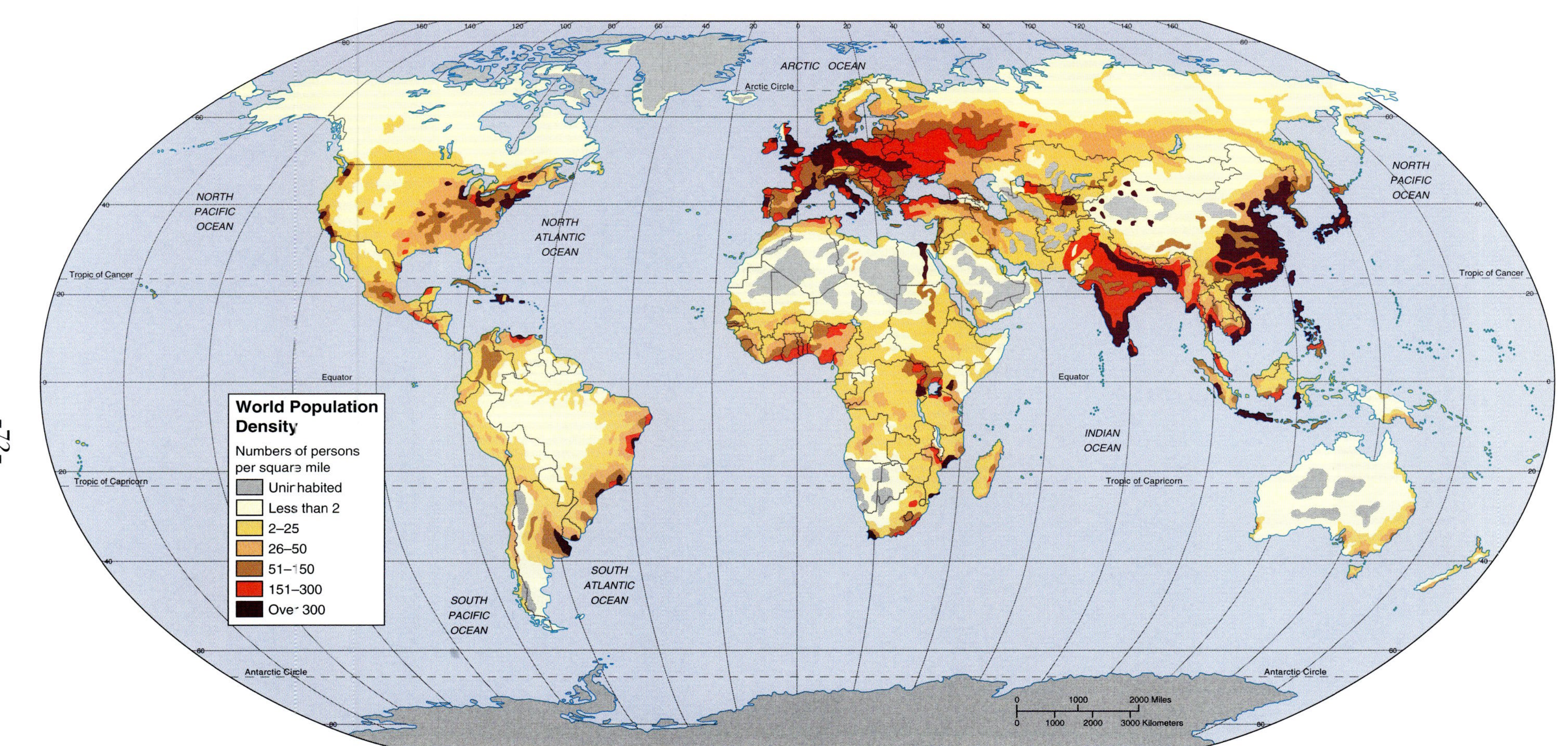
World Population Density
Numbers of persons per square mile
Uninhabited
Less than 2
2–25
26–50
51–150
151–300
Over 300
ARCTIC OCEAN
Arctic Circle
NORTH PACIFIC OCEAN
NORTH ATLANTIC OCEAN
SOUTH PACIFIC OCEAN
SOUTH ATLANTIC OCEAN
INDIAN OCEAN
NORTH PACIFIC OCEAN
Tropic of Cancer
Equator
Tropic of Capricorn
Antarctic Circle
0 1000 2000 Miles
0 1000 2000 3000 Kilometers

No feature of human activity is more reflective of geographic relationships than where people live. In the areas of densest populations, a mixture of natural and human factors has combined to allow maximum food production, maximum urbanization, and maximum centralization of economic activities. Three great concentrations of human population appear on the map—East Asia, South Asia, and Europe—with a fourth, lesser concentration in eastern North America. While population growth is relatively slow in three of these population clusters, in the fourth—South Asia—growth is still rapid and South Asia is expected to become even more densely populated in the early years of the twenty-first century, while density of the other regions is expected to remain about as it now appears. In Europe and North America, the relatively stable population growth rates are the result of economic development that has caused population growth to level off within the last century. In East Asia, the growth rates have also begun to decline. In the case of Japan, Taiwan, the Koreas, and other more highly developed nations of the Pacific Rim, the reduced growth is the result of economic development. In China, at least until recently, lowered population growth rates have resulted from strict family planning. The areas of future high density of population, in addition to those already existing, are likely to be in Middle and South America and in Central Africa, where population growth rates are well above the world average.

Map 48 World Migrations

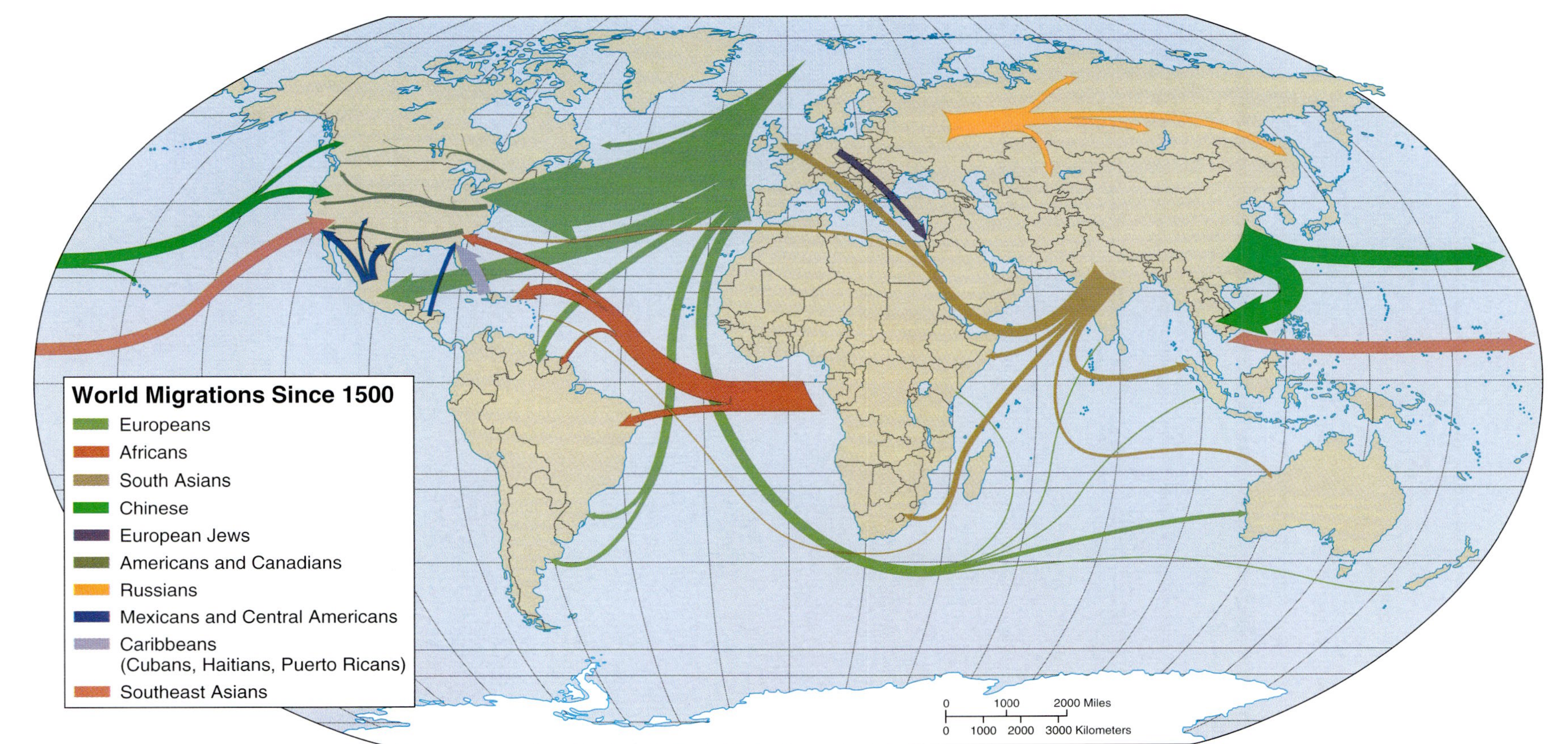
World Migrations Since 1500
Europeans
Africans
South Asians
Chinese
European Jews
Americans and Canadians
Russians
Mexicans and Central Americans
Caribbeans
(Cubans, Haitians, Puerto Ricans)
Southeast Asians
0 1000 2000 Miles
0 1000 2000 3000 Kilometers

Migration has had a significant effect on world geography, contributing to cultural change and development, to the diffusion of ideas and innovations, and to the complex mixture of people and cultures found in the world today. *Internal migration* occurs within the boundaries of a country; *external migration* is movement from one country or region to another. Over the last 50 years, the most important migrations in the world have been internal, largely the rural-to-urban migration that has been responsible for the recent rise of global urbanization. Prior to the mid-twentieth century, three types of external migrations were most important: *voluntary,* most often in search of better conditions and opportunities; *involuntary* or *forced,* involving people who have been driven from their homelands by war, political unrest, or environmental disasters, or who have been transported as slaves or prisoners; and *imposed,* not entirely forced but which conditions make highly advisable. Human migrations in recorded history have been responsible for major changes in the patterns of languages, religions, ethnic composition, and economies. Particularly during the last 500 years, migrations of both the voluntary and involuntary or forced type have literally reshaped the human face of the earth.

Map 49 World Urban Populations

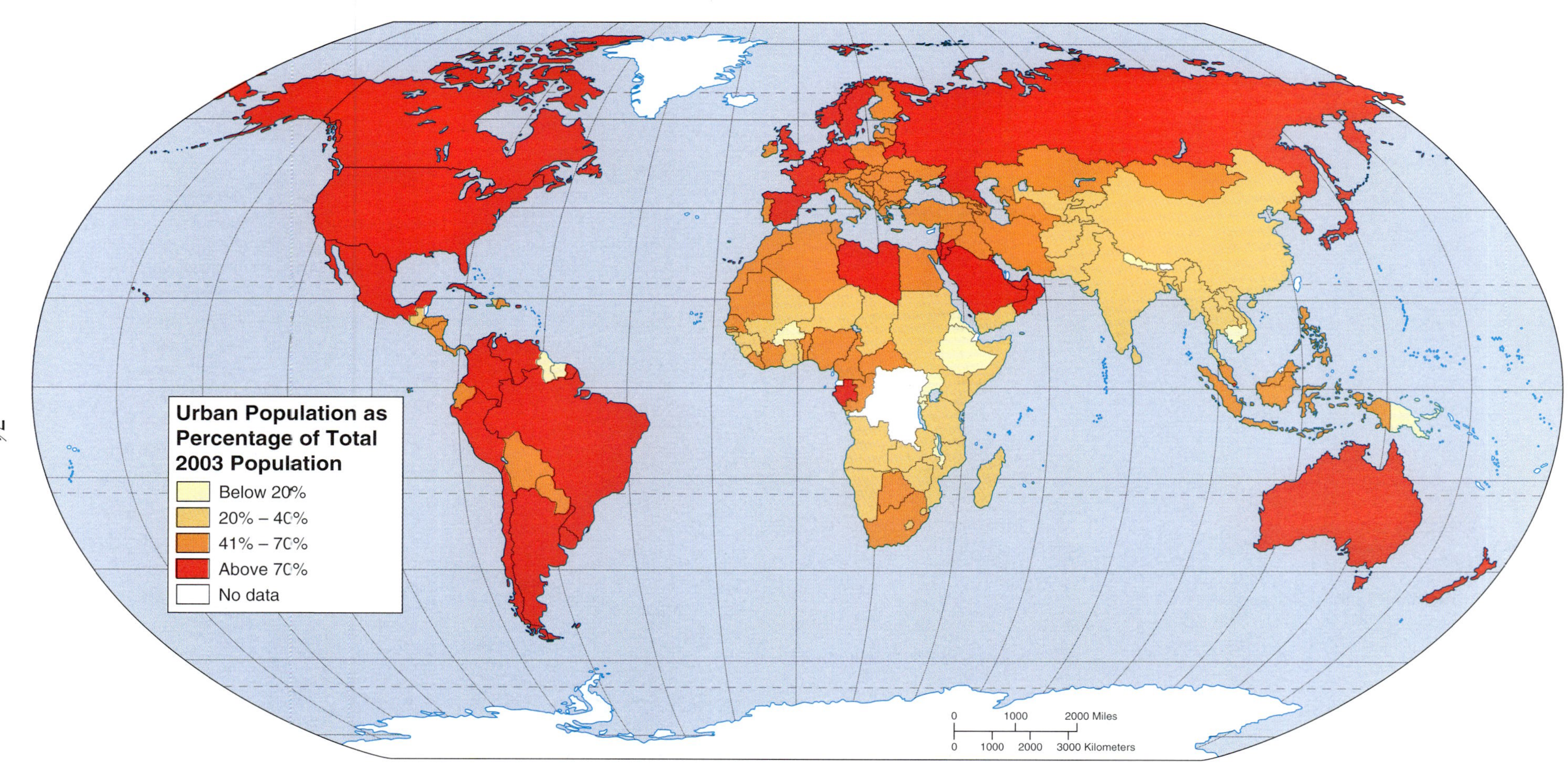
Urban Population as Percentage of Total 2003 Population
Below 20%
20% – 40%
41% – 70%
Above 70%
No data
0 1000 2000 Miles
0 1000 2000 3000 Kilometers

The degree to which a region's population is concentrated in urban areas is a major indicator of a number of things: the potential for environmental impact, the level of economic development, and the problems associated with human concentrations. Urban dwellers are rapidly becoming the norm among the world's people and rates of urbanization are increasing worldwide, with the greatest increases in urbanization taking place in developing regions. Whether in developed or developing countries, those who live in cities exert an influence on the environment, politics, economics, and social systems that go far beyond the confines of the city itself. Acting as the focal points for the flow of goods and ideas, cities draw resources and people not just from their immediate hinterland but from the entire world. This process creates far-reaching impacts as resources are extracted, converted through industrial processes, and transported over great distances to metropolitan regions, and as ideas spread or *diffuse* along with the movements of people to cities and the flow of communication from them. The significance of urbanization can be most clearly seen, perhaps, in North America where, in spite of vast areas of relatively unpopulated land, well over 90 percent of the population lives in urban areas.

Map 50 Population Growth Rates

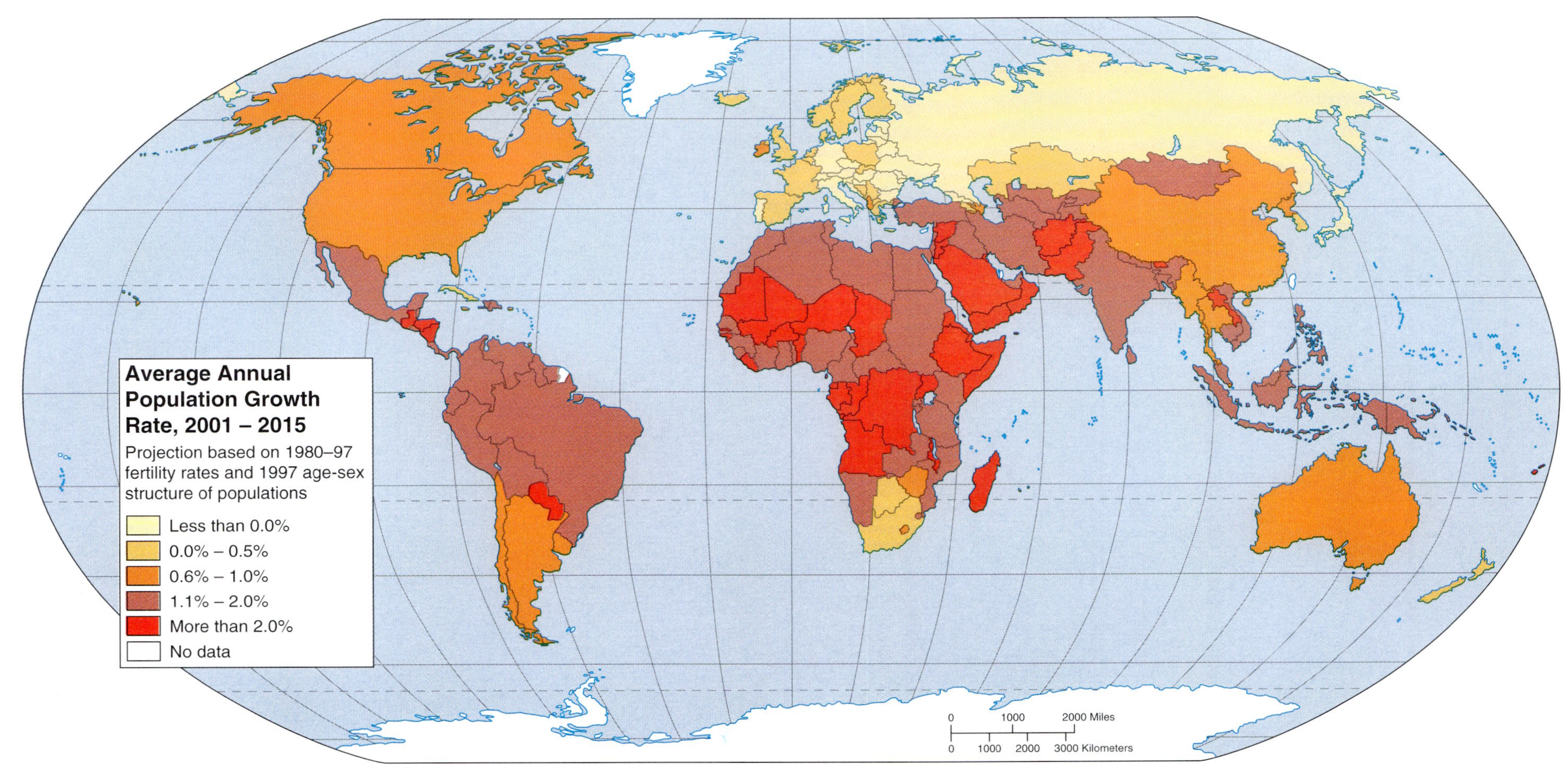

Average Annual Population Growth Rate, 2001 – 2015
Projection based on 1980–97 fertility rates and 1997 age-sex structure of populations
Less than 0.0%
0.0% – 0.5%
0.6% – 1.0%
1.1% – 2.0%
More than 2.0%
No data
0
1000
2000 Miles
0
1000
2000
3000 Kilometers

Of all the statistical measurements of human population, the rate of population growth is the most important. The growth rate of a population is a combination of natural change (births and deaths), in-migration, and out-migration; it is obtained by adding the number of births to the number of immigrants during a year and subtracting from that total the sum of deaths and emigrants for the same year. For a specific country, this figure will determine many things about the country's future ability to feed, house, educate, and provide medical services to its citizens. Some of the countries with the largest populations (such as India) also have high growth rates. Since these countries tend to be in developing regions, the combination of high population and high growth rates poses special problems for continuing economic development and carries heightened risks of environmental degradation. Many people believe that the rapidly expanding world population is a potential crisis that may cause environmental and human disaster by the middle of the twenty-first century.

Map 51 Total Fertility Rates

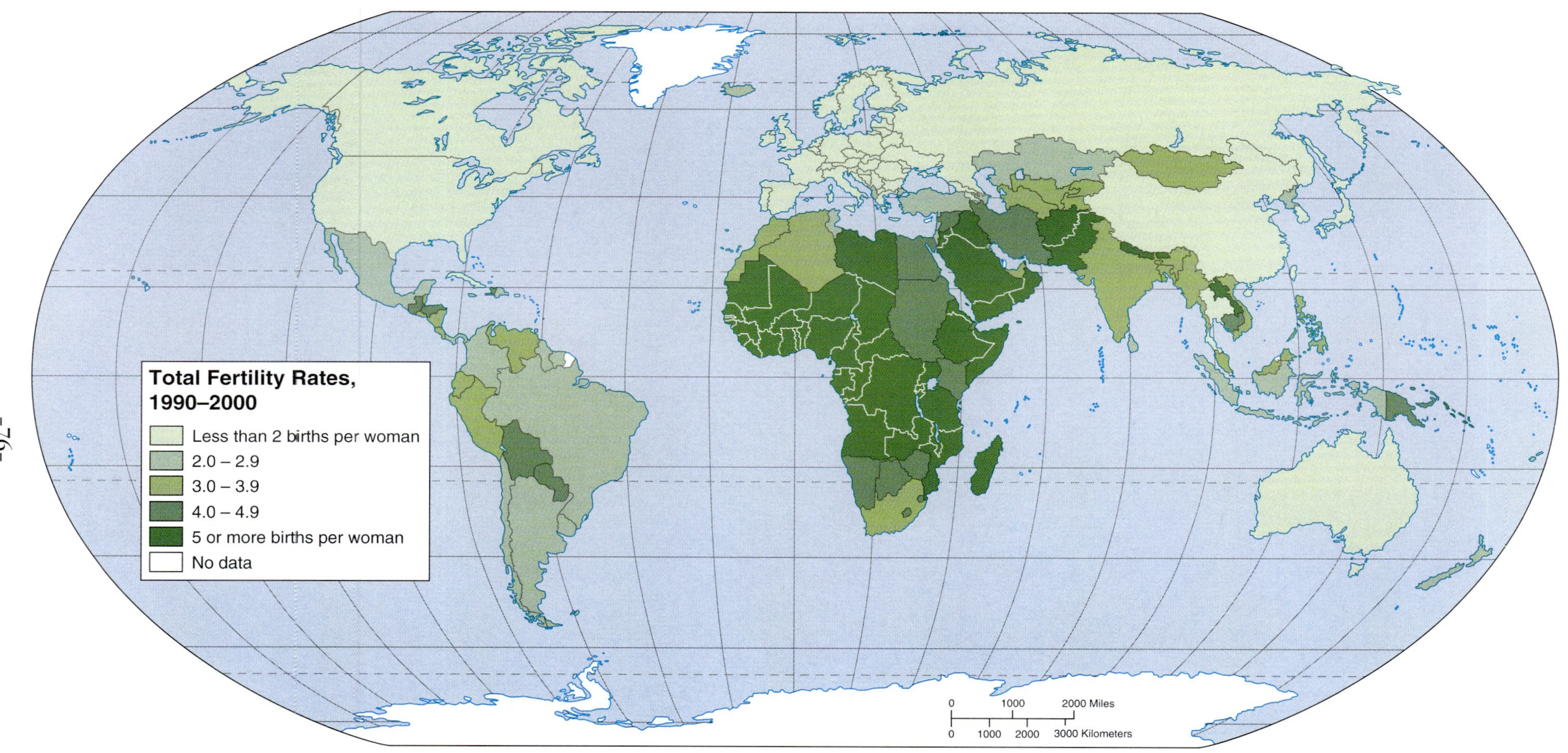

Total Fertility Rates, 1990–2000
Less than 2 births per woman
2.0 – 2.9
3.0 – 3.9
4.0 – 4.9
5 or more births per woman
No data
0 1000 2000 Miles
0 1000 2000 3000 Kilometers

The fertility rate measures the number of children that a woman is expected to bear during her lifetime, based on the age-specific fertility figures of women between 15 and 40 (the normal childbearing years). While fertility rates tell us a great deal about present population growth, with high fertility rates indicating high population growth rates, they are also indicative of potential or projected growth. A country whose women can be expected to bear many children is a country with enormous potential for population growth in the future. Given present fertility rates, for example, the number of offspring from the average German woman over the next three generations (the total number of children, grandchildren, and great-grandchildren) will be 7. During the same three generations, the average American woman will have a total of 17 children, grandchildren, and great-grandchildren. But during this time, assuming that present fertility rates are maintained, the average woman in sub-Saharan Africa will have *258* children, grandchildren, and great-grandchildren. You might be interested in working out some potential population growth rates over two or three generations, using the data as presented on the map.

Note: Total fertility rate figures are based on yearly age-specific fertility rate estimates from 1990–2000.

Map 52 Infant Mortality Rates

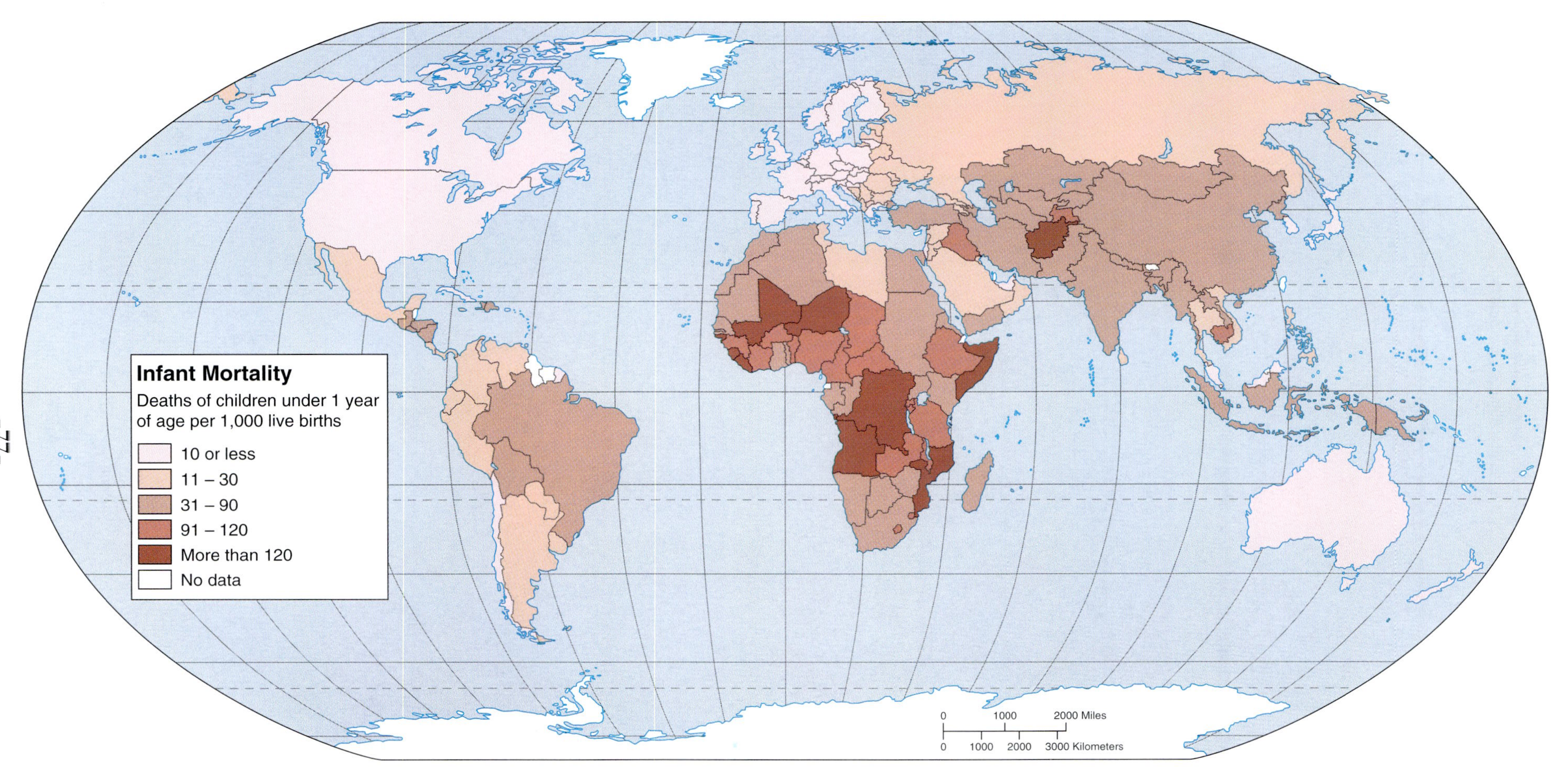

Infant Mortality
Deaths of children under 1 year of age per 1,000 live births
10 or less
11 – 30
31 – 90
91 – 120
More than 120
No data
0 1000 2000 Miles
0 1000 2000 3000 Kilometers

Infant mortality rates are calculated by dividing the number of children born in a given year who die before their first birthday by the total number of children born that year and then multiplying by 1,000; this shows how many infants have died for every 1,000 births. Infant mortality rates are prime indicators of economic development. In highly developed economies, with advanced medical technologies, sufficient diets, and adequate public sanitation, infant mortality rates tend to be quite low. By contrast, in less developed countries, with the disadvantages of poor diet, limited access to medical technology, and the other problems of poverty, infant mortality rates tend to be high.

Although worldwide infant mortality has decreased significantly during the last two decades, many regions of the world still experience infant mortality above the 10 percent level (100 deaths per 1,000 live births). Such infant mortality rates represent not only human tragedy at its most basic level, but also are powerful inhibiting factors for the future of human development. Comparing infant mortality rates in the mid-latitudes and the tropics shows that children in most African countries are more than ten times as likely to die within a year of birth as children in European countries.

Map 53 Average Life Expectancy at Birth

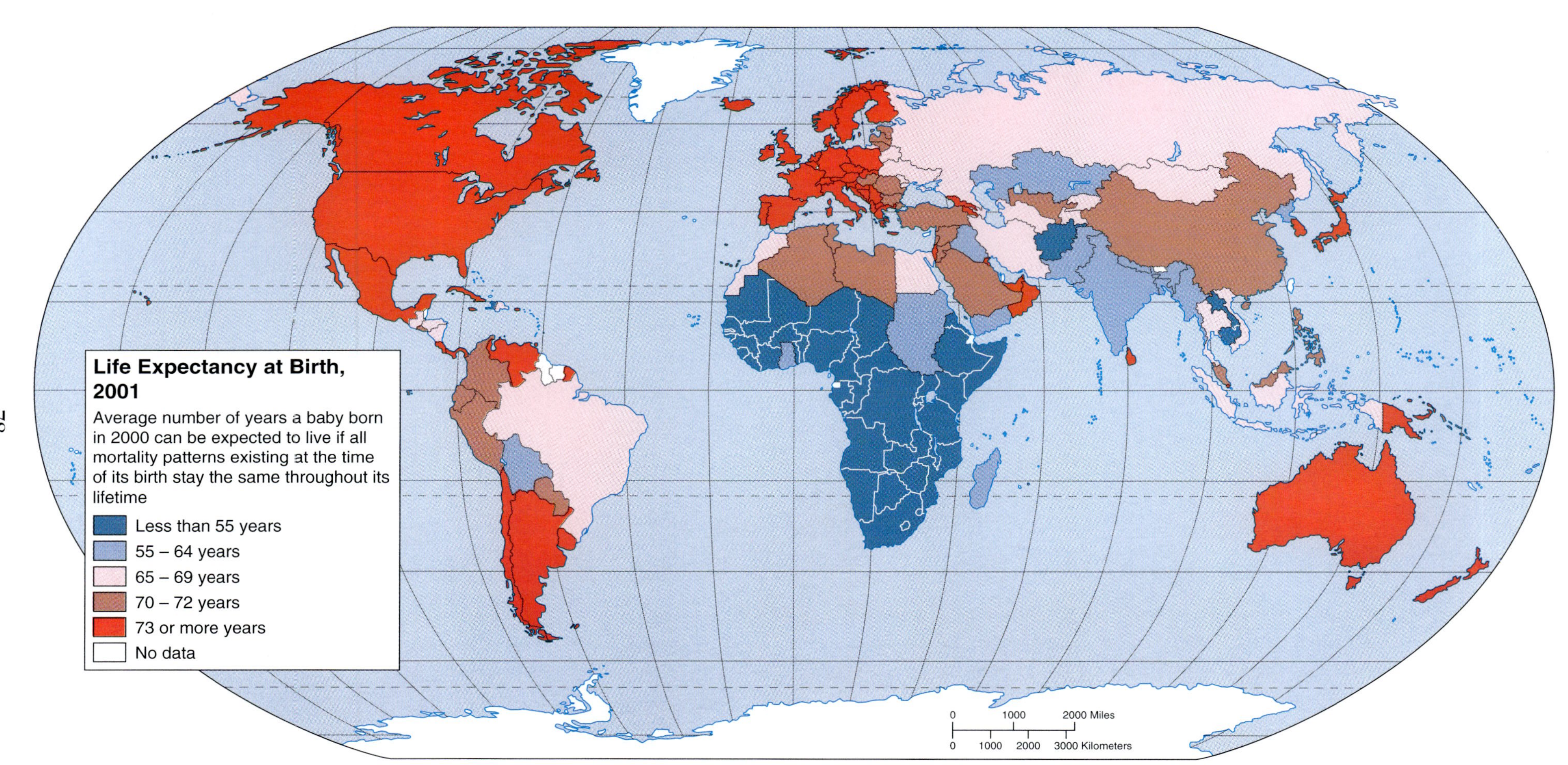

Life Expectancy at Birth, 2001
Average number of years a baby born in 2000 can be expected to live if all mortality patterns existing at the time of its birth stay the same throughout its lifetime
Less than 55 years
55 – 64 years
65 – 69 years
70 – 72 years
73 or more years
No data
0 1000 2000 Miles
0 1000 2000 3000 Kilometers

Average life expectancy at birth is a measure of the average longevity of the population of a country. Like all average measures, it is distorted by extremes. For example, a country with a high mortality rate among children will have a low average life expectancy. Thus, an average life expectancy of 45 years does not mean that everyone can be expected to die at the age of 45. More normally, what the figure means is that a substantial number of children die between birth and 5 years of age, thus reducing the average life expectancy for the entire population. In spite of the dangers inherent in misinterpreting the data, average life expectancy (along with infant mortality and several other measures) is a valid way of judging the relative health of a population. It reflects the nature of the health care system, public sanitation and disease control, nutrition, and a number of other key human need indicators. As such, it is a measure of well-being that is significant in indicating economic development.

Map 54 Population by Age Group

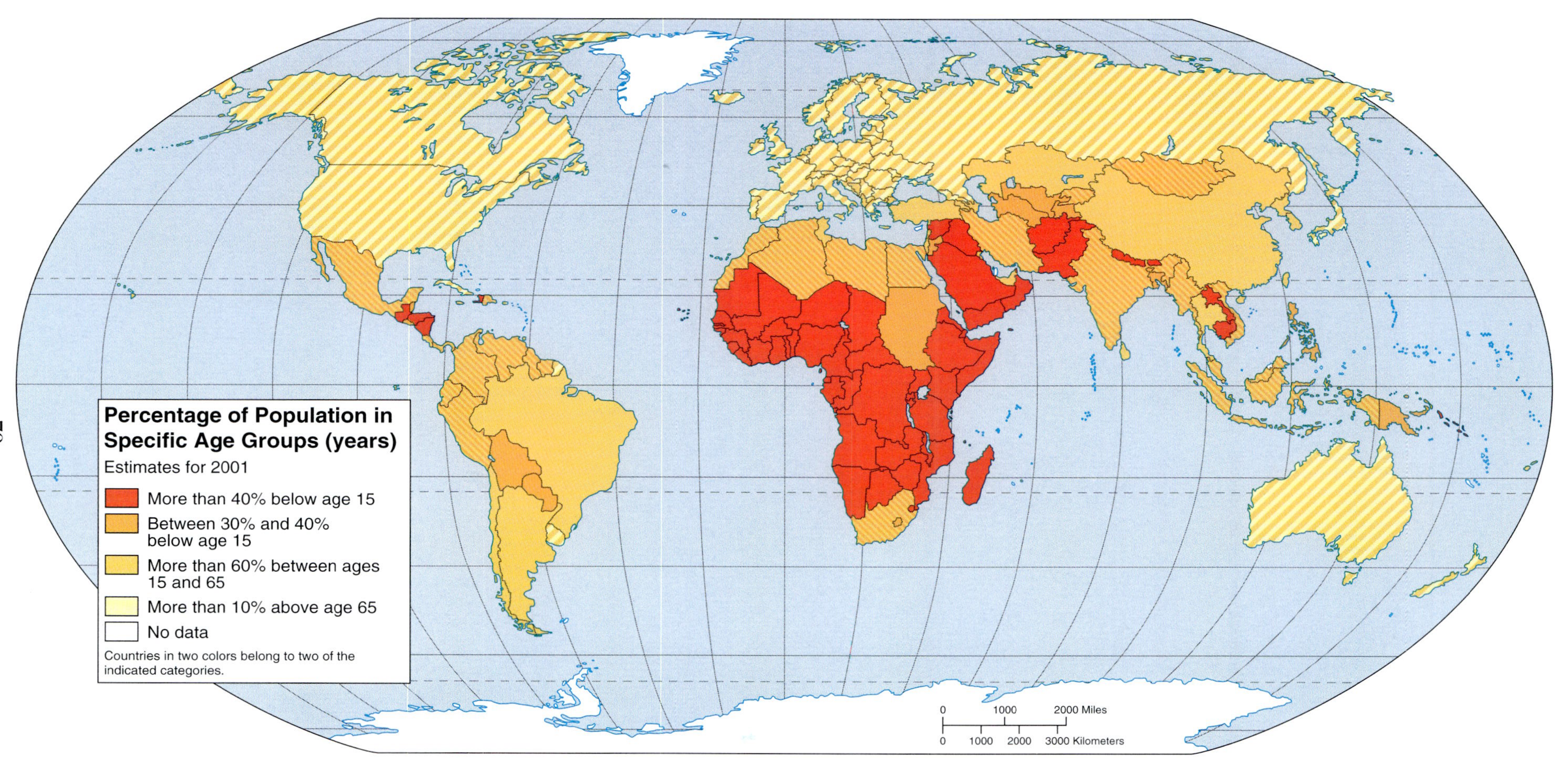

Percentage of Population in Specific Age Groups (years)
Estimates for 2001
More than 40% below age 15
Between 30% and 40% below age 15
More than 60% between ages 15 and 65
More than 10% above age 65
No data
Countries in two colors belong to two of the indicated categories.
0 1000 2000 Miles
0 1000 2000 3000 Kilometers

Of all the measurements that illustrate the dynamics of a population, age distribution may be the most significant, particularly when viewed in combination with average growth rates. The particular relevance of age distribution is that it tells us what to expect from a population in terms of growth over the next generation. If, for example, approximately 40–50 percent of a population is below the age of 15, that suggests that in the next generation about one-quarter of the total population will be women of childbearing age. When age distribution is combined with fertility rates (the average number of children born per woman in a population), an especially valid measurement of future growth potential may be derived. A simple example: Nigeria, with a 2002 population of 130 million, has 43.6 percent of its population below the age of 15 and a fertility rate of 5.5; the United States, with a 2002 population of 280 million, has 21 percent of its population below the age of 15 and a fertility rate of 2.07. During the period in which those women presently under the age of 15 are in their childbearing years, Nigeria can be expected to add a total of approximately 155 million persons to its total population. Over the same period, the United States can be expected to add only 61 million.

Section B Economy

Map 55 World Land Use, A.D. 1500
Map 56 World Land Use, A.D. 2000
Map 57 World Transportation Patterns
Map 58 Rich and Poor Countries: Gross National Income
Map 59 Economic Growth: GDP Change Per Capita
Map 60 Total Labor Force
Map 61 Female Labor Force
Map 62 Employment by Sector
Map 63 Agricultural Production Per Capita
Map 64 Exports of Primary Products
Map 65 Dependence on Trade
Map 66 Per Capita Income
Map 67 Purchasing Power Parity
Map 68 Energy Production Per Capita
Map 69 Energy Requirements Per Capita
Map 70 World Daily Per Capita Food Supply

Map 55 World Land Use, A.D. 1500

Europeans began to explore the world in the late 1400s. They encountered many independent people with self-sustaining economies at that time. Foraging people practiced hunting and gathering, utilizing the wild forms of plants and animals in their environments. Horticultural people practiced a simple form of agriculture using hoes or digging sticks as their basic tools. They sometimes cleared their land by burning and then planted crops. Pastoralists herded animals as their basic subsistence pattern. Complex state-level societies, such as the Mongols, had pastoralism as their base. Intensive agriculturalists based their societies on complicated irrigation systems and/or the plow and draft animals. Wheat and rice were two kinds of crops that supported large populations.

World Land Use
A.D. 1500
Foraging
Pastoralism
Horticulture
Intensive agriculture

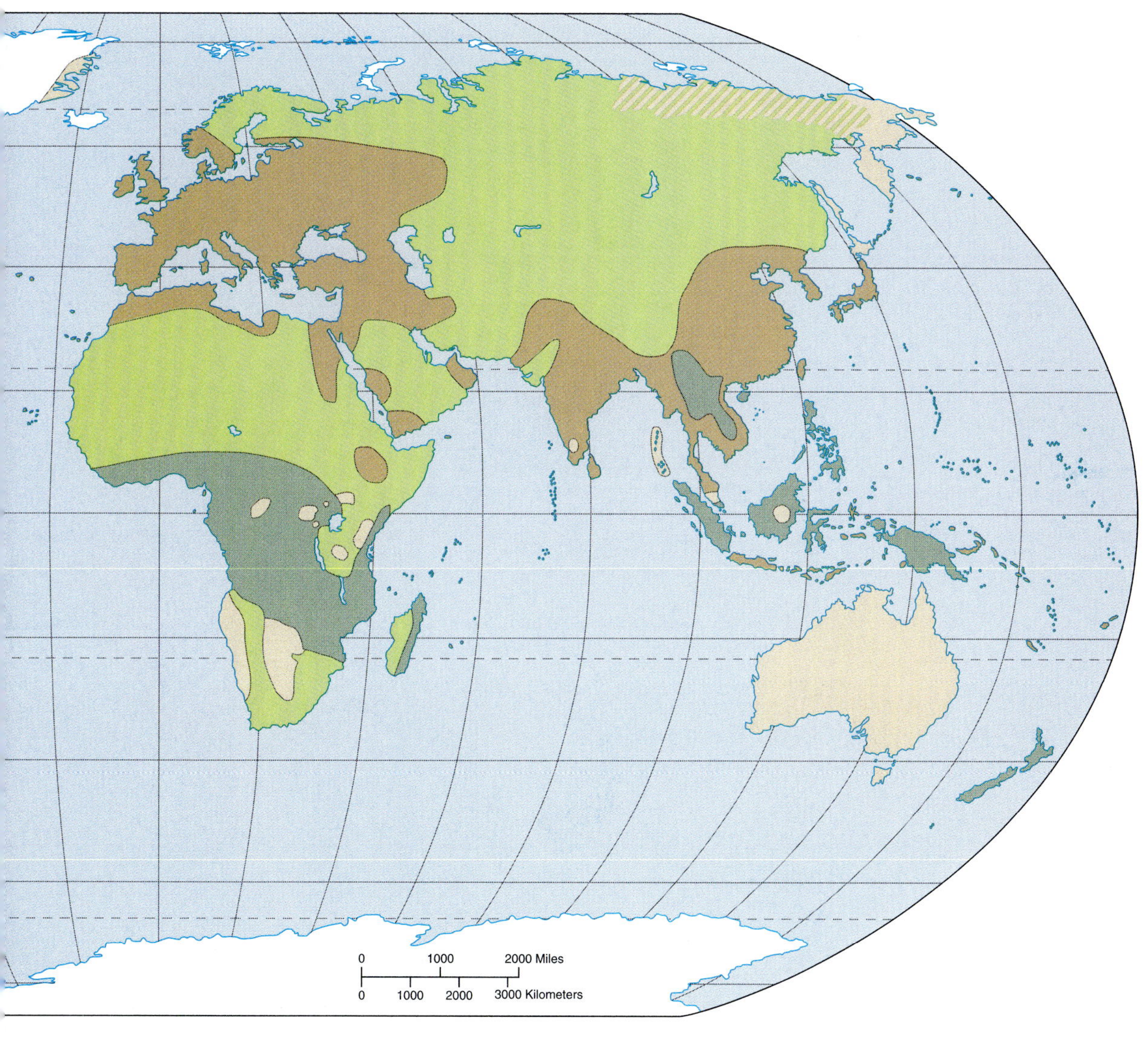
0
1000
2000 Miles
0
1000
2000
3000 Kilometers

Map 56 World Land Use, A.D. 2000

Land uses can be categorized as lying somewhere on a scale between extensive uses, in which human activities are dispersed over relatively large areas, and intensive uses, in which human activities are concentrated in relatively small areas. Many of the most important land use patterns of the world (such as urbanization, industry, mining, or transportation) are intensive and therefore relatively small in area and not easily seen on maps of this scale. Hence, even in the areas identified as "Manufacturing and Commerce" on the map there are many land uses that are not strictly industrial or commercial in nature, and, in fact, more extensive land uses (farming, residential, open space) may actually cover more ground than the inten-

World Land Use
Predominant Activities by Region
Manufacturing and Commerce
Commercial Crop and Livestock Agriculture
Intensive Subsistence Crop and Livestock Agriculture, including Plantations
Tropical Shifting Subsistence Agriculture
Livestock Ranching
Dryland Nomadic Livestock Herding
Forestry, Fishing, Hunting and Gathering, Recreation and Tourism (Commercial)
Nomadic Herding, Forestry, Fishing, Hunting (Primarily Subsistence)
Fishing Grounds (Commercial and Subsistence)
No Major Economic Activity
NORTH PACIFIC OCEAN
NORTH ATLANTIC OCEAN
SOUTH PACIFIC OCEAN
SOUTH ATLANTIC OCEAN
Tropic of Cancer
Equator
Antarctic Circle

sive industrial or commercial activities. On the other hand, the more extensive land uses, like agriculture and forestry, tend to dominate the areas in which they are found. Thus, primary economic activities such as agriculture and forestry tend to dominate the world map of land use because of their extensive character. Much of this map is, therefore, a map that shows the global variations in agricultural patterns. Note, among other things, the differences between land use patterns in the more developed countries of the temperate zones and the less developed countries of the tropics.

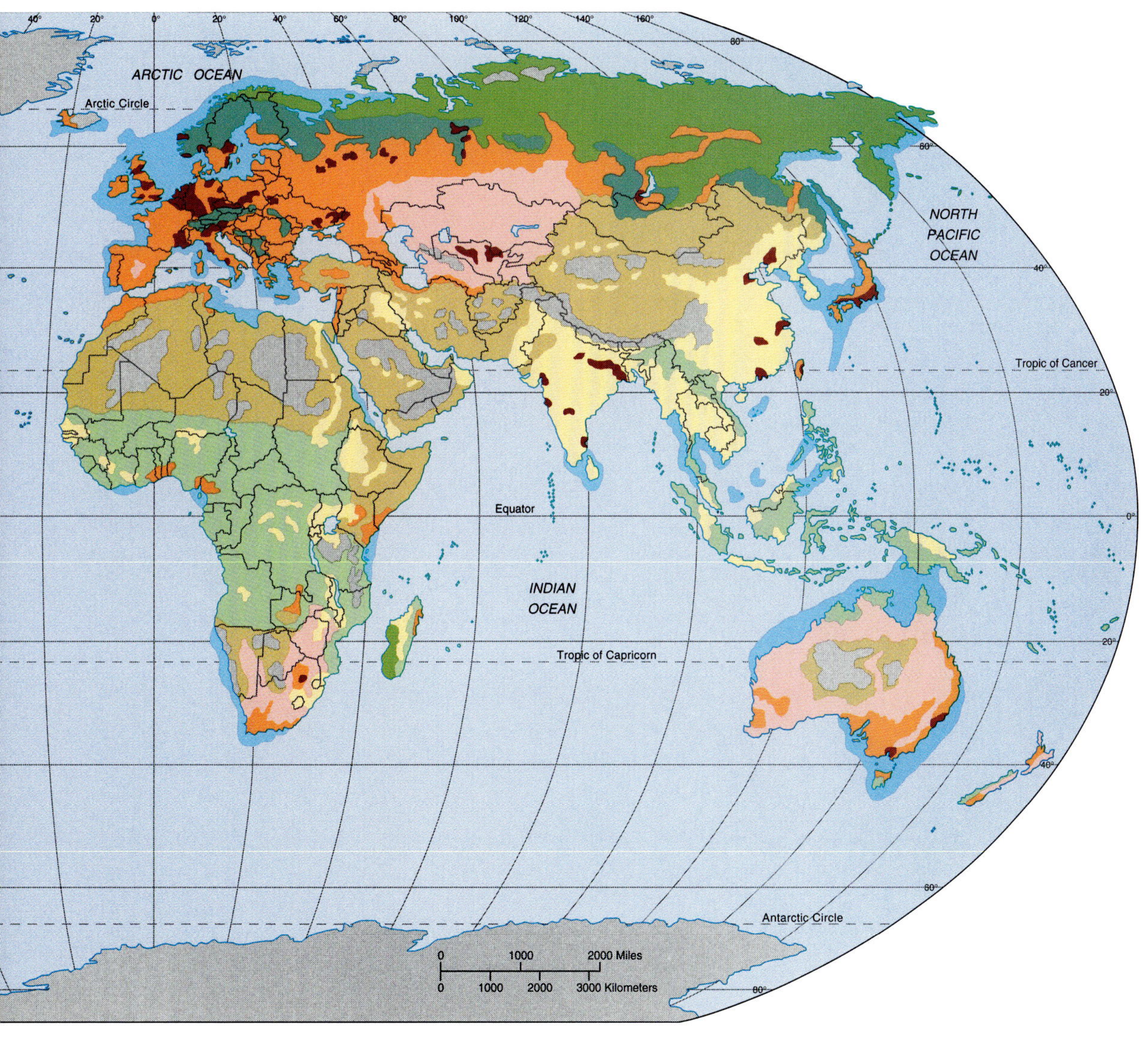
ARCTIC OCEAN
Arctic Circle
NORTH PACIFIC OCEAN
Tropic of Cancer
Equator
INDIAN OCEAN
Tropic of Capricorn
Antarctic Circle
0 1000 2000 Miles
0 1000 2000 3000 Kilometers

Map 57 World Transportation Patterns

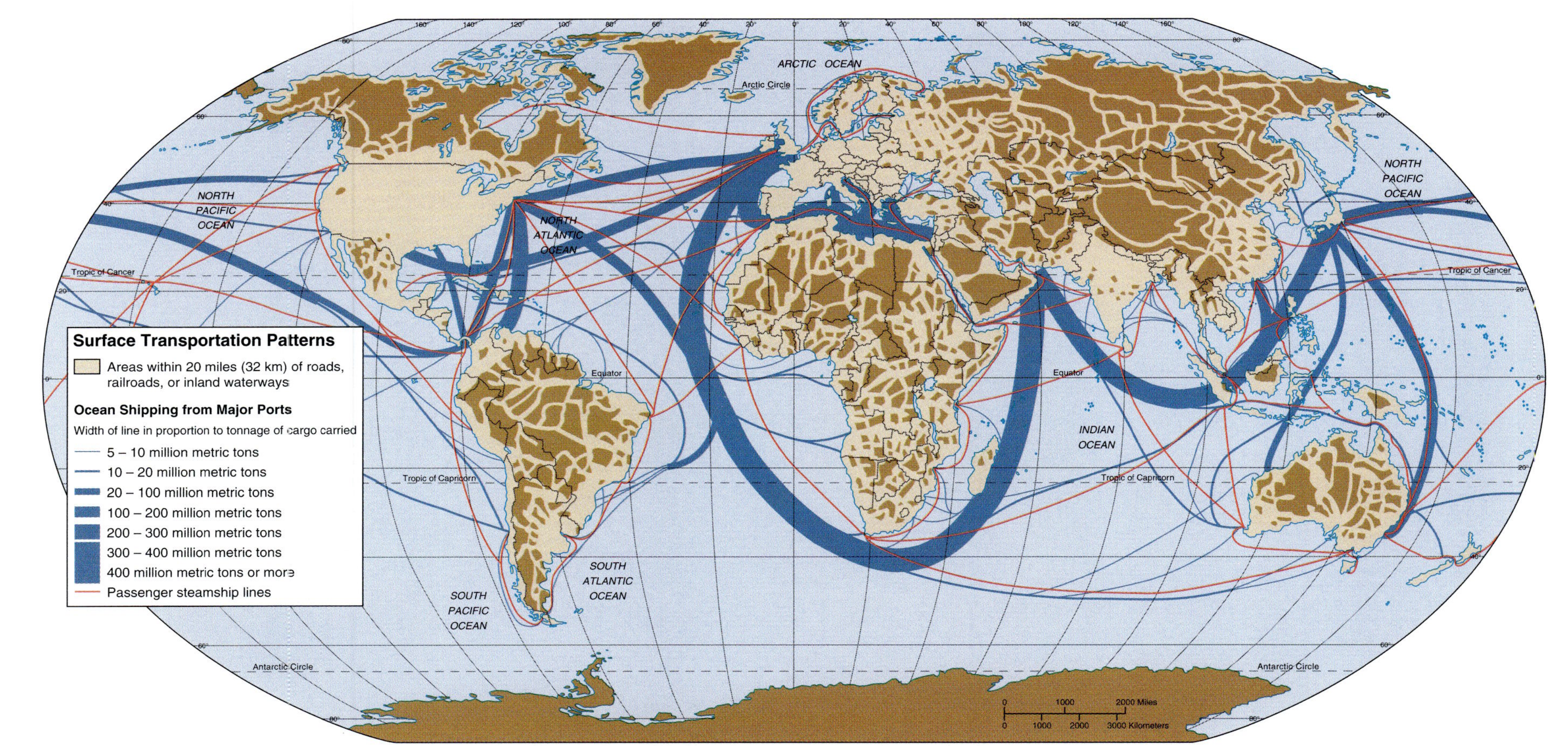

Surface Transportation Patterns
Areas within 20 miles (32 km) of roads, railroads, or inland waterways
Ocean Shipping from Major Ports
Width of line in proportion to tonnage of cargo carried
5 – 10 million metric tons
10 – 20 million metric tons
20 – 100 million metric tons
100 – 200 million metric tons
200 – 300 million metric tons
300 – 400 million metric tons
400 million metric tons or more
Passenger steamship lines
ARCTIC OCEAN
Arctic Circle
NORTH PACIFIC OCEAN
NORTH ATLANTIC OCEAN
NORTH PACIFIC OCEAN
Tropic of Cancer
Equator
Tropic of Capricorn
INDIAN OCEAN
SOUTH ATLANTIC OCEAN
SOUTH PACIFIC OCEAN
Antarctic Circle
0 1000 2000 Miles
0 1000 2000 3000 Kilometers

As a form of land use, transportation is second only to agriculture in its coverage of the earth's surface and is one of the clearest examples in the human world of a *network*, a linked system of lines allowing flows from one place to another. The global transportation network and its related communication web is responsible for most of the *spatial interaction,* or movement of goods, people, and ideas between places. As the chief mechanism of spatial interaction, transportation is linked firmly with the concept of a shrinking world and the development of a global community and economy. Because transportation systems require significant modification of the earth's surface, transportation is also responsible for massive alterations in the quantity and quality of water, for major soil degradations and erosion, and (indirectly) for the air pollution that emanates from vehicles utilizing the transportation system. In addition, as improved transportation technology draws together places on the earth that were formerly remote, it allows people to impact environments a great distance away from where they live.

Map 58 Rich and Poor Countries: Gross National Income

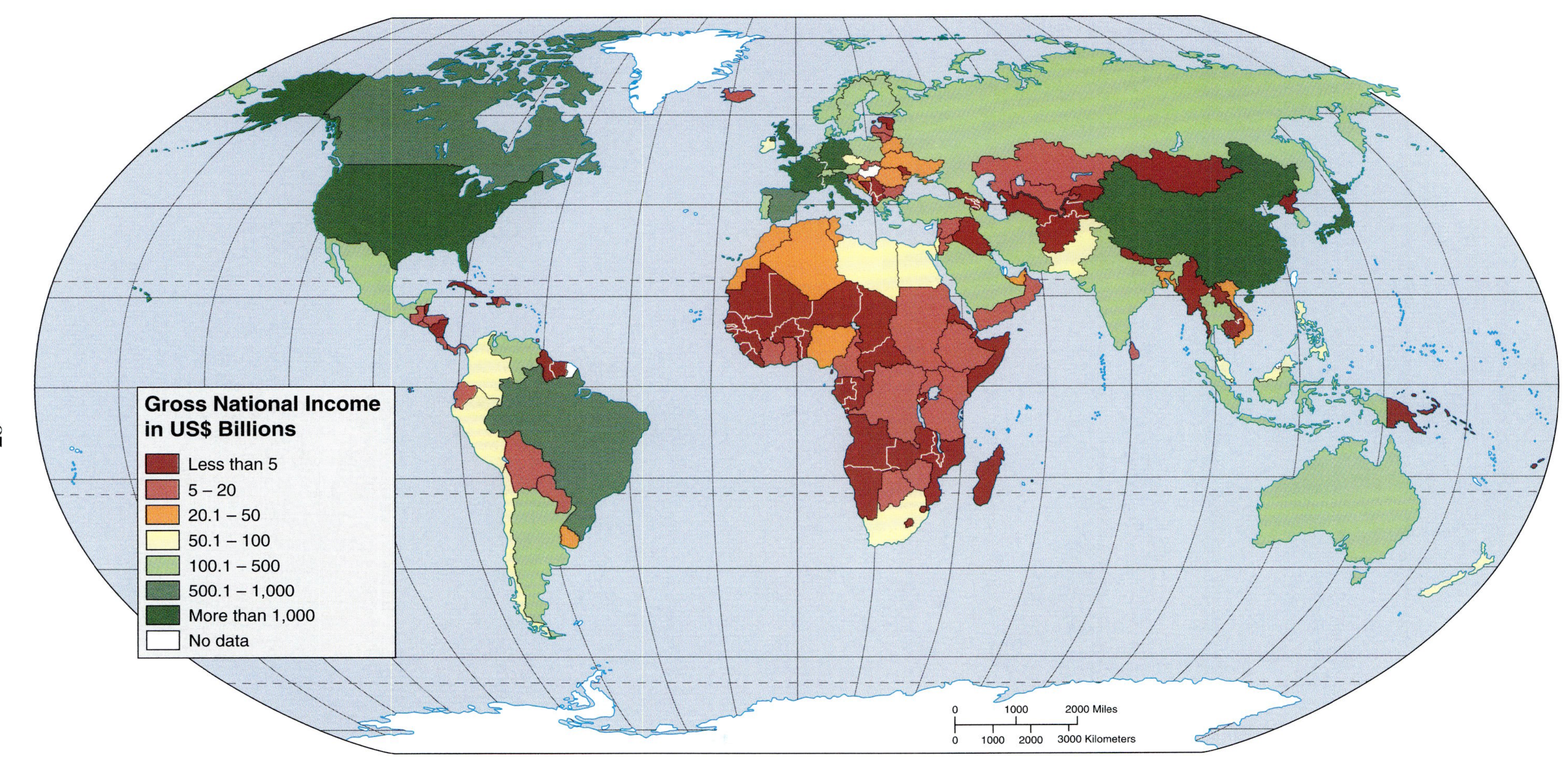

Gross National Income in US$ Billions
Less than 5
5 – 20
20.1 – 50
50.1 – 100
100.1 – 500
500.1 – 1,000
More than 1,000
No data
0 1000 2000 Miles
0 1000 2000 3000 Kilometers

Gross National Income (GNI) is the broadest measure of national income and measures the total claims of a country's residents to all income from domestic and foreign products during a year. Although GNI is often misleading and commonly incomplete, it is often used by economists, geographers, political scientists, policy makers, development experts, and others not only as a measure of relative well-being but also as an instrument of assessing the effectiveness of economic and political policies. What is wrong with GNI? First of all, it does not take into account a number of real economic factors, such as environmental deterioration, the accumulation or degradation of human and social capital, or the value of household work. Yet in spite of these deficiencies, GNI is still a reasonable way to assess the relative wealth of nations: the vast differences in wealth that separate the poorest countries from the richest. One of the more striking features of the map is the evidence it presents that such a small number of countries possess so many of the world's riches (keeping in mind that GNI provides no measure of the distribution of wealth within a country).

Map 59 Economic Growth: GDP Change Per Capita

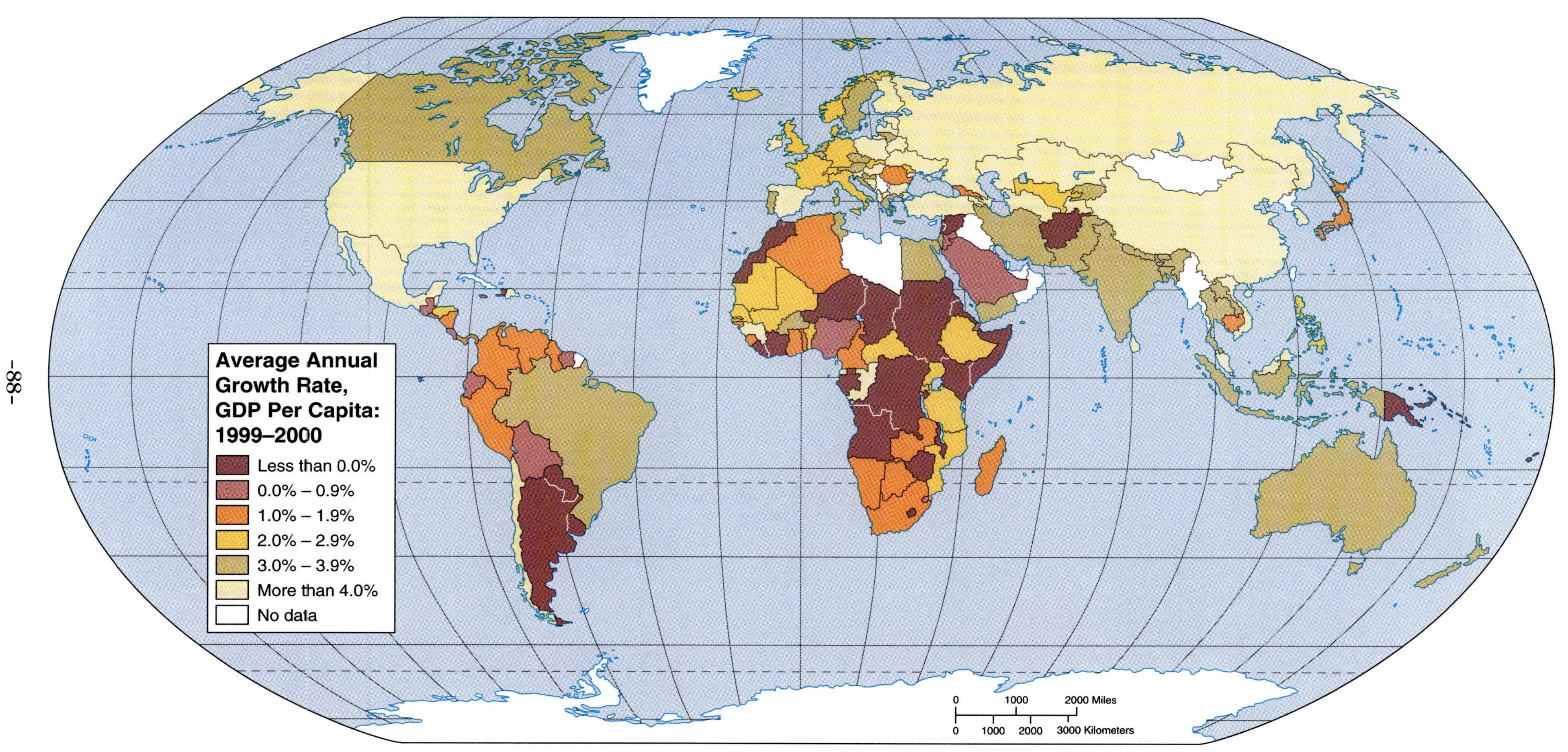
Average Annual
Growth Rate,
GDP Per Capita:
1999–2000
Less than 0.0%
0.0% – 0.9%
1.0% – 1.9%
2.0% – 2.9%
3.0% – 3.9%
More than 4.0%
No data
0 1000 2000 Miles
0 1000 2000 3000 Kilometers

As more and more of the world's countries move into the international trade mainstream, the share of the total global production under the control of developing countries increases. During the last decade for which these data are available, developing economies in South, Southeast, and East Asia grew at rates higher than the growth rates of "richer" countries in Europe and North and South America. This should not necessarily be viewed as a case of the poor catching up with the rich; in fact, it shows the huge impact that even relatively small production increases will have in countries with small GNIs and GDPs.

Map 60 Total Labor Force

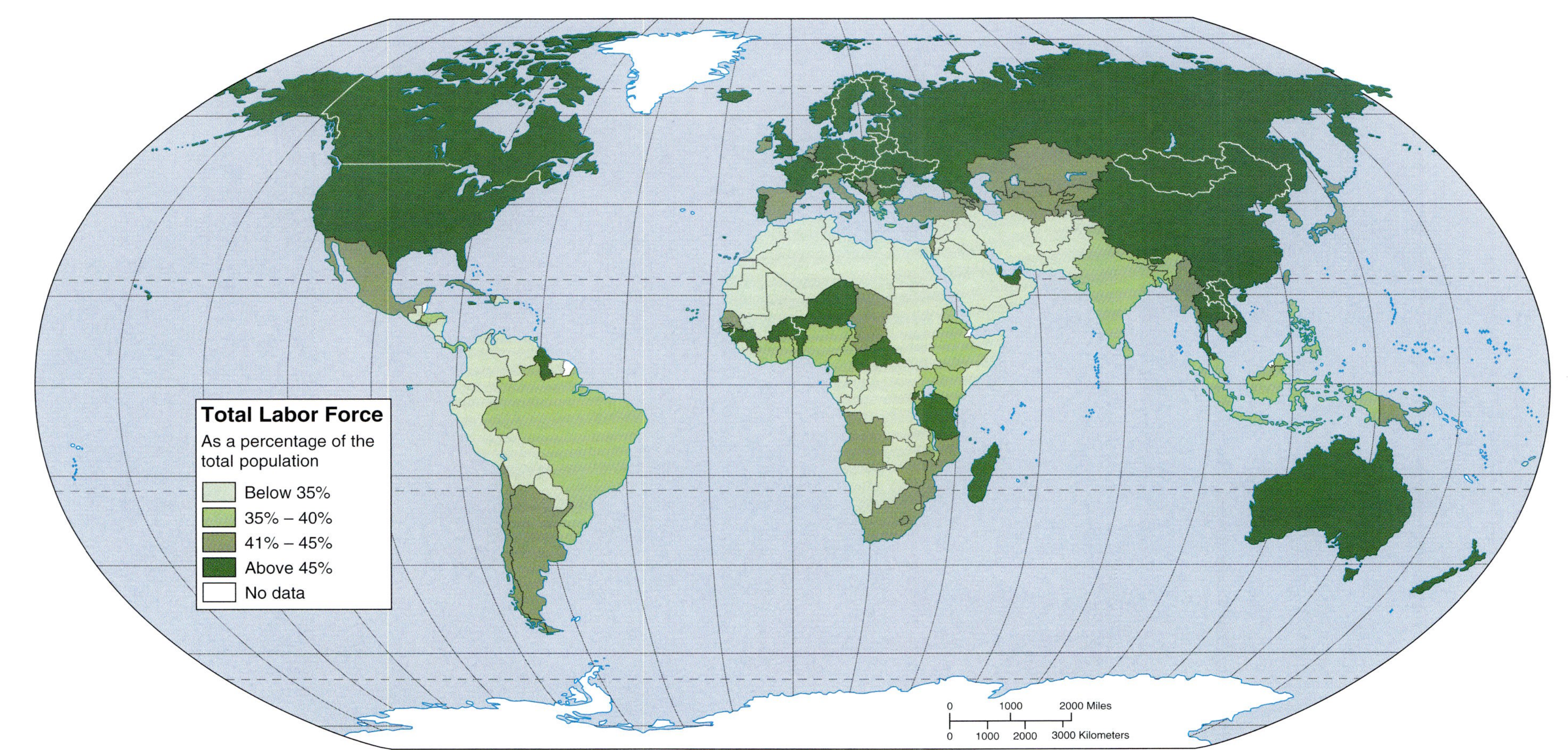
Total Labor Force
As a percentage of the total population
Below 35%
35% – 40%
41% – 45%
Above 45%
No data
0 1000 2000 Miles
0 1000 2000 3000 Kilometers

The term *labor force* refers to the economically active portion of a population, that is, all people who work or are without work but are available for and are seeking work to produce economic goods and services. The total labor force thus includes both the employed and the unemployed (as long as they are actively seeking employment). Labor force is considered a better indicator of economic potential than employment/unemployment figures, since unemployment figures will include experienced workers with considerable potential who are temporarily out of work. Unemployment figures will also incorporate persons seeking employment for the first time (many recent college graduates, for example). Generally, countries with higher percentages of total population within the labor force will be countries with higher levels of economic development. This is partly a function of levels of education and training and partly a function of the age distribution of populations. In developing countries, substantial percentages of the total population are too young to be part of the labor force. Also in developing countries a significant percentage of the population consists of women engaged in household activities or subsistence cultivation. These people seldom appear on lists of either employed or unemployed seeking employment and are the world's forgotten workers.

Map 61 Female Labor Force

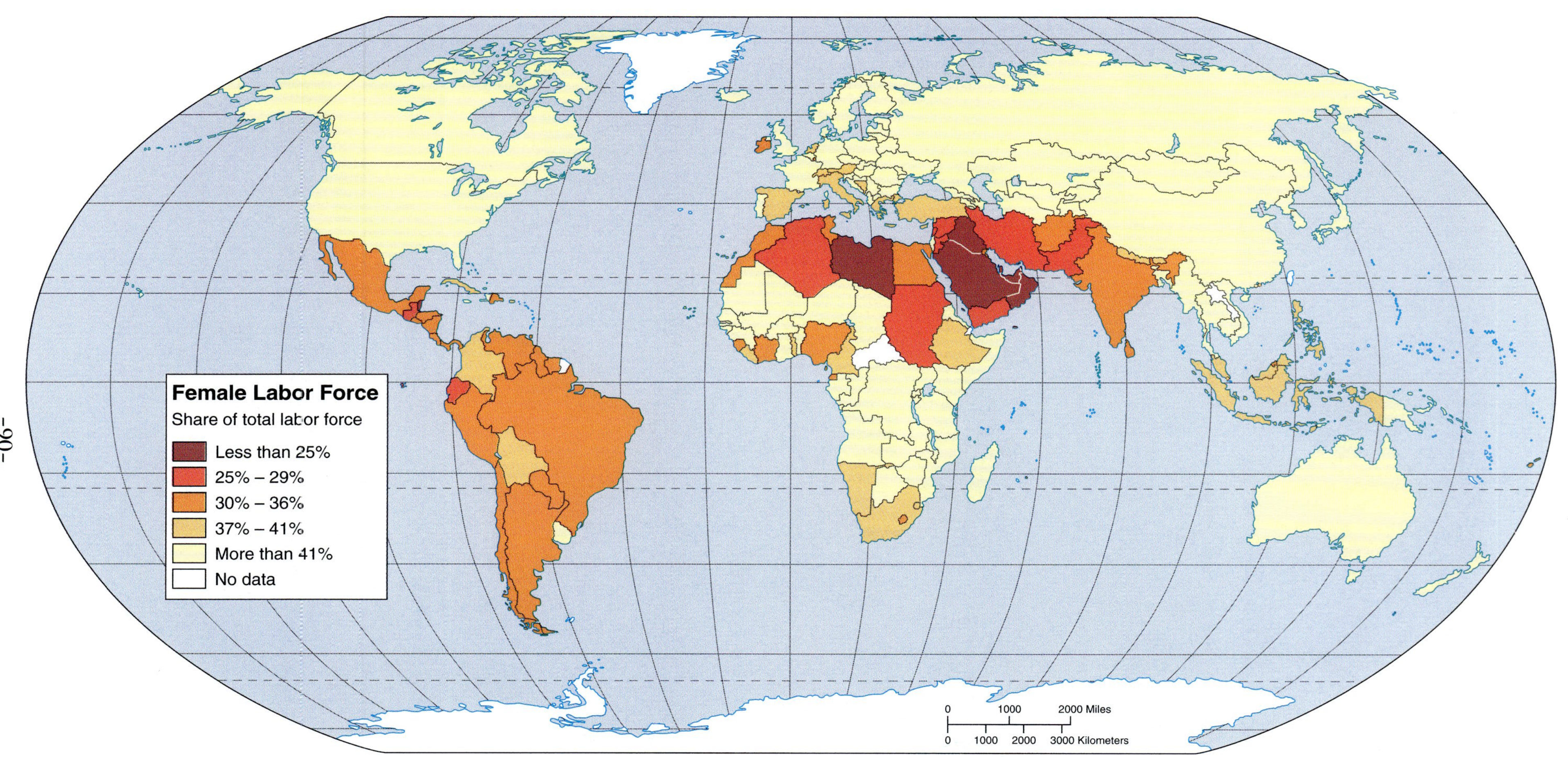
Female Labor Force
Share of total labor force
Less than 25%
25% – 29%
30% – 36%
37% – 41%
More than 41%
No data
0
1000
2000 Miles
0
1000
2000
3000 Kilometers

The percentage of the labor force that is composed of women is an intriguing measure of economic development. In general, countries with higher levels of economic development have larger percentages of women in the "formal" labor force (which excludes household and subsistence agricultural workers, among others). But a considerable number of countries with low percentages of women in the labor force rank somewhere in the middle on the economic development scale. There are two primary reasons why fewer women work in the formal sectors in these countries. One of the reasons is cultural bias. For example, in Latino regions of Middle and South America and in Islamic countries of North Africa and Southwest Asia, cultural bias against women tends to keep them out of the workplace and in the home, where they engage in nonreported household activities. A second reason for the absence of women from the labor force has to do with the structure of national or regional economies. In Native American regions of Middle and Southeast Asia, the role of women in subsistence agriculture is a significant one but is not reported as "employment," just as household activities are not reported as employment. Ultimately, the real significance of the percentage of females in the labor force may be as an indicator of a country's *potential* development and room for growth in those nonhousehold and nonsubsistence economic activities in which women are currently underemployed.

Map 62 Employment by Sector

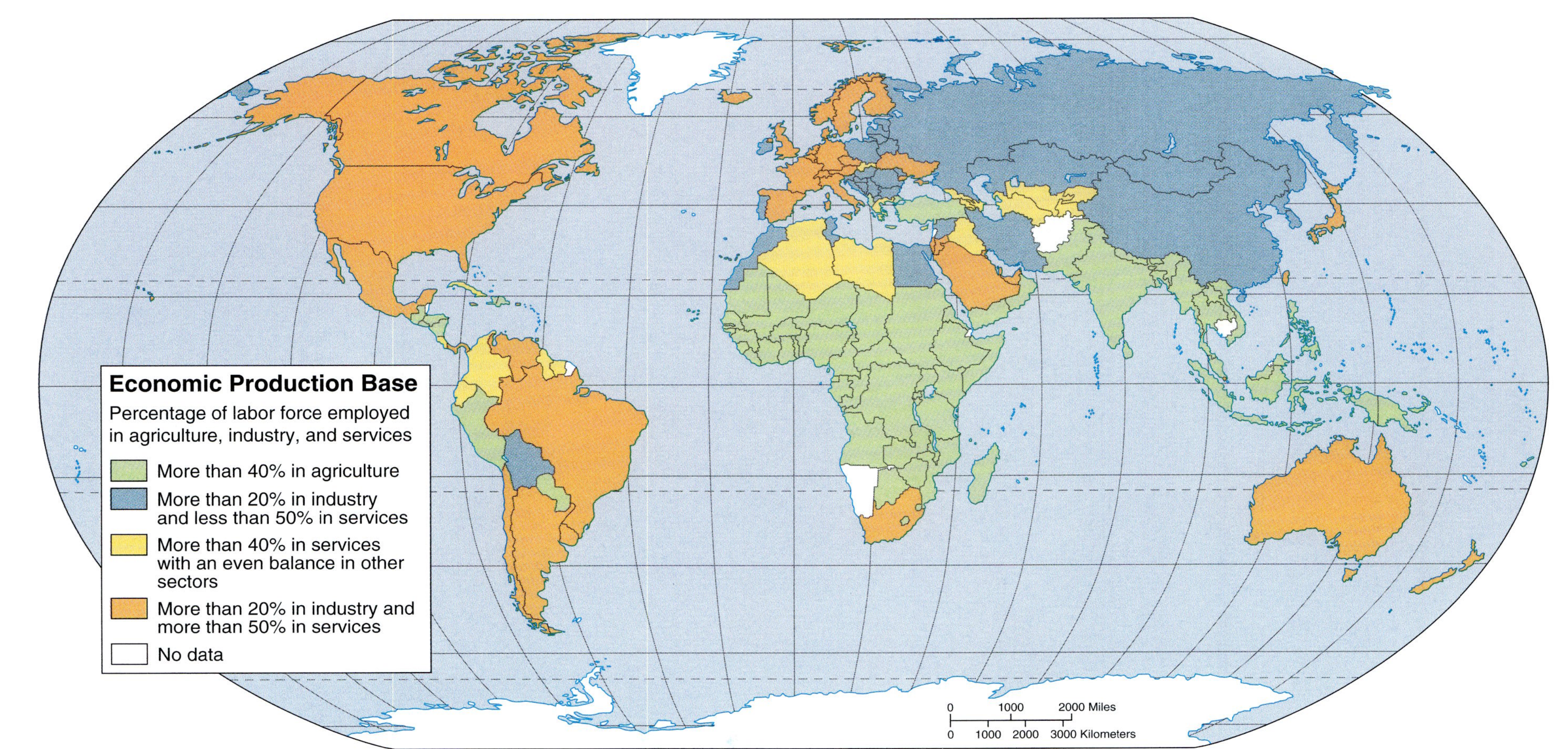
Economic Production Base
Percentage of labor force employed in agriculture, industry, and services
More than 40% in agriculture
More than 20% in industry and less than 50% in services
More than 40% in services with an even balance in other sectors
More than 20% in industry and more than 50% in services
No data
0 1000 2000 Miles
0 1000 2000 3000 Kilometers

The employment structure of a country's population is one of the best indicators of the country's position on the scale of economic development. At one end of the scale are those countries with more than 40 percent of their labor force employed in agriculture. These are almost invariably the least developed, with high population growth rates, poor human services, significant environmental problems, and so on. In the middle of the scale are two types of countries: those with more than 20 percent of their labor force employed in industry and those with a fairly even balance among agricultural, industrial, and service employment but with at least 40 percent of their labor force employed in service activities. Generally, these countries have undergone the industrial revolution fairly recently and are still developing an industrial base while building up their service activities. This category also includes countries with a disproportionate share of their economies in service activities primarily related to resource extraction. On the other end of the scale from the agricultural economies are countries with more than 20 percent of their labor force employed in industry and more than 50 percent in service activities. These countries are, for the most part, those with a highly automated industrial base and a highly mechanized agricultural system (the "postindustrial," developed countries). They also include, particularly in Middle and South America and Africa, industrializing countries that are also heavily engaged in resource extraction as a service activity.

Map 63 Agricultural Production Per Capita

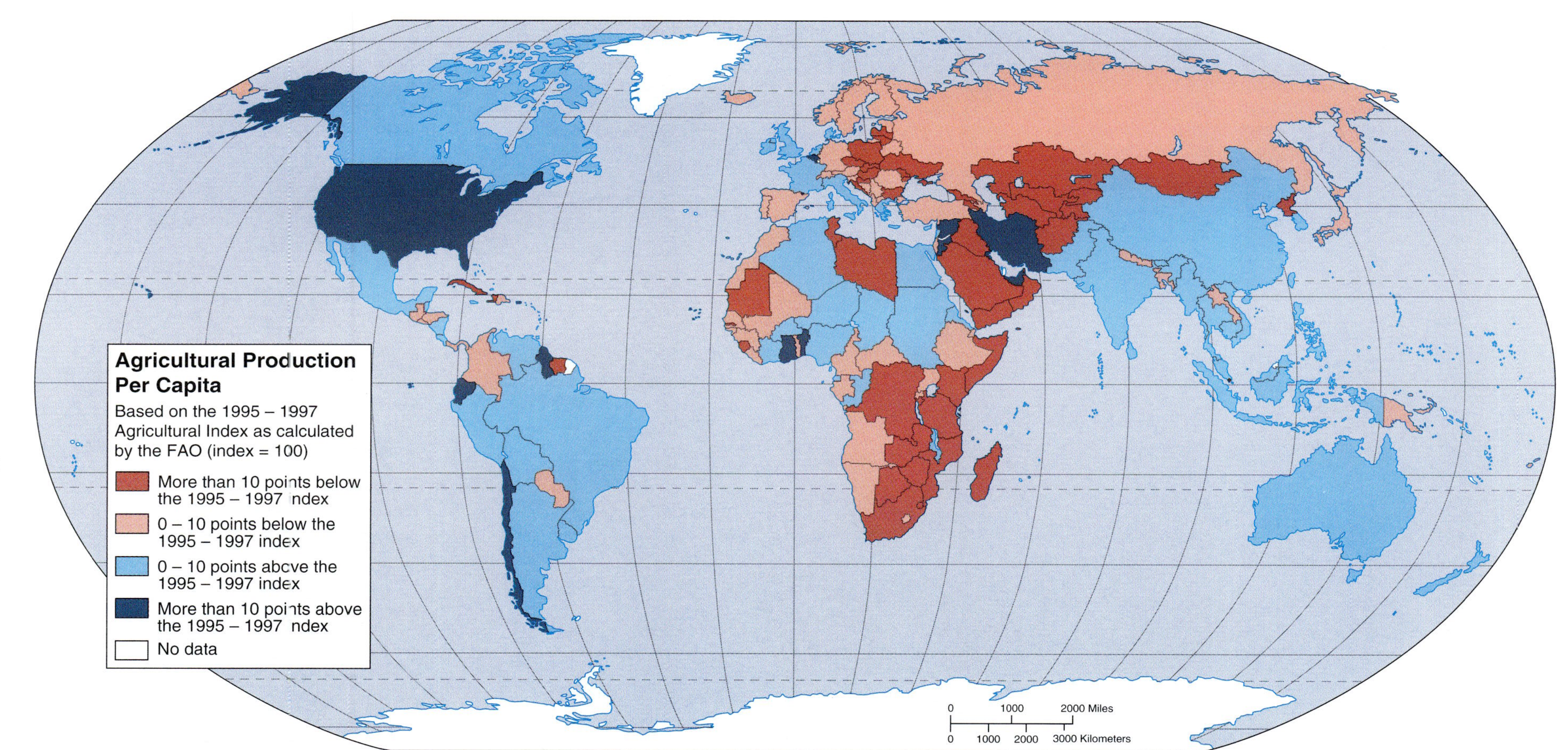

Agricultural Production Per Capita
Based on the 1995 – 1997 Agricultural Index as calculated by the FAO (index = 100)
More than 10 points below the 1995 – 1997 index
0 – 10 points below the 1995 – 1997 index
0 – 10 points above the 1995 – 1997 index
More than 10 points above the 1995 – 1997 index
No data
0 1000 2000 Miles
0 1000 2000 3000 Kilometers

Agricultural production includes the value of all crop and livestock products originating within a country for the base period of 1995–1997. The index value portrays the disposable output (after deductions for livestock feed and seed for planting) of a country's agriculture in comparison with the base period 1989–1991. Thus, the production values show not only the relative ability of countries to produce food but also show whether or not that ability has increased or decreased over a 10-year period. In general, global food production has kept up with or very slightly exceeded population growth. However, there are significant regional variations in the trend of food production keeping up with or surpassing population growth. For example, agricultural production in Africa and in Middle America has fallen, while production in South America, Asia, and Europe has risen. In the case of Africa, the drop in production reflects a population growing more rapidly than agricultural productivity. Where rapid increases in food production per capita exist (as in certain countries in South America, Asia, and Europe), most often the reason is the development of new agricultural technologies that have allowed food production to grow faster than population. In much of Asia, for example, the so-called Green Revolution of new, highly productive strains of wheat and rice made positive index values possible. Also in Asia, the cessation of major warfare allowed some countries (Cambodia, Laos, and Vietnam) to show substantial increases over the 1982–1984 index. In some cases, a drop in production per capita reflects government decisions to limit production in order to maintain higher prices for agricultural products. The United States and Japan fall into this category.

Map 64 Exports of Primary Products

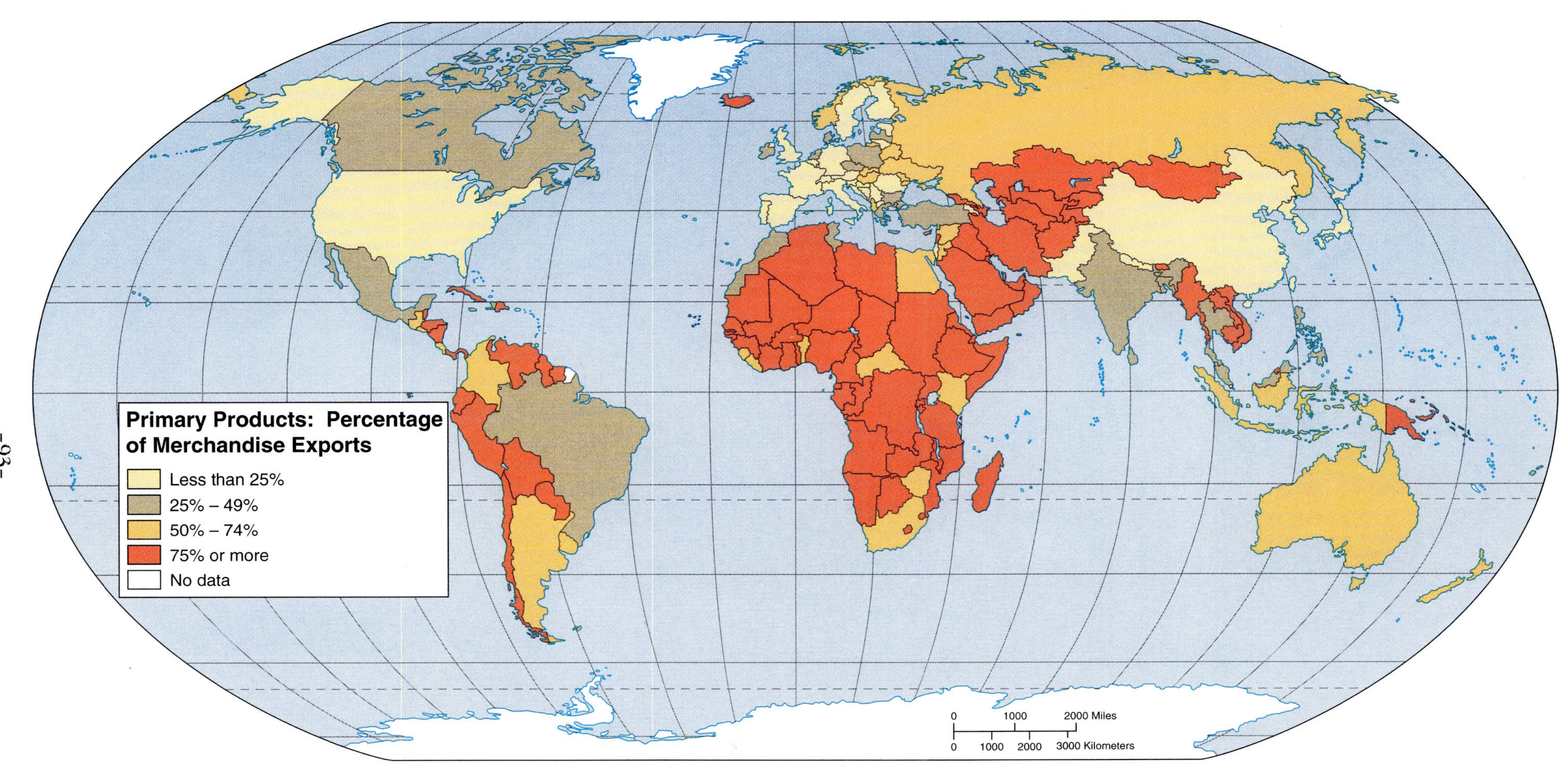
Primary Products: Percentage of Merchandise Exports
Less than 25%
25% – 49%
50% – 74%
75% or more
No data
0 1000 2000 Miles
0 1000 2000 3000 Kilometers

Primary products are those that require additional processing before they enter the consumer market: metallic ores that must be converted into metals and then into metal products such as automobiles or refrigerators; forest products such as timber that must be converted to lumber before they become suitable for construction purposes; and agricultural products that require further processing before being ready for human consumption. It is an axiom in international economics that the more a country relies on primary products for its export commodities, the more vulnerable its economy is to market fluctuations. Those countries with only primary products to export are hampered in their economic growth. A country dependent on only one or two products for export revenues is unprotected from economic shifts, particularly a changing market demand for its products. Imagine what would happen to the thriving economic status of the oil-exporting states of the Persian Gulf, for example, if an alternate source of cheap energy were found. A glance at this map shows that those countries with the lowest levels of economic development tend to be concentrated on primary products and, therefore, have economies that are especially vulnerable to economic instability.

Map 65 Dependence on Trade

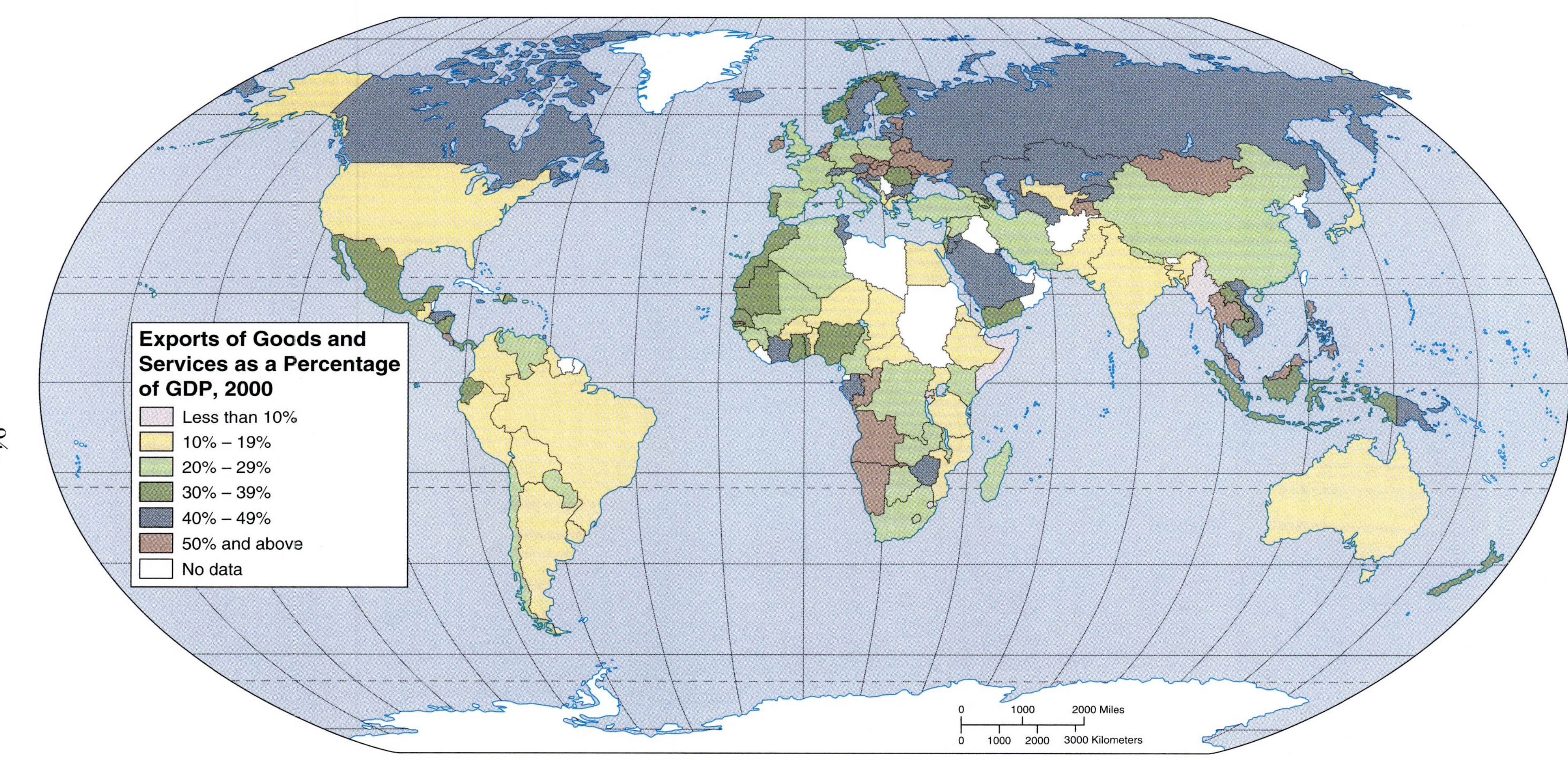
Exports of Goods and Services as a Percentage of GDP, 2000
Less than 10%
10% – 19%
20% – 29%
30% – 39%
40% – 49%
50% and above
No data
0 1000 2000 Miles
0 1000 2000 3000 Kilometers

As the global economy becomes more and more a reality, the economic strength of virtually all countries is increasingly dependent upon trade. For many developing nations, with relatively abundant resources and limited industrial capacity, exports provide the primary base upon which their economies rest. Even countries like the United States, Japan, and Germany, with huge and diverse economies, depend on exports to generate a significant percentage of their employment and wealth. Without imports, many products that consumers want would be unavailable or more expensive; without exports, many jobs would be eliminated. But exports alone do not provide the full story on trade dependence; part of what a map such as this masks is "what kind of exports?" For the more developed parts of the world, exports tend to be industrial products, perhaps along with some few raw materials (the United States and Russia are exceptions here in that they export a significant quantity of raw materials). But for the lesser developed countries, the exports are largely in the raw materials category. While this, as noted, provides jobs, it also means that countries may not have the necessary quantity of raw materials with which to develop their own industries and further their economic development.

Map 66 Per Capita Income

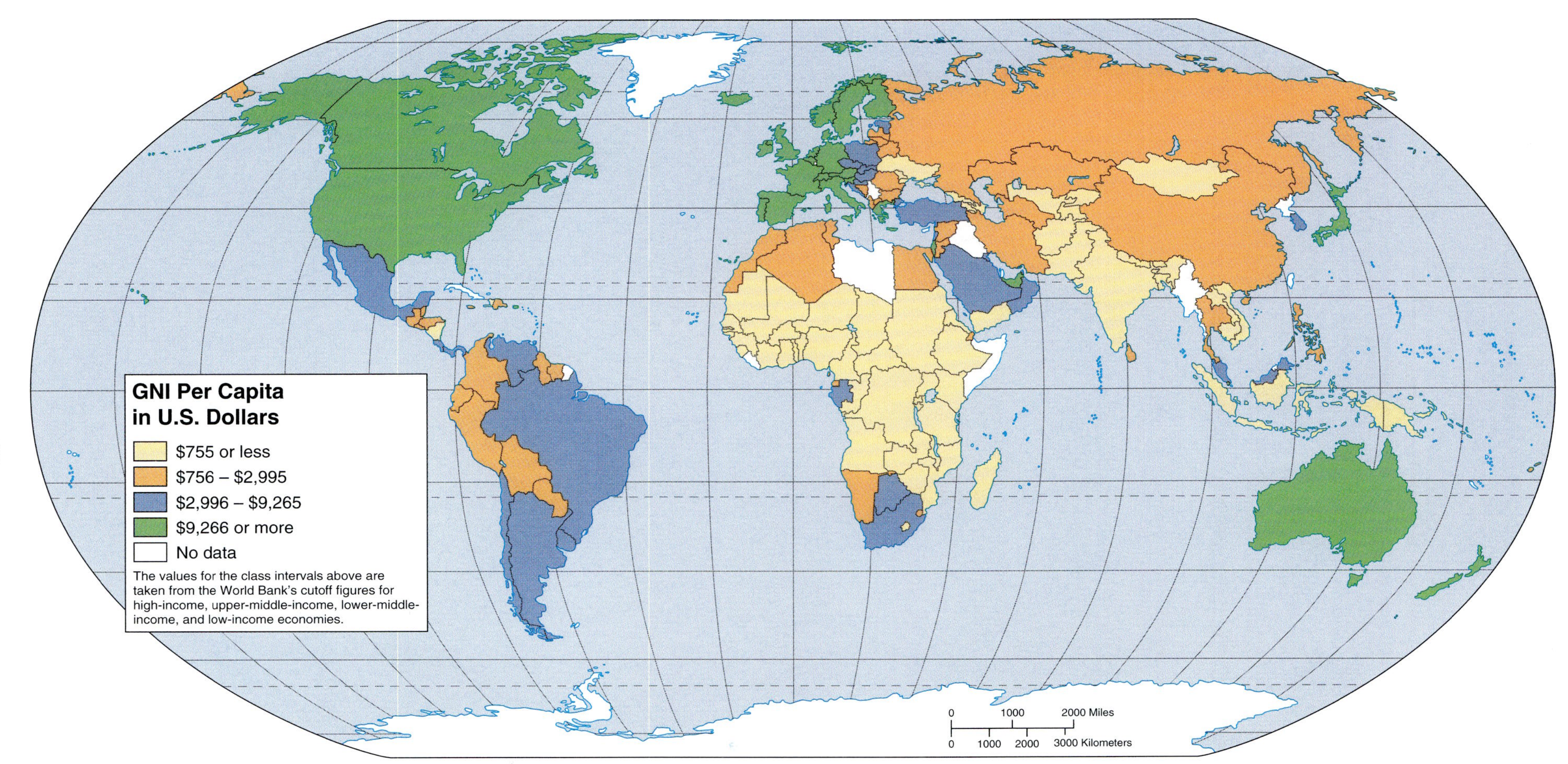
GNI Per Capita in U.S. Dollars
$755 or less
$756 – $2,995
$2,996 – $9,265
$9,266 or more
No data
The values for the class intervals above are taken from the World Bank's cutoff figures for high-income, upper-middle-income, lower-middle-income, and low-income economies.
0 1000 2000 Miles
0 1000 2000 3000 Kilometers

Gross National Income (GNI) in either absolute or per capita form should be used cautiously as a yardstick of economic strength, because it does not measure the distribution of wealth among a population. There are countries (most notably, the oil-rich countries of the Middle East) where per capita GNI is high but where the bulk of the wealth is concentrated in the hands of a few individuals, leaving the remainder in poverty. Even within countries in which wealth is more evenly distributed (such as those in North America or Western Europe), there is a tendency for dollars or pounds sterling or francs or marks to concentrate in the bank accounts of a relatively small percentage of the population. Yet the maldistribution of wealth tends to be greatest in the less developed countries, where the per capita GNI is far lower than in North America and Western Europe, and poverty is widespread. In fact, a map of GNI per capita offers a reasonably good picture of comparative economic well-being. It should be noted that a low per capita GNI does not automatically condemn a country to low levels of basic human needs and services. There are a few countries, such as Costa Rica and Sri Lanka, that have relatively low per capita GNI figures but rank comparatively high in other measures of human well-being, such as average life expectancy, access to medical care, and literacy.

Map 67 Purchasing Power Parity

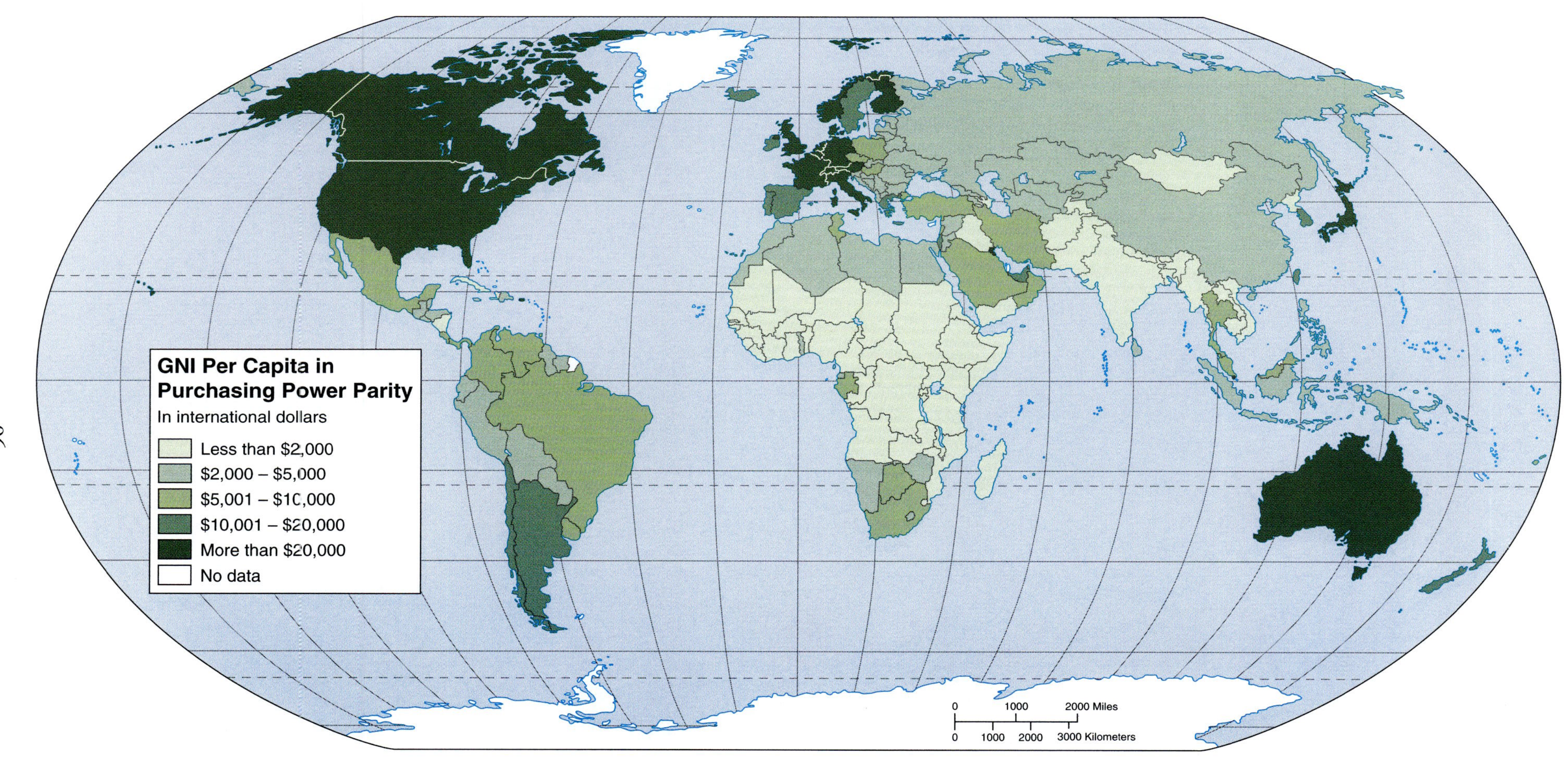
GNI Per Capita in Purchasing Power Parity
In international dollars
Less than $2,000
$2,000 – $5,000
$5,001 – $10,000
$10,001 – $20,000
More than $20,000
No data
0 1000 2000 Miles
0 1000 2000 3000 Kilometers

Among all the economic measures that separate the "haves" from the "have-nots," per capita Purchasing Power Parity (PPP) may be the most meaningful. Per capita GNP and GDP (Gross Domestic Product) figures, and even per capita income, have the limitation of seldom reflecting the true purchasing power of a country's currency at home. In order to get around this limitation, international economists seeking to compare national currencies developed the PPP measure, which shows the level of goods and services that holders of a country's money can acquire locally. By converting all currencies to the "international dollar," the World Bank and other organizations using PPP can now show more truly comparative values, since the new currency value shows the number of units of a country's currency required to buy the same quantity of goods and services in the local market as one U.S. dollar would buy in an average country. The use of PPP currency values can alter the perceptions about a country's true comparative position in the world economy. PPP provides a valid measurement of the ability of a country's population to provide for itself the things that people in the developed world take for granted: adequate food, shelter, clothing, education, and access to medical care. A glance at the map shows a clear-cut demarcation between temperate and tropical zones, with most of the countries with a PPP above $5,000 in the midlatitude zones and most of those with lower PPPs in the tropical and equatorial regions.

Map 68 Energy Production Per Capita

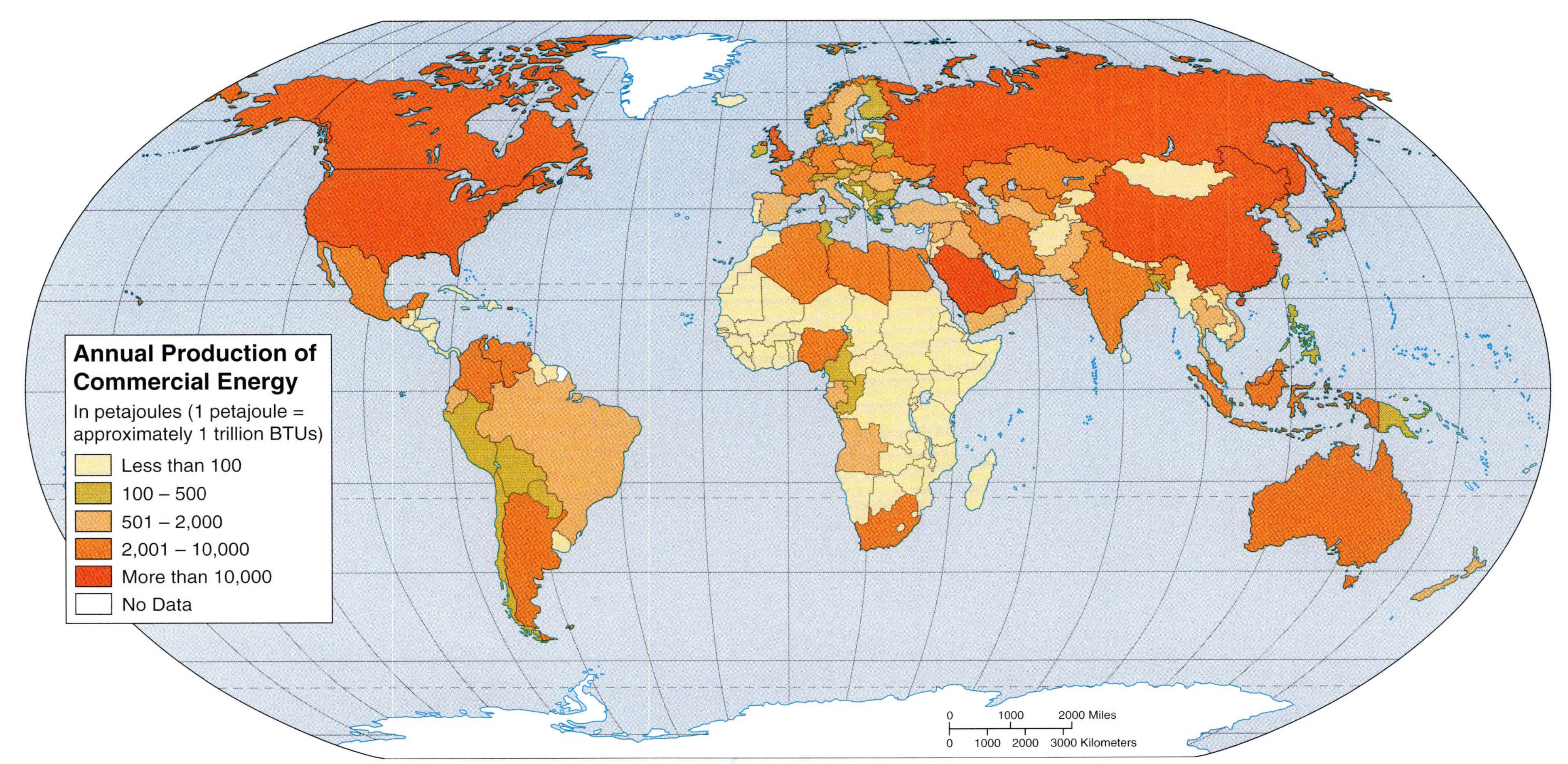

Annual Production of Commercial Energy
In petajoules (1 petajoule = approximately 1 trillion BTUs)
Less than 100
100 – 500
501 – 2,000
2,001 – 10,000
More than 10,000
No Data
0 1000 2000 Miles
0 1000 2000 3000 Kilometers

The production of commercial energy in all its forms—solid fuels (primarily coal), liquid fuels (primarily petroleum), natural gas, geothermal, wind, solar, hydroelectric, and nuclear—is a good measure of a country's ability to produce sufficient quantities of energy to meet domestic demands or to provide a healthy export commodity—or, in some instances, both. Commercial energy production is also a measure of the level of economic development, although a fairly subjective one. With exceptions, wealthier countries produce more energy from all sources than do poorer countries. Countries such as Japan and many European states rank among the world's wealthiest but are energy-poor and produce relatively little of their own energy. They have the ability, however, to pay for it. On the other hand, countries such as those of the Persian Gulf or the oil-producing states of Middle and South America may rank relatively low on the scale of economic development but rank high as producers of energy. The map does not show the enormous amounts of energy from noncommercial sources (traditional fuels like firewood and animal dung) used by the world's poor, particularly in Middle and South America, Africa, South Asia, and East Asia. In these regions, firewood and animal dung may account for more actual energy production than coal or oil. Indeed, for many in the developing world, the real energy crisis is a shortage of wood for cooking and heating.

Map 69 Energy Consumption Per Capita

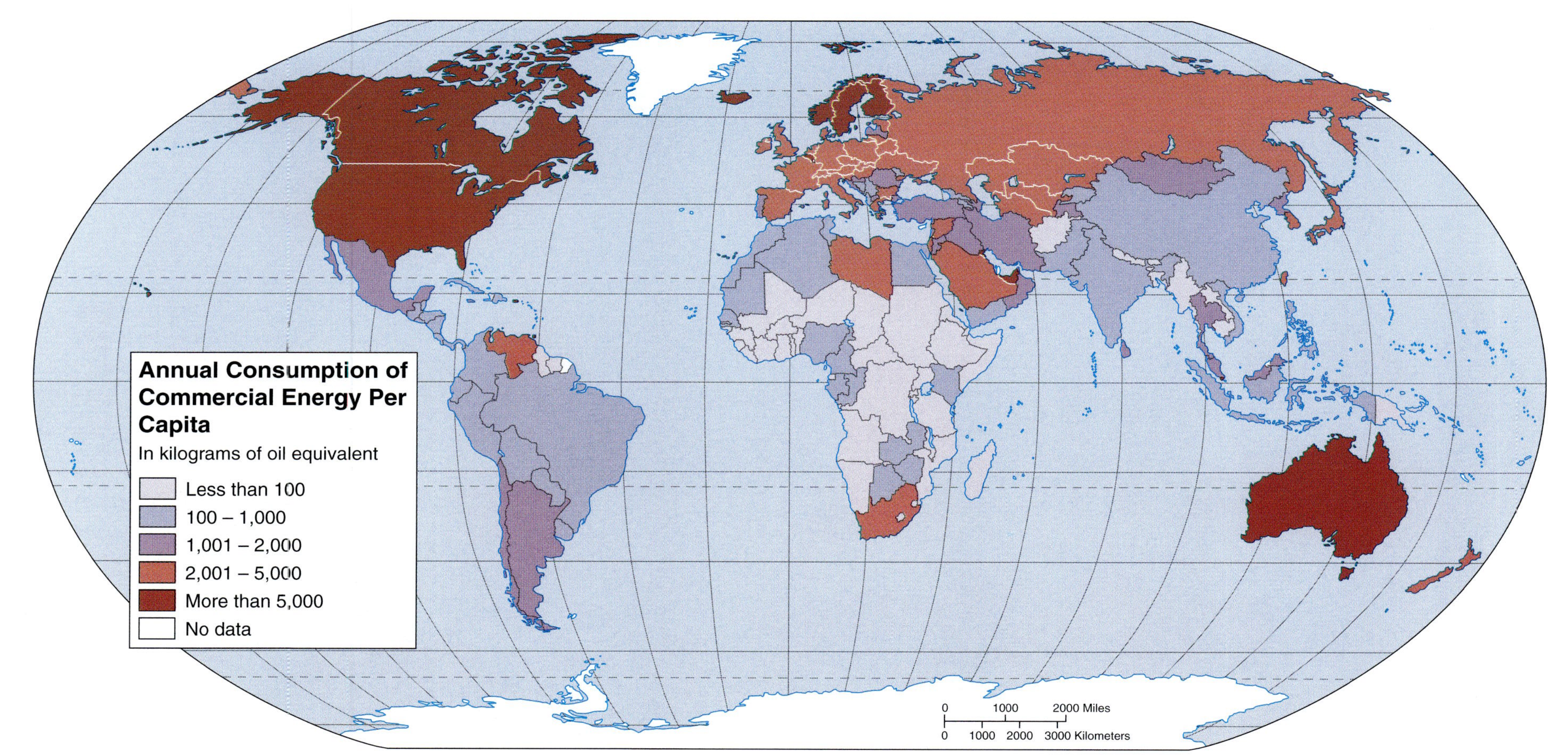

Annual Consumption of Commercial Energy Per Capita
In kilograms of oil equivalent
Less than 100
100 – 1,000
1,001 – 2,000
2,001 – 5,000
More than 5,000
No data
0 1000 2000 Miles
0 1000 2000 3000 Kilometers

Of all the quantitative measures of economic well-being, energy consumption per capita may be the most expressive. All of the countries defined by the World Bank as having high incomes consume at least 100 gigajoules of commercial energy (the equivalent of about 3.5 metric tons of coal) per person per year, with some, such as the United States and Canada, having consumption rates in the 300 gigajoule range (the equivalent of more than 10 metric tons of coal per person per year). With the exception of the oil-rich Persian Gulf states, where consumption figures include the costly "burning off" of excess energy in the form of natural gas flares at wellheads, most of the highest-consuming countries are in the Northern Hemisphere, concentrated in North America and Western Europe. At the other end of the scale are low-income countries, whose consumption rates are often less than 1 percent of those of the United States and other high consumers. These figures do not, of course, include the consumption of noncommercial energy—the traditional fuels of firewood, animal dung, and other organic matter—widely used in the less developed parts of the world.

Map 70 World Daily Per Capita Food Supply

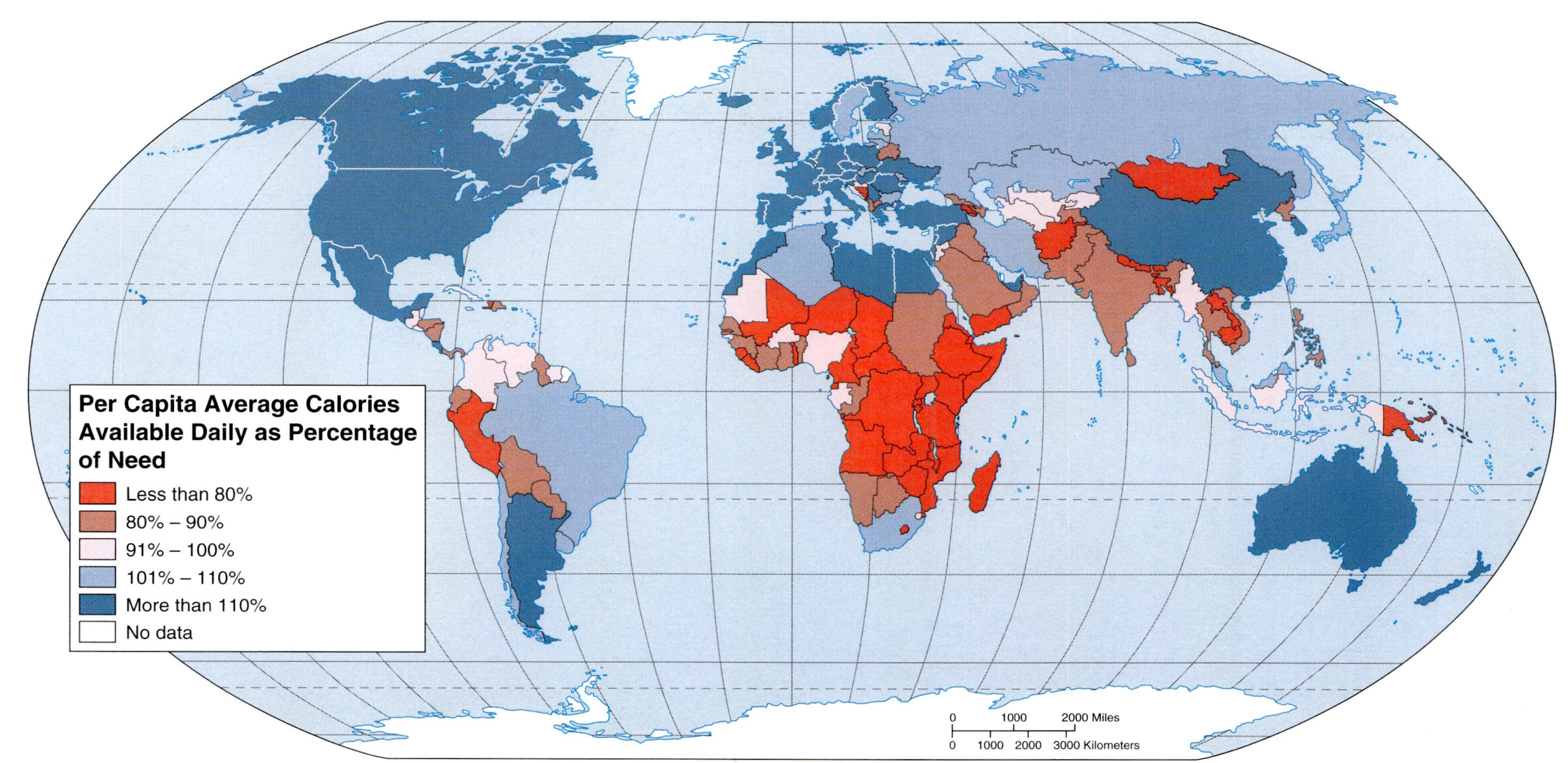
Per Capita Average Calories Available Daily as Percentage of Need
Less than 80%
80% – 90%
91% – 100%
101% – 110%
More than 110%
No data
0 1000 2000 Miles
0 1000 2000 3000 Kilometers

The data shown on this map indicate the presence or absence of critical food shortages. While they do not necessarily indicate the presence of starvation or famine, they certainly do indicate potential problem areas for the next decade. The measurements are in calories from all food sources: domestic production, international trade, drawdown on stocks or food reserves, and direct foreign contributions or aid. The quantity of calories available is that amount, estimated by the UN's Food and Agriculture Organization (FAO), that actually reaches consumers. The calories actually consumed may be lower than the figures shown, depending on how much is lost in a variety of ways: in home storage (to pests such as rats and mice), in preparation and cooking, through consumption by pets and domestic animals, and as discarded foods, for example. The former practice in such maps was to evaluate available calories as a percentage of "need" or minimum daily requirements to maintain health. Such a statistical measure was virtually impossible to standardize for the variety of human types in the world and for such variables as age and sex distribution. A newer form of measure—available calories as a percentage of the world average available—eliminates many of the problems of the former set of numbers while still maintaining a good relative picture of global hunger.

Section C Human Society

Map 71 World Religions
Map 72 Household and Family Structures
Map 73 Kinship Structures
Map 74 Child Malnutrition
Map 75 Primary School Enrollment
Map 76 Illiteracy Rate
Map 77 Female/Male Inequality in Education and Employment
Map 78 The Quality of Life: The Human Development Index

Map 71 World Religions

Religious adherence is one of the fundamental defining characteristics of *human culture*, the style of life adopted by a people and passed from one generation to the next. More than just a set of behavioral patterns having to do with worship and ceremony, religion is a vital conditioner of the ways that people deal with one another, with their institutions, and with the environments they occupy. In many areas of the world, the ways in which people make a

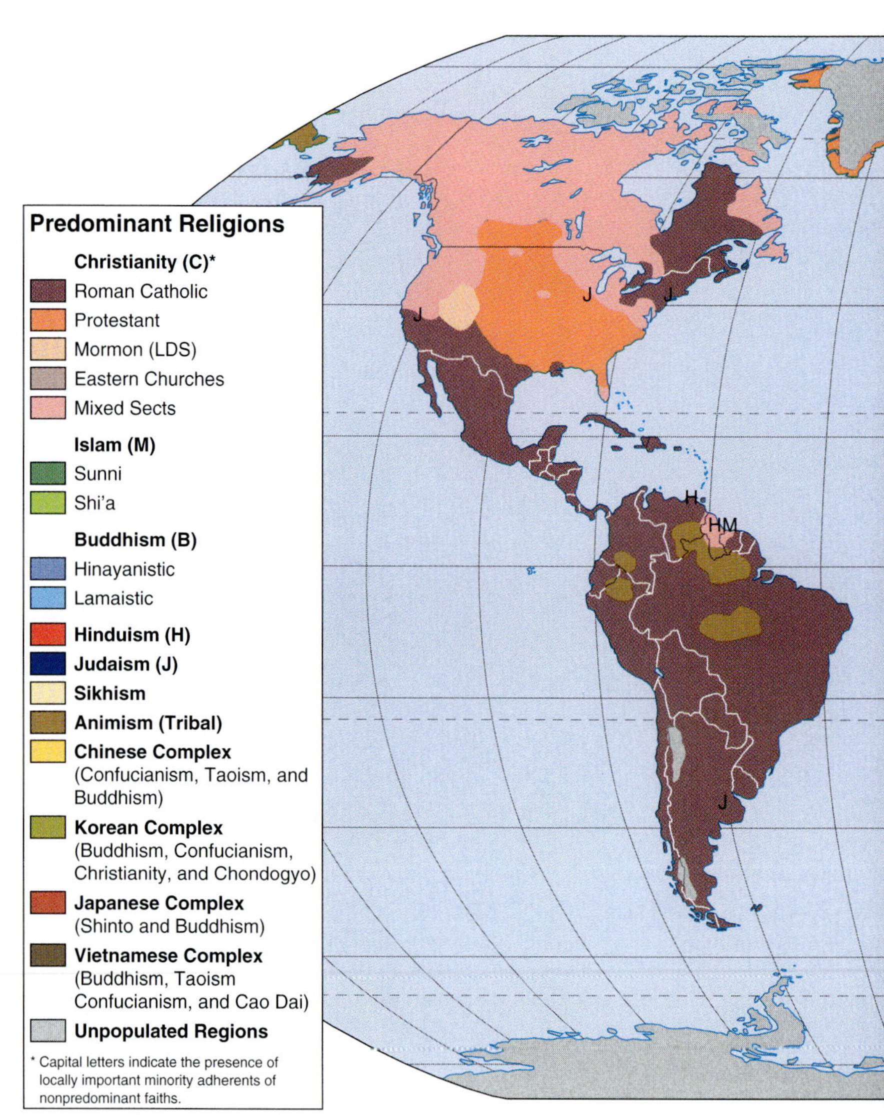

Predominant Religions
Christianity (C)*
Roman Catholic
Protestant
Mormon (LDS)
Eastern Churches
Mixed Sects
Islam (M)
Sunni
Shi'a
Buddhism (B)
Hinayanistic
Lamaistic
Hinduism (H)
Judaism (J)
Sikhism
Animism (Tribal)
Chinese Complex
(Confucianism, Taoism, and Buddhism)
Korean Complex
(Buddhism, Confucianism, Christianity, and Chondogyo)
Japanese Complex
(Shinto and Buddhism)
Vietnamese Complex
(Buddhism, Taoism Confucianism, and Cao Dai)
Unpopulated Regions
* Capital letters indicate the presence of locally important minority adherents of nonpredominant faiths.
J
J
J
H
HM
J

living, the patterns of occupation that they create on the land, and the impacts that they make on ecosystems are the direct consequences of their adherence to a religious faith. An examination of the map in the context of international and intranational conflict will also show that tension between countries and the internal stability of states is also a function of the spatial distribution of religion.

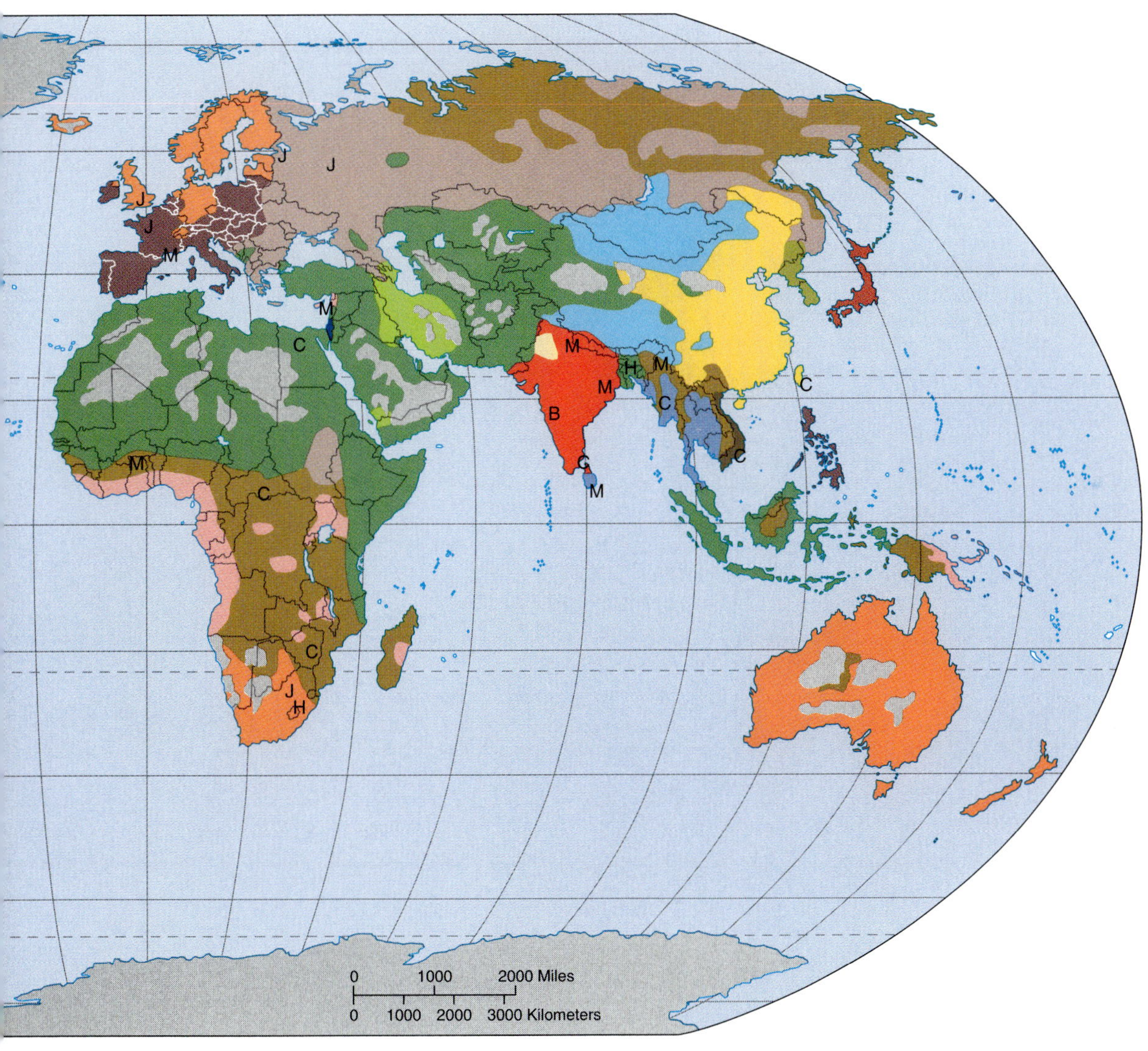

J
J
J
J
M
M
C
M
M
B
C
M
H
M
C
C
C
M
C
C
J
H
0 1000 2000 Miles
0 1000 2000 3000 Kilometers

Map 72 Household and Family Structures

Nuclear families are composed of a married couple and their children. They are found all over the world in many different kinds of cultural systems. Foraging peoples and industrial people find that nuclear families make for efficient and mobile households. Even when different forms of households are preferred in a society, nuclear families may still exist. For example, in traditional intensive agricultural societies, like India, people found it useful to live in larger households in which three generations—the grandparents, their married sons and their wives, and their children—all resided together and shared the work. When the old-

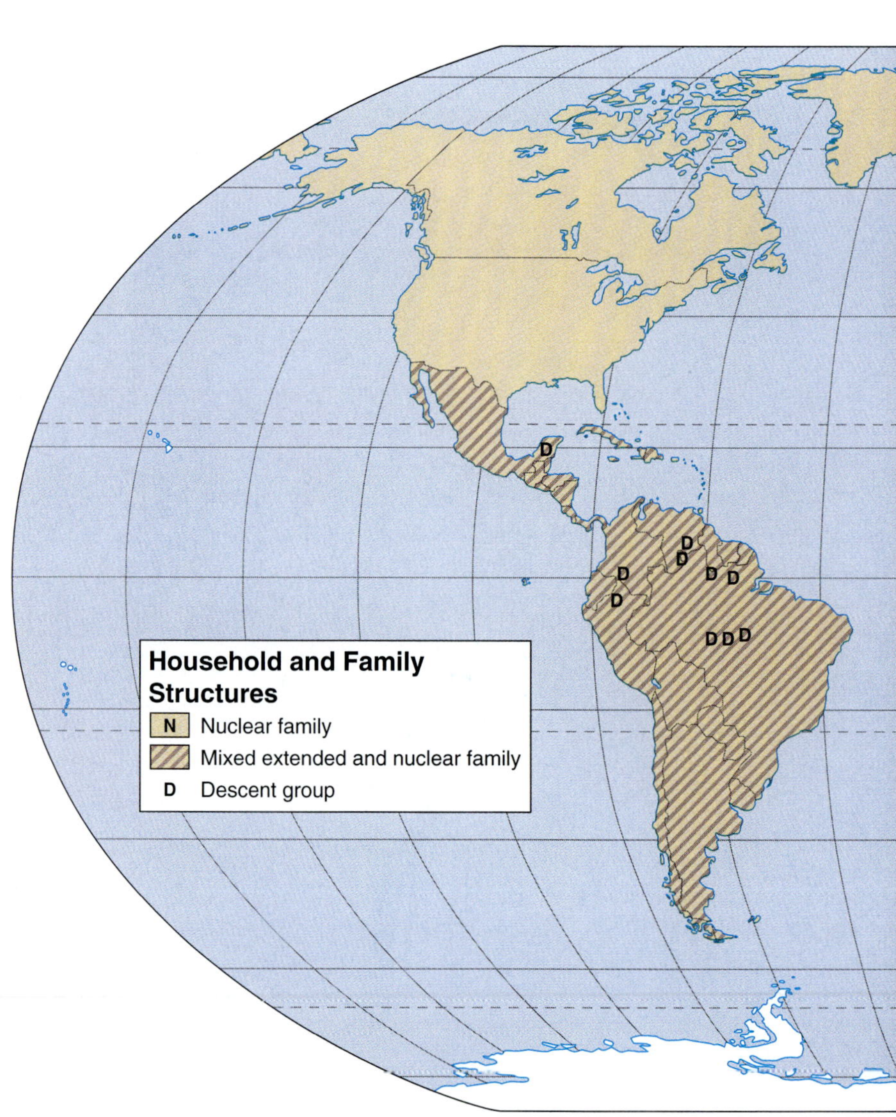

Household and Family Structures
N Nuclear family
Mixed extended and nuclear family
D Descent group
D

est generation died, however, the sons sometimes divided the household and thus lived in nuclear families. Descent groups, such as lineages or clans, are a different sort of social structural unit that exists in perpetuity. Descent groups often own land or herds in common and assign labor to subunits. They are common in tribal societies in which horticulture or pastoralism is practiced. The map provides an overview of the last 100 years of typical household patterns.

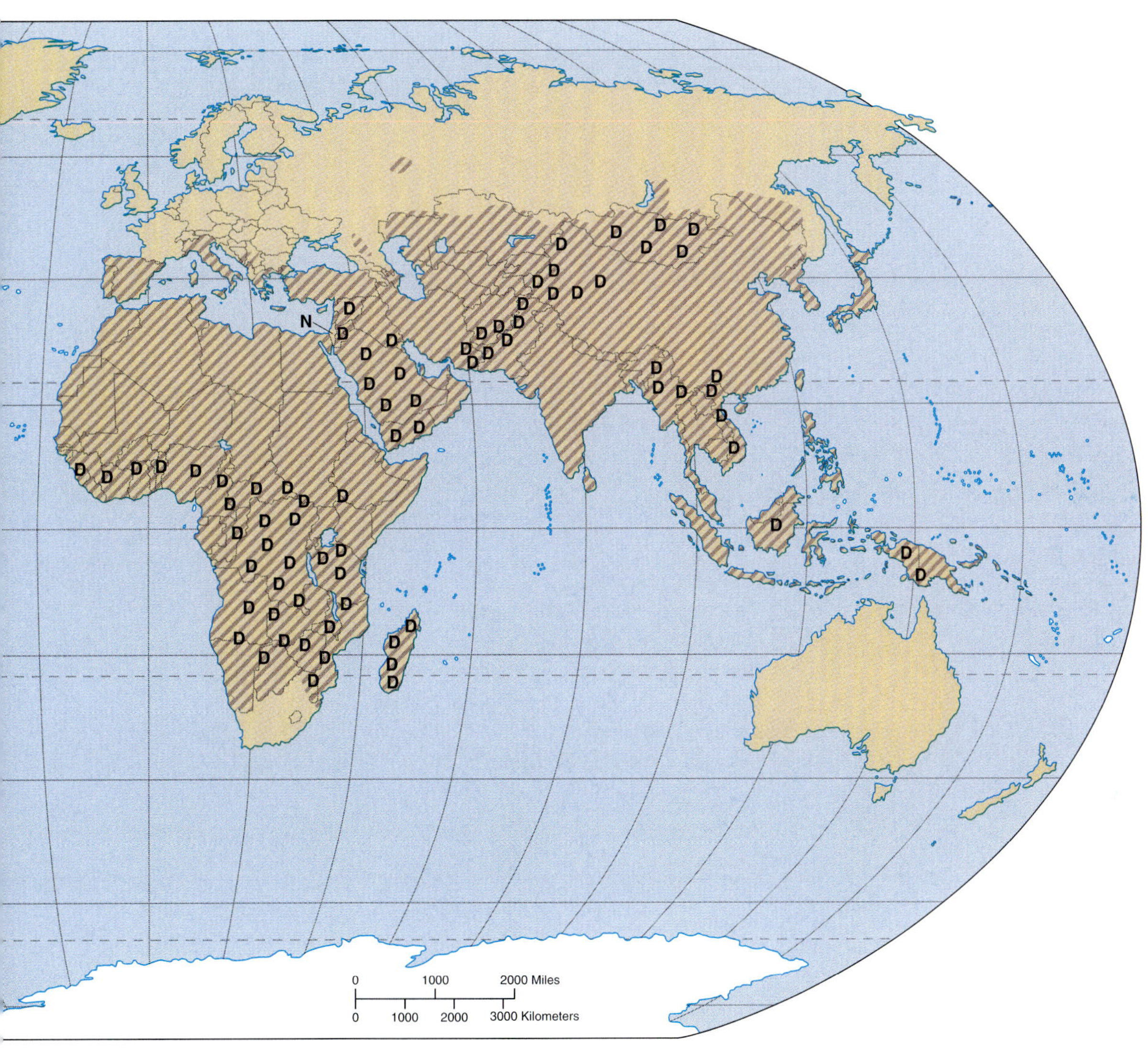
0
1000
2000 Miles
0
1000
2000
3000 Kilometers

Map 73 Kinship Structures

Monogamy, in which a person has only one spouse at a time, is a common form of marriage. Monogamy is found all over the world even though it is not always the preferred form of marriage. Polygyny, a man married to two or more women at the same time, has traditionally been allowed and even favored in many parts of the world. Often, however, only wealthy and powerful men can afford more than one wife. Polyandry, a woman married to two or

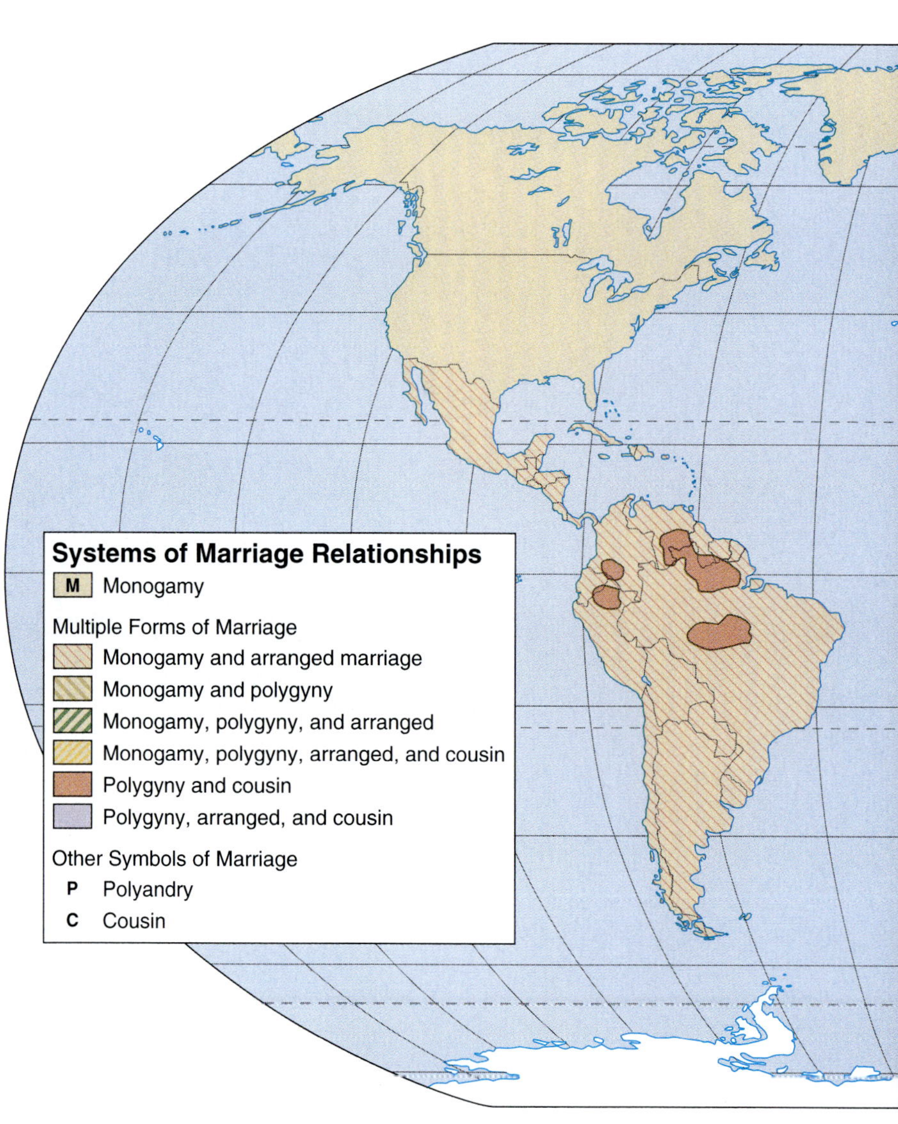

Systems of Marriage Relationships
M Monogamy
Multiple Forms of Marriage
Monogamy and arranged marriage
Monogamy and polygyny
Monogamy, polygyny, and arranged
Monogamy, polygyny, arranged, and cousin
Polygyny and cousin
Polygyny, arranged, and cousin
Other Symbols of Marriage
P Polyandry
C Cousin

men at the same time, is very rare and is found in some parts of South Asia. Marriage has not usually been an individual's choice. In much of the world, families play an important role in arranging marriages. In tribal societies, it is often considered most appropriate to marry someone who is classified as a cross or parallel cousin. The map provides an overview of the last 100 years of traditional marriage patterns and preferences.

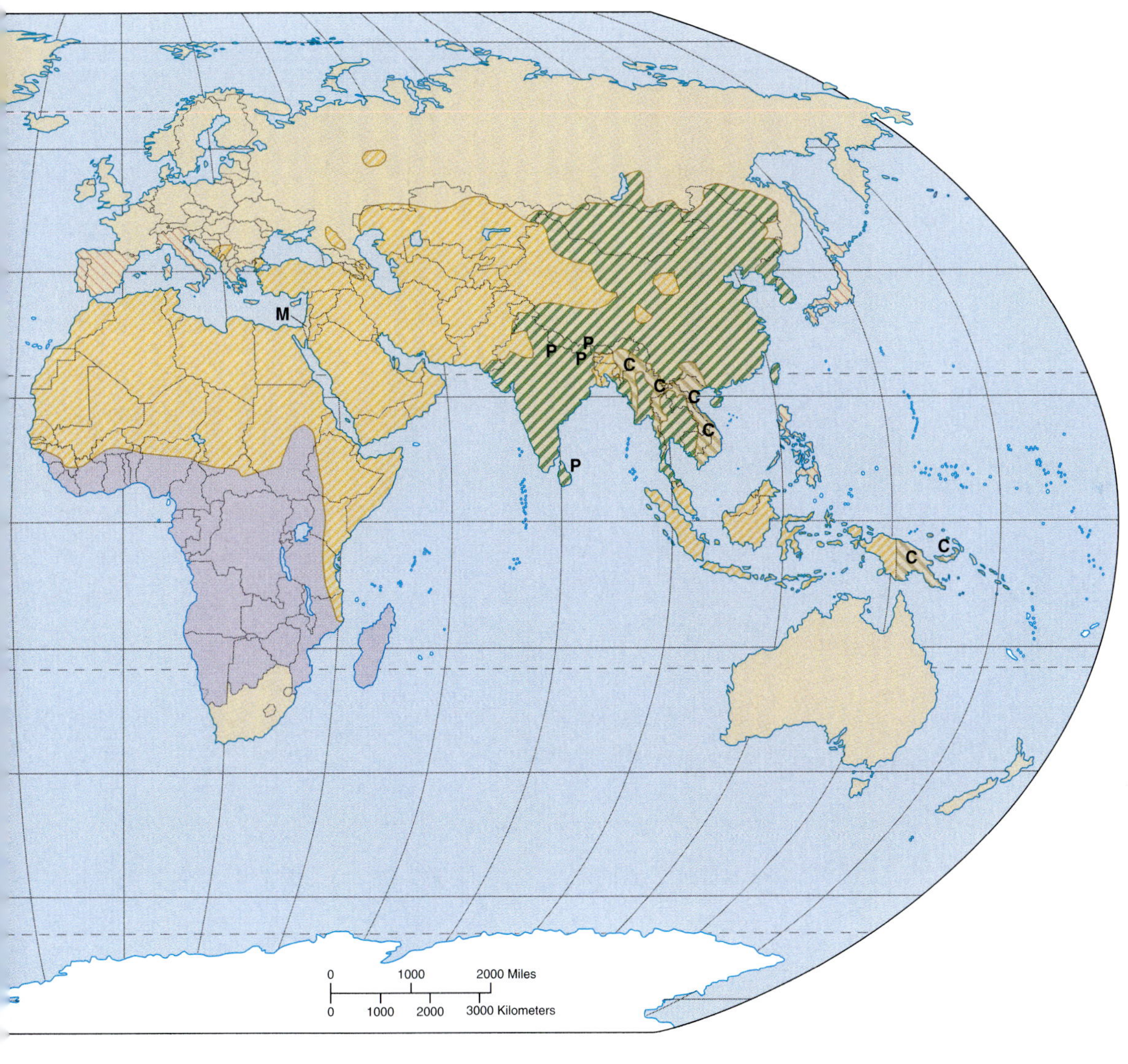

M
P
P
P
P
C
C
C
C
C
C
0
1000
2000 Miles
0
1000
2000
3000 Kilometers

Map 74 Child Malnutrition

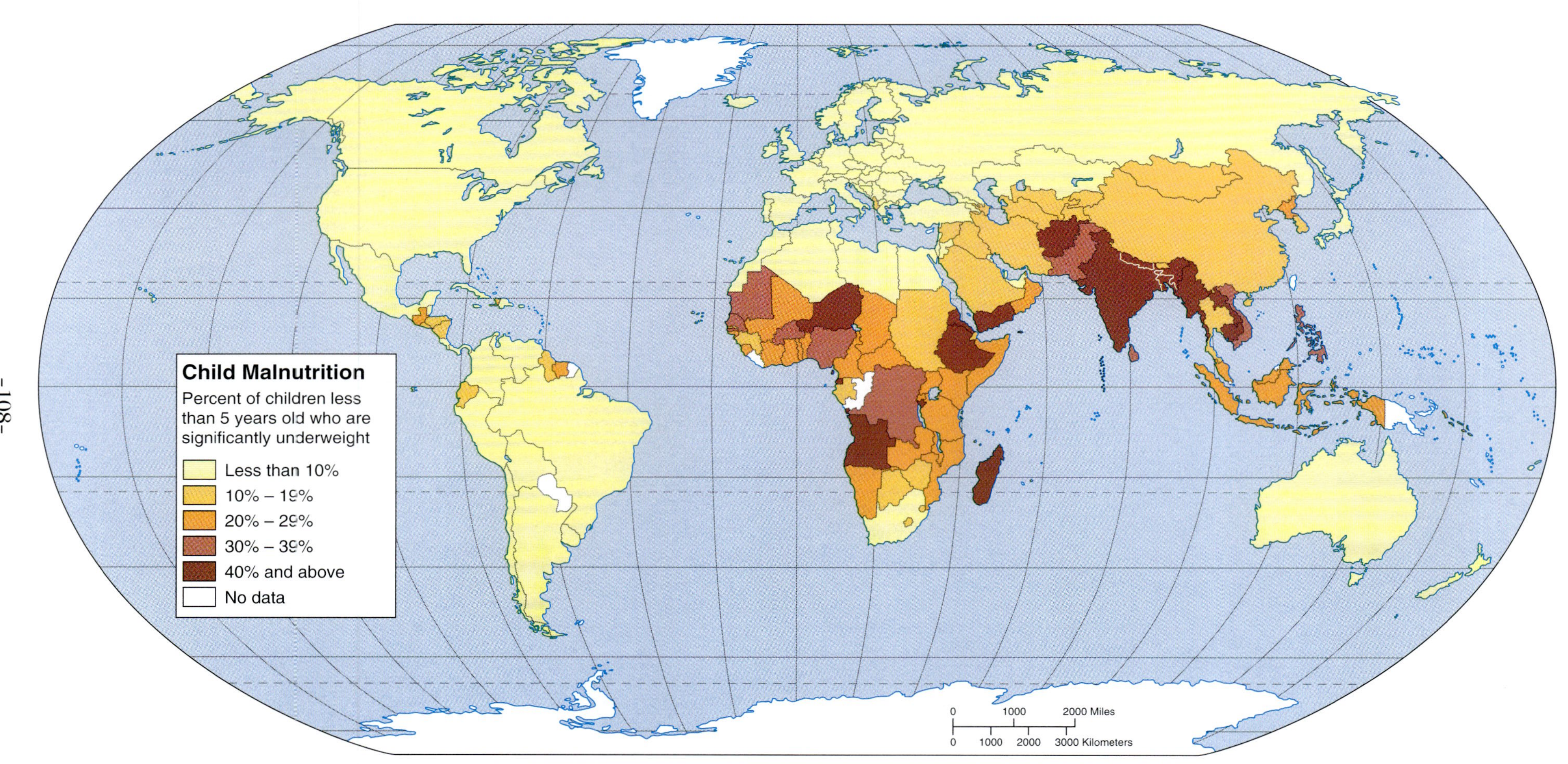

Child Malnutrition
Percent of children less than 5 years old who are significantly underweight
Less than 10%
10% – 19%
20% – 29%
30% – 39%
40% and above
No data
0 1000 2000 Miles
0 1000 2000 3000 Kilometers

The weight of poverty is not evenly spread among the members of a population, falling disproportionately upon the weakest and most disadvantaged members of society. In most societies, these individuals are children, particularly female children. Children simply do not compete as successfully as adults for their (meager) share of the daily food supply. Where food shortages prevail, children tend to have the quality of their future lives severely compromised by poor nutrition, which, in a downward spiral, robs them of the energy necessary to compete more effectively for food. Children who are inadequately fed are less likely to do well in school, are more prone to debilitating disease, and will more often become a drain on scarce societal resources than well-fed children.

Map 75 Primary School Enrollment

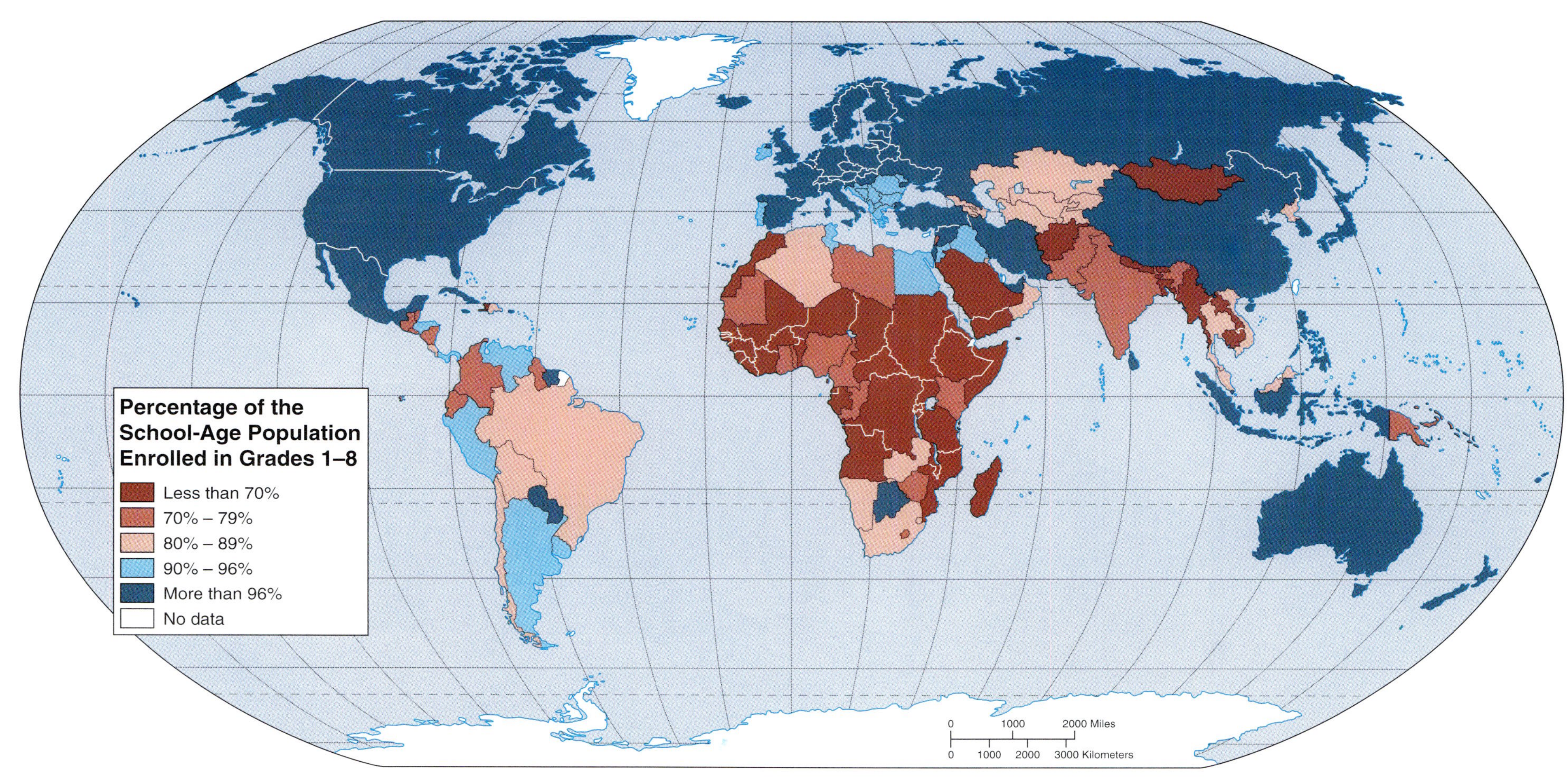

Percentage of the School-Age Population Enrolled in Grades 1–8
Less than 70%
70% – 79%
80% – 89%
90% – 96%
More than 96%
No data
0 1000 2000 Miles
0 1000 2000 3000 Kilometers

Like many of the other measures illustrated in this atlas, primary school enrollment is a clear reflection of the division of the world into "have" and "have-not" countries. It is also a measure that has changed more rapidly over the last decade than demographic and other indicators of development, as countries of even very modest means have made concerted attempts to attain relatively high percentages of primary school enrollment. That they have been able to do so is good evidence of the fact that reasonably respectable levels of human development are feasible at even modest income levels.

High primary school enrollment is also a reflection of the worldwide opinion that a major element in economic development is a well-educated, literate population. The links between human progress, as typified by higher levels of education, and economic growth are not automatic, however, and those countries without programs for maintaining the headway gained by improved education may be on the road to failure in terms of economic development.

Map 76 Illiteracy Rate

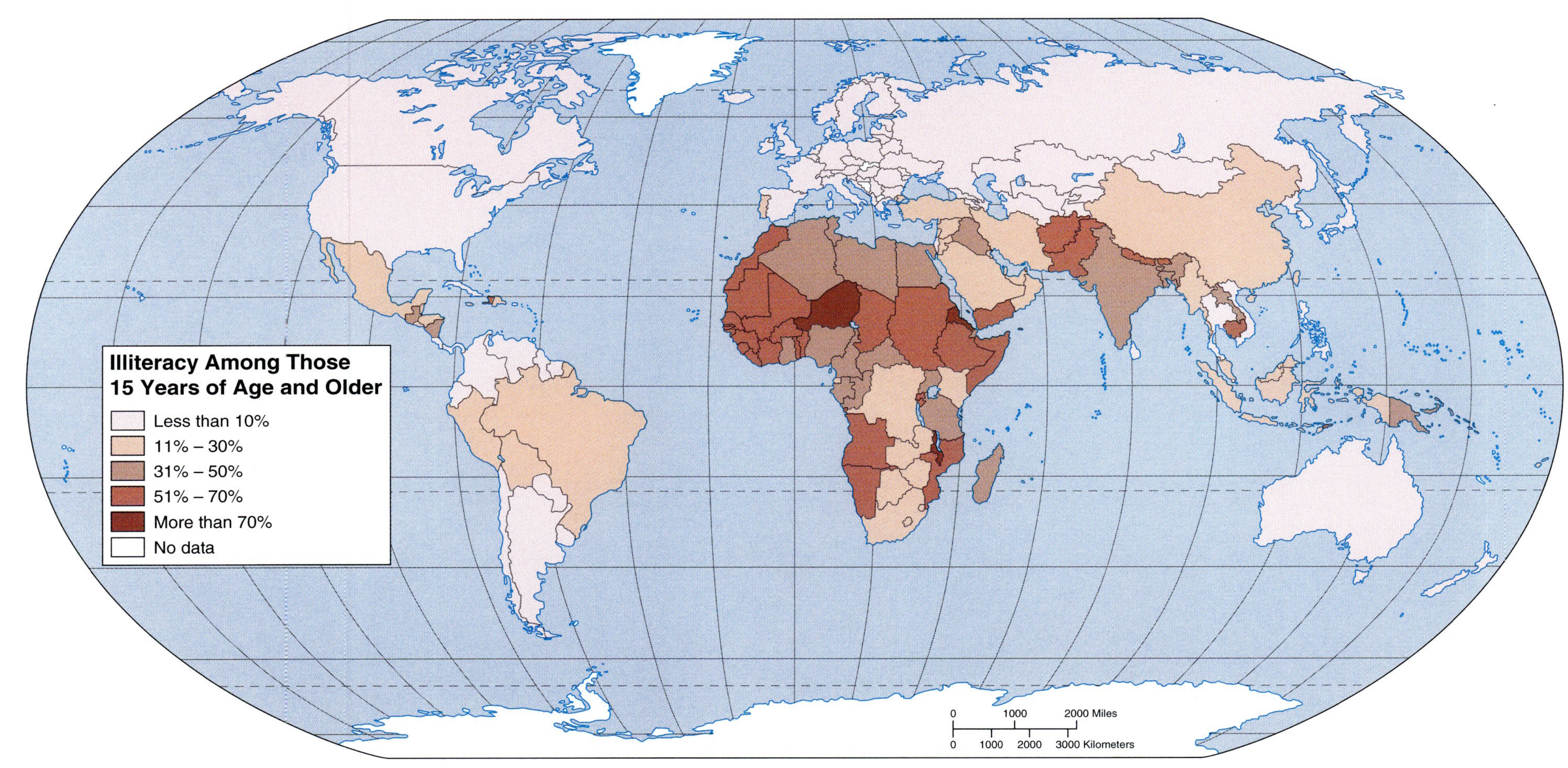

Illiteracy Among Those 15 Years of Age and Older
Less than 10%
11% – 30%
31% – 50%
51% – 70%
More than 70%
No data
0 1000 2000 Miles
0 1000 2000 3000 Kilometers

The gains in living standards that developing countries have experienced during the last two decades are manifested in two major areas: life expectancy and literacy. The increase in global literacy is largely the consequence of an increase in primary school enrollment, particularly throughout Middle and South America, Africa, and Asia. Worldwide, education is perceived as a way to advance economic status. Unfortunately, although gains have been made, there are still countries where illiteracy rates—particularly among the women of the population—are well above global norms. The long-term potential of these countries is severely compromised as a result.

A word of caution: Most countries view their literacy or illiteracy rates as hallmarks of their status in the world community and there is, therefore, a tendency to overstate or overestimate literacy (or, conversely, to underestimate illiteracy). In the United States for example, the stated illiteracy rate is less than 2 percent. Yet many experts indicate that somewhere between 10 percent and 15 percent of the U.S. population may, in fact, be functionally illiterate—that is, unable to read street signs, advertisements, or newspapers.

Map 77 Female/Male Inequality in Education and Employment

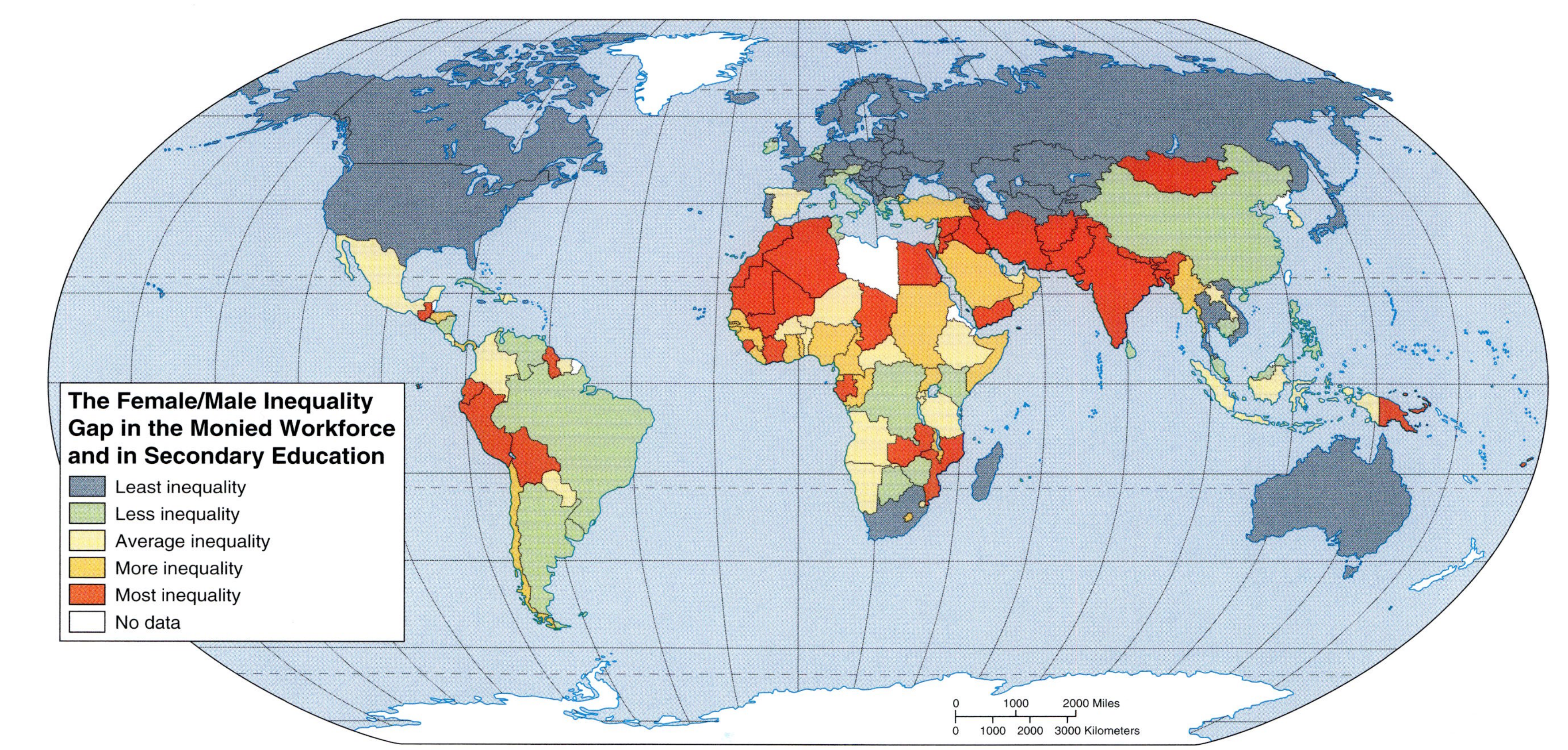
The Female/Male Inequality Gap in the Monied Workforce and in Secondary Education
Least inequality
Less inequality
Average inequality
More inequality
Most inequality
No data
0 1000 2000 Miles
0 1000 2000 3000 Kilometers

While women in developed countries, particularly in North America and Europe, have made significant advances in socioeconomic status in recent years, in most of the world they suffer from significant inequality when compared with their male counterparts. Although women have received the right to vote in most of the world's countries, in over 90 percent of these countries that right has only been granted in the last 50 years. In most regions, literacy rates for women still fall far short of those for men; In Africa and Asia, for example, only about half as many women are literate as are men. Women marry considerably younger than men and attend school for shorter periods of time. Inequalities in education and employment are perhaps the most telling indicators of the unequal status of women in most of the world. Lack of secondary education in comparison with men prevents women from entering the workforce with equally high-paying jobs. Even where women are employed in positions similar to those held by men, they still tend to receive less compensation. The gap between rich and poor involves not only a clear geographic differentiation, but a clear gender differentiation as well.

Map 78 The Quality of Life: The Human Development Index

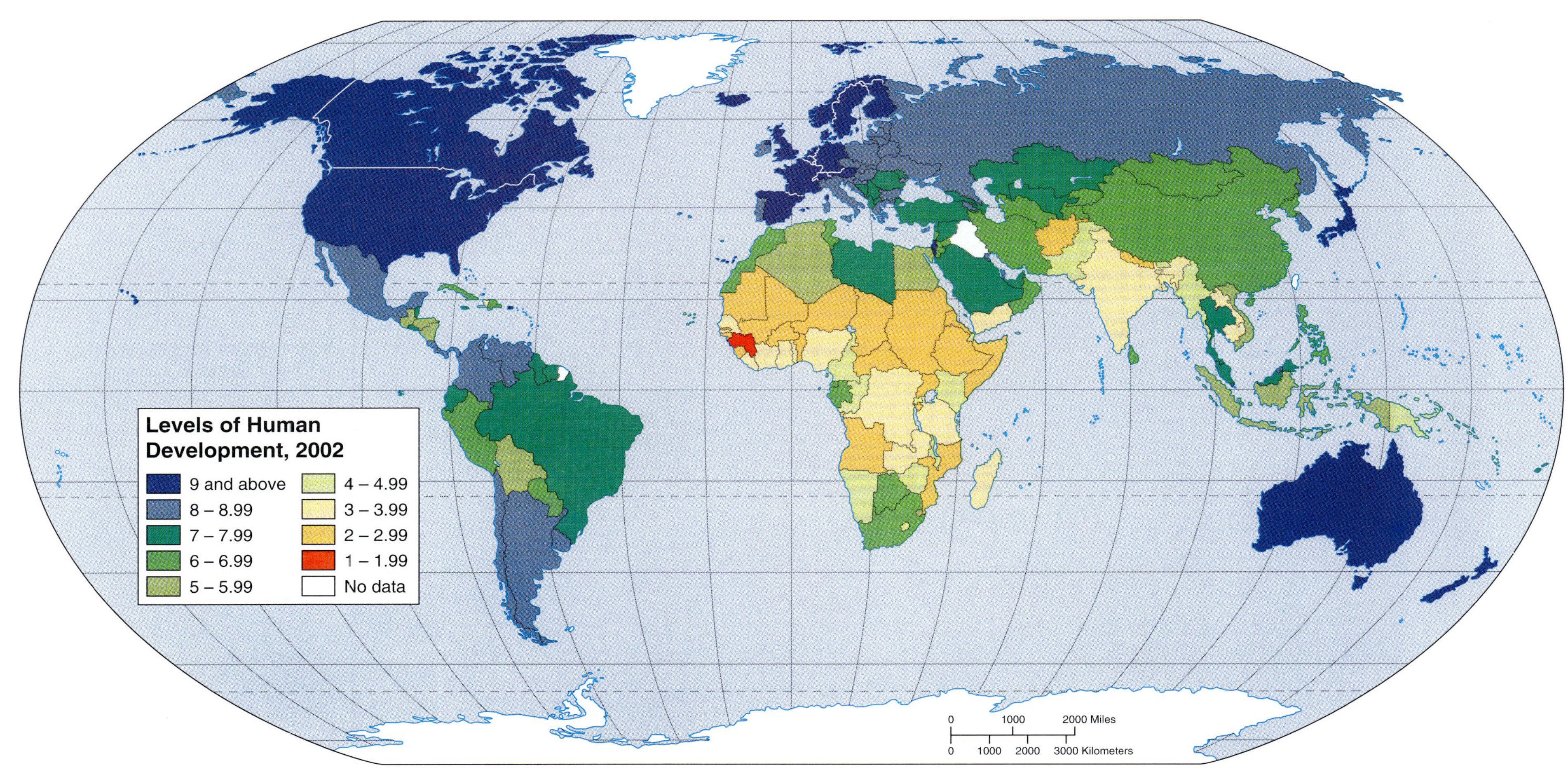

Levels of Human Development, 2002
9 and above
8 – 8.99
7 – 7.99
6 – 6.99
5 – 5.99
4 – 4.99
3 – 3.99
2 – 2.99
1 – 1.99
No data
0 1000 2000 Miles
0 1000 2000 3000 Kilometers

The development index upon which this map is based takes into account a wide variety of demographic, health, and educational data, including population growth, per capita gross domestic product, longevity, literacy, and years of schooling. The map reveals significant improvement in the quality of life in Middle and South America, although it is questionable whether the gains made in those regions can be maintained in the face of the dramatic population increases expected over the next 30 years. More clearly than anything else, the map illustrates the near-desperate situation in Africa and South Asia. In those regions, the unparalle ed growth in population threatens to overwhelm all efforts to improve the quality of life. In Africa, for example, the population is increasing by 20 million persons per year. With nearly 45 percent of the continent's population aged 15 years or younger, this growth rate will accelerate as the women reach childbearing age. Africa, along with South Asia, faces the very difficult challenge of providing basic access to health care, education, and jobs for a rapidly increasing population. The map also illustrates the striking difference in quality of life between those who inhabit the world's equatorial and tropical regions and those fortunate enough to live in the temperate zones, where the qualify of life is significantly higher.

Section D Political Systems

Map 79 Political Systems
Map 80 Sovereign States: Duration of Independence
Map 81 The Emergence of the State
Map 82 Organized States and Chiefdoms, A.D. 1500
Map 83 European Colonialism, 1500-2000
Map 84 The Middle East: Territorial Changes, 1918-Present
Map 85 Africa: Colonial to Independence, 1910-2000
Map 86 Asia: Colonialism to Independence, 1930-2000
Map 87 Global Distribution of Minority Groups
Map 88 World Refugee Population
Map 89 Post-Cold War International Alliances
Map 90 Nations with Nuclear Weapons
Map 91 Military Expenditures as a Percentage of Gross National Product
Map 92 Size of Armed Forces

Map 79 Political Systems

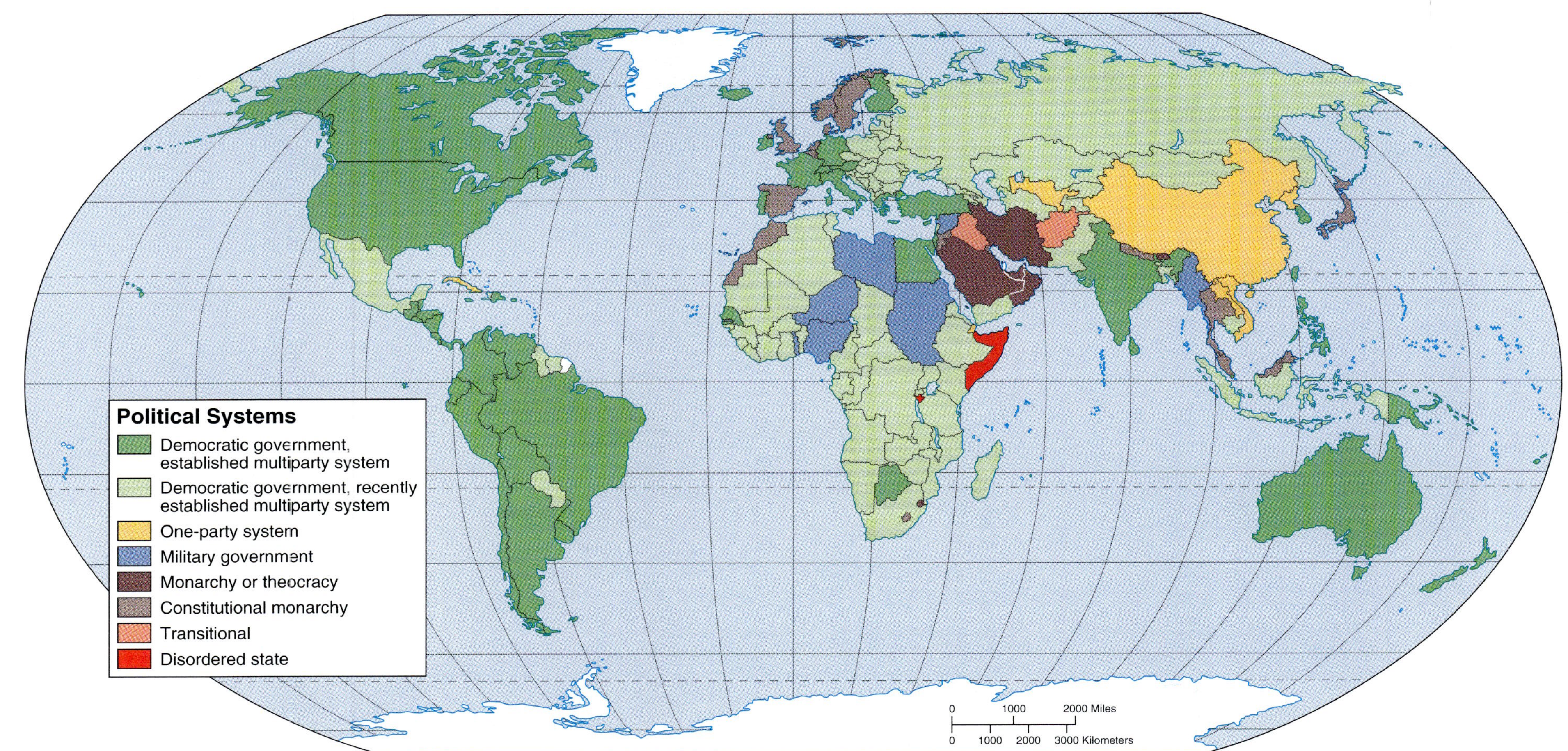
Political Systems
Democratic government, established multiparty system
Democratic government, recently established multiparty system
One-party system
Military government
Monarchy or theocracy
Constitutional monarchy
Transitional
Disordered state
0 1000 2000 Miles
0 1000 2000 3000 Kilometers

The world map of political systems has changed dramatically during the last decade. The categories of political systems shown on the map are subject to some interpretation: established multiparty democracies are those in which elections by secret ballot with adult suffrage are and have been long-term features of the political landscape; recently established multiparty democracies are those in which the characteristic features of multiparty democracies have only recently emerged. The former Soviet satellites of eastern Europe and the republics that formerly constituted the USSR are in this category; so are states in emerging regions that are beginning to throw off the single-party rule that often followed the violent upheavals of the immediate postcolonial governmental transitions. The other categories are more or less obvious. One-party systems are states where single-party rule is constitutionally guaranteed or where a one-party regime is a fact of political life. Monarchies are countries with heads of state who are members of a royal family; some countries with monarchs do not fall into this category because their monarchs are titular heads of state only. Theocracies are countries in which rule is within the hands of a priestly or clerical class; today, this means primarily Islamic countries such as Iran. Military governments are frequently organized around a junta that has seized control of the government from civil authority; such states are often technically transitional, that is, the military claims that it will return the reins of government to civil authority when order is restored. Finally, disordered states are countries so beset by civil war or widespread ethnic conflict that no organized government can be said to exist within them.

Map 80 Sovereign States: Duration of Independence

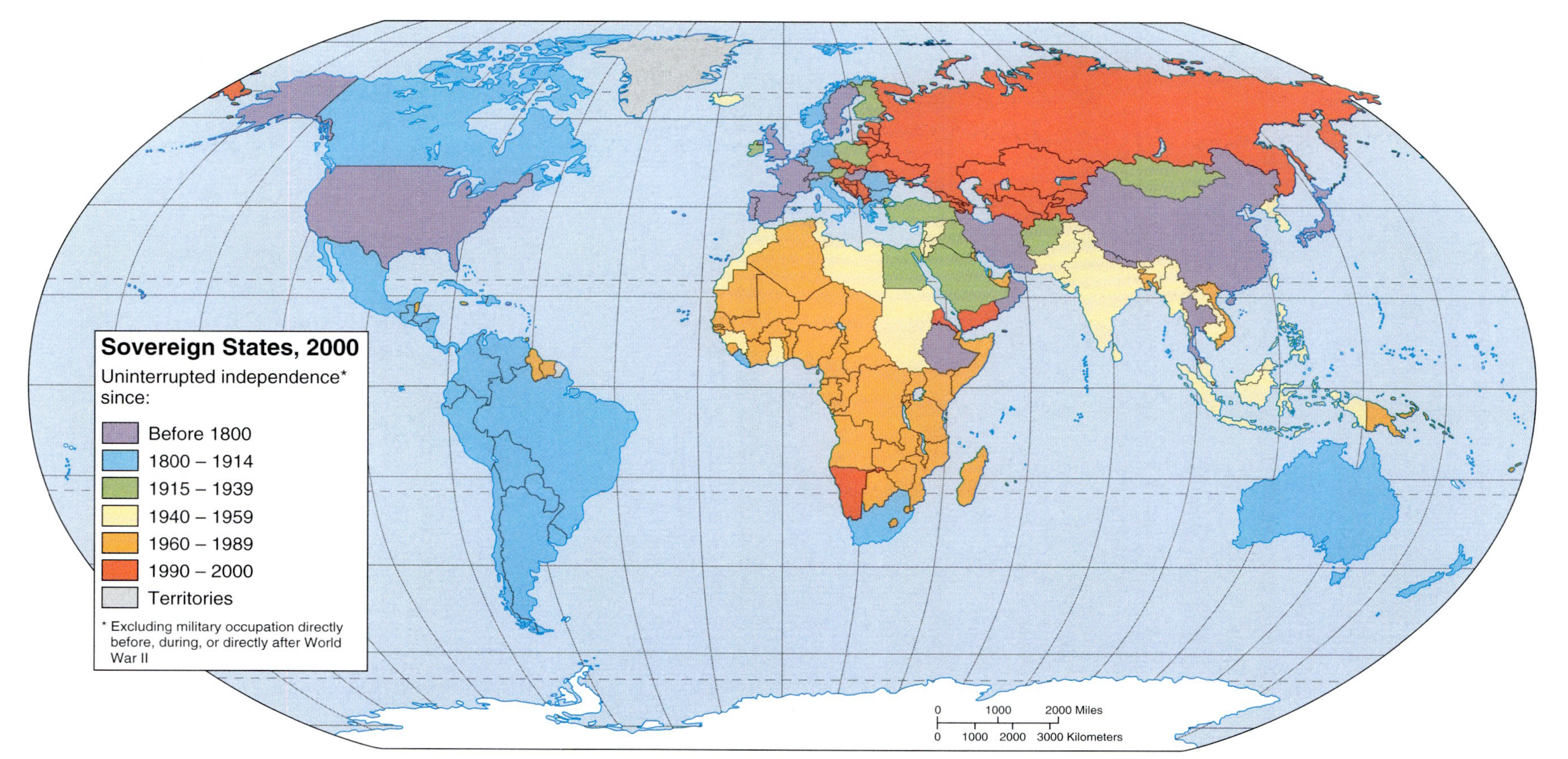
Sovereign States, 2000
Uninterrupted independence* since:
Before 1800
1800 – 1914
1915 – 1939
1940 – 1959
1960 – 1989
1990 – 2000
Territories
* Excluding military occupation directly before, during, or directly after World War II
0 1000 2000 Miles
0 1000 2000 3000 Kilometers

Most countries of the modern world, including such major states as Germany and Italy, became independent after the beginning of the nineteenth century. Of the world's current countries, only 27 were independent in 1800. (Ten of the 27 were in Europe; the others were Afghanistan, China, Colombia, Ethiopia, Haiti, Iran, Japan, Mexico, Nepal, Oman, Paraguay, Russia, Taiwan, Thailand, Turkey, the United States, and Venezuela.) Following 1800, there have been four great periods of national independence. During the first of these (1800–1914), most of the mainland countries of the Americas achieved independence. During the second period (1915–1939), the countries of Eastern Europe emerged as independent entities. The third period (1940–1959) includes World War II and the years that followed, when independence for African and Asian nations that had been under control of colonial powers first began to occur. During the fourth period (1960–1989), independence came to the remainder of the colonial African and Asian nations, as well as to former colonies in the Caribbean and the South Pacific. More than half of the world's countries came into being as independent political entities during this period. Finally, in the last decade (199–02000), the breakup of the existing states of the Soviet Union, Yugoslavia, and Czechoslovakia created 22 countries where only 3 had existed before, and the newest independent state, East Timor, gained independence from Indonesia in 2001.

Map 81 The Emergence of the State

Agriculture is the basis of the development of the state, a form of complex political organization. Archaeologists believe that agriculture allows for larger concentrations of population. Farmers do not need to be as mobile as hunters and gatherers to make a living. Ideas about access to land and ownership change as people develop social and political hierarchies. Social stratification based on wealth and power creates different classes or groups, some of whom no longer work the land. An agricultural surplus supports those who perform other functions for society, such as craftsmen and priests. Thus, over time, egalitarian foraging peoples shifted to state-level societies in some parts of the world. For more information about complex political organization, see Map 82. Compare also Maps 26 and 31.

The Emergence of the State
Hunters and gatherers
Farming peoples
Chiefdoms
States
WOODLAND FARMERS
CARIBBEAN FARMERS
TEOTIHUACÁN STATE
MAYA
MESOAMERICAN CIVILIZATION
NORTH ANDEAN CHIEFDOMS
SAVANNAH FARMERS
FARMING TRIBES
CHIMU STATE
CENTRAL ANDEAN CIVILIZATION
Area of detail
MOCHE
CAJAMARCA
RECUAY
LIMA
HUARPA
WARU
PACIFIC OCEAN
TIAHUANACO
ATACAMEÑO
0 250 500 Miles
0 250 500 Kilometers

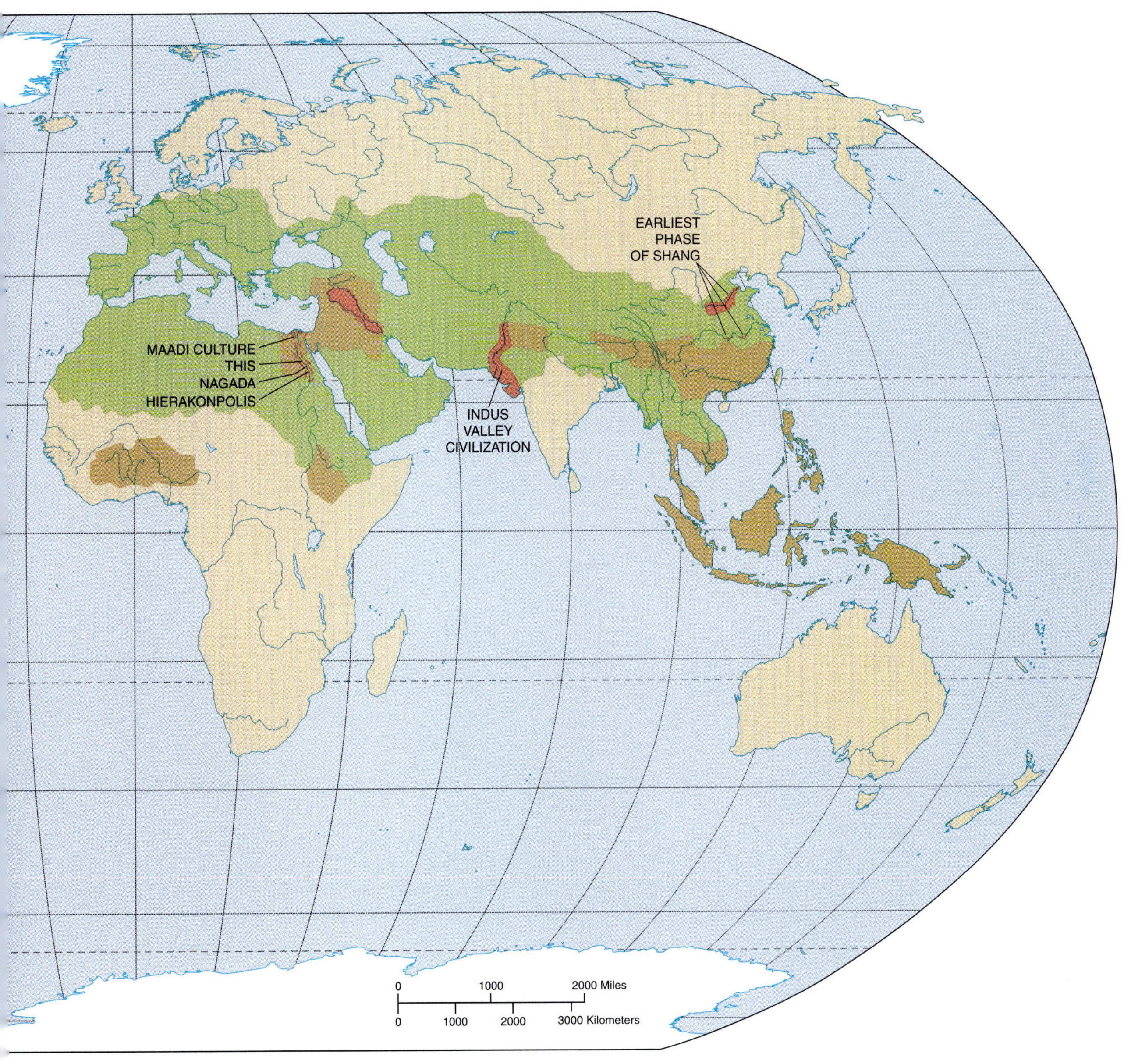
EARLIEST
PHASE
OF SHANG
MAADI CULTURE
THIS
NAGADA
HIERAKONPOLIS
INDUS
VALLEY
CIVILIZATION
0
1000
2000 Miles
0
1000
2000
3000 Kilometers

Map 82 Organized States and Chiefdoms, A.D. 1500

When the Europeans began to explore the world in the fifteenth through seventeenth centuries, they found complex political organizations in many places. Both chiefdoms and states are large-scale forms of political organization in which some people have privileged access to power, wealth, and prestige. Chiefdoms are kin-based societies in which redistribution is

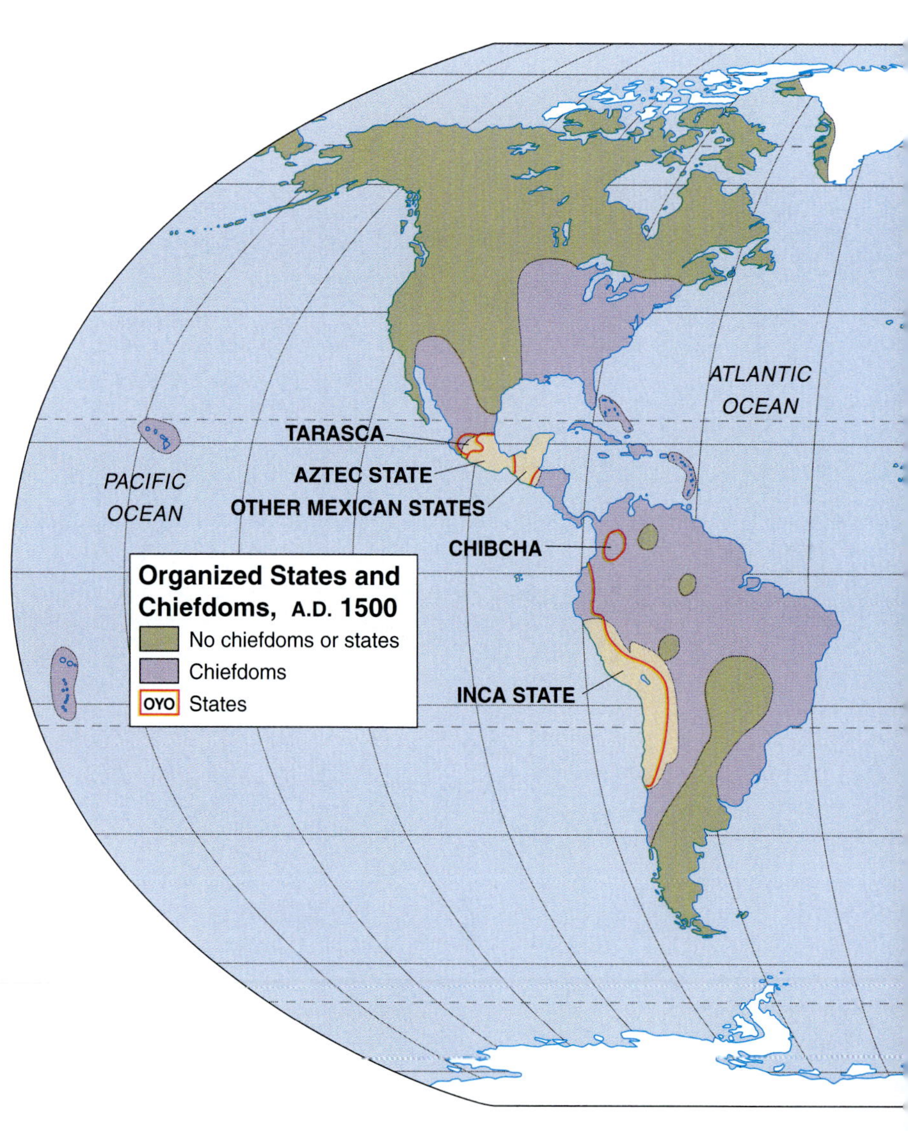

ATLANTIC OCEAN
PACIFIC OCEAN
TARASCA
AZTEC STATE
OTHER MEXICAN STATES
CHIBCHA
INCA STATE
Organized States and Chiefdoms, A.D. 1500
No chiefdoms or states
Chiefdoms
OYO
States

the major economic pattern. States are organized in terms of socioeconomic classes, headed by a centralized government that is led by an elite. States include a full-time bureaucracy and specialized subsystems for such activities as military action, taxation, and social control.

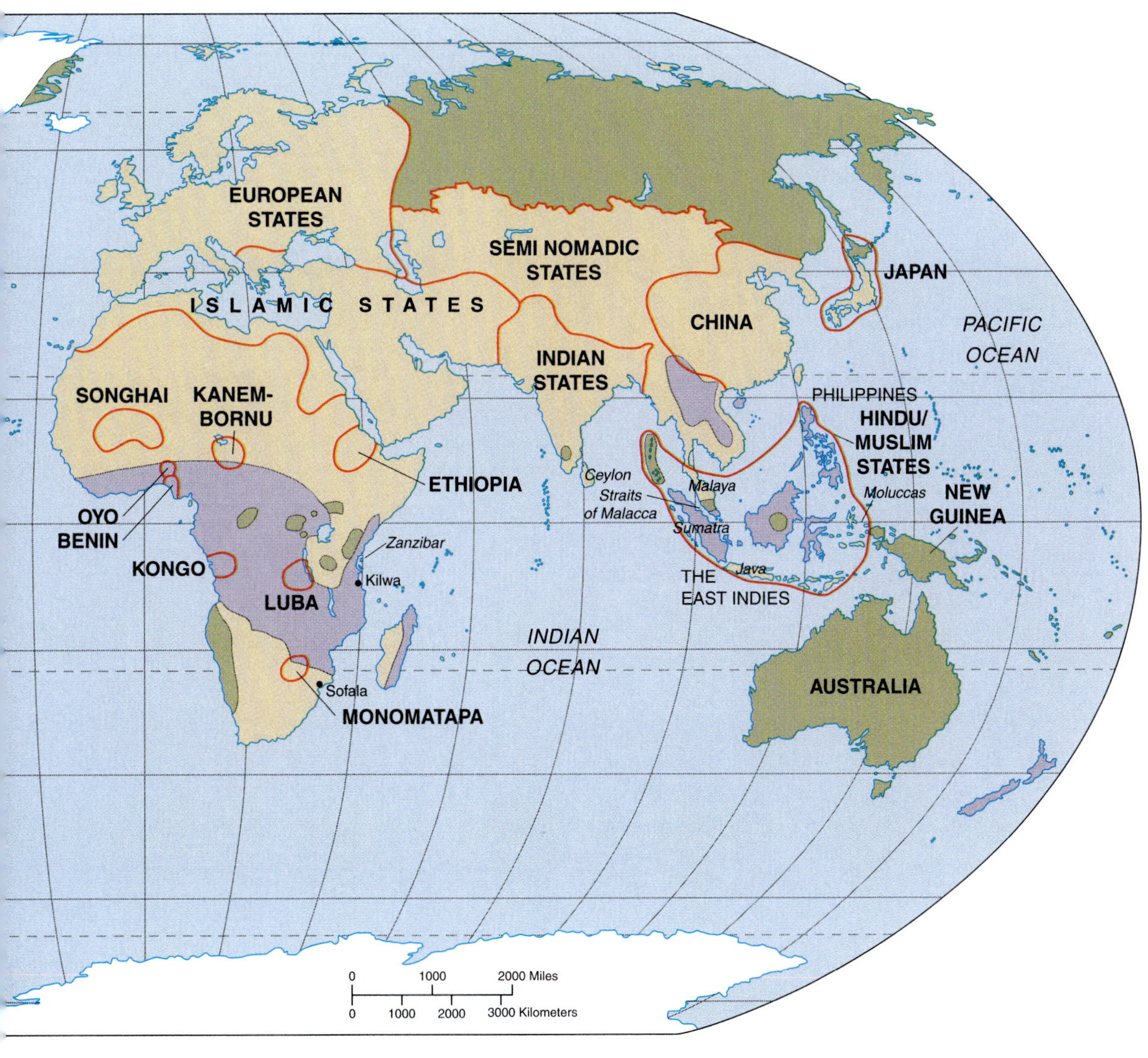
EUROPEAN STATES
SEMI NOMADIC STATES
ISLAMIC STATES
JAPAN
CHINA
PACIFIC OCEAN
INDIAN STATES
SONGHAI
KANEM-BORNU
PHILIPPINES
HINDU/ MUSLIM STATES
ETHIOPIA
Ceylon
Straits of Malacca
Malaya
Moluccas
NEW GUINEA
OYO
BENIN
Sumatra
Zanzibar
KONGO
Kilwa
Java
THE EAST INDIES
LUBA
INDIAN OCEAN
AUSTRALIA
Sofala
MONOMATAPA
0 1000 2000 Miles
0 1000 2000 3000 Kilometers

Map 83 European Colonialism A.D. 1500–2000

European nations have controlled many parts of the world during the last 500 years. The period of European expansion began when European explorers sailed the oceans in search of new trading routes and ended after World War II when many colonies in Africa and Asia gained independence.

ALASKA
RUPERT'S LAND
NEW FRANCE
NEWFOUNDLAND
NOVA SCOTIA
LOUISIANA
THIRTEEN COLONIES
NEW SPAIN
SPANISH FLORIDA
BAHAMAS
HAITI
CUBA
PUERTO RICO
JAMAICA
GUADELOUPE
MARTINIQUE
BARBADOS
BRITISH HONDURAS
DUTCH GUIANA
FRENCH GUIANA
NEW GRANADA
GALAPAGOS ISLANDS
BRAZIL
PERU
PERU
LA PLATA
European Colonialism
A.D. 1500 – 2000
Belgian
British
Danish
Dutch
French
German
Italian
Japanese
Japanese controlled
Portuguese
Russian
Spanish
United States
U.S.S.R.
U.S.S.R. controlled

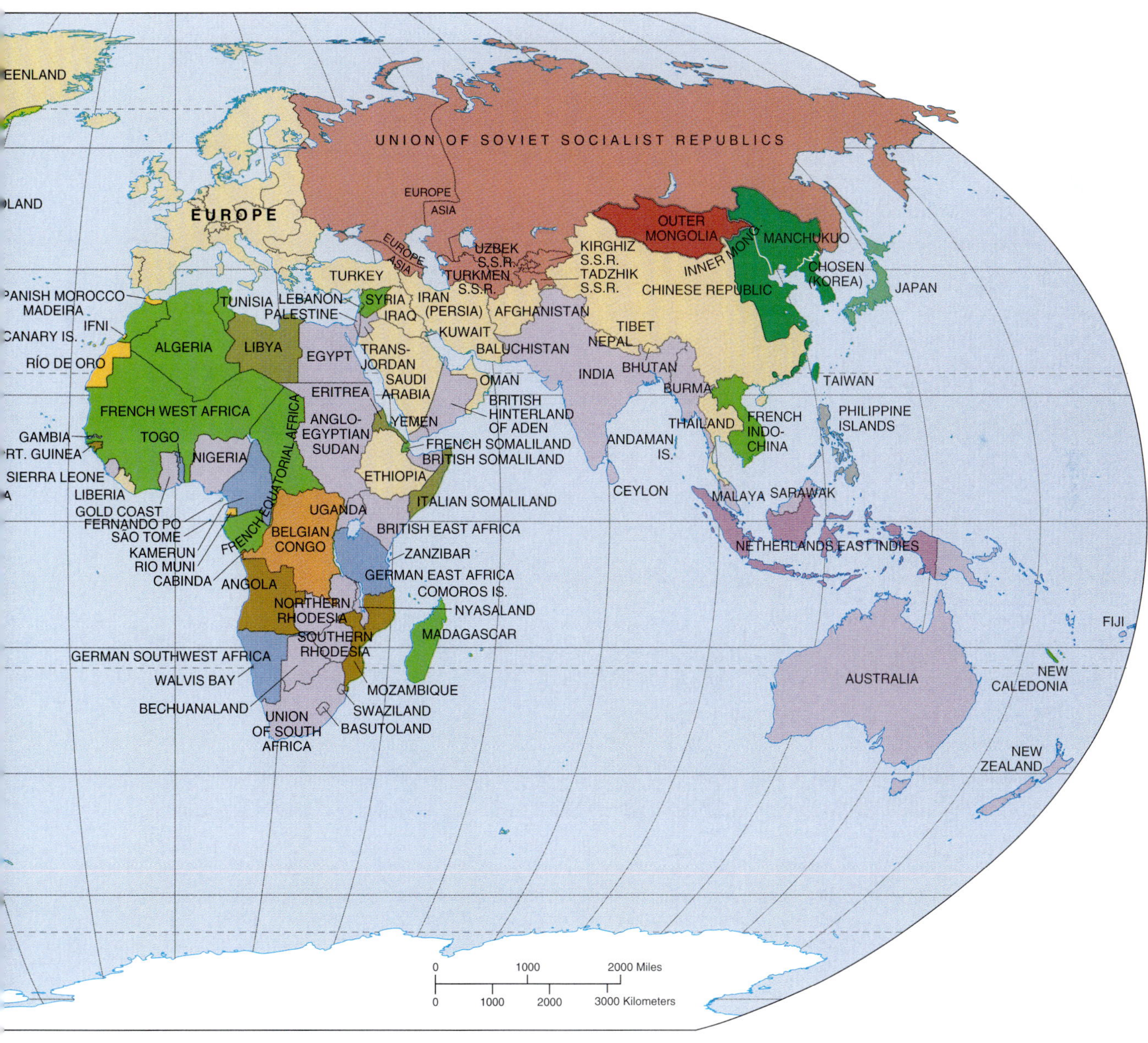
UNION OF SOVIET SOCIALIST REPUBLICS
EUROPE
ASIA
EUROPE
OUTER MONGOLIA
MANCHUKUO
INNER MONG.
CHOSEN (KOREA)
JAPAN
UZBEK S.S.R.
KIRGHIZ S.S.R.
TADZHIK S.S.R.
TURKMEN S.S.R.
CHINESE REPUBLIC
TURKEY
SYRIA
IRAN (PERSIA)
IRAQ
AFGHANISTAN
TUNISIA
LEBANON
PALESTINE
MADEIRA
IFNI
CANARY IS.
RÍO DE ORO
ALGERIA
LIBYA
EGYPT
TRANS-JORDAN
KUWAIT
BALUCHISTAN
TIBET
NEPAL
BHUTAN
INDIA
SAUDI ARABIA
OMAN
BURMA
TAIWAN
ERITREA
BRITISH HINTERLAND OF ADEN
PHILIPPINE ISLANDS
FRENCH WEST AFRICA
ANGLO-EGYPTIAN SUDAN
YEMEN
THAILAND
FRENCH INDO-CHINA
GAMBIA
TOGO
FRENCH SOMALILAND
BRITISH SOMALILAND
ANDAMAN IS.
NIGERIA
SIERRA LEONE
ETHIOPIA
LIBERIA
FRENCH EQUATORIAL AFRICA
ITALIAN SOMALILAND
CEYLON
MALAYA
SARAWAK
GOLD COAST
FERNANDO PO
SÃO TOMÉ
UGANDA
BRITISH EAST AFRICA
KAMERUN
RIO MUNI
CABINDA
BELGIAN CONGO
ZANZIBAR
NETHERLANDS EAST INDIES
ANGOLA
GERMAN EAST AFRICA
COMOROS IS.
NORTHERN RHODESIA
NYASALAND
MADAGASCAR
FIJI
SOUTHERN RHODESIA
GERMAN SOUTHWEST AFRICA
AUSTRALIA
NEW CALEDONIA
WALVIS BAY
MOZAMBIQUE
BECHUANALAND
UNION OF SOUTH AFRICA
SWAZILAND
BASUTOLAND
NEW ZEALAND
0 1000 2000 Miles
0 1000 2000 3000 Kilometers

Map 84 The Middle East: Territorial Changes, 1918–Present

TERRITORIAL CHANGES IN THE MIDDLE EAST, WORLD WAR I TO PRESENT
Ottoman Empire to World War I
British control
French control
Kurdish homelands
International boundaries in 1994
Istanbul (Constantinople)
BLACK SEA
GEORGIA
RUSSIA
CASPIAN SEA
ARMENIA
AZERBAIJAN
GREECE
AEGEAN SEA
Ankara
TURKEY
Tabriz
LEBANON AND SYRIA
Ottoman Empire to 1920
French (1920–1944)
Independent 1944
CRETE
MEDITERRANEAN SEA
CYPRUS from Ottoman Empire to British control 1878 Independent 1960
SYRIA
Euphrates River
Tigris River
LEBANON
Beirut
Damascus
ISRAEL
Ottoman Empire to 1920
UK (1920–1948)
Tel Aviv
Amman
Jerusalem
Baghdad
IRAQ
UK (1920–1932)
Tehran
IRAN
(named Persia until 1935)
AFGHANISTAN
LIBYA
Ottoman Empire to 1911
Italian colony (1911–1943)
UK–French Protectorate (1943–1951)
Alexandria
Cairo
Suez
Suez Canal British control to 1956
INSET
JORDAN
Ottoman Empire to 1920
UK (1920–1946)
Hejaz Nedj (to 1926)
Basra
Abadan
KUWAIT
UK (1899–1961)
Kuwait
BAHRAIN
UK (1861–1971)
PAKISTAN
Strait of Hormuz
OMAN
Nile River
EGYPT
Ottoman Empire to 1885
UK Protectorate (1885–1936)
SAUDI ARABIA
PERSIAN GULF
U.A.E.
UK (1820s–1971)
Muscat
Medina
Riyadh
Abu Dhabi
QATAR
UK 1868–1971
RED SEA
Jiddah
Mecca
King Saud expanded territory (1901–1936)
Asir (1917–1934)
OMAN
UK (1891–1971)
CHAD
SUDAN
YEMEN (Independent 1918)
YEMEN
INDIAN OCEAN
ERITREA
UK 1868–1971
Independent as (South) Yemen 1967
Merged with (North) Yemen 1990
Aden
GULF OF ADEN
ETHIOPIA
DJIBOUTI
SOMALIA
200 Miles
200 Kilometers
LEBANON
Beirut
Damascus
SYRIA
ISRAELI SECURITY ZONE
GOLAN HEIGHTS
Sea of Galilee
MEDITERRANEAN SEA
Jordan River
Tel Aviv
WEST BANK
Amman
Jerusalem
Allenby Bridge
Jericho
GAZA
Dead Sea
ISRAEL
JORDAN
EGYPT
SINAI PENINSULA
Eilat
Aqaba
SAUDI ARABIA
50 Miles
50 Kilometers

The Middle East, encompassing the northeastern part of Africa and southwestern Asia, has experienced a turbulent history. In the last century alone, many of the region's countries have gone from being ruled by the Turkish Ottoman Empire, to being dependencies of Great Britain or France, to being independent. Having experienced the Crusades and colonial domination by European powers, the region's predominantly Islamic countries are now resentful of interference in the region's affairs by countries with a European and/or Christian heritage. The tension between Israel (settled largely in the late nineteenth and twentieth centuries by Jews of predominantly European background) and its neighbors is a matter of European-Middle Eastern cultural stress as well as a religious conflict between Islamic Arab culture and Judaism. In fact, in addition to those who are native born, many Israeli Jews today trace their origins to Mediterranean Arab and/or Islamic countries of Southwest Asia from which they emigrated beginning in the 1950s.

Map 85 Africa: Colonialism to Independence, 1910–2000

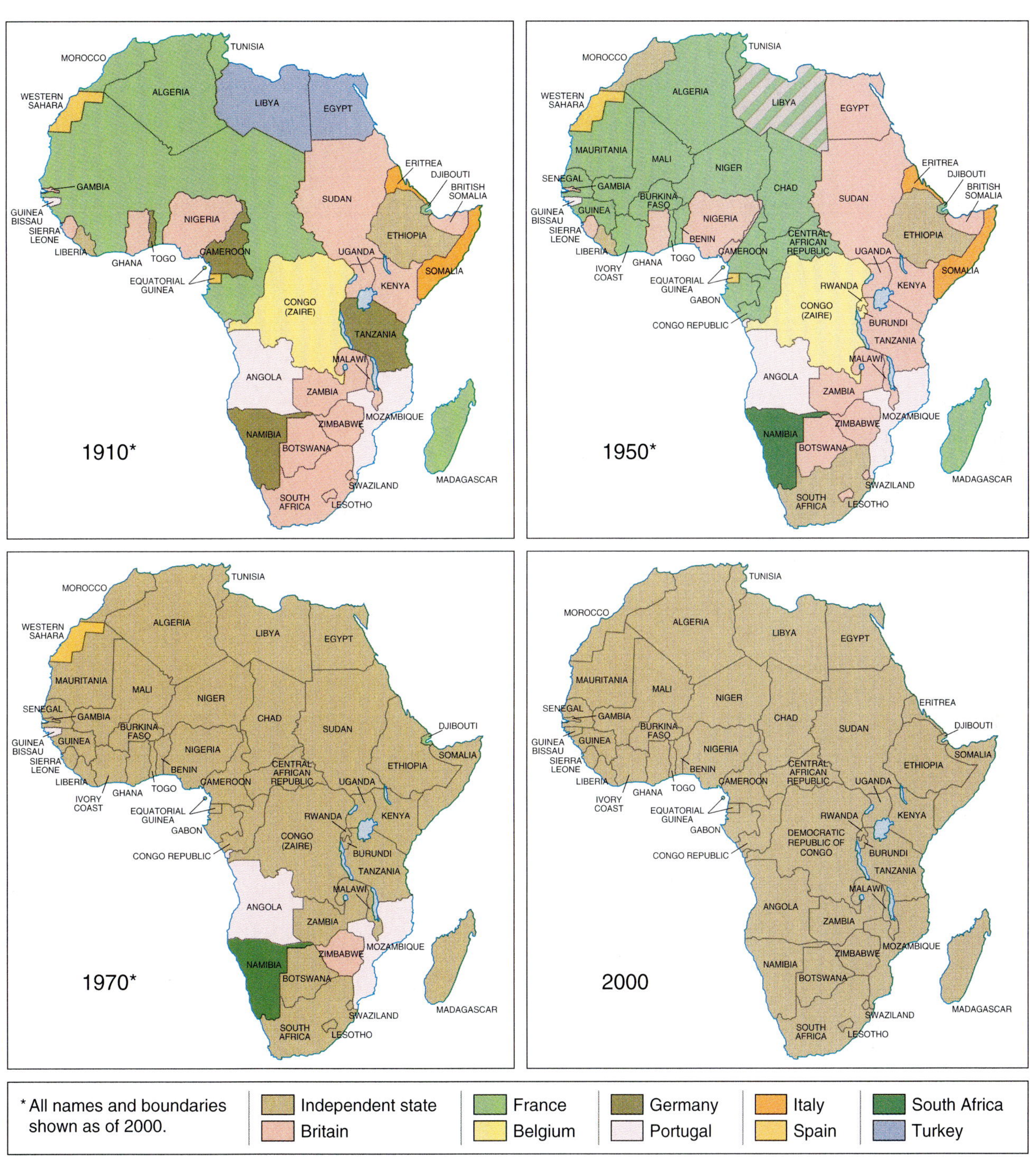
1910*
MOROCCO
TUNISIA
WESTERN SAHARA
ALGERIA
LIBYA
EGYPT
ERITREA
DJIBOUTI
BRITISH SOMALIA
GAMBIA
GUINEA BISSAU
SIERRA LEONE
LIBERIA
GHANA
TOGO
NIGERIA
CAMEROON
EQUATORIAL GUINEA
SUDAN
ETHIOPIA
UGANDA
SOMALIA
KENYA
CONGO (ZAIRE)
TANZANIA
MALAWI
ANGOLA
ZAMBIA
MOZAMBIQUE
NAMIBIA
ZIMBABWE
BOTSWANA
MADAGASCAR
SWAZILAND
SOUTH AFRICA
LESOTHO
1950*
MAURITANIA
MALI
NIGER
CHAD
SENEGAL
BURKINA FASO
GUINEA
BENIN
IVORY COAST
CENTRAL AFRICAN REPUBLIC
GABON
CONGO REPUBLIC
RWANDA
BURUNDI
1970*
2000
DEMOCRATIC REPUBLIC OF CONGO
* All names and boundaries shown as of 2000.
Independent state
Britain
France
Belgium
Germany
Portugal
Italy
Spain
South Africa
Turkey

In few parts of the world has the transition from colonialism to independence been as abrupt as on the African continent. Unlike the states of Middle and South America, which generally achieved independence from their colonial masters in the early nineteenth century, most African states did not become independent until the twentieth century, often not until after World War II. In part because they retain borders that are legacies of their former colonial status, many of these recently created African states are beset by internal problems related to tribal and ethnic conflicts.

Map 86 Asia: Colonialism to Independence, 1930–2000

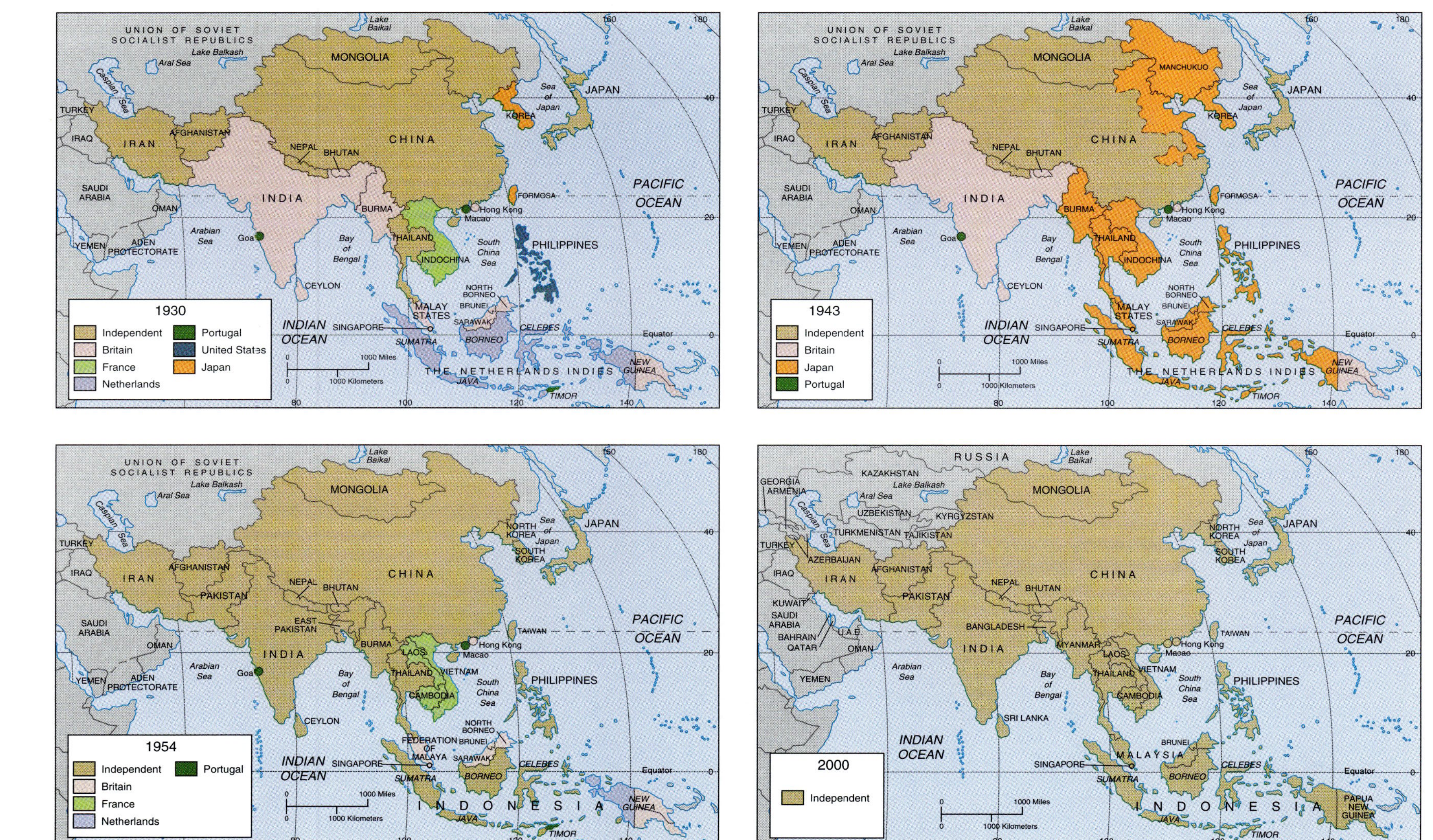

1930
Independent
Britain
France
Netherlands
Portugal
United States
Japan
UNION OF SOVIET SOCIALIST REPUBLICS
MONGOLIA
CHINA
INDIA
JAPAN
KOREA
FORMOSA
PHILIPPINES
INDOCHINA
THAILAND
BURMA
MALAY STATES
THE NETHERLANDS INDIES
NEW GUINEA
PACIFIC OCEAN
INDIAN OCEAN
1943
MANCHUKUO
1954
NORTH KOREA
SOUTH KOREA
TAIWAN
VIETNAM
LAOS
CAMBODIA
FEDERATION OF MALAYA
PAKISTAN
EAST PAKISTAN
INDONESIA
2000
RUSSIA
KAZAKHSTAN
UZBEKISTAN
KYRGYZSTAN
TURKMENISTAN
TAJIKISTAN
AZERBAIJAN
GEORGIA
ARMENIA
BANGLADESH
MYANMAR
SRI LANKA
MALAYSIA
PAPUA NEW GUINEA

Asian countries, like those in Africa, have recently emerged from a colonial past. With the exception of China, Japan, and Thailand, virtually all Asian nations were until not long ago under the colonial control of Great Britain, France, Spain, the Netherlands, or the United States. For a short period of time between 1930 and 1945, Japan itself was a colonial power with considerable territories on the Asian mainland. The unraveling of colonial control in Asia, particularly in South and Southeast Asia, has precipitated internal conflicts in the newly independent states that make up a significant part of the political geography of the region. The last vestiges of European colonialism in Asia disappeared with the cession of Hong Kong (1997) and Macau (1999) to China.

Map 87 Global Distribution of Minority Groups

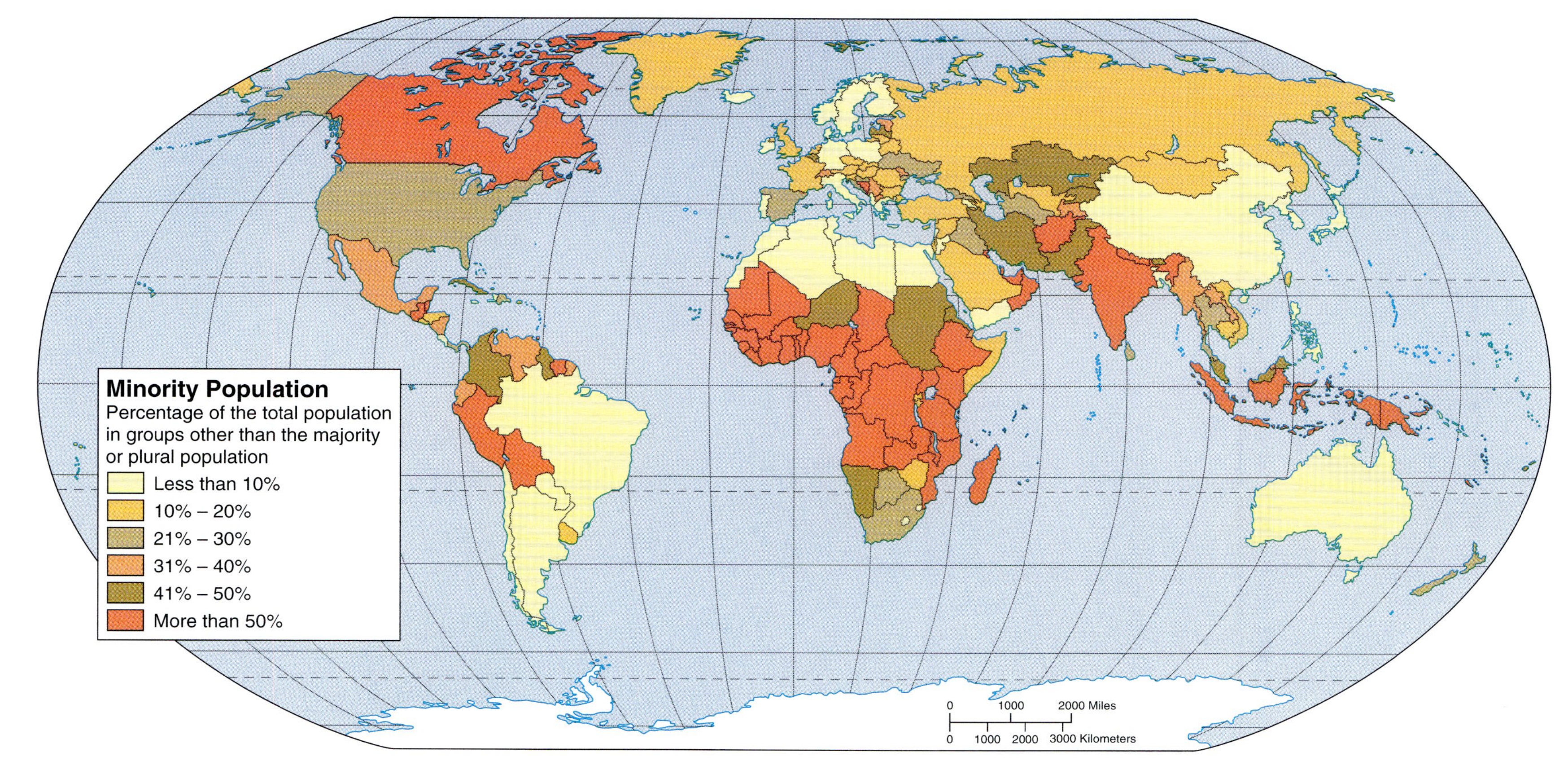

Minority Population
Percentage of the total population in groups other than the majority or plural population
Less than 10%
10% – 20%
21% – 30%
31% – 40%
41% – 50%
More than 50%
0 1000 2000 Miles
0 1000 2000 3000 Kilometers

The presence of minority ethnic, national, or racial groups within a country's population can add a vibrant and dynamic mix to the whole. Plural societies with a high degree of cultural and ethnic diversity should, according to some social theorists, be among the world's most healthy. Unfortunately, the reality of the situation is quite different from theory or expectation. The presence of significant minority populations played an important role in the disintegration of the Soviet Union, and the continuing existence of minority populations within the former Soviet republics threatened the viability and stability of those young political units. In Africa, national boundaries were drawn by colonial powers without regard for the geographical distribution of ethnic groups, and the continuing tribal conflicts that have resulted hamper both economic and political development.

Map 88 World Refugee Population

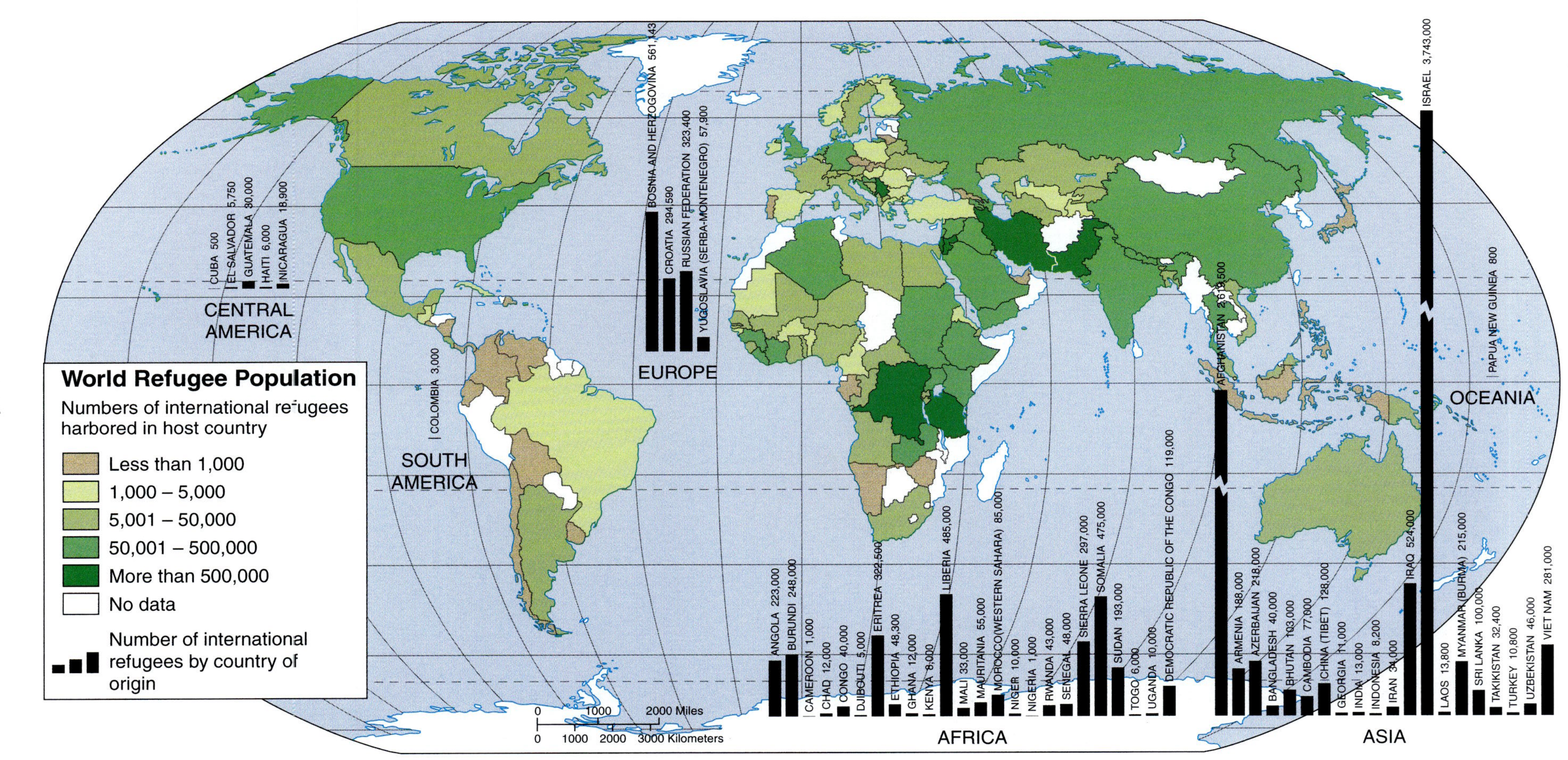

World Refugee Population
Numbers of international refugees harbored in host country
Less than 1,000
1,000 – 5,000
5,001 – 50,000
50,001 – 500,000
More than 500,000
No data
Number of international refugees by country of origin
CENTRAL AMERICA
CUBA 500
EL SALVADOR 5,750
GUATEMALA 30,000
HAITI 6,000
NICARAGUA 18,900
SOUTH AMERICA
COLOMBIA 3,000
EUROPE
BOSNIA AND HERZOGOVINA 561,143
CROATIA 294,590
RUSSIAN FEDERATION 323,400
YUGOSLAVIA (SERBA-MONTENEGRO) 57,900
AFRICA
ANGOLA 223,000
BURUNDI 248,000
CAMEROON 1,000
CHAD 12,000
CONGO 40,000
DJIBOUTI 5,000
ERITREA 322,500
ETHIOPIA 48,300
GHANA 12,000
KENYA 8,000
LIBERIA 485,000
MALI 33,000
MAURITANIA 55,000
MOROCCO(WESTERN SAHARA) 85,000
NIGER 10,000
NIGERIA 1,000
RWANDA 43,000
SENEGAL 48,000
SIERRA LEONE 297,000
SOMALIA 475,000
SUDAN 193,000
TOGO 6,000
UGANDA 10,000
DEMOCRATIC REPUBLIC OF THE CONGO 119,000
ASIA
AFGHANISTAN 2,619,500
ARMENIA 188,000
AZERBAIJAN 218,000
BANGLADESH 40,000
BHUTAN 103,000
CAMBODIA 77,000
CHINA (TIBET) 128,000
GEORGIA 11,000
INDIA 13,000
INDONESIA 8,200
IRAN 34,000
IRAQ 524,000
ISRAEL 3,743,000
LAOS 13,800
MYANMAR (BURMA) 215,000
SRI LANKA 100,000
TAKIKISTAN 32,400
TURKEY 10,800
UZBEKISTAN 46,000
VIET NAM 281,000
OCEANIA
PAPUA NEW GUINEA 800
0 1000 2000 Miles
0 1000 2000 3000 Kilometers

Refugees are persons who have been driven from their homes, normally by armed conflict, and have sought refuge by relocating. The most numerous refugees have traditionally been international refugees, who have crossed the political boundaries of their homelands into other countries. This refugee population is recognized by international agencies, and the countries of refuge are often rewarded financially by those agencies for their willingness to take in externally displaced persons. In recent years, largely because of an increase in civil wars, there have been growing numbers of internally displaced persons—those who leave their homes but stay within their country of origin. There are no rewards for harboring such internal refugee populations.

Map 89 Post–Cold War International Alliances

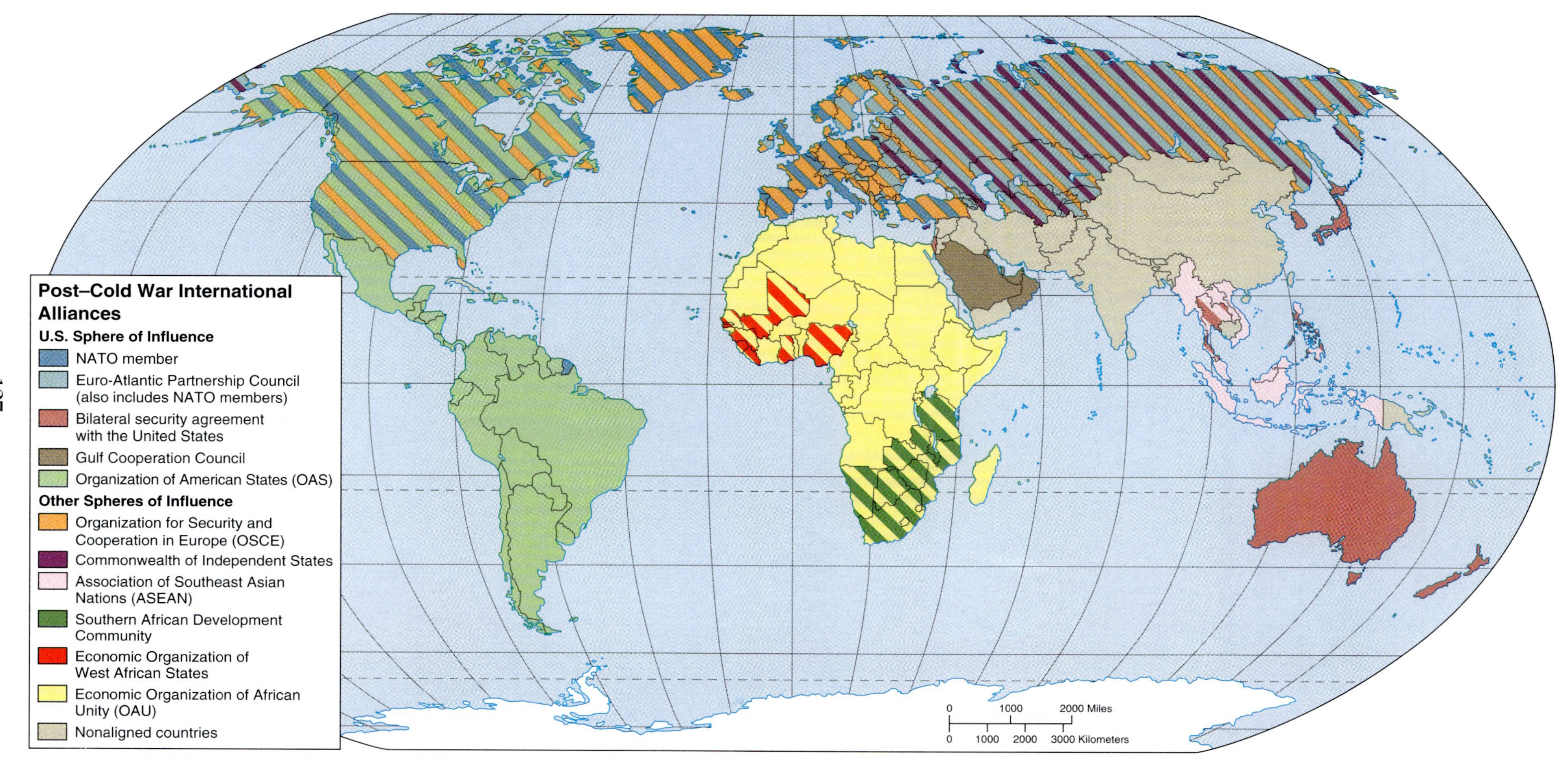

Post–Cold War International Alliances
U.S. Sphere of Influence
NATO member
Euro-Atlantic Partnership Council (also includes NATO members)
Bilateral security agreement with the United States
Gulf Cooperation Council
Organization of American States (OAS)
Other Spheres of Influence
Organization for Security and Cooperation in Europe (OSCE)
Commonwealth of Independent States
Association of Southeast Asian Nations (ASEAN)
Southern African Development Community
Economic Organization of West African States
Economic Organization of African Unity (OAU)
Nonaligned countries
0 1000 2000 Miles
0 1000 2000 3000 Kilometers

When the Warsaw Pact dissolved in 1992, the North Atlantic Treaty Organization (NATO) was left as the only major military alliance in the world. Some former Warsaw Pact members (Czech Republic, Hungary, and Poland) have joined NATO and others are petitioning for entry. The bipolar division of the world into two major military alliances is over, at least temporarily, leaving the United States alone as the world's dominant political and military power. But other international alliances such as the Commonwealth of Independent States (including most of the former republics of the Soviet Union) will continue to be important.

Map 90 Nations with Nuclear Weapons

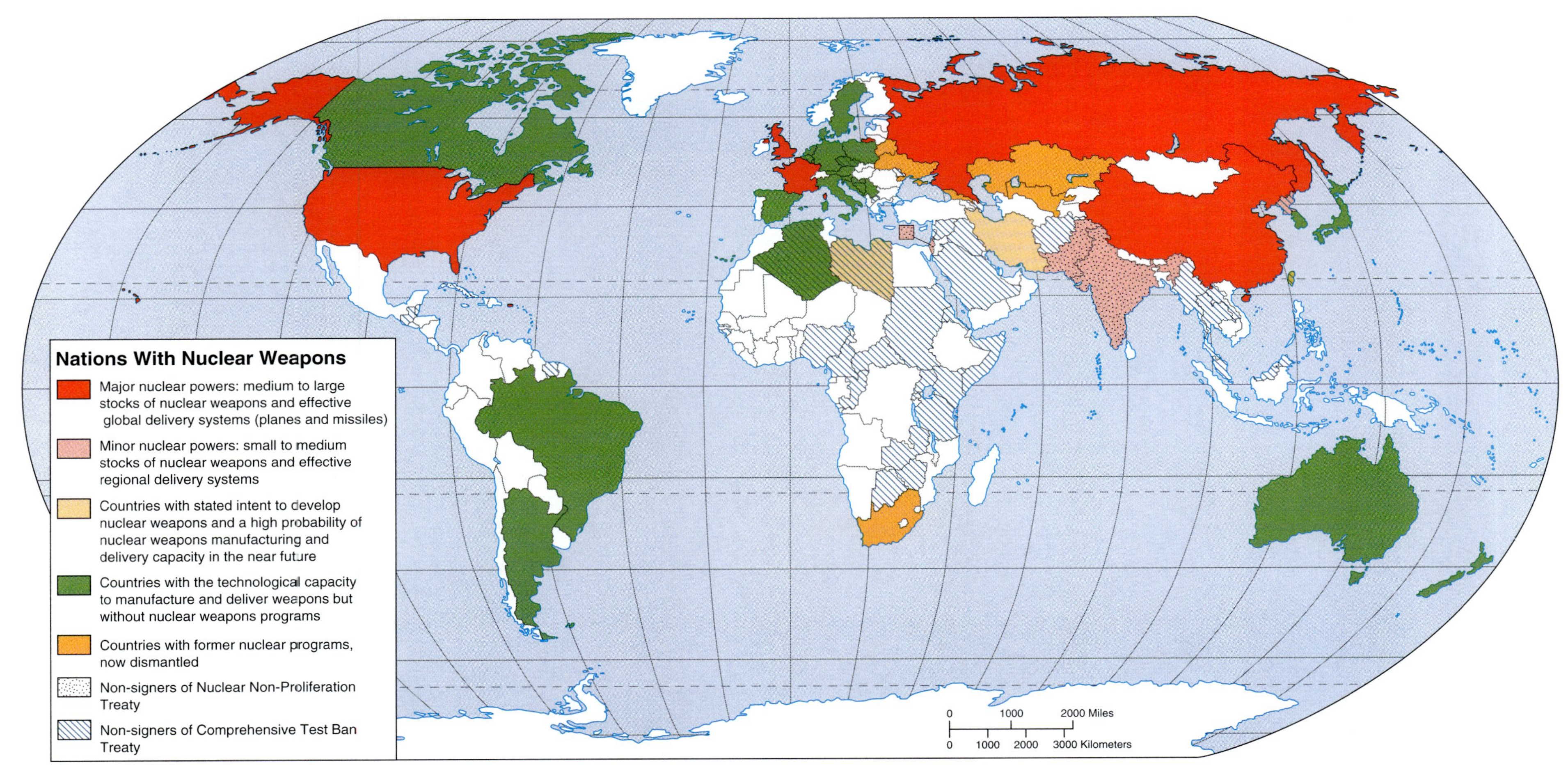

Nations With Nuclear Weapons
Major nuclear powers: medium to large stocks of nuclear weapons and effective global delivery systems (planes and missiles)
Minor nuclear powers: small to medium stocks of nuclear weapons and effective regional delivery systems
Countries with stated intent to develop nuclear weapons and a high probability of nuclear weapons manufacturing and delivery capacity in the near future
Countries with the technological capacity to manufacture and deliver weapons but without nuclear weapons programs
Countries with former nuclear programs, now dismantled
Non-signers of Nuclear Non-Proliferation Treaty
Non-signers of Comprehensive Test Ban Treaty
0 1000 2000 Miles
0 1000 2000 3000 Kilometers

Since 1980, the number of countries possessing the capacity to manufacture and deliver nuclear weapons has grown dramatically, increasing the chances of accidental nuclear exchanges. In addition to the traditional nuclear powers of the United States, Russia, China, the United Kingdom, and France, some newly independent former Soviet republics (Ukraine, Kazakhstan, Uzbekistan, and Georgia) may retain some of the weapons systems from the old Soviet Union. Also, four other countries are now judged by many authorities to possess nuclear weapons capability: Israel, India, Pakistan, and South Africa. While the stockpile of weapons of these countries is small (ranging from a minimum of 510 weapons in Pakistan to a maximum of 50–200 weapons in Israel), the proliferation of countries capable of using nuclear warheads in wartime threatens global security. In addition to countries that already possess the capacity to make and deliver nuclear weapons, seven other countries—Argentina, Brazil, Iran, Iraq, Libya, North Korea, and Taiwan—have or recently have had active nuclear weapons programs and may possess nuclear weapons capacity. Finally, there are countries—virtually all of them in the developed economies of the world—that possess the technological capacity to manufacture nuclear weapons and delivery systems but have chosen not to develop nuclear weapons programs. These countries include, among others, Canada, most western and eastern European countries (other than Britain or France), South Korea, Japan, Australia, and New Zealand.

Map 91 Military Expenditures as a Percentage of Gross National Product

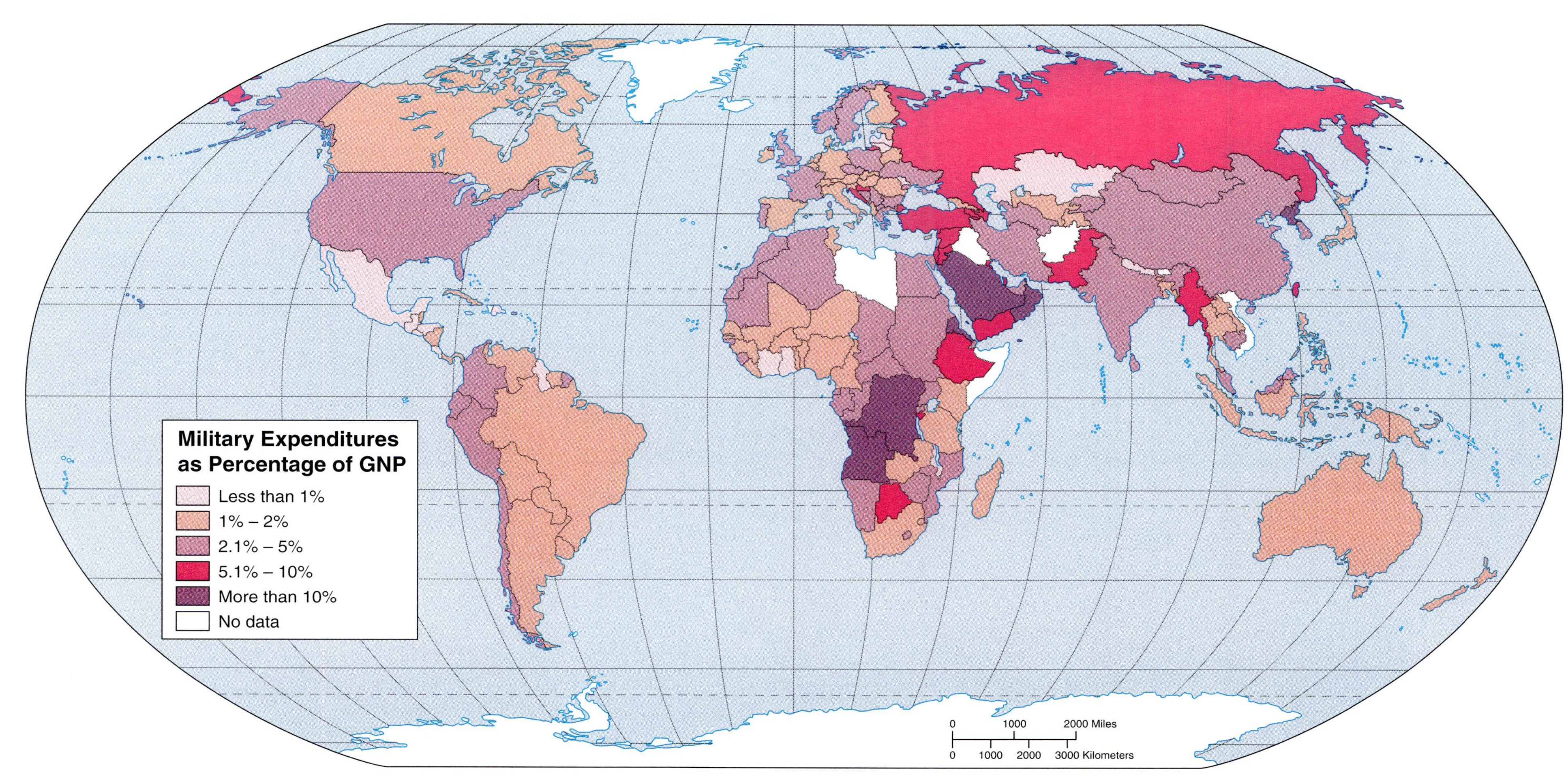
Military Expenditures as Percentage of GNP
Less than 1%
1% – 2%
2.1% – 5%
5.1% – 10%
More than 10%
No data
0 1000 2000 Miles
0 1000 2000 3000 Kilometers

Many countries devote a significant proportion of their total central governmental expenditures to defense: weapons, personnel, and research and development of military hardware. A glance at the map reveals that there are a number of regions in which defense expenditures are particularly high, reflecting the degree of past and present political tension between countries. The clearest example is the Middle East. The steady increase in military expenditures by developing countries is one of the most alarming (and least well-known) worldwide defense issues. Where the end of the cold war has meant a substantial reduction of military expenditures for the countries in North America and Europe and for Russia, in many of the world's developing countries military expenditures have risen between 15 percent and 20 percent per year for the past few years, averaging out to 7.5 percent per year for the past quarter-century. Even though many developing countries still spend less than 5 percent of their gross national product on defense, these funds could be put to different uses in such human development areas as housing, land reform, health care, and education.

Map 92 Size of Armed Forces

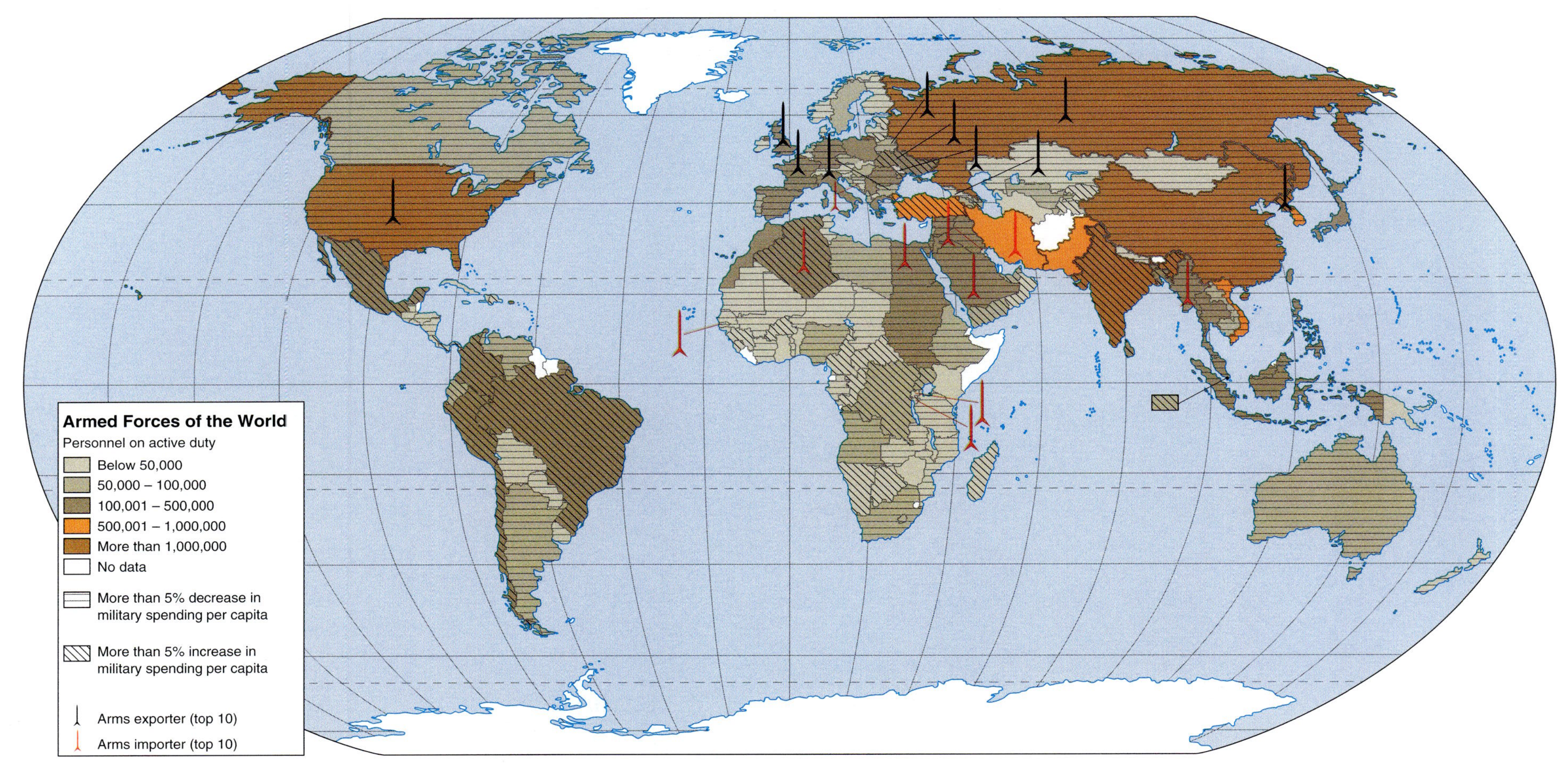
Armed Forces of the World
Personnel on active duty
Below 50,000
50,000 – 100,000
100,001 – 500,000
500,001 – 1,000,000
More than 1,000,000
No data
More than 5% decrease in military spending per capita
More than 5% increase in military spending per capita
Arms exporter (top 10)
Arms importer (top 10)

While the size of a country's armed forces is still an indicator of national power on the international scene, it is no longer as important as it once was. The increasing high technology of military hardware allows smaller numbers of military personnel to be more effective. There are some countries, such as China, with massive numbers of military personnel but with relatively limited military power because of a lack of modern weaponry. Additionally, the use of rapid transportation allows personnel to be deployed about the globe or any region of it quickly; this also increases effectiveness of highly trained and well-armed smaller military units. Nevertheless, the world is still a long way from the predicted "push-button warfare" that many experts have long anticipated. Indeed, the pattern of the last few years has been for most military conflicts to involve ground troops engaged in fairly traditional patterns of operation. Even in the 1991 Persian Gulf conflict and the war to disarm Iraq in 2003, with their highly-publicized "smart bombs," the bulk of the military operations that ended the conflicts were carried out by infantry and armor operating on the ground and supported by traditional air cover using conventional weaponry. Thus, while the size of a country's armed forces may not be as important as it once was, it is still a major factor in measuring the ability of nations to engage successfully in armed conflict.

Part VI

The Changing World: Environment and Culture

Map 93 Global Air Pollution: Sources and Wind Currents
Map 94 Major Polluters and Common Pollutants
Map 95 Global Carbon Dioxide Emissions
Map 96 Pollution of the Oceans
Map 97 Cropland Per Capita: Changes, 1987-1997
Map 98 Annual Change in Forest Cover, 1990-1995
Map 99 Global Hotspots of Biodiversity
Map 100 The Loss of Biodiversity: Globally Threatened Animal Species
Map 101 The Loss of Biodiversity: Globally Threatened Plant Species
Map 102 The Risks of Desertification
Map 103 Global Soil Degradation
Map 104 The Degree of Human Disturbance

Map 93 Global Air Pollution: Sources and Wind Currents

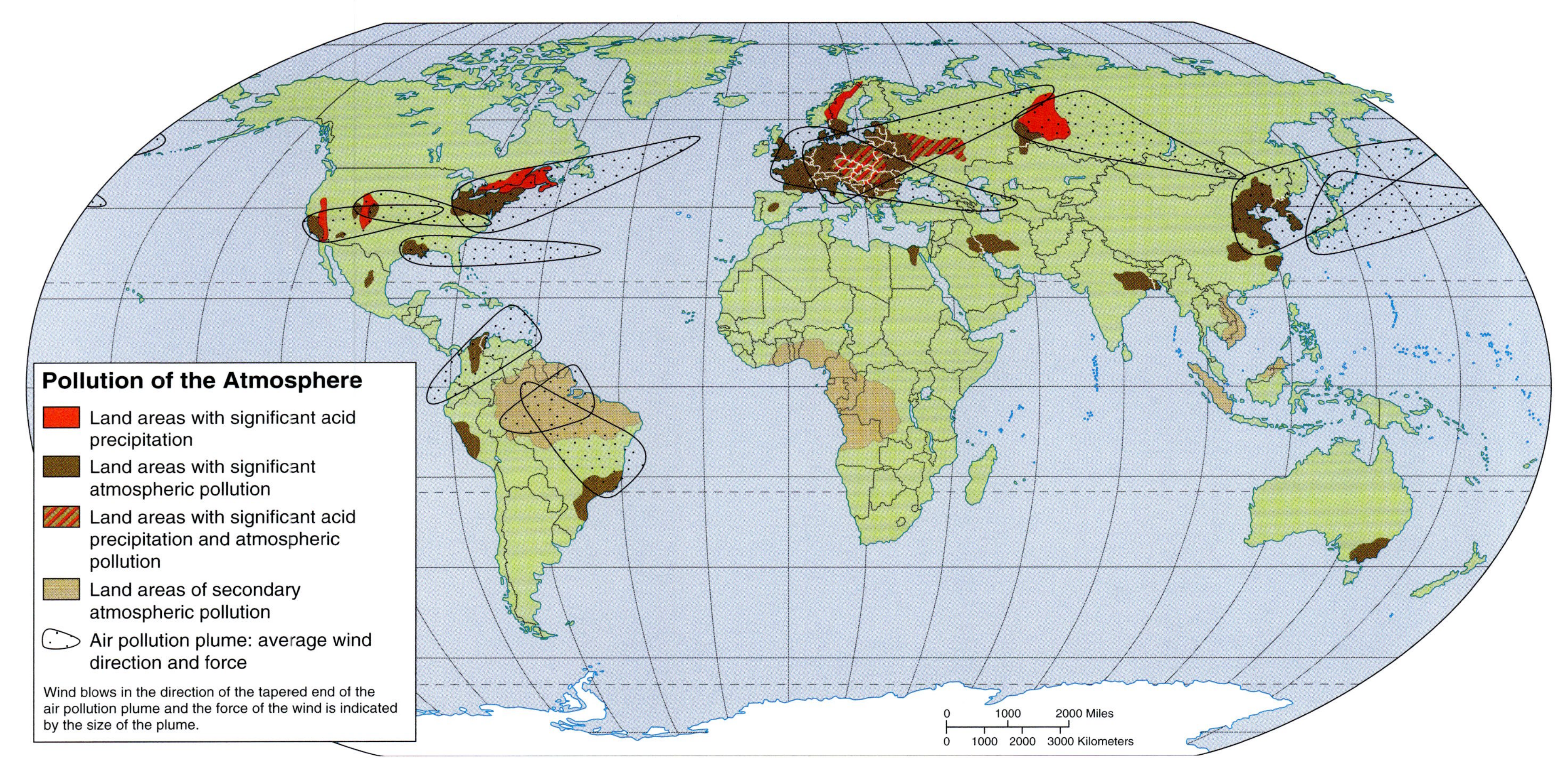

Pollution of the Atmosphere
Land areas with significant acid precipitation
Land areas with significant atmospheric pollution
Land areas with significant acid precipitation and atmospheric pollution
Land areas of secondary atmospheric pollution
Air pollution plume: average wind direction and force
Wind blows in the direction of the tapered end of the air pollution plume and the force of the wind is indicated by the size of the plume.
0 1000 2000 Miles
0 1000 2000 3000 Kilometers

Almost all processes of physical geography begin and end with the flows of energy and matter among land, sea, and air. Because of the primacy of the atmosphere in this exchange system, air pollution is potentially one of the most dangerous human modifications in environmental systems. Pollutants such as various oxides of nitrogen or sulfur cause the development of acid precipitation, which damages soil, vegetation, and wildlife and fish. Air pollution in the form of smog is often dangerous for human health. And most atmospheric scientists believe that the efficiency of the atmosphere in retaining heat—the so-called greenhouse effect—is being enhanced by increased carbon dioxide, methane, and other gases produced by agricultural and industrial activities. The result, they fear, will be a period of global warming that will dramatically alter climates in all parts of the world.

Map 94 Major Polluters and Common Pollutants

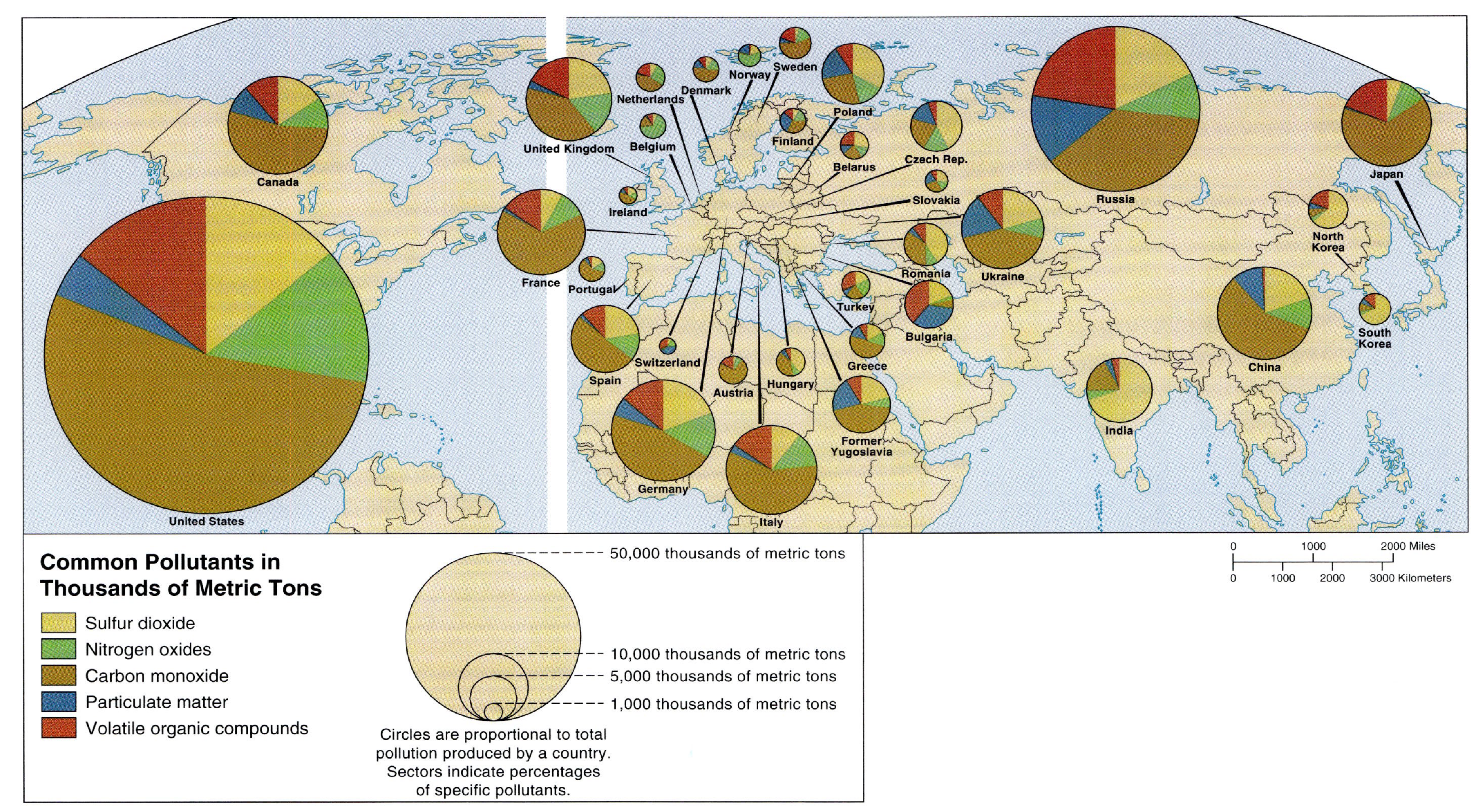

Canada
United States
United Kingdom
Netherlands
Belgium
Denmark
Norway
Sweden
Finland
Poland
Belarus
Czech Rep.
Slovakia
Ireland
France
Portugal
Spain
Switzerland
Germany
Austria
Italy
Hungary
Turkey
Romania
Bulgaria
Greece
Former Yugoslavia
Ukraine
Russia
India
China
North Korea
South Korea
Japan
0 1000 2000 Miles
0 1000 2000 3000 Kilometers
Common Pollutants in Thousands of Metric Tons
Sulfur dioxide
Nitrogen oxides
Carbon monoxide
Particulate matter
Volatile organic compounds
50,000 thousands of metric tons
10,000 thousands of metric tons
5,000 thousands of metric tons
1,000 thousands of metric tons
Circles are proportional to total pollution produced by a country. Sectors indicate percentages of specific pollutants.

More than 90 percent of the world's total of anthropogenic (human-generated) air pollutants come from the heavily populated industrial regions of North America, Europe, South Asia (primarily in India), and East Asia (mainly in China, Japan, and the two Koreas). This map shows the origins of the five most common pollutants: sulfur dioxide, nitrogen oxide, carbon monoxide, particulate matter, and volatile organic compounds. These substances are produced both by industry and by the combustion of fossil fuels that generate electricity and power trains, planes, automobiles, buses, and trucks. In addition to combining with other components of the atmosphere and with one another to produce smog, they are the chief ingredients in acid accumulations in the atmosphere, which ultimately result in acid deposition, either as acid precipitation or dry acid fallout. Like other forms of pollutants, these air pollutants do not recognize political boundaries, and regions downwind of major polluters receive large quantities of pollutants from areas over which they often have no control.

Map 95 Global Carbon Dioxide Emissions

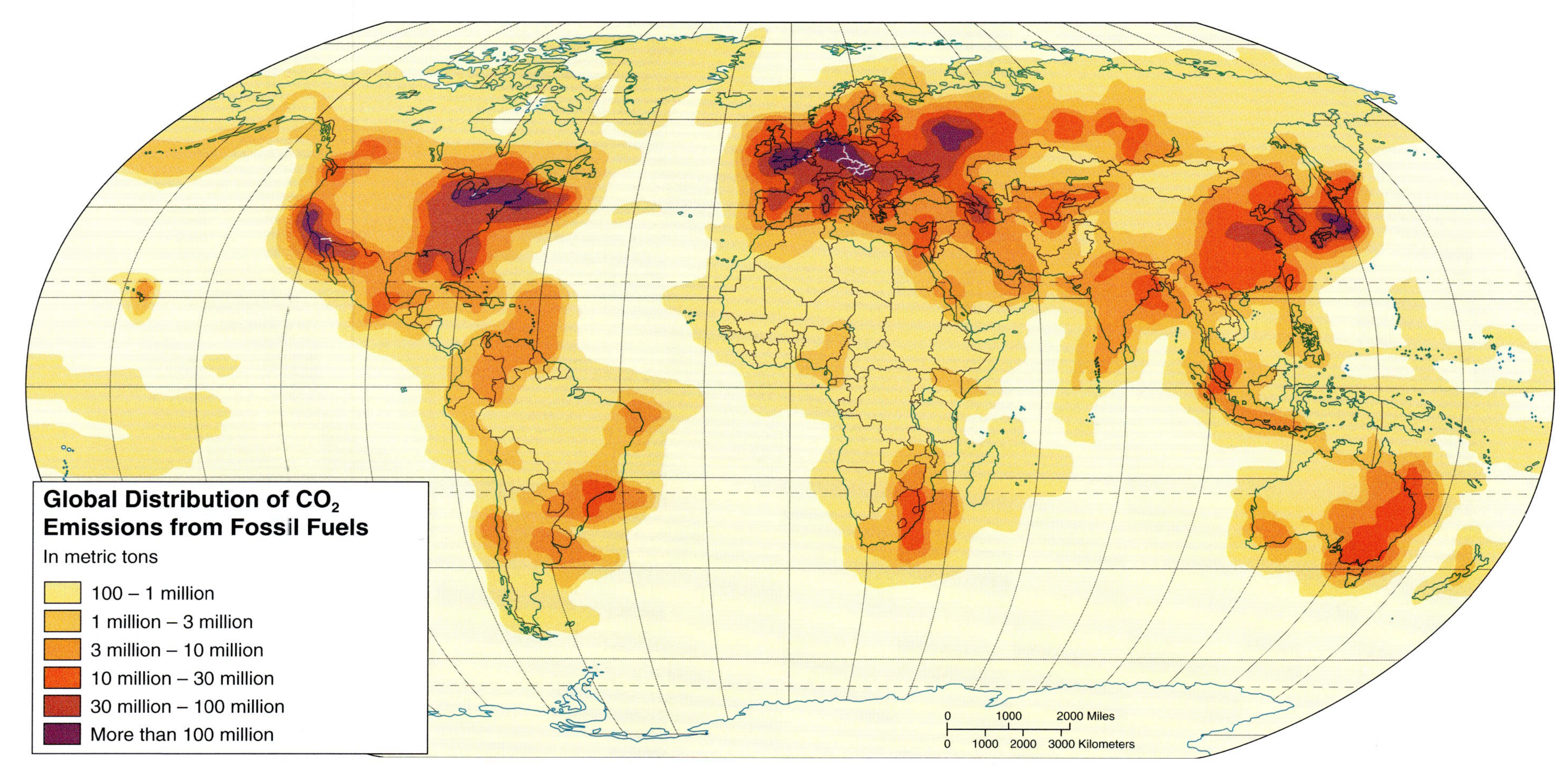

Global Distribution of CO_2 Emissions from Fossil Fuels
In metric tons
100 – 1 million
1 million – 3 million
3 million – 10 million
10 million – 30 million
30 million – 100 million
More than 100 million
0 1000 2000 Miles
0 1000 2000 3000 Kilometers

One of the most important components of the atmosphere is the gas carbon dioxide (CO^2), the byproduct of animal respiration, of decomposition, and of combustion. During the past 200 years, atmospheric CO^2 has risen dramatically, largely as the result of the tremendous increase in fossil fuel combustion brought on by the industrialization of the world's economy and the burning and clearing of forests by the expansion of farming. While CO^2 by itself is relatively harmless, it is an important "greenhouse gas." The gases in the atmosphere act like the panes of glass in a greenhouse roof, allowing light in but preventing heat from escaping. The greenhouse capacity of the atmosphere is crucial for organic life and is a purely natural component of the global energy cycle. But too much CO^2 and other greenhouse gases such as methane could cause the earth's atmosphere to warm up too much, producing the global warming that atmospheric scientists are concerned about. Researchers estimate that if greenhouse gases such as CO^2 continue to increase at their present rates, the earth's mean temperature could rise between 1.5 and 4.5 degrees Celsius by the middle of the next century. Such a rise in global temperatures would produce massive alterations in the world's climate patterns.

Map 96 Pollution of the Oceans

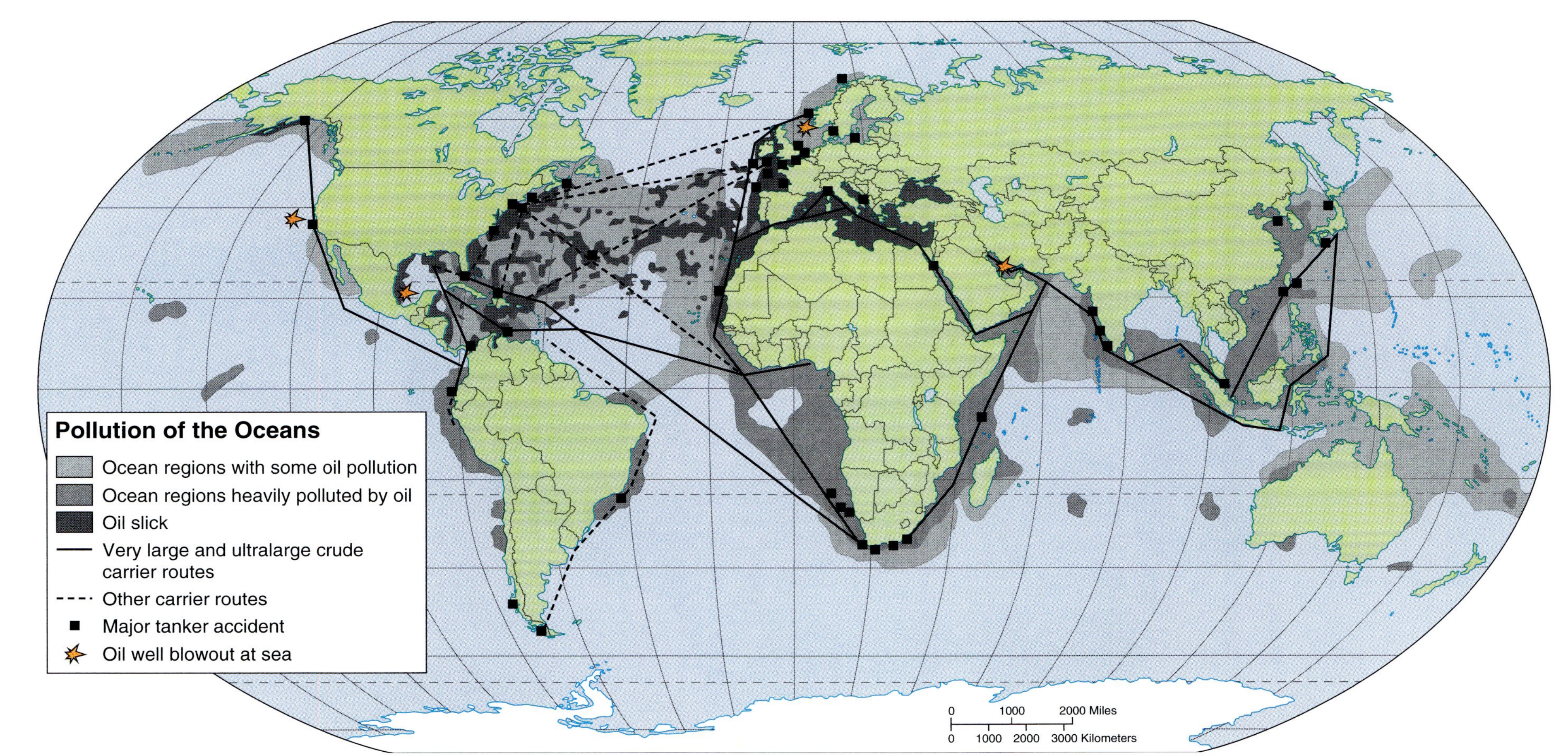

Pollution of the Oceans
Ocean regions with some oil pollution
Ocean regions heavily polluted by oil
Oil slick
Very large and ultralarge crude carrier routes
Other carrier routes
Major tanker accident
Oil well blowout at sea
0 1000 2000 Miles
0 1000 2000 3000 Kilometers

The pollution of the world's oceans has long been a matter of concern to physical geographers, oceanographers, and other environmental scientists. The great circulation systems of the ocean are one of the controlling factors of the earth's natural environment, and modifications to those systems have unknown consequences. This map is based on what we can measure: (1) areas of oceans where oil pollution has been proven to have inflicted significant damage to ocean ecosystems and life-forms (including phytoplankton, the oceans' primary food producers, equivalent to land-based vegetation) and (2) areas of oceans where unusually high concentrations of hydrocarbons from oil spills may have inflicted some damage to the oceans' biota. A glance at the map shows that there are few areas of the world's oceans where some form of pollution is not a part of the environmental system. What the map does not show in detail, because of the scale, are the dramatic consequences of large individual pollution events: the wreck of the *Exxon Valdez* and the polluting of Prince William Sound, or the environmental devastation produced by the 1991 Gulf War in the Persian Gulf.

Map 97 Cropland Per Capita: Changes, 1987–1997

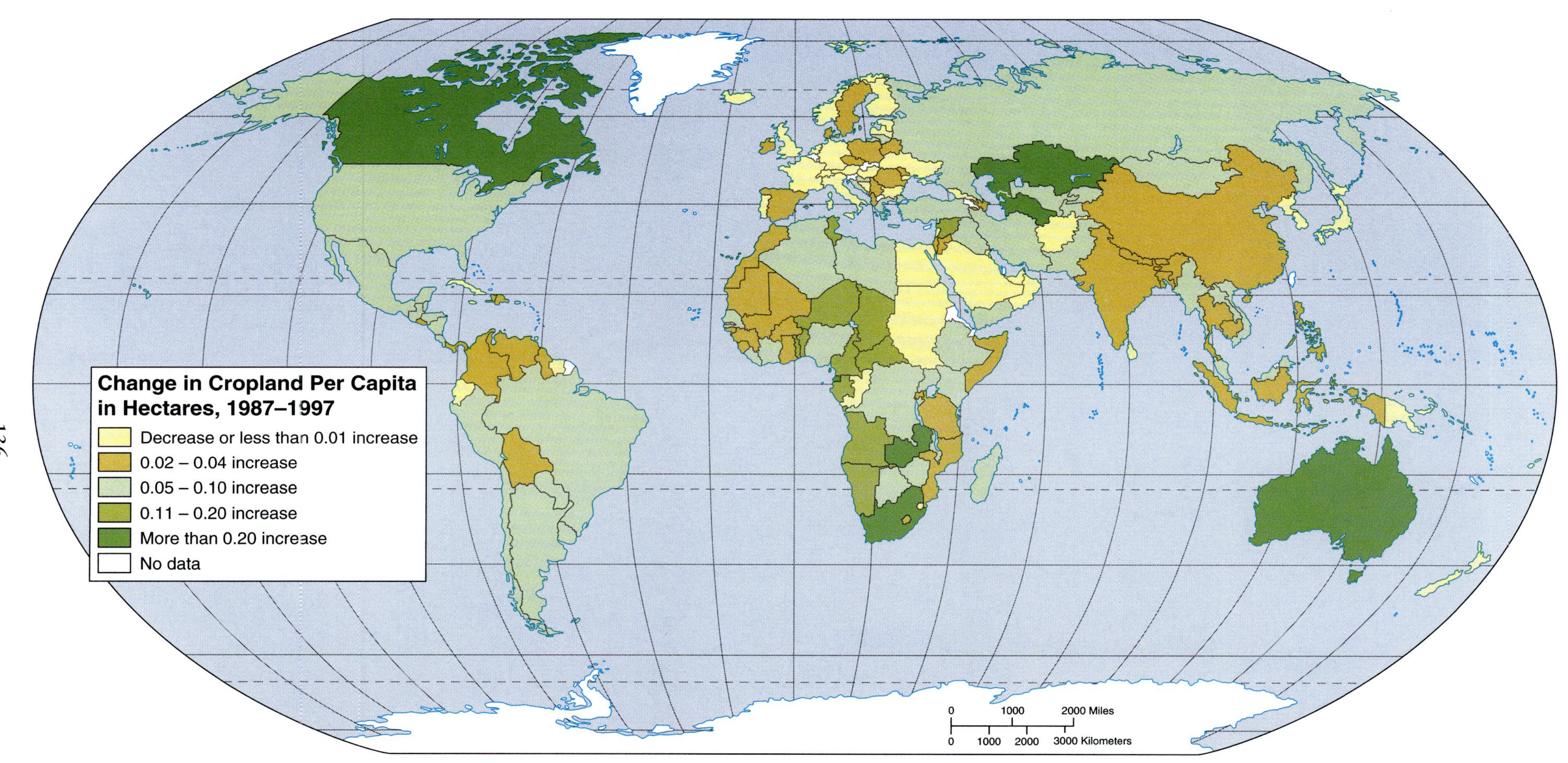
Change in Cropland Per Capita in Hectares, 1987–1997
Decrease or less than 0.01 increase
0.02 – 0.04 increase
0.05 – 0.10 increase
0.11 – 0.20 increase
More than 0.20 increase
No data
0
1000
2000 Miles
0
1000
2000
3000 Kilometers

As population has increased rapidly throughout the world, the area of cultivated land has increased at the same time; in fact, the amount of farmland per person has gone up slightly. Unfortunately, the figures that show this also tell us that since most of the best (or even good) agricultural land in 1985 was already under cultivation, most of the agricultural area added since the early 1980s involves land that would have been viewed as marginal by the fathers and grandfathers of present farmers—marginal in that it was too dry, too wet, too steep to cultivate, too far from a market, and so on. The continued expansion of agricultural area is one reason that serious famine and starvation have struck only a few regions of the globe. But land, more than any other resource we deal with, is finite, and the expansion cannot continue indefinitely. Future gains in agricultural production are most probably going to come through more intensive use of existing cropland, heavier applications of fertilizers and other agricultural chemicals, and genetically engineered crops requiring heavier applications of energy and water, than from an increase in the amount of the world's cropland.

Map 98 Annual Change in Forest Cover, 1990-1995

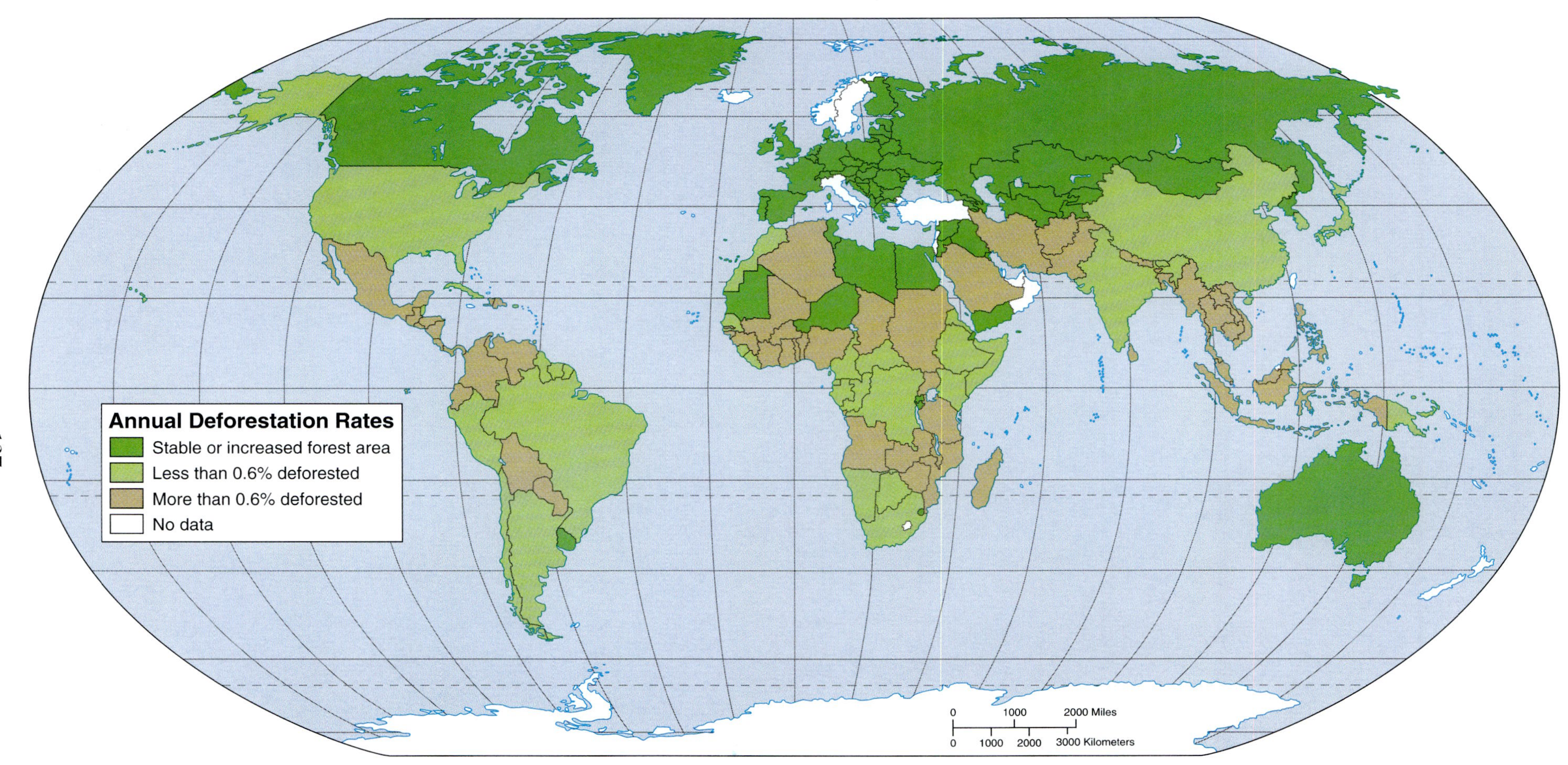
Annual Deforestation Rates
Stable or increased forest area
Less than 0.6% deforested
More than 0.6% deforested
No data
0 1000 2000 Miles
0 1000 2000 3000 Kilometers

One of the most discussed environmental problems is that of deforestation. For most people, deforestation means clearing of tropical rain forests for agricultural purposes. Yet nearly as much forest land per year—much of it in North America, Europe, and Russia—is impacted by commercial lumbering as is cleared by tropical farmers and ranchers. Even in the tropics, much of the forest clearance is undertaken by large corporations producing high-value tropical hardwoods for the global market in furniture, ornaments, and other fine wood products. Still, it is the agriculturally driven clearing of the great rain forests of the Amazon Basin, west and central Africa, Middle America, and Southeast Asia that draws public attention. Although much concern over forest clearance focuses on the relationship between forest clearance and the reduction in the capacity of the world's vegetation system to absorb carbon dioxide (and thus delay global warming), of just as great concern are issues having to do with the loss of biodiversity (large numbers of plants and animals), the near-total destruction of soil systems, and disruptions in water supply that accompany clearing.

Map 99 Global Hotspots of Biodiversity

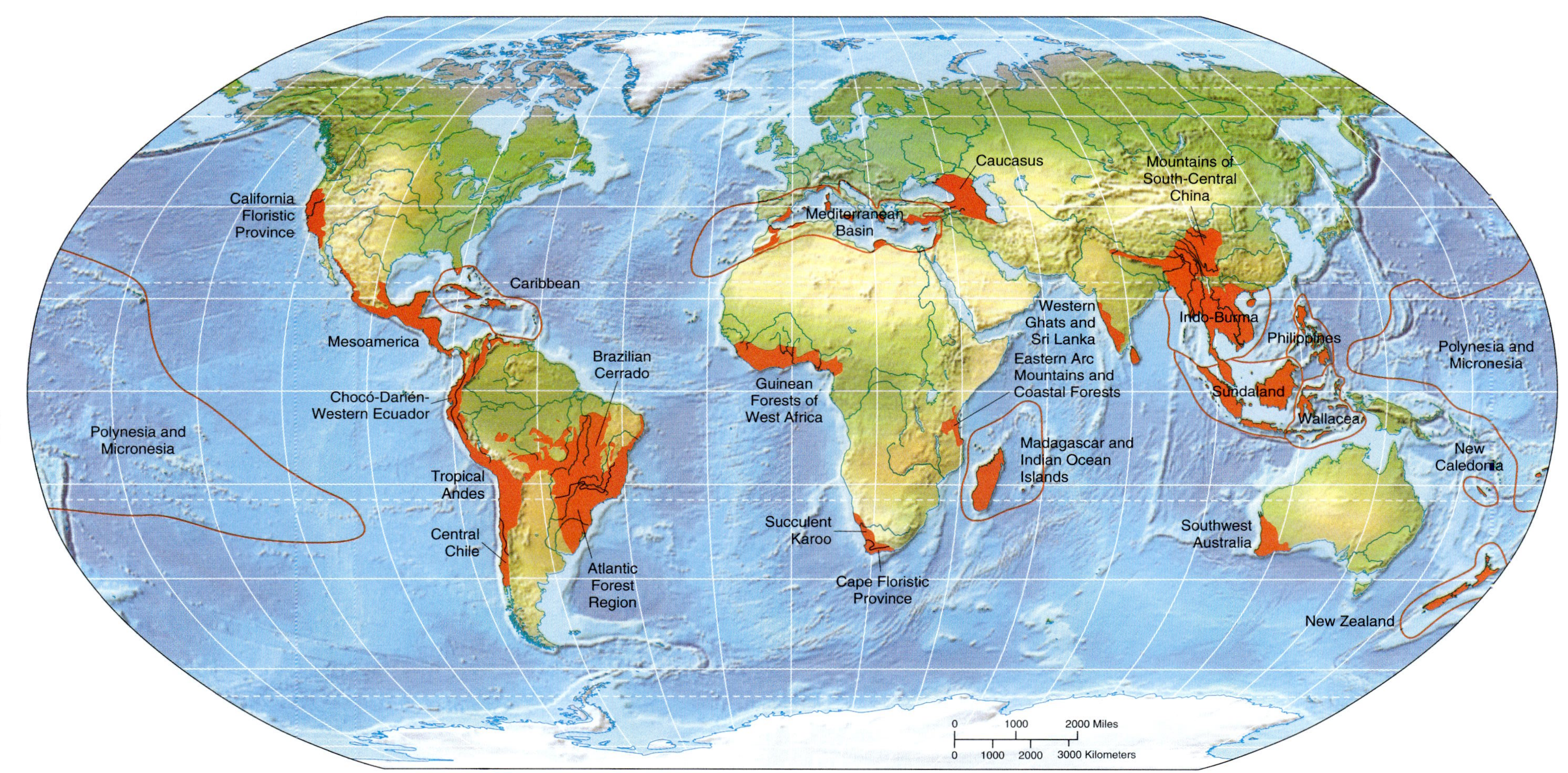

California Floristic Province
Caribbean
Mesoamerica
Brazilian Cerrado
Chocó-Darién-Western Ecuador
Polynesia and Micronesia
Tropical Andes
Central Chile
Atlantic Forest Region
Mediterranean Basin
Caucasus
Guinean Forests of West Africa
Succulent Karoo
Cape Floristic Province
Western Ghats and Sri Lanka
Eastern Arc Mountains and Coastal Forests
Madagascar and Indian Ocean Islands
Mountains of South-Central China
Indo-Burma
Philippines
Sundaland
Wallacea
Polynesia and Micronesia
New Caledonia
Southwest Australia
New Zealand
0 1000 2000 Miles
0 1000 2000 3000 Kilometers

Where we have normally thought of tropical forest basins such as Amazonia as the worlds most biologically diverse ecosystems, recent research has discovered the surprising fact that a number of hotspots of biological diversity exist outside the major tropical forest regions. These hotspot regions contain slightly less than 2 percent of the worlds total land area but may contain up to 60 percent of the total worlds terrestrial species of plants and animals. Geographically, the hotspot areas are characterized by vertical zonation (that is, they tend to be hilly to mountainous regions), long known to be a factor in biological complexity. They are also in coastal locations or near large bodies of water, locations that stimulate climatic variability and, hence, b ological complexity. Although some of the hotspots are sparsely populated, others, such as Sundaland, are occupied by some of the worlds densest populations. Protection of the rich biodiversity of these hotspots is, most biologists feel, of crucial importance to the preservation of the worlds biological heritage.

Map 100 The Loss of Biodiversity: Globally Threatened Animal Species

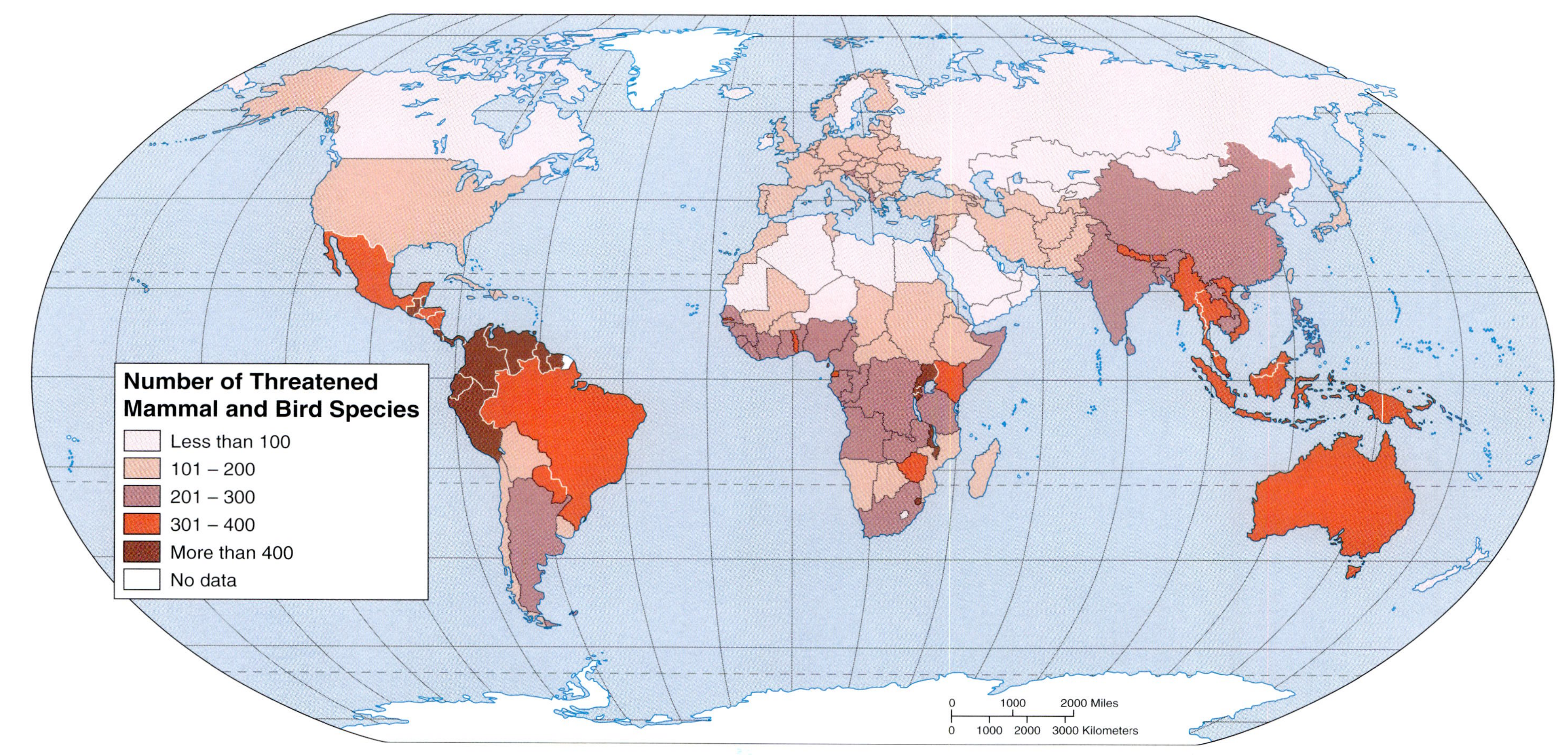
Number of Threatened
Mammal and Bird Species
Less than 100
101 – 200
201 – 300
301 – 400
More than 400
No data
0 1000 2000 Miles
0 1000 2000 3000 Kilometers

Threatened species are those in grave danger of going extinct. Their populations are becoming restricted in range, and the size of the populations required for sustained breeding is nearing a critical minimum. *Endangered species* are in immediate danger of becoming extinct. Their range is already so reduced that the animals may no longer be able to move freely within an ecozone, and their populations are at the level where the species may no longer be able to sustain breeding. Most species become threatened first and then endangered as their range and numbers continue to decrease. When people think of animal extinction, they think of large herbivorous species like the rhinoceros or fierce carnivores like lions, tigers, or grizzly bears. Certainly these animals make almost any list of endangered or threatened species. But there are literally hundreds of less conspicuous animals that are equally threatened. Extinction is normally nature's way of informing a species that it is inefficient. But conditions in the late twentieth century are controlled more by human activities than by natural evolutionary processes. Species that are endangered or threatened fall into that category because, somehow, they are competing with us or with our domesticated livestock for space and food. And in that competition the animals are always going to lose.

Map 101 The Loss of Biodiversity: Globally Threatened Plant Species

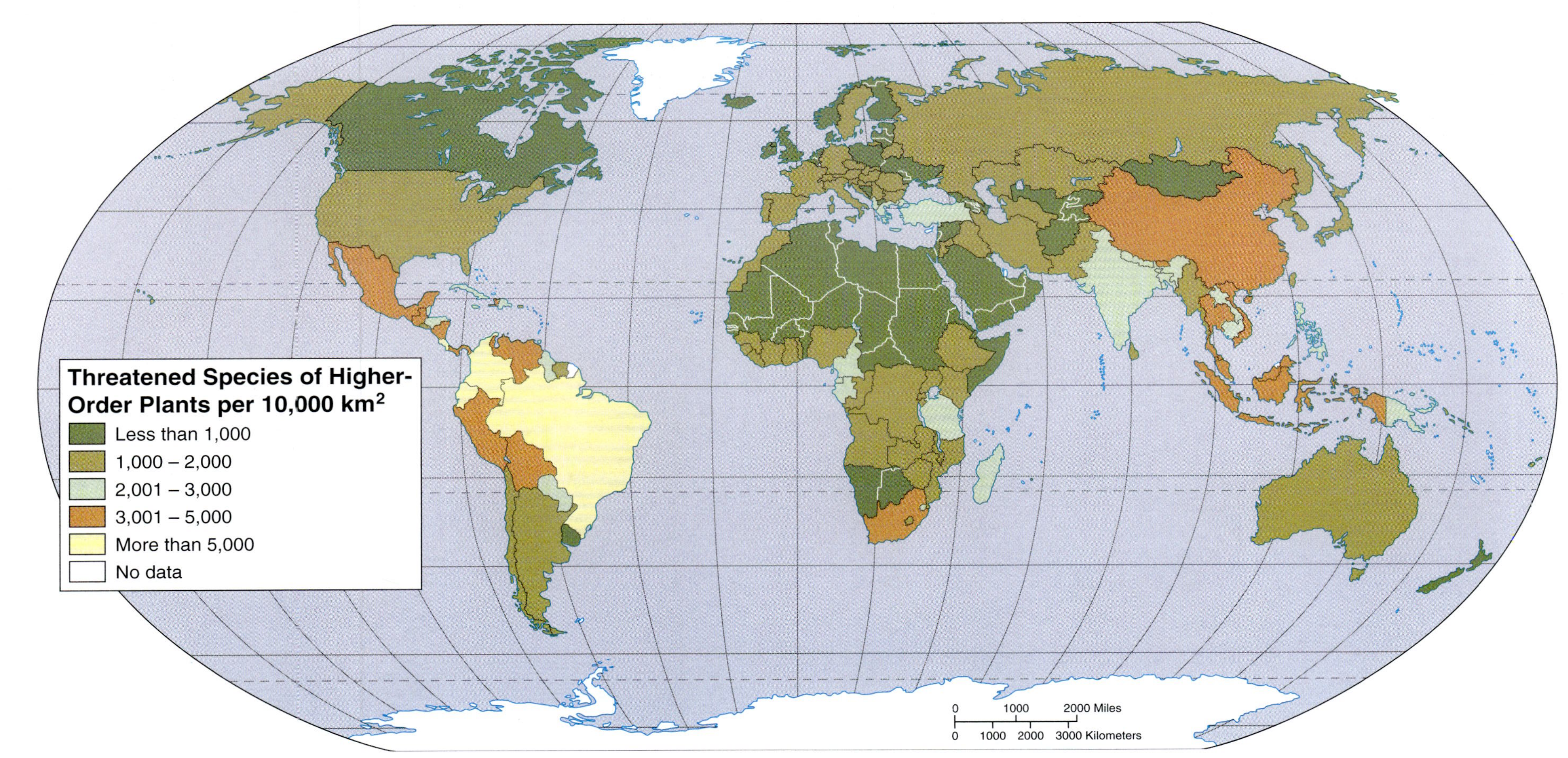
Threatened Species of Higher-Order Plants per 10,000 km²
Less than 1,000
1,000 – 2,000
2,001 – 3,000
3,001 – 5,000
More than 5,000
No data
0 1000 2000 Miles
0 1000 2000 3000 Kilometers

While most people tend to be more concerned about the animals on threatened and endangered species lists, the fact is that many more plants are in jeopardy, and the loss of plant life is, in all ecological regions, a more critical occurrence than the loss of animal populations. Plants are the primary producers in the ecosystem; that is, plants produce the food upon which all other species in the food web, including human beings, depend for sustenance. It is plants from which many of our critical medicines come, and it is plants that maintain the delicate balance between soil and water in most of the world's regions. When environmental scientists speak of a loss of biodiversity, what they are most often describing is a loss of the richness and complexity of plant life that lends stability to ecosystems. Systems with more plant life tend to be more stable than those with less. For these and other reasons, the scientific concern over extinction is greater when applied to plants than to animals. It is difficult for people to become as emotional over a teak tree as they would over an elephant. But as great a tragedy as the loss of the elephant would be, the loss of the teak would be greater.

Map 102 The Risks of Desertification

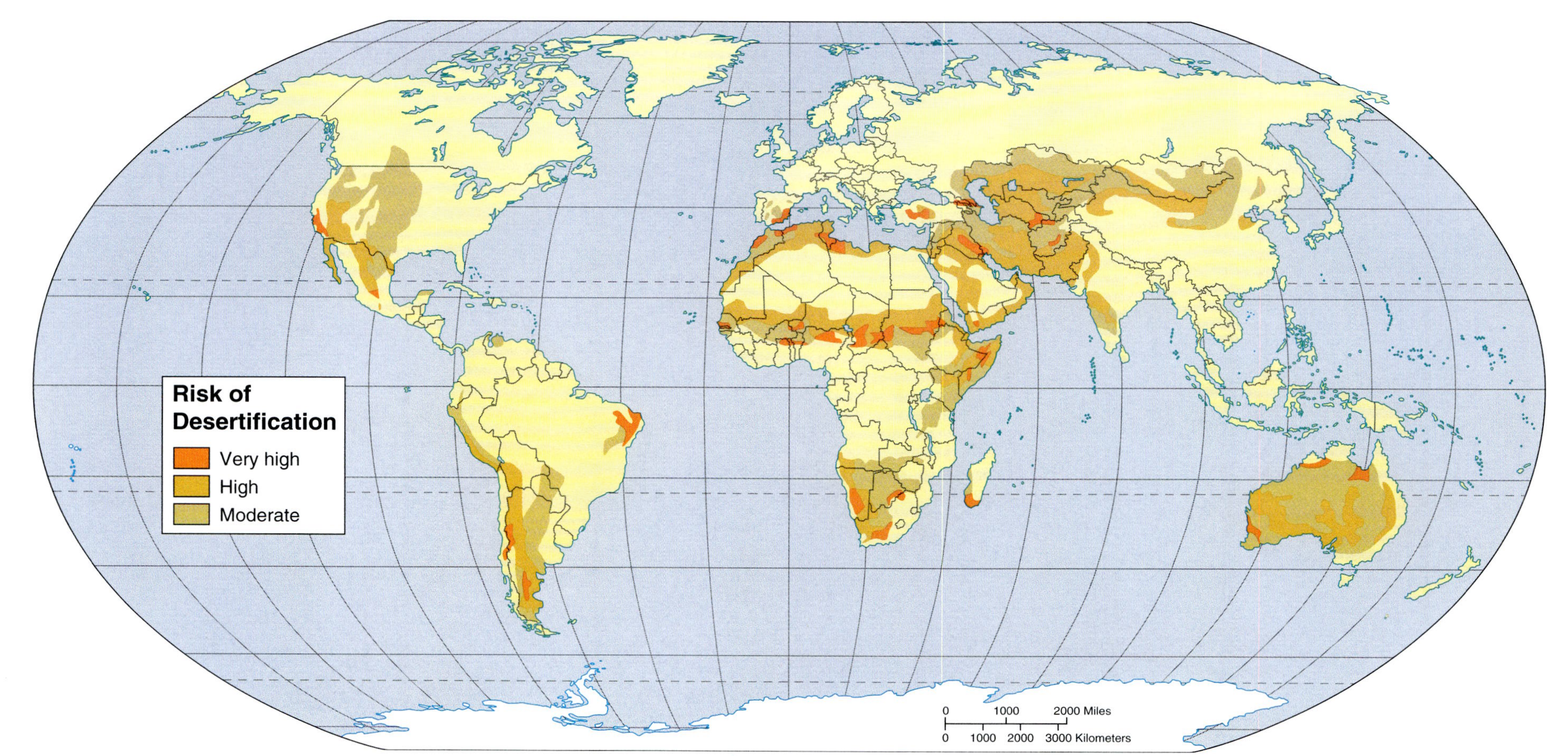
Risk of Desertification
Very high
High
Moderate
0 1000 2000 Miles
0 1000 2000 3000 Kilometers

The awkward-sounding term "desertification" refers to a reduction in the food-producing capacity of drylands through vegetation, soil, and water changes that culminate in either a drier climate or in soil and plant systems that are less efficient in their use of water. Most of the world's existing drylands—the shortgrass steppes, the tropical savannas, the bunchgrass regions of the desert fringe—are fairly intensively used for agriculture and are, therefore, subject to the kinds of pressures that culminate in desertification. Most desertification is a natural process that occurs near the margins of desert regions. It is caused by dehydration of the soil's surface layers during periods of drought and by high water loss through evaporation in an environment of high temperature and high winds. This natural process is greatly enhanced by human agricultural activities that expose topsoil to wind and water erosion. Among the most important practices that cause desertification are (1) overgrazing of rangelands, resulting from too many livestock on too small an area of land; (2) improper management of soil and water resources in irrigation agriculture, leading to accelerated erosion and to salt buildup in the soil; (3) cultivation of marginal terrain with soils and slopes that are unsuitable for farming; (4) surface disturbances of vegetation (clearing of thorn scrub, mesquite, chaparral, and similar vegetation) without soil protection efforts being made or replanting being done; and (5) soil compaction by agricultural implements, domesticated livestock, and rain falling on an exposed surface.

Map 103 Global Soil Degradation

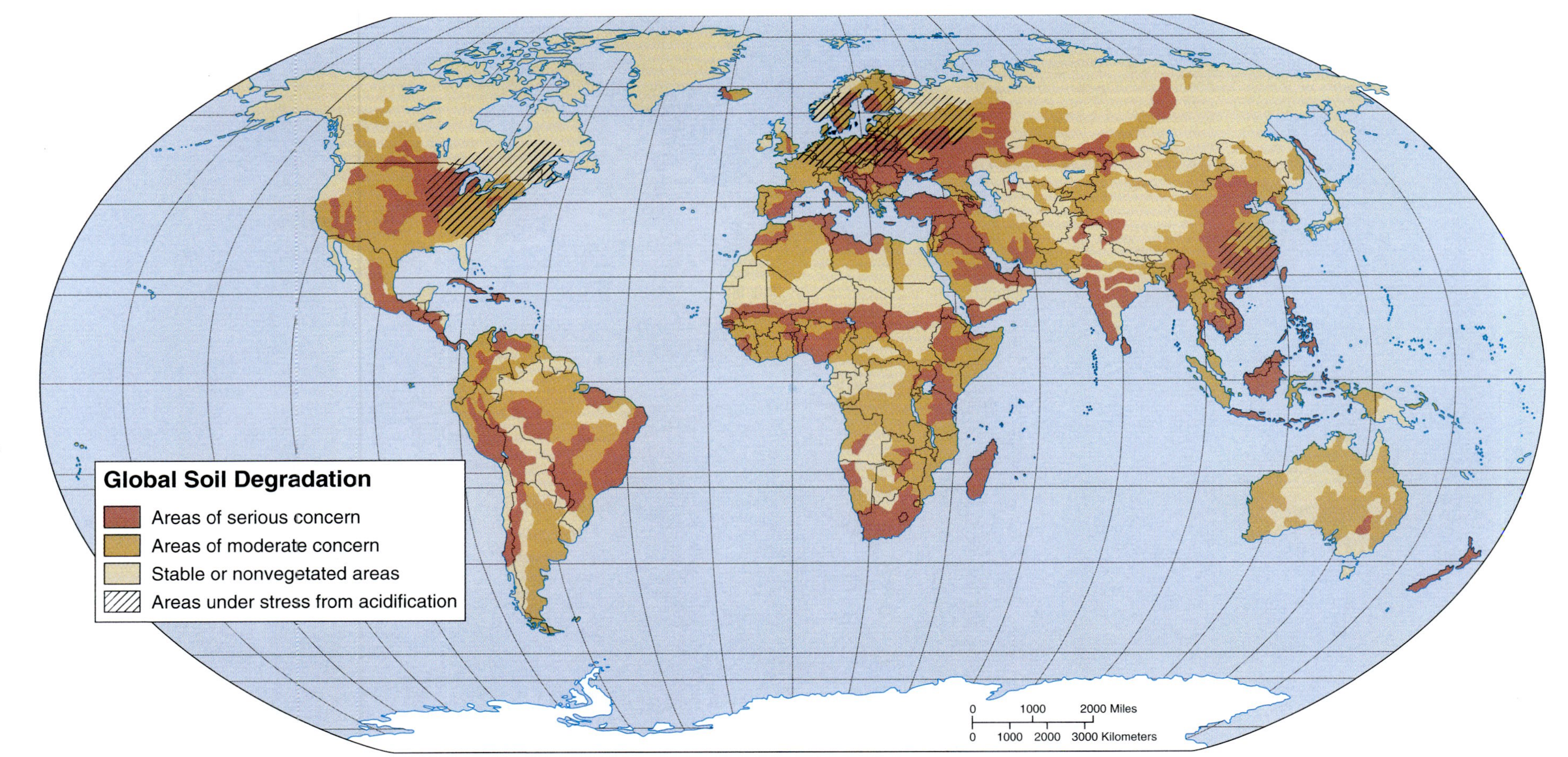
Global Soil Degradation
Areas of serious concern
Areas of moderate concern
Stable or nonvegetated areas
Areas under stress from acidification
0 1000 2000 Miles
0 1000 2000 3000 Kilometers

Recent research has shown that more than 3 billion acres of the world's surface suffer from serious soil degradation, with more than 22 million acres so severely eroded or poisoned with chemicals that they can no longer support productive crop agriculture. Most of this soil damage has been caused by poor farming practices, overgrazing of domestic livestock, and deforestation. These activities strip away the protective cover of natural vegetation forests and grasslands, allowing wind and water erosion to remove the topsoil that contains necessary nutrients and soil microbes for plant growth. But millions of acres of topsoil have been degraded by chemicals as well. In some instances these chemicals are the result of overapplication of fertilizers, herbicides, pesticides, and other agricultural chemicals. In other instances, chemical deposition from industrial and urban wastes and from acid precipitation has poisoned millions of acres of soil. As the map shows, soil erosion and pollution are not problems just in developing countries with high population densities and increasing use of marginal lands. They also afflict the more highly developed regions of mechanized, industrial agriculture. While many methods for preventing or reducing soil degradation exist, they are seldom used because of ignorance, cost, or perceived economic inefficiency.

Map 104 The Degree of Human Disturbance

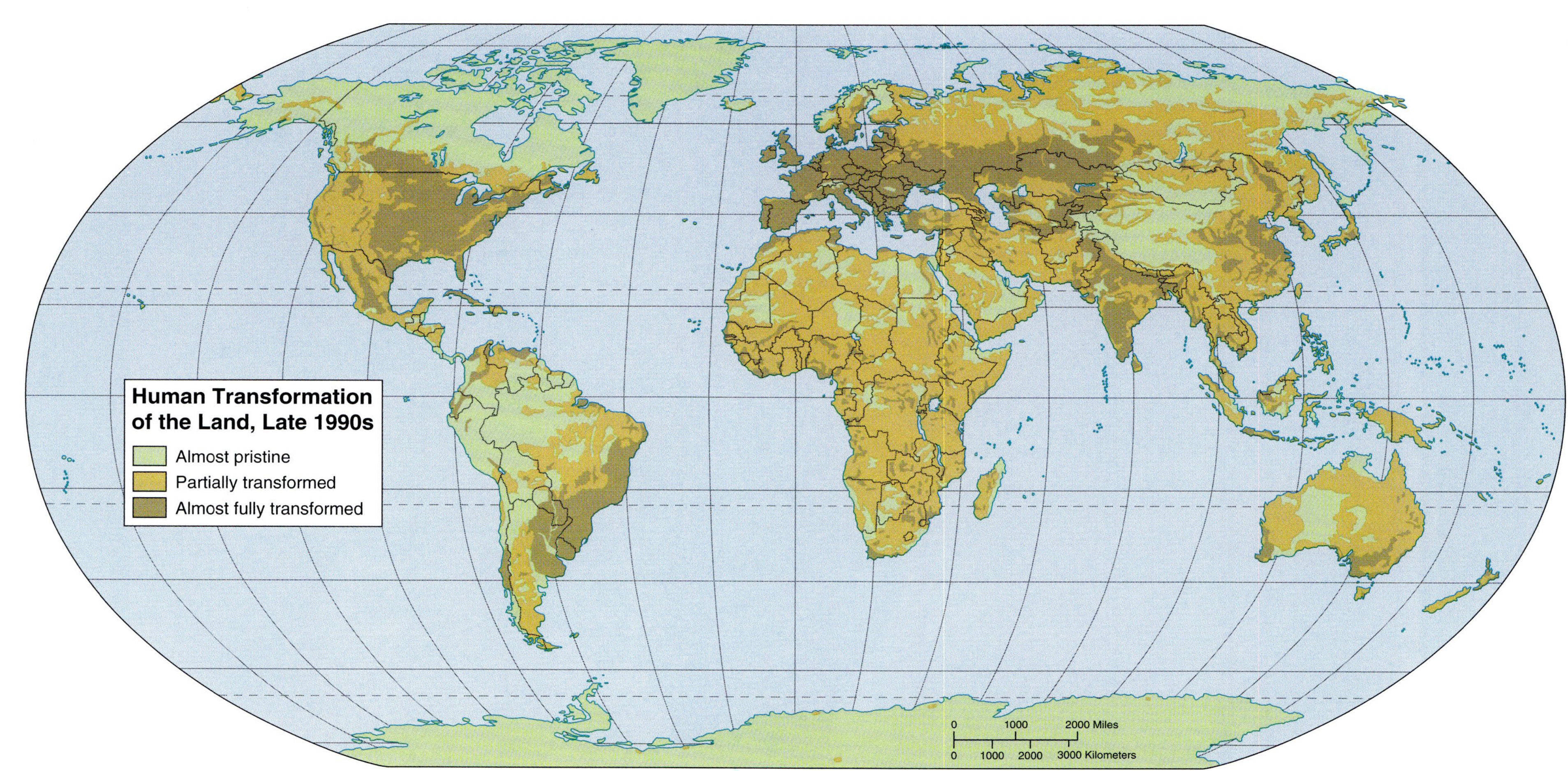
Human Transformation of the Land, Late 1990s
Almost pristine
Partially transformed
Almost fully transformed
0 1000 2000 Miles
0 1000 2000 3000 Kilometers

The data on human disturbance have been gathered from a wide variety of sources, some of them conflicting and not all of them reliable. Nevertheless, at a global scale this map fairly depicts the state of the world in terms of the degree to which humans have modified its surface. The almost pristine areas, covered with natural vegetation, generally have population densities under 10 persons per square mile. These areas are, for the most part, in the most inhospitable parts of the world: too high, too dry, too cold for permanent human habitation in large numbers. The partially transformed areas are normally agricultural areas, either subsistence (such as shifting cultivation) or extensive (such as livestock grazing). They often contain areas of secondary vegetation, regrown after removal of original vegetation by humans. They are also sometimes marked by a density of livestock in excess of carrying capacity, leading to overgrazing, which further alters the condition of the vegetation. The almost fully transformed areas are those of permanent and intensive agriculture and urban settlement. The primary vegetation of these regions has been removed, with no evidence of regrowth or with current vegetation that is quite different from natural (potential) vegetation. Soils are in a state of depletion and degradation, and, in drier lands, desertification is a factor of human occupation. The disturbed areas match closely those areas of the world with the densest human populations.

Part VII

World Regions

Map 105 North America: Physical Features
Map 106 North America: Political Divisions
Map 107a Indian Reservations, United States
Map 107b Indian Reserves, Canada
Map 108 South America: Physical Features
Map 109 South America: Political Divisions
Map 110 Europe: Physical Features
Map 111 Europe: Political Divisions
Map 112 Asia: Physical Features
Map 113 Asia: Political Divisions
Map 114 Africa: Physical Features
Map 115 Africa: Political Divisions
Map 116 Australia and Oceania: Physical Features
Map 117 Australia and Oceania: Political Divisions

Map 105 North America: Physical Features

ARCTIC OCEAN
BEAUFORT SEA
Pt. Barrow
BROOKS RANGE
Arctic Circle
QUEEN ELIZABETH ISLANDS
ELLESMERE ISLAND
BANKS ISLAND
Viscount Melville Sound
VICTORIA ISLAND
BOOTHIA PENINSULA
GREENLAND (DENMARK)
Cape York
Baffin Bay
BAFFIN ISLAND
Davis Strait
Mackenzie R.
Great Bear Lake
Mt. Logan 18,551 ft.
Mt. St. Elias 18,008 ft.
SOUTHAMPTON ISLAND
Hudson Strait
Cape Chidley
UNGAVA PENINSULA
Hudson Bay
Great Slave Lake
SITKA ISLAND
ROCKY CORDILLERAN MOUNTAINS
COAST MOUNTAINS
Peace R.
Athabasca Lake
Reindeer Lake
Athabaska R.
Nelson R.
CANADA
James Bay
LABRADOR PENINSULA
Strait of Belle Isle
Cape Race
QUEEN CHARLOTTE ISLANDS
Saskatchewan R.
N. Saskatchewan R.
S. Saskatchewan R.
Fraser R.
Lake Winnipeg
LAURENTIAN HIGHLANDS
St. Lawrence R.
Gulf of St. Lawrence
CAPE BRETON ISLAND
GASPÉ PENINSULA
VANCOUVER ISLAND
Lake Nipigon
Lake of the Woods
Lake Superior
Montreal
Ottawa
Cape Sable
Mt. Rainier 14,410 ft.
Missouri R.
Yellowstone R.
Columbia R.
CASCADE RANGE
COAST RANGES
Snake R.
GREAT PLAINS
Red R.
Lake Huron
Lake Michigan
L. Ontario
L. Erie
APPALACHIAN MOUNTAINS
Connecticut R.
Cape Cod
Hudson R.
New York
Philadelphia
Delaware R.
Washington, D.C.
Potomac R.
Chesapeake Bay
Roanoke R.
Cape Hatteras
Grand Teton 13,770'
Mt. Shasta 14,162 ft.
Great Salt Lake
MOUNTAINS AND HIGHLANDS
UNITED STATES
Des Moines R.
Chicago
Detroit
Missouri R.
Platte R.
Wabash R.
Ohio R.
Illinois R.
Sacramento R.
San Joaquin R.
GREAT BASIN
SIERRA NEVADA
Mt. Whitney 14,494 ft.
Colorado R.
Pike's Peak 14,110'
Arkansas R.
Canadian R.
Red R.
Mississippi R.
Tennessee R.
Savannah R.
BERMUDA
ATLANTIC OCEAN
Los Angeles
Rio Grande
GUADALUPE ISLAND
Colorado R.
Rio Grande
SIERRA MADRE OCCIDENTAL
SIERRA MADRE ORIENTAL
Gulf of California
Lake Okeechobee
Miami
Straits of Florida
BAHAMAS
Gulf of Mexico
Tropic of Cancer
Cabo San Lucas
Havana
CUBA
DOMINICAN REPUBLIC
HAITI
Yucatan Channel
WEST INDIES
PACIFIC OCEAN
MEXICO
ISLA REVILLAGIGEDO
Campeche Bay
Yucatan Peninsula
JAMAICA
Mexico City
Popocatepetl 17,887 ft.
Orizaba Peak 18,406 ft.
BELIZE
Gulf of Honduras
CARIBBEAN SEA
HONDURAS
GUATEMALA
NICARAGUA
EL SALVADOR
COSTA RICA
PANAMA
Gulf of Panama
ISLA DEL COCO
ISLA DE MALPELO
0 500 1000 Miles
0 500 1000 Kilometers
ST. LAWRENCE ISLAND
Bering Strait
BERING SEA
ALASKA
PRIBILOF ISLANDS
Mt. McKinley 20,320 ft.
ALASKA RANGE
Yukon R.
Fairbanks
Anchorage
Bristol Bay
Mt. Logan 18,551 ft.
YUKON
ALEUTIAN ISLANDS
ALASKA PENINSULA
KODIAK ISLAND
Mt. St. Elias 18,008 ft.
Gulf of Alaska
Juneau
500 Miles
500 Kilometers
KAUAI
NIIHAU
OAHU
HAWAII
MOLOKAI
MAUI
LANAI
KAHOOLAWE
PACIFIC OCEAN
HAWAII
0 50 100 Miles
0 50 100 Kilometers
National capital
City
Elevation
Feet
3000
1500
300
0
Sea level
0
100
1000
Below sea level

Map 106 North America: Political Divisions

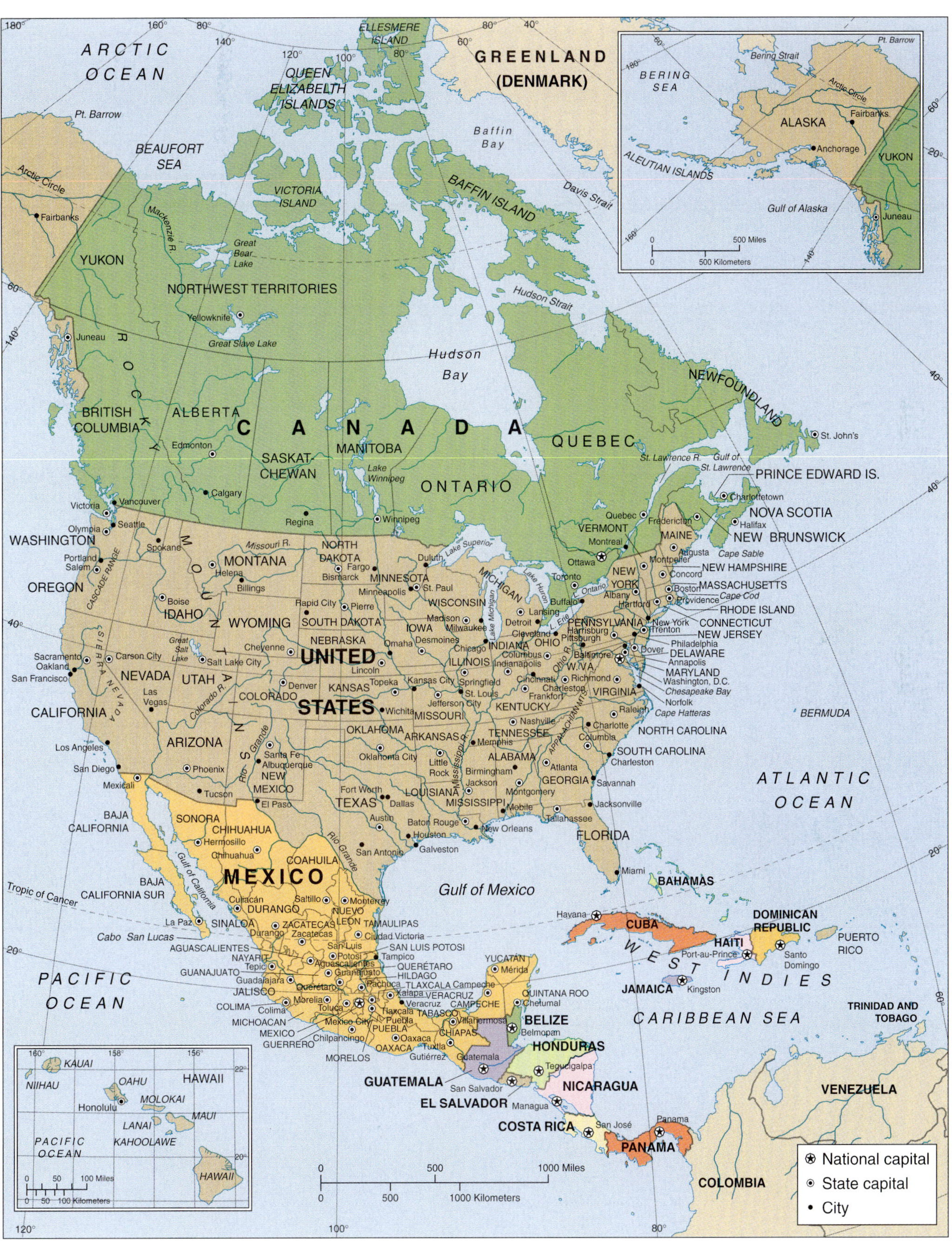

ARCTIC OCEAN
GREENLAND (DENMARK)
QUEEN ELIZABETH ISLANDS
ELLESMERE ISLAND
BEAUFORT SEA
Baffin Bay
BAFFIN ISLAND
VICTORIA ISLAND
YUKON
NORTHWEST TERRITORIES
Hudson Bay
BRITISH COLUMBIA
ALBERTA
SASKATCHEWAN
MANITOBA
ONTARIO
QUEBEC
NEWFOUNDLAND
PRINCE EDWARD IS.
NOVA SCOTIA
NEW BRUNSWICK
CANADA
UNITED STATES
MEXICO
Gulf of Mexico
ATLANTIC OCEAN
PACIFIC OCEAN
CARIBBEAN SEA
WEST INDIES
BAHAMAS
CUBA
HAITI
DOMINICAN REPUBLIC
PUERTO RICO
JAMAICA
BELIZE
GUATEMALA
HONDURAS
EL SALVADOR
NICARAGUA
COSTA RICA
PANAMA
VENEZUELA
COLOMBIA
TRINIDAD AND TOBAGO
BERMUDA
ALASKA
BERING SEA
ALEUTIAN ISLANDS
Gulf of Alaska
HAWAII
National capital
State capital
City
0 500 1000 Miles
0 500 1000 Kilometers

Map 107a Indian Reservations, United States

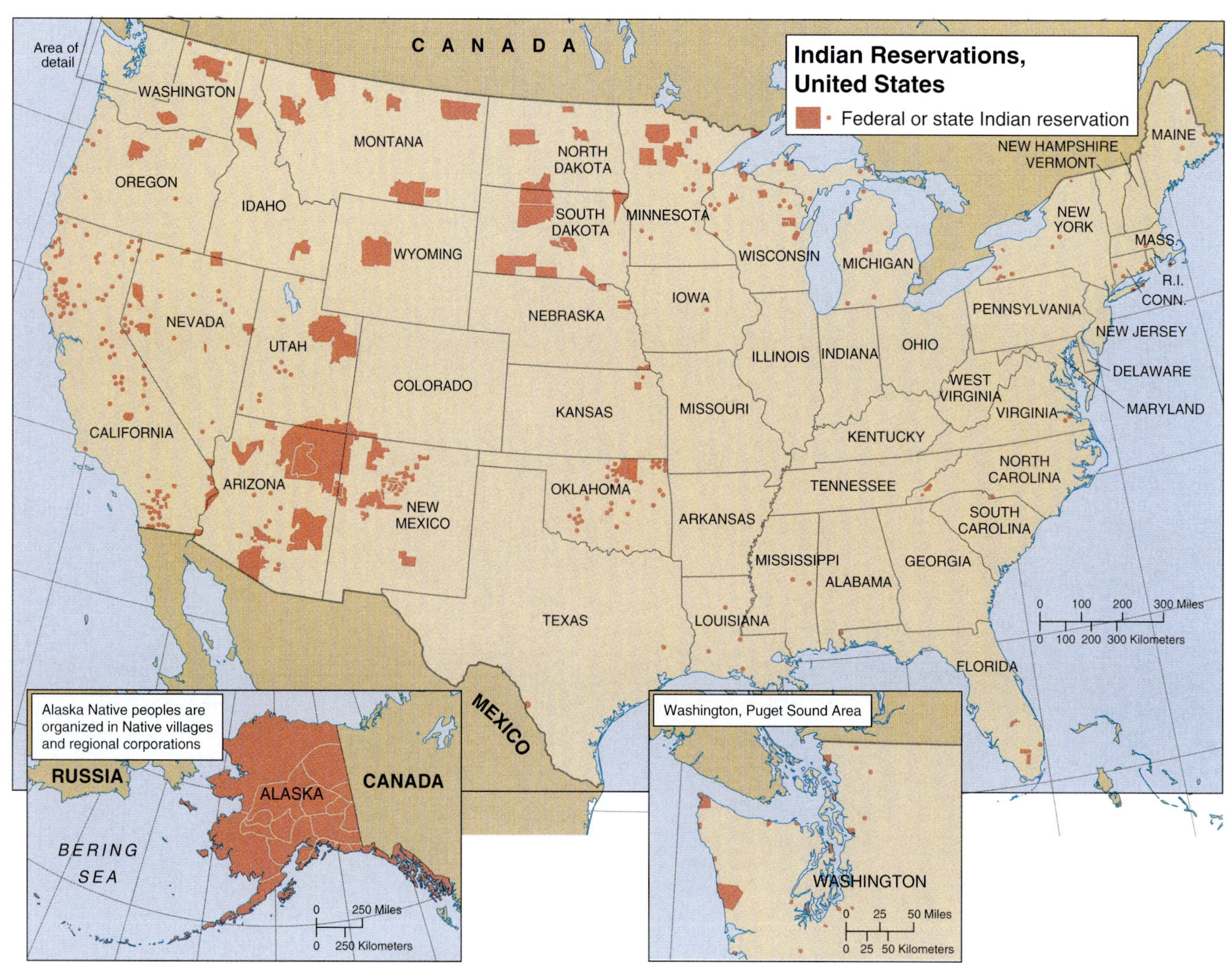

Indian Reservations, United States
Federal or state Indian reservation
CANADA
MEXICO
WASHINGTON
OREGON
CALIFORNIA
NEVADA
IDAHO
MONTANA
WYOMING
UTAH
ARIZONA
COLORADO
NEW MEXICO
NORTH DAKOTA
SOUTH DAKOTA
NEBRASKA
KANSAS
OKLAHOMA
TEXAS
MINNESOTA
IOWA
MISSOURI
ARKANSAS
LOUISIANA
WISCONSIN
ILLINOIS
MICHIGAN
INDIANA
OHIO
KENTUCKY
TENNESSEE
MISSISSIPPI
ALABAMA
GEORGIA
FLORIDA
SOUTH CAROLINA
NORTH CAROLINA
VIRGINIA
WEST VIRGINIA
PENNSYLVANIA
NEW YORK
MAINE
NEW HAMPSHIRE
VERMONT
MASS.
R.I.
CONN.
NEW JERSEY
DELAWARE
MARYLAND
Area of detail
0 100 200 300 Miles
0 100 200 300 Kilometers
Alaska Native peoples are organized in Native villages and regional corporations
RUSSIA
ALASKA
CANADA
BERING SEA
0 250 Miles
0 250 Kilometers
Washington, Puget Sound Area
WASHINGTON
0 25 50 Miles
0 25 50 Kilometers

Tribes with federal or state reservations are shown.

Map 107b Indian Reserves, Canada

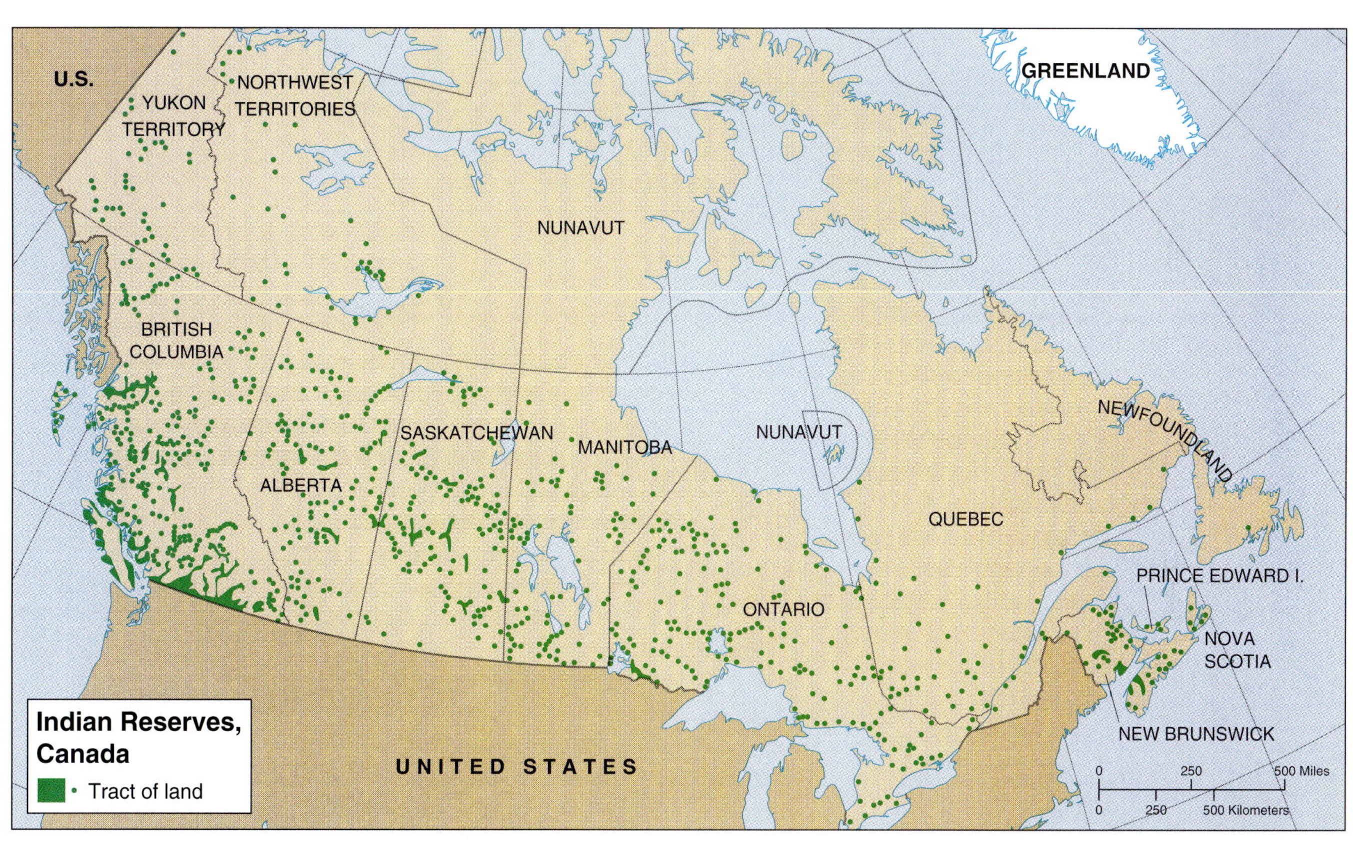
U.S.
YUKON TERRITORY
NORTHWEST TERRITORIES
NUNAVUT
GREENLAND
BRITISH COLUMBIA
ALBERTA
SASKATCHEWAN
MANITOBA
NUNAVUT
NEWFOUNDLAND
QUEBEC
ONTARIO
PRINCE EDWARD I.
NOVA SCOTIA
NEW BRUNSWICK
UNITED STATES
Indian Reserves, Canada
Tract of land
0 250 500 Miles
0 250 500 Kilometers

Dots show the general locations of 2,283 tracts of land held by about 600 First Nations. Inuit and Metis lands are not included. Nunavut is Canada's newest territory, ratified in 1993. Inuit comprise about 85 percent of its population.

Map 108 South America: Physical Features

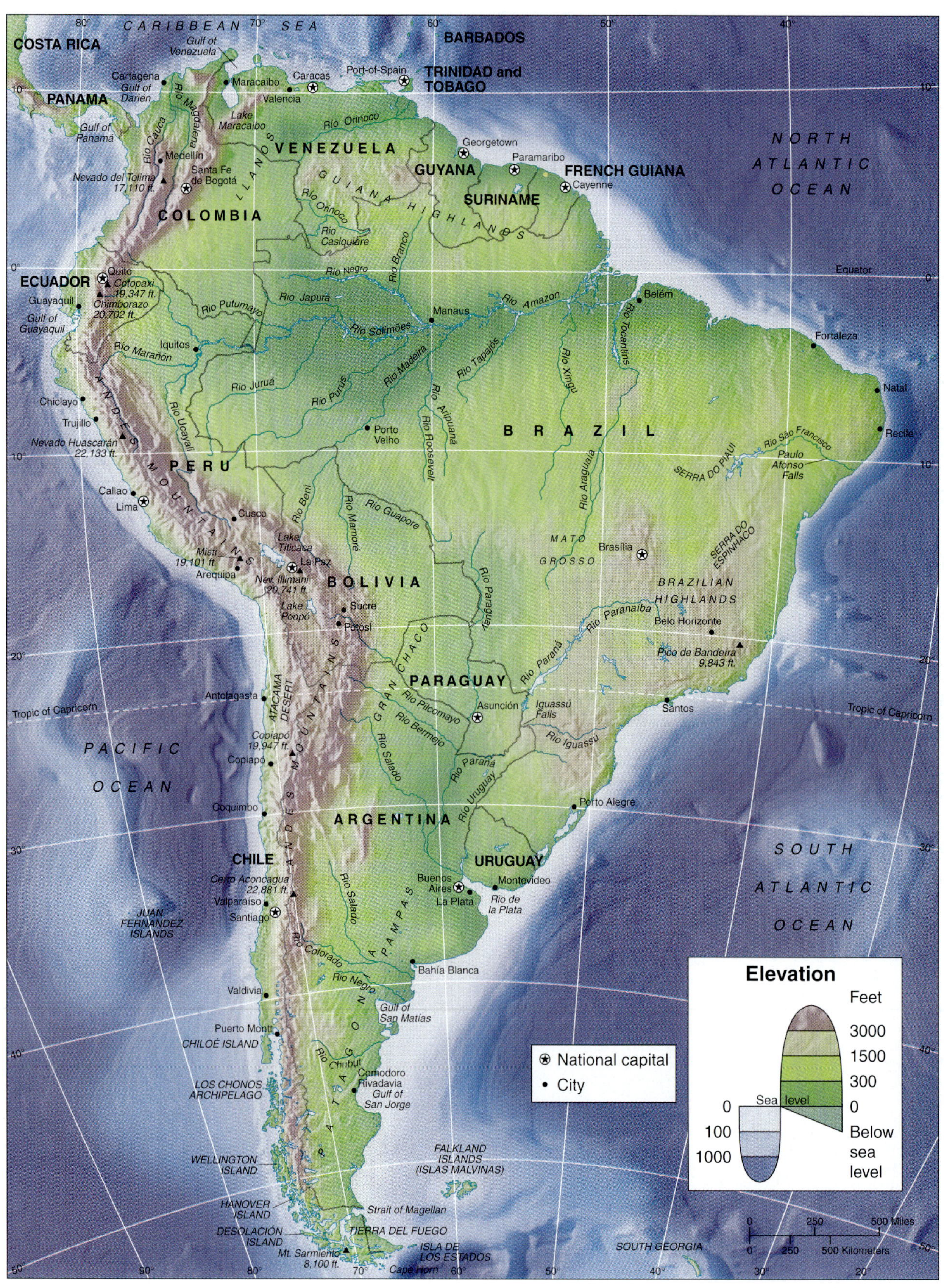

CARIBBEAN SEA
COSTA RICA
Gulf of Venezuela
BARBADOS
Cartagena
Gulf of Darién
Maracaibo
Caracas
Port-of-Spain
TRINIDAD and TOBAGO
PANAMA
Valencia
Lake Maracaibo
Río Orinoco
Gulf of Panamá
Río Cauca
Río Magdalena
Medellín
VENEZUELA
Georgetown
Paramaribo
NORTH ATLANTIC OCEAN
Nevado del Tolima 17,110 ft.
Santa Fe de Bogotá
LLANOS
GUYANA
FRENCH GUIANA
Cayenne
GUIANA HIGHLANDS
SURINAME
Río Orinoco
Río Casiquiare
COLOMBIA
Río Branco
Equator
Río Negro
ECUADOR
Quito
Cotopaxi 19,347 ft.
Chimborazo 20,702 ft.
Guayaquil
Gulf of Guayaquil
Río Putumayo
Río Japurá
Manaus
Río Amazon
Belém
Río Solimões
Río Tocantins
Fortaleza
Iquitos
Río Marañón
Río Xingu
Río Tapajós
Río Madeira
Río Juruá
Río Purús
Río Aripuanã
Natal
Chiclayo
Trujillo
Nevado Huascarán 22,133 ft.
Río Ucayali
Porto Velho
Río Roosevelt
BRAZIL
Recife
Río São Francisco
Paulo Afonso Falls
SERRA DO PIAUÍ
PERU
ANDES MOUNTAINS
Río Araguaia
Callao
Lima
Cusco
Río Beni
Río Mamoré
Río Guaporé
MATO GROSSO
Brasília
SERRA DO ESPINHAÇO
Lake Titicaca
La Paz
Misti 19,101 ft.
Arequipa
Nev. Illimani 20,741 ft.
BOLIVIA
Río Paraguay
BRAZILIAN HIGHLANDS
Lake Poopó
Sucre
Potosí
Río Paranaiba
Belo Horizonte
GRAN CHACO
Pico de Bandeira 9,843 ft.
Río Paraná
PARAGUAY
Antofagasta
ATACAMA DESERT
Asunción
Iguassú Falls
Santos
Tropic of Capricorn
Río Pilcomayo
Río Bermejo
PACIFIC OCEAN
Copiapó 19,947 ft.
Copiapó
Río Iguassú
Río Salado
Río Paraná
Río Uruguay
Coquimbo
Porto Alegre
ARGENTINA
SOUTH ATLANTIC OCEAN
CHILE
URUGUAY
Cerro Aconcagua 22,881 ft.
Buenos Aires
Montevideo
Valparaíso
La Plata
Río de la Plata
JUAN FERNÁNDEZ ISLANDS
Santiago
Río Salado
PAMPAS
Río Colorado
Bahía Blanca
Río Negro
Valdivia
Gulf of San Matías
Puerto Montt
CHILOÉ ISLAND
PATAGONIA
Río Chubut
Comodoro Rivadavia
Gulf of San Jorge
LOS CHONOS ARCHIPELAGO
FALKLAND ISLANDS (ISLAS MALVINAS)
WELLINGTON ISLAND
HANOVER ISLAND
Strait of Magellan
DESOLACIÓN ISLAND
TIERRA DEL FUEGO
Mt. Sarmiento 8,100 ft.
ISLA DE LOS ESTADOS
Cape Horn
SOUTH GEORGIA
National capital
City
Elevation
Feet
3000
1500
300
0
Sea level
0
100
1000
Below sea level
0
250
500 Miles
0
250
500 Kilometers
80°
70°
60°
50°
40°
30°
20°
10°
0°
90°

Map 109 South America: Political Divisions

CARIBBEAN SEA
COSTA RICA
PANAMA
BARBADOS
TRINIDAD and TOBAGO
Port-of-Spain
Caracas
Valencia
Maracaibo
Lake Maracaibo
Gulf of Venezuela
Cartagena
Gulf of Darién
Gulf of Panamá
VENEZUELA
Río Orinoco
GUYANA
Georgetown
SURINAME
Paramaribo
FRENCH GUIANA
Cayenne
NORTH ATLANTIC OCEAN
COLOMBIA
Medellín
Santa Fe de Bogotá
Cali
LLANOS
GUIANA HIGHLANDS
Boa Vista do Rio Branco
RORAIMA
AMAPÁ
Macapá
Equator
ECUADOR
Quito
Guayaquil
Gulf of Guayaquil
Belém
São Luis
Fortaleza
RIO GRANDE DO NORTE
Natal
João Pessoa
Recife
Manaus
Rio Amazon
PARÁ
Rio Xingu
MARANHÃO
Teresina
CEARÁ
PIAUÍ
PARAÍBA
PERNAMBUCO
ALAGOAS
Maceió
SERGIPE
Aracaju
Salvador
BAHIA
Iquitos
AMAZONAS
Rio Madeira
Chiclayo
Trujillo
ACRE
Rio Branco
Porto Velho
RONDÔNIA
BRAZIL
Palmas
TOCANTINS
PERU
ANDES MOUNTAINS
Callao
Lima
Cusco
MATO GROSSO
Cuiabá
GOIÁS
Brasília
Goiânia
BRAZILIAN HIGHLANDS
Lake Titicaca
La Paz
Arequipa
BOLIVIA
Sucre
Potosí
MATO GROSSO DO SUL
Campo Grande
MINAS GERAIS
Belo Horizonte
ESPIRITU SANTO
Vitória
SÃO PAULO
São Paulo
Santos
RIO DE JANEIRO
Rio de Janeiro
Tropic of Capricorn
PARAGUAY
Asunción
Antofagasta
JUJUY
Jujuy
Salta
SALTA
CHACO
FORMOSA
Formosa
Resistencia
SANTIAGO DEL ESTERO
Santiago
TUCUMAN
Tucumán
CATAMARCA
Catamarca
MISIONES
Posadas
Corrientes
CORRIENTES
SANTA FE
PARANÁ
Rio Paraná
Curitiba
SANTA CATARINA
Florianópolis
RIO GRANDE DO SUL
Porto Alegre
PACIFIC OCEAN
Copiapó
Coquimbo
LA RIOJA
La Rioja
SAN JUAN
San Juan
ARGENTINA
Córdoba
CORDOBA
ENTRE RIOS
Paraná
Rosario
URUGUAY
Montevideo
CHILE
San Luis
SAN LUIS
Mendoza
MENDOZA
Buenos Aires
La Plata
Río de la Plata
Valparaíso
Santiago
Santa Rosa
LA PAMPA
PAMPAS
BUENOS AIRES
NEUQUÉN
Neuquén
Río Colorado
Bahía Blanca
RÍO NEGRO
Viedma
Gulf of San Matías
Valdivia
Puerto Montt
Rawson
CHUBUT
Comodoro Rivadavia
Gulf of San Jorge
SOUTH ATLANTIC OCEAN
SANTA CRUZ
FALKLAND ISLANDS (ISLAS MALVINAS)
Río Gallegos
Strait of Magellan
TIERRA DEL FUEGO
ISLA DE LOS ESTADOS
SOUTH GEORGIA
National capital
State capital
City
0 250 500 Miles
0 250 500 Kilometers

Map 110 Europe: Physical Features

Elevation
Feet
3000
1500
300
0
Below sea level
Sea level
0
100
1000
National capital
City
0
250
500 Miles
0
250
500 Kilometers
GREENLAND
ARCTIC OCEAN
Denmark Strait
Arctic Circle
Reykjavik
ICELAND
FAEROE ISLANDS
SHETLAND ISLANDS
ORKNEY ISLANDS
HEBRIDES
UNITED KINGDOM
GRAMPIAN MTS.
NORTH SEA
Firth of Forth
North Channel
IRELAND
IRISH SEA
Dublin
Newcastle
Leeds
Liverpool
Manchester
Birmingham
St. George's Channel
Lands End
Thames R.
London
ISLES OF SCILLY
Strait of Dover
English Channel
NETHERLANDS
The Hague
Amsterdam
Rotterdam
Antwerp
BELGIUM
Brussels
Lille
Bonn
GERMANY
Hamburg
Elbe
Weser R.
Berlin
Frankfurt
ERZGEBIRGE
Prague
CZECH REP.
Luxembourg
LUX.
Rhine R.
Stuttgart
Munich
Seine R.
Paris
FRANCE
Bay of Biscay
SWITZ.
Bern
JURA MTS.
ALPS
MASSIF CENTRAL
Rhone R.
MONACO
Marseille
Monaco
Gulf of Lyon
Gulf of Genoa
Po
Cape Finisterre
PORTUGAL
Lisbon
Madrid
ANDORRA
SPAIN
PYRENEES
Barcelona
BALEARIC IS.
CORSICA
SARDINIA
Cabo De Sao Vicente
Strait of Gibraltar
MADEIRA ISLANDS
CANARY ISLANDS
ATLANTIC OCEAN
NORWAY
Oslo
Vestfjord
SWEDEN
Lake Vanern
Lake Vattern
Stockholm
GOTLAND
OLAND
Skagerrak
Kattegat
DENMARK
Copenhagen
Gulf of Bothnia
FINLAND
Helsinki
Gulf of Finland
Tallinn
ESTONIA
BALTIC SEA
Gulf of Riga
LATVIA
Riga
LITHUANIA
Vilnius
RUSSIA
POLAND
Warsaw
BELARUS
Minsk
PRIPYAT MARSHES
UKRAINE
Kiev
Dnepr R.
Dnipropetrovs'k
SLOVAKIA
Bratislava
Vienna
AUSTRIA
HUNGARY
Budapest
CARPATHIAN MTS.
MOLDOVA
Chisinau
ROMANIA
TRANSYLVANIAN ALPS
Bucharest
SLOVENIA
Ljubljana
Zagreb
CROATIA
Belgrade
BOSNIA AND HERZEGOVINA
Sarajevo
SERBIA AND MONTENEGRO
DINARIC ALPS
Danube R.
BULGARIA
Sofia
Skopje
MACEDONIA
Tirane
ALBANIA
ADRIATIC SEA
ITALY
Rome
APENNINES
Naples
TYRRHENIAN SEA
SICILY
IONIAN SEA
GREECE
Athens
AEGEAN SEA
CRETE
MALTA
MEDITERRANEAN SEA
Tunis
TUNISIA
Algiers
Rabat
ATLAS MOUNTAINS
MOROCCO
ALGERIA
Tripoli
LIBYA
MAURITANIA
EGYPT
Cairo
Nile R.
RED SEA
Istanbul
Bosporus
BLACK SEA
SEA OF AZOV
Ankara
TURKEY
L. Van
Nicosia
CYPRUS
Beirut
LEBANON
ISRAEL
Tel-Aviv
Jerusalem
Amman
JORDAN
Damascus
SYRIA
IRAQ
Baghdad
Tigris R.
Euphrates R.
KUWAIT
Kuwait
Persian Gulf
BAHRAIN
QATAR
Abu Dhabi
UNITED ARAB EMIRATES
SAUDI ARABIA
Riyadh
IRAN
Tehran
ZAGROS MOUNTAINS
ELBURZ MOUNTAINS
AZERBAIJAN
Baku
ARMENIA
Yerevan
GEORGIA
Tbilisi
CAUCASUS
CASPIAN SEA
CASPIAN DEPRESSION
TURKMENISTAN
Ashkhabad
KARAKUMY DESERT
Amu Darya
UZBEKISTAN
ARAL SEA
Syr Darya
KAZAKSTAN
Volgograd
Volga R.
Don R.
Moscow
Nizhniy-Novgorod
Lake Rybinsk
Lake Ladoga
Lake Onega
St. Petersburg
WHITE SEA
Dvina R.
RUSSIA
URAL MOUNTAINS
Yekaterinburg
Chelyabinsk

Map 111 Europe: Political Divisions

National capital
City
GREENLAND
ARCTIC OCEAN
ATLANTIC OCEAN
0 250 500 Miles
0 250 500 Kilometers
ICELAND
Reykjavik
Arctic Circle
Bospor
Murmansk
Gulf of Riga
WHITE SEA
Arkhangelsk
URAL MOUNTAINS
Omsk
Yekaterinburg
Chelyabinsk
RUSSIA
SWEDEN
FINLAND
NORWAY
Gulf of Bothnia
Bergen
Oslo
Stavenger
Uppsala
Stockholm
Goteborg
Turku
Helsinki
Tallinn
ESTONIA
St. Petersburg
Nizhniy-Novgorod
Volga R.
Samara
KAZAKSTAN
Moscow
LATVIA
Riga
BALTIC SEA
UNITED KINGDOM
Glasgow
Belfast
Newcastle
IRISH SEA
Leeds
IRELAND
Dublin
Liverpool
Manchester
Birmingham
London
DENMARK
Copenhagen
LITHUANIA
Vilnius
Minsk
BELARUS
RUSSIA
Kaliningrad
Gdansk
NETHERLANDS
The Hague
Amsterdam
Rotterdam
Antwerp
Hamburg
Berlin
POLAND
Warsaw
Don R.
Volgograd
UZBEKISTAN
Strait of Dover
English Channel
BELGIUM
Brussels
Le Havre
Lille
Essen
Bonn
GERMANY
Frankfurt
Luxembourg
Rhine R.
Prague
Katowice
Kiev
Kharkiv
UKRAINE
Dnipropetrovs'k
Donetsk
Volga R.
Astrakhan
Paris
LUX.
FRANCE
Stuttgart
CZECH REP.
SLOVAKIA
Bratislava
Vienna
Munich
Lyon
SWITZERLAND
Bern
AUSTRIA
Budapest
MOLDOVA
Chisinau
SEA OF AZOV
CASPIAN SEA
TURKMENISTAN
Ashkhabad
Bordeaux
Ljubljana
HUNGARY
Zagreb
SLOVENIA
Milan
Turin
Venice
CROATIA
ROMANIA
Bucharest
Danube R.
Bilbao
Valladolid
ANDORRA
MONACO
Marseille
Monaco
BOSNIA AND HERZEGOVINA
Sarajevo
Belgrade
GEORGIA
Tbilisi
Baku
Yerevan
ARMENIA
AZERBAIJAN
PORTUGAL
Lisbon
Madrid
SPAIN
Valencia
Seville
Barcelona
BALEARIC IS
CORSICA
ITALY
Rome
Naples
ADRIATIC SEA
SERBIA AND MONTENEGRO
Sofia
BULGARIA
Tirane
Skopje
MACEDONIA
ALBANIA
Istanbul
Ankara
Tehran
Strait of Gibraltar
SARDINIA
TYRRHENIAN SEA
GREECE
Athens
AEGEAN SEA
TURKEY
IRAN
Rabat
Algiers
MEDITERRANEAN SEA
IONIAN SEA
Tunis
MALTA
Nicosia
CYPRUS
Beirut
LEBANON
Damascus
SYRIA
Tigris R.
Baghdad
Euphrates R.
IRAQ
TUNISIA
ISRAEL
Tel-Aviv
Jerusalem
Amman
JORDAN
KUWAIT
Kuwait
MOROCCO
Tripoli
ALGERIA
Persian Gulf
BAHRAIN
Abu Dhabi
QATAR
UNITED ARAB EMIRATES
Cairo
SAUDI ARABIA
Riyadh
LIBYA
EGYPT
Nile R.
RED SEA
MAURITANIA
MALI

Map 112 Asia: Physical Features

National capital
City
ATLANTIC OCEAN
ARCTIC OCEAN
ICELAND
GREENLAND
ALASKA (USA)
Bering Strait
ST. LAWRENCE ISLAND
BERING SEA
WRANGELL ISLAND
EAST SIBERIAN SEA
NEW SIBERIAN ISLANDS
LAPTEV SEA
SEVERNAYA ZEMLYA
ZEMLYA FRANTSA IOSIFA
NOVAYA ZEMLYA
SVALBARD
BARENTS SEA
KARA SEA
Arctic Circle
IRELAND
UNITED KINGDOM
London
NORTH SEA
NORWAY
SWEDEN
Gulf of Bothnia
FINLAND
DENMARK
Copenhagen
NETH.
BELG.
Paris
FRANCE
LUX.
GERMANY
Berlin
SWITZ.
ALPS
Danube R.
POLAND
Prague
Warsaw
CZECH REP.
AUSTRIA
Vienna
SLOVENIA
SLOVAKIA
CROATIA
HUNGARY
Budapest
B-H
Rome
ITALY
SERBIA
ROMANIA
MACEDONIA
ALBANIA
Sofiya
BULGARIA
Bucharest
MOLDOVA
GREECE
BALTIC SEA
Stockholm
St.Petersburg
ESTONIA
LATVIA
LITHUANIA
Ladozhkoye Ozero
Onezhkoye Ozero
RUSSIA
Moscow
Rostov
Nizhniy Novgorod
UKRAINE
Kiev
Dnepr R.
Don R.
Donetsk
Rostov na Donu
SEA OF AZOV
BLACK SEA
Istanbul
Ankara
TURKEY
Volga R.
Samara
Arkhangelsk
Sev. Dvina
URAL MOUNTAINS
Yekaterinburg
Ural R.
Astrakhan
CAUCASUS MTS.
Mt. Elbrus 18,510 ft.
GEORGIA
Tbilisi
ARMENIA
Yerevan
Baku
AZERBAIJAN
CASPIAN SEA
MEDITERRANEAN SEA
CYPRUS
LEBANON
ISRAEL
Beirut
Damascus
Aleppo
SYRIA
Alexandria
EGYPT
Cairo
Jerusalem
Tel Aviv
Amman
JORDAN
TOROS DAGLARI
Tabriz
IRAQ
Baghdad
Euphrates R.
Tigris R.
Nile R.
ARABIAN DESERT
RED SEA
AL HIJAZ ASIR
KUWAIT
Kuwait
SAUDI ARABIA
ARABIAN DESERT
Riyadh
BAHRAIN
QATAR
Al Manamah
Ad Dawhah
Persian Gulf
UNITED ARAB EMIRATES
Abu Dhabi
Straits of Hormuz
Gulf of Oman
Muscat
OMAN
RUB AL KHALI
SUDAN
ERITREA
Sanaa
YEMEN
Aden
Bab el Mandeb
DJIBOUTI
Gulf of Aden
ETHIOPIA
SOMALIA
ARABIAN SEA
IRAN
Tehran
ELBURZ MTS.
ZAGROS MTS.
Shiraz
PLATEAU OF IRAN
Mashad
TURKMENISTAN
Ashkabad
UZBEKISTAN
Amu Darya
Syr Darya
ARAL SEA
KIRGHIZ STEPPE
KAZAKSTAN
Akmola
Ishim R.
Irtysh R.
Omsk
Tomsk
Novosibirsk
Krasnoyarsk
Irkutsk
Lake Balkash
Alma-Ata
Gora Kommunizma 24,590 ft.
Tashkent
Samarkand
Dushanbe
Bishkek
KYRGYZSTAN
TAJIKISTAN
PAMIRS
TIEN SHAN
TARIM BASIN
TAKLA MAKAN
ALTUN SHAN
KUNLUN SHAN
AFGHANISTAN
Kabul
HINDU KUSH
KARAKORAM
K2 (Godwin-Austen) 28,250 ft.
Peshawar
Islamabad
Srinagar
Rawalpindi
Lahore
SULAIMAN RANGE
Indus R.
PAKISTAN
Karachi
Gulf of Kutch
GREAT INDIAN DESERT
Nanda Devi 25,645 ft.
Delhi
New Delhi
NEPAL
Kathmandu
Kanchenjunga 28,208 ft.
Mt. Everest 29,028 ft.
HIMALAYAS
PLATEAU OF TIBET
Lhasa
BHUTAN
Thimphu
Brahmaputra R.
Ganges R.
Ahmadabad
INDIA
DECCAN PLATEAU
Gulf of Khambhat
Bombay
WESTERN GHATS
EASTERN GHATS
Godavari R.
Hyderabad
Krishna R.
Bangalore
Madras
Calicut
Gulf of Mannar
Colombo
SRI LANKA
Calcutta
Dhaka
BANGLADESH
Bay of Bengal
ANDAMAN ISLANDS
NICOBAR ISLANDS
INDIAN OCEAN
Equator
WESTERN SIBERIAN LOWLAND
Ob R.
Yenisey R.
Podkammenaya Tunguska
Angara R.
CENTRAL SIBERIAN PLATEAU
RUSSIA
Lena R.
VERKHOYANSKIY RANGE
Indigirka R.
Kolyma R.
GYDAN RANGE
KAMCHATKA RANGE
Klyuchevskaya 15,584 ft.
Okhotsk
SEA OF OKHOTSK
Yakutsk
DZHUGDZHUR MOUNTAINS
STANOVOY MOUNTAINS
Lake Baikal
YABLONOVYY RANGE
SAYAN RANGE
ALTAI MTS.
Komsomolsk
SAKHALIN
Tatar Strait
KURIL ISLANDS
HOKKAIDO
Amur R.
Khabarovsk
SIKHOTE ALIN
GREATER KHINGAN RANGE
Harbin
Vladivostok
Changchun
Ulan Bator
MONGOLIA
GOBI DESERT
SEA OF JAPAN
HONSHU
JAPAN
Tokyo
Yokohama
Kyoto
Osaka
Kobe
SHIKOKU
Kitayushu
KYUSHU
Shenyang
NORTH KOREA
Pyongyang
Seoul
SOUTH KOREA
Korea Strait
Tianjin
Beijing
Qingdao
Huang
Lanzhou
CHINA
Chengdu
Yangtze (Chiang Jiang)
Chongqing
Nanjing
Wuhan
Shanghai
EAST CHINA SEA
NANSEI SHOTO
Fuzhou
Taiwan Strait
Taipei
TAIWAN
PACIFIC OCEAN
Gongga Shan 24,790 ft.
Kunming
Phou Bia 9,249 ft.
NAN LING MTS.
Guangzhou
Hong Kong
Luzon Strait
PHILIPPINE SEA
PHILIPPINES
LUZON
Manila
SAMAR
MINDORO
LEYTE
PANAY
NEGROS
PALAWAN
MINDINAO
SULU SEA
SULU ISLANDS
HALMAHERA
CELEBES SEA
CELEBES
Irrawaddy R.
Mandalay
MYANMAR (BURMA)
Salween R.
Rangoon
Moulmein
THAILAND
Bangkok
Gulf of Thailand
LAOS
Viangchan
Mekong R.
Hanoi
Gulf of Tonkin
Hue
VIETNAM
CAMBODIA
Phnom Penh
Ho Chi Minh
SOUTH CHINA SEA
Bandar Seri Begawan
BRUNEI
Straits of Malacca
Kuala Lumpur
MALAYSIA
SINGAPORE
BORNEO
Elevation
Feet
3000
1500
300
0
Sea level
0
100
1000
Below sea level
0
500
1000 Miles
0
500
1000 Kilometers
MADAGASCAR
THAILAND
Straits of Malacca
Bandar Seri Begawan
BRUNEI
SULU ISLANDS
CELEBES SEA
HALMAHERA
Equator
NEW GUINEA
PAPUA NEW GUINEA
Kuala Lumpur
MALAYSIA
SINGAPORE
BORNEO
CELEBES
SUMATRA
INDONESIA
EAST TIMOR
AUSTRALIA
INDIAN OCEAN
Jakarta
JAVA
0
500
1000 Miles
0
500
1000 Kilometers

Asia: Political Divisions

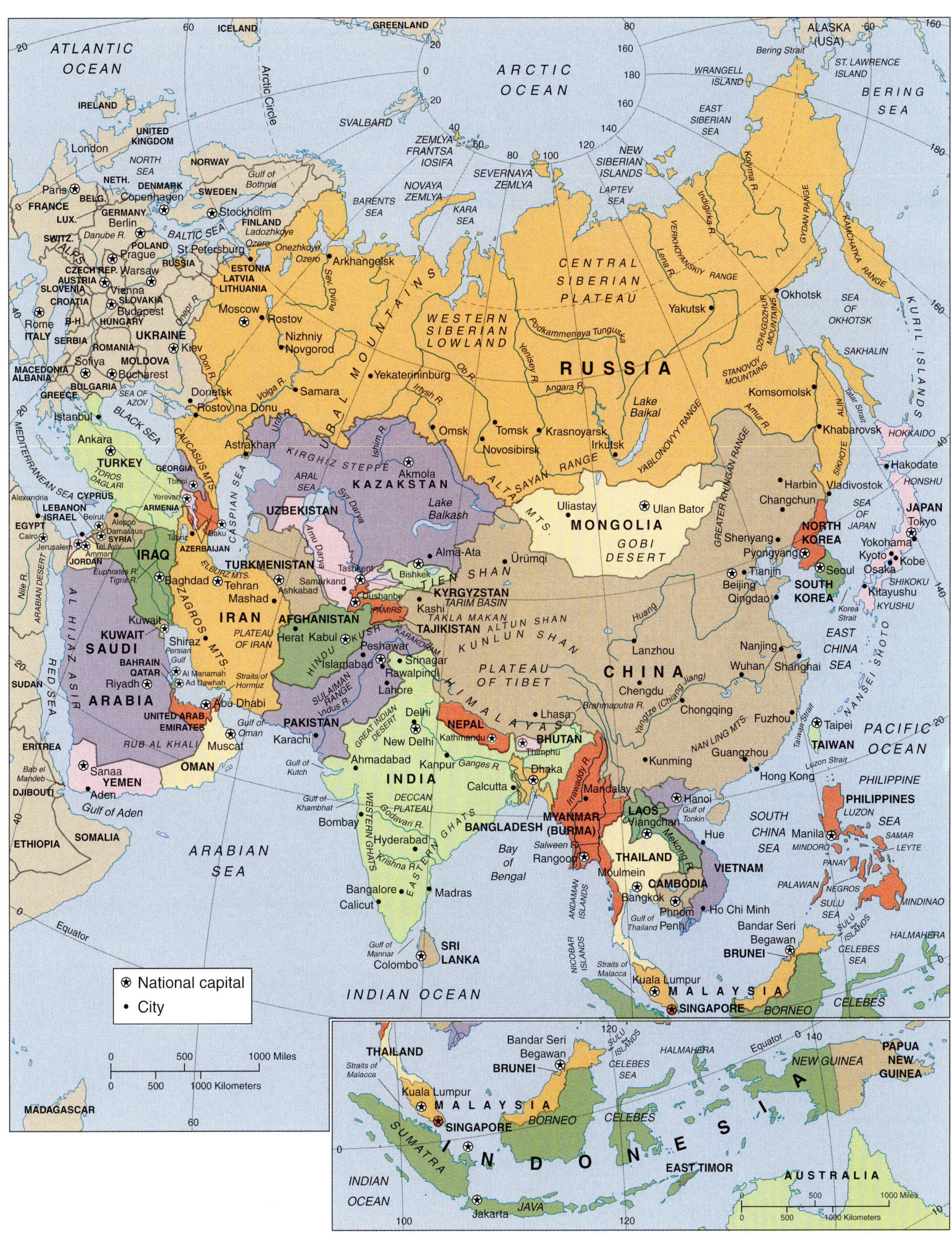
ATLANTIC OCEAN
ARCTIC OCEAN
ICELAND
GREENLAND
ALASKA (USA)
Bering Strait
ST. LAWRENCE ISLAND
BERING SEA
WRANGELL ISLAND
EAST SIBERIAN SEA
NEW SIBERIAN ISLANDS
LAPTEV SEA
SEVERNAYA ZEMLYA
ZEMLYA FRANTSA IOSIFA
SVALBARD
NOVAYA ZEMLYA
BARENTS SEA
KARA SEA
Arctic Circle
IRELAND
UNITED KINGDOM
London
NORTH SEA
NORWAY
SWEDEN
Gulf of Bothnia
FINLAND
Stockholm
DENMARK
Copenhagen
NETH.
BELG.
Paris
FRANCE
LUX.
GERMANY
Berlin
SWITZ.
ALPS
Danube R.
POLAND
Prague
CZECH REP.
Warsaw
AUSTRIA
Vienna
SLOVENIA
CROATIA
SLOVAKIA
Budapest
HUNGARY
B-H
Rome
ITALY
SERBIA
ROMANIA
Sofiya
MOLDOVA
Bucharest
MACEDONIA
ALBANIA
BULGARIA
GREECE
BALTIC SEA
St.Petersburg
ESTONIA
LATVIA
LITHUANIA
RUSSIA
Ladozhkoye Ozero
Onezhkoye Ozero
Arkhangelsk
Sev. Dvina
Moscow
Rostov
Nizhniy Novgorod
Dnepr R.
UKRAINE
Kiev
Don R.
Volga R.
Samara
Donetsk
Rostov na Donu
SEA OF AZOV
BLACK SEA
Istanbul
Ankara
TURKEY
TOROS DAGLARI
CAUCASUS MTS.
GEORGIA
Tbilisi
Yerevan
ARMENIA
Baku
AZERBAIJAN
Tabriz
Astrakhan
Ural R.
CASPIAN SEA
MEDITERRANEAN SEA
CYPRUS
LEBANON
ISRAEL
Beirut
Aleppo
Damascus
SYRIA
Tel Aviv
Amman
Jerusalem
JORDAN
Alexandria
Cairo
EGYPT
Nile R.
ARABIAN DESERT
IRAQ
Euphrates R.
Tigris R.
Baghdad
Tehran
ELBURZ MTS.
IRAN
Mashad
ZAGROS MTS.
PLATEAU OF IRAN
Kuwait
KUWAIT
Shiraz
Persian Gulf
SAUDI ARABIA
AL HIJAZ
ASIR
RED SEA
BAHRAIN
QATAR
Al Manamah
Ad Dawhah
Riyadh
Straits of Hormuz
UNITED ARAB EMIRATES
Abu Dhabi
Gulf of Oman
Muscat
OMAN
RUB AL KHALI
Sanaa
YEMEN
Aden
Gulf of Aden
SUDAN
ERITREA
Bab el Mandeb
DJIBOUTI
ETHIOPIA
SOMALIA
ARABIAN SEA
MADAGASCAR
URAL MOUNTAINS
Yekaterinburg
KIRGHIZ STEPPE
ARAL SEA
Syr Darya
Amu Darya
UZBEKISTAN
TURKMENISTAN
Ashkhabad
Samarkand
Tashkent
Dushanbe
KAZAKSTAN
Akmola
Ishim R.
Lake Balkash
Alma-Ata
Bishkek
KYRGYZSTAN
TAJIKISTAN
PAMIRS
Kashi
AFGHANISTAN
Herat
Kabul
HINDU KUSH
Peshawar
Islamabad
Rawalpindi
Srinagar
KARAKORAM
SULAIMAN RANGE
Indus R.
Lahore
PAKISTAN
Karachi
Gulf of Kutch
WESTERN SIBERIAN LOWLAND
Ob R.
Irtysh R.
Omsk
Tomsk
Novosibirsk
Krasnoyarsk
Irkutsk
ALTAI MTS.
SAYAN RANGE
Yenisey R.
Podkammenaya Tunguska
Angara R.
CENTRAL SIBERIAN PLATEAU
RUSSIA
Lena R.
Yakutsk
VERKHOYANSKIY RANGE
Indigirka R.
Kolyma R.
GYDAN RANGE
KAMCHATKA RANGE
Okhotsk
SEA OF OKHOTSK
DZHUGDZHUR MOUNTAINS
STANOVOY MOUNTAINS
Lake Baikal
YABLONOVYY RANGE
Komsomolsk
Amur R.
SAKHALIN
KURIL ISLANDS
Tatar Strait
ALIN
SIKHOTE
Khabarovsk
HOKKAIDO
Hakodate
HONSHU
Vladivostok
Harbin
Changchun
GREATER KHINGAN RANGE
Uliastay
Ulan Bator
MONGOLIA
GOBI DESERT
Ürümqi
TIEN SHAN
TARIM BASIN
TAKLA MAKAN
ALTUN SHAN
KUNLUN SHAN
PLATEAU OF TIBET
HIMALAYAS
Lhasa
Brahmaputra R.
CHINA
Huang
Lanzhou
Chengdu
Chongqing
Yangtze (Chiang Jiang)
Nanjing
Wuhan
Shanghai
Shenyang
Pyongyang
NORTH KOREA
Seoul
SOUTH KOREA
Beijing
Tianjin
Qingdao
SEA OF JAPAN
JAPAN
Tokyo
Yokohama
Kyoto
Kobe
Osaka
Kitayushu
SHIKOKU
KYUSHU
Korea Strait
EAST CHINA SEA
NANSEI SHOTO
Fuzhou
Taiwan Strait
Taipei
TAIWAN
PACIFIC OCEAN
NAN LING MTS.
Guangzhou
Kunming
Hong Kong
Luzon Strait
PHILIPPINE SEA
PHILIPPINES
LUZON
Manila
MINDORO
SAMAR
LEYTE
PANAY
NEGROS
PALAWAN
MINDINAO
SULU SEA
SULU ISLANDS
CELEBES SEA
HALMAHERA
SOUTH CHINA SEA
Gulf of Tonkin
Hanoi
LAOS
Viangchan
Hue
Mekong R.
VIETNAM
Ho Chi Minh
CAMBODIA
Phnom Penh
Gulf of Thailand
THAILAND
Bangkok
Moulmein
Rangoon
Salween R.
MYANMAR (BURMA)
Mandalay
Irrawaddy R.
ANDAMAN ISLANDS
NICOBAR ISLANDS
Straits of Malacca
Kuala Lumpur
MALAYSIA
SINGAPORE
BORNEO
CELEBES
Bandar Seri Begawan
BRUNEI
NEPAL
Kathmandu
BHUTAN
Thimphu
Delhi
New Delhi
GREAT INDIAN DESERT
Kanpur
Ganges R.
Dhaka
Calcutta
BANGLADESH
Bay of Bengal
Ahmadabad
INDIA
Gulf of Khambhat
DECCAN PLATEAU
Bombay
WESTERN GHATS
EASTERN GHATS
Godavari R.
Hyderabad
Krishna R.
Bangalore
Madras
Calicut
Gulf of Mannar
Colombo
SRI LANKA
INDIAN OCEAN
Equator
National capital
City
500
1000 Miles
1000 Kilometers
THAILAND
Straits of Malacca
Kuala Lumpur
MALAYSIA
SINGAPORE
BORNEO
Bandar Seri Begawan
BRUNEI
SULU ISLANDS
CELEBES SEA
HALMAHERA
Equator
NEW GUINEA
PAPUA NEW GUINEA
CELEBES
SUMATRA
INDONESIA
EAST TIMOR
JAVA
Jakarta
INDIAN OCEAN
AUSTRALIA

Map 114 Africa: Physical Features

ATLANTIC OCEAN
PORTUGAL
SPAIN
FRANCE
ITALY
SERBIA
BULGARIA
ALBANIA
MACEDONIA
GREECE
BLACK SEA
RUSSIA
GEORGIA
ARMENIA
AZERBAIJAN
CASPIAN SEA
TURKEY
ASIA MINOR
TURKMENISTAN
IRAN
CYPRUS
SYRIA
LEBANON
ISRAEL
IRAQ
JORDAN
KUWAIT
Persian Gulf
SAUDI ARABIA
ARABIAN PENINSULA
BAHRAIN
QATAR
UNITED ARAB EMIRATES
YEMEN
Gulf of Aden
Strait of Gibraltar
MEDITERRANEAN SEA
Algiers
Tunis
TUNISIA
Gulf of Gabes
Rabat
MOROCCO
Jebel Toubkal 13,665 ft.
ATLAS MOUNTAINS
CANARY ISLANDS
GRAND ERG OCCIDENTAL
ERG IGUIDI
ALGERIA
Tripoli
Khalij Bay
Banghazi
Alexandria
Cairo
Al Fayyum
LIBYA
LIBYAN DESERT
Asyut
Nile R.
ARABIAN DESERT
SINAI PENINSULA
EGYPT
Aswan
Lake Nasser
RED SEA
NUBIAN DESERT
Al Khufra Oasis
WESTERN SAHARA
Tropic of Cancer
Dakhla
EL DJOUF
AHAGGAR MTS
Mt. Tahat 9,541 ft.
Cape Blanc
MAURITANIA
Nouakchott
Cape Vert
MALI
SAHARA
Pic Tousidé 10,712 ft.
TIBESTI MASSIF
SAHEL
Tombouctou
Sénégal R.
SENEGAL
Dakar
Gambie R.
GAMBIA
Banjul
Bissau
GUINEA-BISSAU
GUINEA
Conakry
Freetown
SIERRA LEONE
Monrovia
LIBERIA
Niger R.
NIGER
CHAD
Bur Sudan
ERITREA
Asmera
Bamako
BURKINA FASO
Niamey
Ouagadougou
Lake Chad
Kano
N'Djamena
Omdurman
Khartoum
DARFUR
Al Fashir
Jabal Marrah 10,131 ft.
Bab el Mandeb
Black Volta R.
White Volta R.
BENIN
NIGERIA
Abuja
Ras Dashen Terara 15,158 ft.
DJIBOUTI
Djibouti
Gees Gwardafuy
IVORY COAST
GHANA
TOGO
Lake Volta
Ibadan
Benue R.
Logone R.
Chari R.
SUDAN
Blue Nile
White Nile
Addis Ababa
Harer
Hargeysa
ETHIOPIAN PLATEAU
ETHIOPIA
SOMALIA
SUDD
Mountain Nile
Abidjan
Accra
Lomé
Porto Novo
Lagos
Cape Palmas
Volta R.
Gulf of Guinea
CAMEROON
CENTRAL AFRICAN REPUBLIC
Bangui
Douala
Malabo
Yaoundé
EQUATORIAL GUINEA
Equator
SÃO TOMÉ AND PRINCIPE
Libreville
Cape Lopez
GABON
Ubangi R.
Uele R.
CONGO BASIN
Congo R.
RUWENZORI MTS.
Lake Albert
UGANDA
Lake Rudolf
Jubba R.
Mogadishu
Kisangani
Kampala
Mt. Elgon 14,178 ft.
KENYA
Mt. Kenya 17,058 ft.
Lake Edward
Lake Victoria
CONGO REPUBLIC
DEMOCRATIC REPUBLIC OF THE CONGO
RWANDA
Kigali
Nairobi
Brazzaville
Kinshasa
Kasai R.
Boma
Bujumbura
BURUNDI
Mt. Kilimanjaro 19,340 ft.
MASAI STEPPE
Mombasa
INDIAN OCEAN
ZANZIBAR
Dodoma
Lake Tanganyika
Dar es Salaam
Cuango R.
Luanda
ASCENSION ISLAND
ATLANTIC OCEAN
TANZANIA
ALDABRA ISLANDS
COSMOLEDO ISLANDS
Lake Nyasa
ANGOLA
Lubumbashi
Benguela
Ruvuma R.
COMOROS
Moroni
Cape d'Ambre
MALAWI
Lilongwe
ZAMBIA
Lusaka
Zambezi R.
Moçambique
Mozambique Channel
Namibe
Cubango R.
ST. HELENA
Cape Fria
Okavongo R.
Harare
Okavango Swamp
ZIMBABWE
MOZAMBIQUE
Toamasino
Antananarivo
MADAGASCAR
NAMIBIA
Windhoek
BOTSWANA
Limpopo R.
Tropic of Capricorn
Walvis Bay
Kalahari Desert
Gaborone
GREAT NAMALAND
Pretoria
Johannesburg
Maputo
Mbabane
Vaal R.
Kimberly
SWAZILAND
Maseru
LESOTHO
DRAKENSBERG
Durban
SOUTH AFRICA
Cape Ste. Marie
Cape Town
Cape of Good Hope
Cape Agulhas
Port Elizabeth
Elevation
Feet
3000
1500
300
0
Sea level
0
100
1000
Below sea level
National capital
City
0 250 500 750 1000 Miles
0 250 500 750 1000 Kilometers

Map 115 Africa: Political Divisions

ATLANTIC OCEAN
MEDITERRANEAN SEA
INDIAN OCEAN
Gulf of Guinea
MOROCCO
ALGERIA
TUNISIA
LIBYA
EGYPT
WESTERN SAHARA
MAURITANIA
MALI
NIGER
CHAD
SUDAN
ERITREA
DJIBOUTI
ETHIOPIA
SOMALIA
SENEGAL
GAMBIA
GUINEA-BISSAU
GUINEA
SIERRA LEONE
LIBERIA
IVORY COAST
BURKINA FASO
GHANA
TOGO
BENIN
NIGERIA
CAMEROON
CENTRAL AFRICAN REPUBLIC
EQUATORIAL GUINEA
SÃO TOMÉ AND PRINCIPE
GABON
CONGO REPUBLIC
DEMOCRATIC REPUBLIC OF THE CONGO
UGANDA
KENYA
RWANDA
BURUNDI
TANZANIA
ANGOLA
ZAMBIA
MALAWI
MOZAMBIQUE
ZIMBABWE
NAMIBIA
BOTSWANA
SOUTH AFRICA
LESOTHO
SWAZILAND
MADAGASCAR
COMOROS
National capital
City
0 250 500 750 1000 Miles
0 250 500 750 1000 Kilometers

Map 116 Australia and Oceania: Physical Features

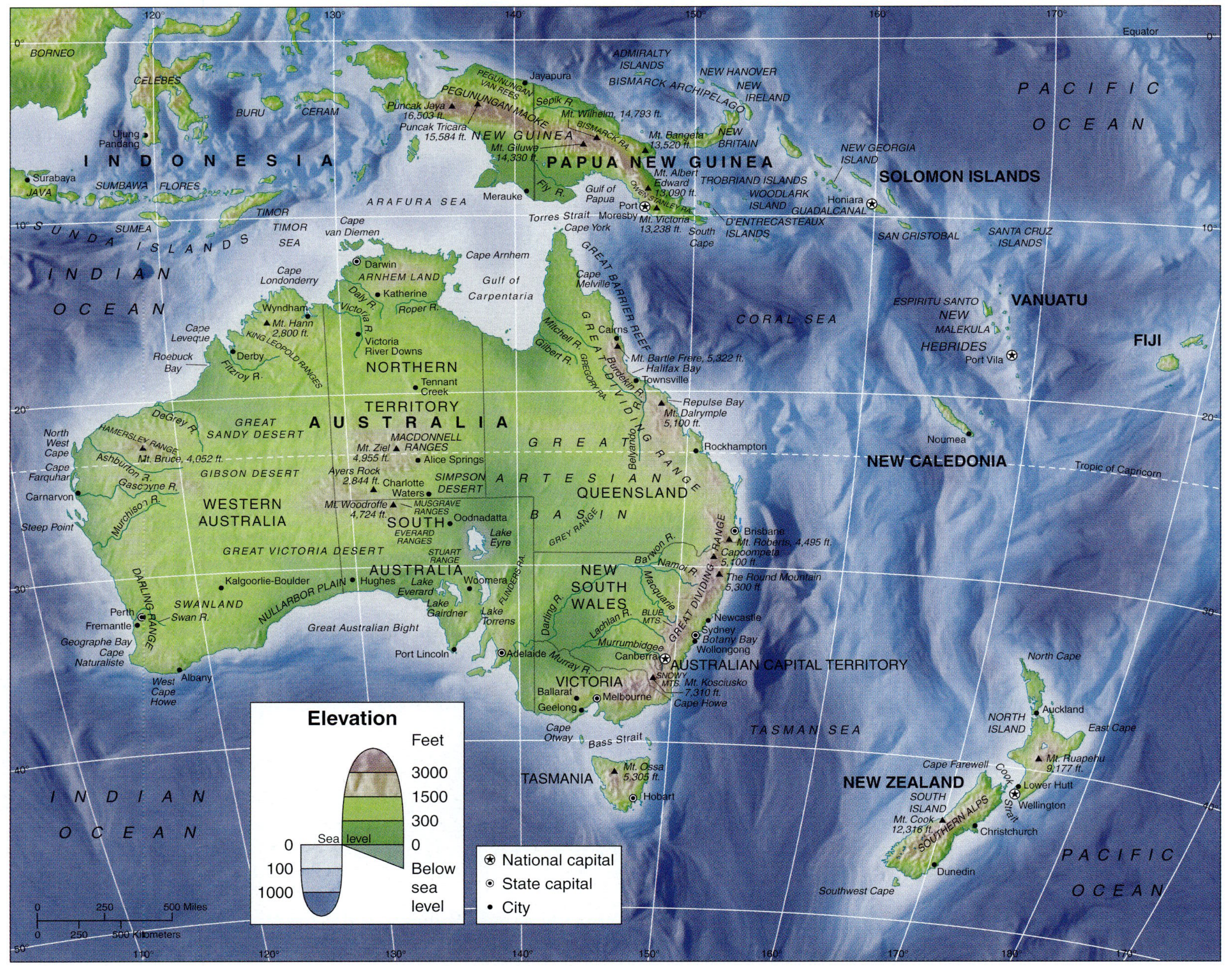

PACIFIC OCEAN
INDIAN OCEAN
INDONESIA
PAPUA NEW GUINEA
NEW GUINEA
SOLOMON ISLANDS
VANUATU
FIJI
NEW CALEDONIA
NEW ZEALAND
AUSTRALIA
WESTERN AUSTRALIA
NORTHERN TERRITORY
SOUTH AUSTRALIA
QUEENSLAND
NEW SOUTH WALES
VICTORIA
TASMANIA
AUSTRALIAN CAPITAL TERRITORY
BORNEO
CELEBES
BURU
CERAM
JAVA
SUMBAWA
FLORES
SUMEA
TIMOR
SUNDA ISLANDS
TIMOR SEA
ARAFURA SEA
CORAL SEA
TASMAN SEA
Gulf of Carpentaria
Gulf of Papua
Torres Strait
Bass Strait
Cook Strait
Great Australian Bight
ADMIRALTY ISLANDS
BISMARCK ARCHIPELAGO
NEW HANOVER
NEW IRELAND
NEW BRITAIN
NEW GEORGIA ISLAND
TROBRIAND ISLANDS
WOODLARK ISLAND
GUADALCANAL
D'ENTRECASTEAUX ISLANDS
SAN CRISTOBAL
SANTA CRUZ ISLANDS
ESPIRITU SANTO
NEW MALEKULA
HEBRIDES
NORTH ISLAND
SOUTH ISLAND
GREAT BARRIER REEF
GREAT DIVIDING RANGE
GREAT ARTESIAN BASIN
GREAT SANDY DESERT
GIBSON DESERT
GREAT VICTORIA DESERT
SIMPSON DESERT
NULLARBOR PLAIN
SWANLAND
ARNHEM LAND
MACDONNELL RANGES
MUSGRAVE RANGES
EVERARD RANGES
STUART RANGE
FLINDERS RA.
GREY RANGE
GREGORY RA.
KING LEOPOLD RANGES
HAMERSLEY RANGE
DARLING RANGE
BLUE MTS.
SNOWY MTS.
SOUTHERN ALPS
PEGUNUNGAN VAN REES
PEGUNUNGAN MAOKE
BISMARCK RA.
OWEN STANLEY RA.
Puncak Jaya 16,503 ft.
Puncak Tricara 15,584 ft.
Mt. Wilhelm 14,793 ft.
Mt. Giluwe 14,330 ft.
Mt. Bangeta 13,520 ft.
Mt. Albert Edward 13,090 ft.
Mt. Victoria 13,238 ft.
Mt. Hann 2,800 ft.
Mt. Bruce 4,052 ft.
Mt. Ziel 4,955 ft.
Ayers Rock 2,844 ft.
Mt. Woodroffe 4,724 ft.
Mt. Bartle Frere 5,322 ft.
Mt. Dalrymple 5,100 ft.
Mt. Roberts 4,495 ft.
Capoompeta 5,100 ft.
The Round Mountain 5,300 ft.
Mt. Kosciusko 7,310 ft.
Mt. Ossa 5,305 ft.
Mt. Ruapehu 9,177 ft.
Mt. Cook 12,316 ft.
Sepik R.
Fly R.
DeGrey R.
Ashburton R.
Gascoyne R.
Murchison R.
Swan R.
Fitzroy R.
Victoria R.
Daly R.
Roper R.
Mitchell R.
Gilbert R.
Burdekin R.
Belyando
Barwon R.
Namoi R.
Macquarie
Darling R.
Lachlan R.
Murrumbidgee
Murray R.
Lake Eyre
Lake Torrens
Lake Gairdner
Lake Everard
Jayapura
Merauke
Port Moresby
Honiara
Port Vila
Noumea
Ujung Pandang
Surabaya
Darwin
Katherine
Victoria River Downs
Tennant Creek
Alice Springs
Charlotte Waters
Oodnadatta
Wyndham
Derby
Roebuck Bay
Carnarvon
Perth
Fremantle
Kalgoorlie-Boulder
Hughes
Woomera
Albany
Port Lincoln
Adelaide
Ballarat
Geelong
Melbourne
Canberra
Wollongong
Botany Bay
Sydney
Newcastle
Brisbane
Rockhampton
Repulse Bay
Halifax Bay
Townsville
Cairns
Hobart
Auckland
Lower Hutt
Wellington
Christchurch
Dunedin
Cape York
Cape Melville
Cape Arnhem
Cape van Diemen
Cape Londonderry
Cape Leveque
North West Cape
Cape Farquhar
Steep Point
Geographe Bay
Cape Naturaliste
West Cape Howe
Cape Otway
Cape Howe
South Cape
North Cape
East Cape
Cape Farewell
Southwest Cape
Equator
Tropic of Capricorn
Elevation
Feet
3000
1500
300
0
Below sea level
Sea level
0
100
1000
National capital
State capital
City
0 250 500 Miles
0 250 500 Kilometers

Map 117 Australia and Oceania: Political Divisions

INDONESIA
PAPUA NEW GUINEA
SOLOMON ISLANDS
VANUATU
FIJI
NEW CALEDONIA
AUSTRALIA
NEW ZEALAND
WESTERN AUSTRALIA
NORTHERN TERRITORY
SOUTH AUSTRALIA
QUEENSLAND
NEW SOUTH WALES
VICTORIA
AUSTRALIAN CAPITAL TERRITORY
TASMANIA
SOUTH ISLAND
BORNEO
NEW GUINEA
BISMARCK ARCHIPELAGO
SUMBA
FLORES
TIMOR SEA
ARAFURA SEA
CORAL SEA
INDIAN OCEAN
NEW HEBRIDES
Equator
Tropic of Capricorn
Torres Strait
Bass Strait
Cook Strait
Gulf of
Repulse Ba
South Cape
Southwest Cape
Cape Naturaliste
Steep P
GIBSON DESERT
GREAT SAND
NULLARBOR PLAIN
GREAT DIVIDING RANGE
GREAT BARRIER REEF
KING LEOPOLD RANGES
HAMERSLEY RANGE
DARLING RANGE
FLINDERS RA.
GREY RANGE
GREGORY RA.
OWEN STANLEY RA.
BISMARCK RA.
PEGUNUNGAN MAOKE
PEGUNUNGAN VAN REES
SOUTHERN ALPS
BLUE MTS
MUSGRAVE
Sepik R.
Fly R.
Daly R.
Victoria R.
Roper R.
Fitzroy R.
DeGrey R.
Ashburton R.
Gascoyne R.
Murchison R.
Swan R.
Mitchell R.
Gilbert R.
Burdekin R.
Darling R.
Lachlan R.
Murrumbidgee
Murray R.
Macquarie
Namoi R.
Barwon R.
Surabaya
Ujung Pandang
Jayapura
Merauke
Port Moresby
Honiara
Port Vila
Suva
Noumea
Darwin
Katherine
Wyndham
Derby
Victoria River Downs
Tennant Creek
Alice Springs
Charlotte Waters
Oodnadatta
Carnarvon
Perth
Fremantle
Albany
Kalgoorlie-Boulder
Hughes
Woomera
Port Lincoln
Adelaide
Melbourne
Ballarat
Geelong
Canberra
Sydney
Wollongong
Newcastle
Brisbane
Rockhampton
Townsville
Cairns
Hobart
Auckland
Lower Hutt
Wellington
Christchurch
Dunedin
National capital
State capital
City
0 250 500 Miles
0 250 500 Kilometers

Part VIII

Geographic Index

Name/Description	Latitude & Longitude	Page	Name/Description	Latitude & Longitude	Page
Abidjan, Cote d'Ivoire (city,nat. cap.)	5N 4W	157	Albert, Lake	2N 30E	156
Abu Dhabi, U.A.E. (city, nat. cap.)	24N 54E	113	Alberta (prov., Can.)	55N 117W	147
Accra, Ghana (city, nat. cap.)	64N 0	157	Albuquerque, NM (city)	35N 107W	147
Aconcagua, Mt. 22,881	38S 78W	150	Aldabra Islands	9S 44E	156
Acre (st., Brazil)	9S 70W	151	Aleppo, Syria (city)	36N 37E	113
Addis Ababa, Ethiopia (city, nat. cap.)	9N 39E	157	Aleutian Islands	55N 175W	146
Adelaide, S. Australia (city, st. cap., Aust.)	35S 139E	159	Alexandria, Egypt (city)	31N 30E	157
Aden, Gulf of	12N 46E	112	Algeria (country)	28N 15E	157
Aden, Yemen (city)	13N 45E	113	Algiers, Algeria (city, nat. cap.)	37N 3E	157
Admiralty Islands	1S 146E	158	Alice Springs, Aust. (city)	24S 134E	159
Adriatic Sea	44N 14E	152	Alma Ata, Kazakhstan (city, nat. cap.)	43N 77E	113
Aegean Sea	39N 25E	152	Alps Mountains	46N 6E	152
Afghanistan (country)	35N 65E	113	Altai Mountains	49N 87E	112
Aguascalientes (st., Mex.)	22N 110W	150	Altun Shan	45N 90E	112
Aguascalientes, Aguas (city, st. cap., Mex.)	22N 102W	150	Amapa (st., Brazil)	2N 52W	151
Agulhas, Cape	35S 20E	156	Amazon (riv., S. Am.)	2S 53W	150
Ahaggar Range	23N 6E	156	Amazonas (st., Brazil)	2S 64W	151
Ahmadabad, India (city)	23N 73E	113	Amman, Jordan (city, nat. cap.)	32N 36E	113
Akmola, Kazakhstan (city)	51N 72E	113	Amsterdam, Netherlands (city)	52N 5E	153
Al Fashir, Sudan (city)	14N 25E	157	Amu Darya (riv., Asia)	40N 62E	112
Al Fayyum, Egypt (city)	29N 31E	157	Amur (riv., Asia)	52N 156E	112
Al Hijaz Range	30N 40E	112	Anchorage, AK (city)	61N 150W	147 inset
Al Khufra Oasis	24N 23E	156	Andaman Islands	12N 92E	113
Alabama (st., US)	33N 87W	147	Andes Mountains	25S 70W	150
Alagoas (st., Brazil)	9S 37W	151	Angara (riv., Asia)	60N 100E	112
Alaska (st., US)	63N 153W	147 inset	Angola (country)	11S 18E	157
Alaska, Gulf of	58N 150W	147 inset	Ankara, Turkey (city, nat. cap.)	40N 33E	113
Alaska Peninsula	57N 155W	146 inset	Annapolis, Maryland (city, st. cap., US)	39N 76W	147
Alaska Range	60N 150W	146 inset	Antananarivo, Madagascar (city, nat. cap.)	19S 48E	157
Albania (country)	41N 20E	153	Antofogasta, Chile (city)	24S 70W	151
Albany, Australia (city)	35S 118E	159	Antwerp, Belgium (city)	51N 4E	153
Albany, New York (city, st. cap., US)	43N 74W	147	Appalachian Mountains	37N 80W	146
Albert Edward, Mt. 13,090	8S 147E	158	Appenines Mountains	32N 14E	152

The geographic index contains approximately 1,500 names of cities, states, countries, rivers, lakes, mountain ranges, oceans, capes, bays, and other geographic features. The name of each geographical feature in the index is accompanied by a geographical coordinate (latitude and longitude) in degrees and by the page number of the primary map on which the geographical feature appears. Where the geographical coordinates are for specific places or points, such as a city or a mountain peak, the latitude and longitude figures give the location of the map symbol denoting that point. Thus, Los Angeles, California, is at 34N and 118W and the location of Mt. Everest is 28N and 87E.

The coordinates for political features (countries or states) or physical features (oceans, deserts) that are areas rather than points are given according to the location of the name of the feature on the map, except in those cases where the name of the feature is separated from the feature (such as a country's name appearing over an adjacent ocean area because of space requirements). In such cases, the feature's coordinates will indicate the location of the center of the feature. The coordinates for the Sahara Desert will lead the reader to the place name "Sahara Desert" on the map; the coordinates for North Carolina will show the center location of the state since the name appears over the adjacent Atlantic Ocean. Finally, the coordinates for geographical features that are lines rather than points or areas will also appear near the center of the text identifying the geographical feature.

Alphabetizing follows general conventions; the names of physical features such as lakes, rivers, mountains are given as: proper name, followed by the generic name. Thus "Mount Everest" is listed as "Everest, Mt." Where an article such as "the," "le," or "al" appears in a geographic name, the name is alphabetized according to the article. Hence, "La Paz" is found under "L" and not under "P."

Geographic Index

Name/Description	Latitude & Longitude	Page	Name/Description	Latitude & Longitude	Page
Arabian Desert	25N 33E	152	Bahia Blanca, Argentina (city)	39S 62W	151
Arabian Peninsula	23N 40E	158	Baikal, Lake	52N 105E	112
Arabian Sea	18N 61E	112	Baja California (st., Mex.)	30N 110W	147
Aracaju, Sergipe (city, st. cap., Braz.)	11S 37W	151	Baja California Sur (st., Mex.)	25N 110W	147
Arafura Sea	9S 133E	158	Baku, Azerbaijan (city, nat. cap.)	40N 50E	153
Araguaia, Rio (riv., Brazil)	13S 50W	150	Balearic Islands	29N 3E	153
Aral Sea	45N 60E	112	Balkash, Lake	47N 75E	112
Arctic Ocean	75N 160W	151	Ballarat, Aust. (city)	38S 144E	159
Arequipa, Peru (city)	16S 71W	151	Baltic Sea	56N 18E	152
Argentina (country)	39S 67W	151	Baltimore, MD (city)	39N 77W	112
Aripuana, Rio (riv., S.Am.)	11S 60W	150	Bamako, Mali (city, nat. cap.)	13N 8W	157
Arizona (st., US)	34N 112W	147	Bandiera Peak 9,843	20S 42W	150
Arkansas (riv., N.Am.)	38N 100W	146	Bangalore, India (city)	13N 75E	113
Arkansas (st., US)	37N 94W	147	Bangeta, Mt. 13,520	6S 147E	158
Arkhangelsk, Russia (city)	75N 160W	153	Banghazi, Libya (city)	32N 20E	157
Armenia (country)	40N 45E	153	Bangkok, Thailand (city, nat. cap.)	14N 100E	113
Arnhem, Cape	11S 139E	158	Bangladesh (country)	23N 92E	113
Arnhem Land	12S 133E	158	Bangui, Cent. African Rep. (city, nat. cap.)	4N 19E	157
As Sudd	9N 26E	156	Banjul, Gambia (city, nat. cap.)	13N 17W	157
Ascension (island)	9S 13W	156	Banks Island	73N 125W	146
Ashburton (riv., Australasia)	23S 115W	112	Barbados (island)	13N 60W	151
Ashkhabad, Turkmenistan (city, nat. cap.)	38N 58E	113	Barcelona, Spain (city)	41N 2E	153
Asia Minor	39N 33E	157	Barents Sea	69N 40E	112
Asmera, Eritrea (city, nat. cap.)	15N 39E	157	Bartle Frere, Mt. 5,322	18S 145W	158
Astrakhan, Russia (city)	46N 48E	153	Barwon (riv., Australasia)	29S 148E	158
Asuncion, Paraguay (city, nat. cap.)	25S 57W	151	Bass Strait	40S 146E	158
Aswan, Egypt (city)	24N 33E	157	Baton Rouge, Louisiana (city, st. cap., US)	30N 91W	147
Asyuf, Egypt (city)	27N 31E	157	Beaufort Sea	72N 135W	146
Atacama Desert	23S 70W	150	Beijing, China (city, nat. cap.)	40N 116E	113
Athabasca (lake, N.Am.)	60N 109W	146	Beirut, Lebanon (city, nat. cap.)	34N 35E	153
Athabaska (riv., N.Am.)	58N 114W	146	Belarus (country)	52N 27E	153
Athens, Greece (city, nat. cap.)	38N 24E	153	Belem, Para (city, st. cap., Braz.)	1S 48W	151
Atlanta, Georgia (city, st. cap., US)	34N 84W	147	Belfast, Northern Ireland (city)	55N 6W	153
Atlantic Ocean	30N 40W	146	Belgium (country)	51N 4E	153
Atlas Mountains	31N 6W	156	Belgrade, Yugoslavia (city, nat. cap.)	45N 21E	153
Auckland, New Zealand (city)	37S 175E	159	Belhuka, Mt. 14,483	50N 86E	112
Augusta, Maine (city, st. cap., US)	44N 70W	147	Belize (country)	18S 88W	147
Austin, Texas (city, st. cap., US)	30N 98W	147	Belle Isle, Strait of	52N 57W	146
Australia (country)	20S 135W	159	Belmopan, Belize (city, nat. cap.)	18S 89W	147
Austria (country)	47N 14E	153	Belo Horizonte, M.G. (city, st. cap., Braz.)	20S 43W	151
Ayers Rock 2,844	25S 131E	158	Belyando (riv., Australasia)	22S 147W	158
Azerbaijan (country)	38N 48E	153	Ben, Rio (riv., S.Am.)	14S 67W	150
Azov, Sea of	48N 36E	152	Bengal, Bay of	15N 90E	112
Bab el Mandeb (strait)	13N 42E	156	Benguela, Angola (city)	13S 13E	157
Baffin Bay	74N 65W	146	Benin (country)	10N 4E	157
Baffin Island	70N 72W	146	Benin City, Nigeria (city)	6N 6E	157
Baghdad, Iraq (city, nat. cap.)	33N 44E	152	Benue (riv., Africa)	8N 9E	156
Bahamas (island)	25N 75W	146	Bergen, Norway (city)	60N 5E	153
Bahia (st., Brazil)	13S 42W	151	Bering Sea	57N 175W	112

Geographic Index

Name/Description	Latitude & Longitude	Page	Name/Description	Latitude & Longitude	Page
Bering Strait	65N 168W	112	Buenos Aires (st., Argentina)	36S 60W	151
Berlin, Germany (city)	52N 13E	153	Buffalo, NY (city)	43N 79W	147
Bermeo, Rio (riv., S.Am.)	25S 61W	150	Bujumbura, Burundi (city, nat. cap.)	3S 29E	157
Bermuda (island)	30S 66W	147	Bulgaria (country)	44N 26E	153
Bhutan (country)	28N 110E	113	Bur Sudan, Sudan (city)	19N 37E	157
Billings, MT (city)	46N 108W	147	Burdekin (riv., Australasia)	19S 146W	158
Birmingham, AL (city)	34N 87W	147	Burkina Faso (country)	11N 2W	157
Birmingham, UK (city)	52N 2W	153	Buru (island)	4S 127E	158
Biscay, Bay of	45N 5W	152	Burundi (country)	4S 30E	157
Bishkek, Kyrgyzstan (city, nat. cap.)	43N 75E	113	Cairns, Aust. (city)	17S 145E	159
Bismarck Archipelago	4S 147E	158	Cairo, Egypt (city, nat. cap.)	30N 31E	157
Bismarck, North Dakota (city, st. cap., US)	47N 101W	147	Calcutta, (Kolkota) India (city)	23N 88E	113
Bismarck Range	6S 145E	158	Calgary, Canada (city)	51N 114W	147
Bissau, Guinea-Bissau (city, nat. cap.)	12N 16W	157	Calicut, India (city)	11N 76E	113
Black Sea	46N 34E	152	California (st., US)	35N 120W	147
Blanc, Cape	21N 18W	156	California, Gulf of	29N 110W	147
Blue Nile (riv., Africa)	10N 36E	156	Callao, Peru (city)	13S 77W	151
Blue Mountains	33S 150E	158	Cambodia (country)	10N 106E	113
Boa Vista do Rio Branco, Roraima (city, st. cap., Braz.)	3N 61W	151	Cameroon (country)	5N 13E	157
Boise, Idaho (city, st. cap., US)	44N 116W	147	Campeche (st., Mex.)	19N 90W	147
Bolivia (country)	17S 65W	151	Campeche Bay	20N 92W	146
Boma, Congo Republic (city)	5S 13E	157	Campeche, Campeche (city, st. cap., Mex.)	19N 90W	147
Bombay, (Mumbai) India (city)	19N 73E	113	Campo Grande, M.G.S. (city, st. cap., Braz.)	20S 55W	151
Bonn, Germany (city, nat. cap.)	51N 7E	153	Canada (country)	52N 100W	147
Boothia Peninsula	71N 94W	146	Canadian (riv., N.Am.)	30N 100W	146
Borneo (island)	0 11E	113	Canary Islands	29N 18W	156
Bosnia-Herzegovina (country)	45N 18E	153	Canberra, Australia (city, nat. cap.)	35S 149E	159
Bosporus, Strait of	41N 29E	152	Cape Breton Island	46N 60W	146
Boston, Massachusetts (city, st. cap., US)	42N 71W	147	Cape Town, South Africa (city)	34S 18E	157
Botany Bay	35S 153E	159	Caracas, Venezuela (city, nat. cap.)	10N 67W	151
Bothnia, Gulf of	62N 20E	152	Caribbean Sea	18N 75W	151
Botswana (country)	23S 25E	157	Carnarvon, Australia (city)	25S 113E	159
Brahmaputra (riv., Asia)	30N 100E	112	Carpathian Mountains	48N 24E	152
Branco, Rio (riv., S.Am.)	3N 62W	150	Carpentaria, Gulf of	14S 140E	158
Brasilia, Brazil (city, nat. cap.)	16S 48W	151	Carson City, Nevada (city, st. cap., US)	39N 120W	147
Bratislava, Slovakia (city, nat. cap.)	48N 17E	153	Cartagena, Colombia (city)	10N 76W	151
Brazil (country)	10S 52W	151	Cascade Range	45N 120W	146
Brazilian Highlands	18S 45W	150	Casiquiare, Rio (riv., S.Am.)	4N 67W	150
Brazzaville, Congo (city, nat. cap.)	4S 15E	157	Caspian Depression	49N 48E	152
Brisbane, Queensland (city, st. cap., Aust.)	27S 153E	159	Caspian Sea	42N 48E	152
Bristol Bay	58N 159W	146 inset	Catamarca (st., Argentina)	25S 70W	151
British Columbia (prov., Can.)	54N 130W	147	Catamarca, Catamarca (city, st. cap., Argen.)	28S 66W	151
Brooks Range	67N 155W	146	Cauca, Rio (riv., S.Am.)	8N 75W	150
Bruce, Mt. 4,052	22S 117W	158	Caucasus Mountains	42N 40E	152
Brussels, Belgium (city, nat. cap.)	51N 4E	153	Cayenne, French Guiana (city, nat. cap.)	5N 52W	151
Bucharest, Romania (city, nat. cap.)	44N 26E	153	Ceara (st., Brazil)	4S 40W	151
Budapest, Hungary (city, nat. cap.)	47N 19E	153	Celebes (island)	0 120E	112
Buenos Aires, Argentina (city, nat. cap.)	34S 58W	151	Celebes Sea	2N 120E	112

Part VIII *(Continued)*

Geographic Index

Name/Description	Latitude & Longitude	Page	Name/Description	Latitude & Longitude	Page
Central African Republic (country)	5N 20E	157	Columbia (riv., N.Am.)	45N 120W	147
Ceram (island)	3S 129E	159	Columbia, South Carolina (city, st. cap., US)	34N 81W	147
Chaco (st., Argentina)	25S 60W	151	Columbus, Ohio (city, st. cap., US)	40N 83W	147
Chad (country)	15N 20E	157	Comodoro Rivadavia, Argentina (city)	68S 70W	151
Chad, Lake	12N 12E	159	Comoros (country)	12S 44E	157
Changchun, China (city)	44N 125E	151	Conakry, Guinea (city, nat. cap.)	9N 14W	153
Chari (riv., Africa)	11N 16E	157	Concord, New Hampshire (city, st. cap., US)	43N 71W	147
Charleston, SC (city)	33N 80W	157	Congo (country)	3S 15E	157
Charleston, West Virginia (city, st. cap., US)	38N 82W	113	Congo (riv., Africa)	3N 22E	156
Charlotte, NC (city)	35N 81W	156	Congo Basin	4N 22E	156
Charlotte Waters, Aust. (city)	26S 135E	147	Congo, Democratic Republic of (country)	5S 15E	157
Charlottetown, P.E.I. (city, prov. cap., Can.)	46N 63W	147	Connecticut (st., US)	43N 76W	147
Chelyabinsk, Russia (city)	55N 61E	147	Connecticut (riv., N.Am.)	43N 76W	146
Chengdu, China (city)	30N 104E	159	Cook, Mt. 12,316	44S 170E	158
Chesapeake Bay	36N 74W	147	Cook Strait	42S 175E	158
Chetumal, Quintana Roo (city, st. cap., Mex.)	19N 88W	153	Copenhagen, Denmark (city, nat. cap.)	56N 12E	153
Cheyenne, Wyoming (city, st. cap., US)	41N 105W	113	Copiapo, Chile (city)	27S 70W	151
Chiapas (st., Mex.)	17N 92W	146	Copiapo, Mt. 19,947	26S 70W	150
Chicago, IL (city)	42N 87W	147	Coquimbo, Chile (city)	30S 70W	151
Chiclayo, Peru (city)	7S 80W	147	Coral Sea	15S 155E	158
Chidley, Cape	60N 65W	147	Cordilleran Highlands	45N 118W	146
Chihuahua (st., Mex.)	30N 110W	147	Cordoba (st., Argentina)	32S 67W	151
Chihuahua, Chihuahua (city, st. cap., Mex.)	29N 106W	151	Cordoba, Cordoba (city, st. cap., Argen.)	32S 64W	151
Chile (country)	32S 75W	146	Corrientes (st., Argentina)	27S 60W	151
Chiloe (island)	43S 74W	147	Corrientes, Corrientes (city, st. cap., Argen.)	27S 59W	151
Chilpancingo, Guerrero (city, st. cap., Mex.)	19N 99W	147	Corsica (island)	42N 9E	153
Chimborazo, Mt. 20,702	2S 79W	151	Cosmoledo Islands	9S 48E	156
China (country)	38N 105E	112	Costa Rica (country)	15N 84W	147
Chisinau, Moldova (city, nat. cap.)	47N 29E	147	Cote d'Ivoire (country)	7N 86W	157
Chongqing, China (city)	30N 107E	112	Cotopaxi, Mt. 19,347	1S 78W	150
Christchurch, New Zealand (city)	43S 173E	151	Crete (island)	36N 25W	152
Chubut (st., Argentina)	44S 70W	151	Croatia (country)	46N 20W	153
Chubut, Rio (riv., S.Am.)	44S 71W	150	Cuango (riv., Africa)	10S 16E	156
Cincinnati, OH (city)	39N 84W	113	Cuba (country)	22N 78W	147
Cleveland (city)	41N 82W	147	Cuiaba, Mato Grosso (city, st. cap., Braz.)	16S 56W	151
Coahuila (st., Mex.)	30N 105W	147	Cuidad Victoria, Tamaulipas (city, st. cap., Mex.)	24N 99W	147
Coast Mountains (Can.)	55N 130W	146	Culiacan, Sinaloa (city, st. cap., Mex.)	25N 107W	147
Coast Ranges (US)	40N 120W	146	Curitiba, Parana (city, st. cap., Braz.)	26S 49W	151
Coco Island	8N 88W	146	Cusco, Peru (city)	14S 72W	151
Cod, Cape	42N 70W	146	Cyprus (island)	36N 34E	152
Colima (st., Mex.)	18N 104W	147	Czech Republic (country)	50N 16E	153
Colima, Colima (city, st. cap., Mex.)	19N 104W	147	d'Ambre, Cape	12S 50E	157
Colombia (country)	4N 73W	151	Dakar, Senegal (city, nat. cap.)	15N 17W	157
Colombo, Sri Lanka (city, nat. cap.)	7N 80E	113	Dakhla, Western Sahara (city)	24N 16W	157
Colorado (riv., N.Am.)	36N 110W	146	Dallas, TX (city)	33N 97W	147
Colorado (st., US)	38N 104W	147	Dalrymple, Mt. 4,190	22S 148E	158
Colorado, Rio (riv., S.Am.)	38S 70W	150	Daly (riv., Australasia)	14S 132E	158
Colorado (Texas) (riv., N.Am.)	30N 100W	146	Damascus, Syria (city, nat. cap.)	34N 36E	153

Geographic Index

Name/Description	Latitude & Longitude	Page	Name/Description	Latitude & Longitude	Page
Danube (riv., Europe)	44N 24E	152	Edward, Lake	0 30E	156
Dar es Salaam, Tanzania (city, nat. cap.)	7S 39E	157	Egypt (country)	23N 30E	157
Darien, Gulf of	9N 77W	150	El Aaiun, Western Sahara (city)	27N 13W	157
Darling (riv., Australasia)	35S 144E	158	El Djouf	25N 15W	156
Darling Range	33S 116W	158	El Paso, TX (city)	32N 106W	147
Darwin, Northern Terr. (city, st. cap., Aust.)	12S 131E	159	El Salvador (country)	15N 90W	147
Davis Strait	57N 59W	146	Elbe (riv., Europe)	54N 10E	152
Deccan Plateau	20N 80E	112	Elburz Mountains	28N 60E	112
DeGrey (riv., Australasia)	22S 120E	158	Elbruz, Mt. 18,510	43N 42E	112
Delaware (st., US)	38N 75W	147	Elgon, Mt. 14,178	1N 34E	156
Delaware (riv., N.Am.)	38N 77W	146	English Channel	50N 0	152
Delhi, India (city)	30N 78E	157	Entre Rios (st., Argentina)	32S 60W	151
Denmark (country)	55N 10E	153	Equatorial Guinea (country)	3N 10E	157
Denmark Strait	67N 27W	152	Erg Iguidi	26N 6W	156
D'Entrecasteaux Islands	10S 153E	158	Erie (lake, N.Am.)	42N 85W	146
Denver, Colorado (city, st. cap., US)	40N 105W	147	Eritrea (country)	16N 38E	157
Derby, Australia (city)	17S 124E	159	Erzegebirge Mountains	50N 14E	152
Des Moines (riv., N.Am.)	43N 95W	146	Espinhaco Mountains	15S 42W	150
Des Moines, Iowa (city, st. cap., US)	42N 92W	147	Espiritu Santo (island)	15S 168E	159
Desolacion Island	54S 73W	150	Espiritu Santo (st., Brazil)	20S 42W	151
Detroit, MI (city)	42N 83W	147	Essen, Germany (city)	52N 8E	153
Dhaka, Bangladesh (city, nat. cap.)	24N 90E	113	Estonia (country)	60N 26E	153
Dinaric Alps	44N 20E	152	Ethiopia (country)	8N 40E	157
Djibouti (country)	12N 43E	157	Ethiopian Plateau	8N 40E	156
Djibouti, Djibouti (city, nat. cap.)	12N 43E	157	Euphrates (riv., Asia)	28N 50E	112
Dnepr (riv., Europe)	50N 34E	152	Everard, Lake	32S 135E	158
Dnipropetrovsk, Ukraine (city)	48N 35E	153	Everard Ranges	28S 135E	158
Dodoma, Tanzania (city)	6S 36E	157	Everest, Mt. 29,028	28N 84E	112
Dominican Republic (country)	20N 70W	147	Eyre, Lake	29S 136E	158
Don (riv., Europe)	53N 39E	152	Faeroe Islands	62N 11W	152
Donetsk, Ukraine (city)	48N 38E	153	Fairbanks, AK (city)	63N 146W	147
Dover, Delaware (city, st. cap., US)	39N 75W	147	Falkland Islands (Islas Malvinas)	52S 60W	150
Dover, Strait of	52N 0	152	Farewell, Cape (NZ)	40S 170E	158
Drakensberg	30S 30E	156	Fargo, ND (city)	47N 97W	147
Dublin, Ireland (city, nat. cap.)	53N 6W	153	Farquhar, Cape	24S 114E	158
Duluth, MN (city)	47N 92W	147	Fiji (country)	17S 178E	159
Dunedin, New Zealand (city)	46S 171E	159	Finisterre, Cape	44N 10W	152
Durango (st., Mex.)	25N 108W	147	Finland (country)	62N 28E	153
Durango, Durango (city, st. cap., Mex.)	24N 105W	147	Finland, Gulf of	60N 20E	152
Durban, South Africa (city)	30S 31E	157	Firth of Forth	56N 3W	152
Dushanbe, Tajikistan (city, nat. cap.)	39N 69E	113	Fitzroy (riv., Australasia)	17S 125E	158
Dvina (riv., Europe)	64N 42E	152	Flinders Range	31S 139E	158
Dzhugdzhur Khrebet	58N 138E	112	Flores (island)	8S 121E	158
East Cape (NZ)	37S 180E	158	Florianopolis, Sta. Catarina (city, st. cap., Braz.)	27S 48W	151
East China Sea	30N 128E	112	Florida (st., US)	28N 83W	147
Eastern Ghats	15N 80E	112	Florida, Strait of	28N 80W	146
Ecuador (country)	3S 78W	151	Fly (riv., Australasia)	8S 143E	158
Edmonton, Alberta (city, prov. cap., Can.)	54N 114W	147	Formosa (st., Argentina)	23S 60W	151

Geographic Index

Name/Description	Latitude & Longitude	Page	Name/Description	Latitude & Longitude	Page
Formosa, Formosa (city, st. cap., Argen.)	27S 58W	151	Guerrero (st., Mex.)	18N 102W	147
Fort Worth, TX (city)	33N 97W	147	Grampian Mountains	57N 4W	152
Fortaleza, Ceara (city, st. cap., Braz.)	4S 39W	151	Gran Chaco	23S 70N	150
France (country)	46N 4E	153	Grand Erg Occidental	29N 0	156
Frankfort, Kentucky (city, st. cap., US)	38N 85W	147	Grand Teton 13,770	45N 112W	146
Frankfurt, Germany (city)	50N 9E	153	Great Artesian Basin	25S 145E	158
Fraser (riv., N.Am.)	52N 122W	146	Great Australian Bight	33S 130E	158
Fredericton, N.B. (city, prov. cap., Can.)	46N 67W	147	Great Barrier Reef	15S 145E	158
Fremantle, Australia (city)	33S 116E	159	Great Basin	39N 117W	146
Freetown, Sierra Leone (city, nat. cap.)	8N 13W	157	Great Bear Lake (lake, N.Am.)	67N 120W	146
French Guiana (country)	4N 52W	151	Great Dividing Range	20S 145E	158
Fria, Cape	18S 12E	156	Great Indian Desert	25N 72E	112
Fuzhou, China (city)	26N 119E	113	Great Namaland	25S 16E	156
Gabes, Gulf of	33N 12E	156	Great Plains	40N 105W	146
Gabes, Tunisia (city)	34N 10E	157	Great Salt Lake (lake, N.Am.)	40N 113W	146
Gabon (country)	2S 12E	157	Great Sandy Desert	23S 125E	158
Gaborone, Botswana (city, nat. cap.)	25S 25E	157	Great Slave Lake (lake, N.Am.)	62N 110W	146
Gairdiner, Lake	32S 136E	158	Great Victoria Desert	30S 125E	158
Galveston, TX (city)	29N 95W	147	Greater Khingan Range	50N 120E	112
Gambia (country)	13N 15W	157	Greece (country)	39N 21E	153
Gambia (riv., Africa)	13N 15W	156	Greenland (Denmark) (country)	78N 40W	147
Ganges (riv., Asia)	27N 85E	112	Gregory Range	18S 145E	158
Gascoyne (riv., Australasia)	25S 115E	158	Grey Range	26S 145E	158
Gaspé Peninsula	50N 70W	146	Guadalajara, Jalisco (city, st. cap., Mex.)	21N 103W	147
Gdansk, Poland (city)	54N 19E	153	Guadalcanal (island)	9S 160E	159
Geelong, Aust. (city)	38S 144E	159	Guadeloupe (island)	29N 120W	146
Gees Gwardafuy (island)	15N 50E	156	Guanajuato (st., Mex.)	22N 100W	147
Genoa, Gulf of	44N 10E	152	Guanajuato, Guanajuato (city, st. cap., Mex.)	21N 101W	147
Geographe Bay	35S 115E	158	Guangzhou, China (city)	23N 113E	113
Georgetown, Guyana (city, nat. cap.)	8N 58W	151	Guapore, Rio (riv., S.Am.)	15S 63W	150
Georgia (country)	42N 44E	153	Guatemala (country)	14N 90W	147
Georgia (st., US)	30N 82W	147	Guatemala, Guatemala (city, nat. cap.)	15N 91W	147
Germany (country)	50N 12E	153	Guayaquil, Ecuador (city)	2S 80W	151
Ghana (country)	8N 3W	157	Guayaquil, Gulf of	3S 83W	150
Gibraltar, Strait of	37N 6W	152	Guianas Highlands	5N 60W	150
Gibson Desert	24S 124E	158	Guinea (country)	10N 10W	157
Gilbert (riv., Australasia)	8S 142E	158	Guinea, Gulf of	3N 0	156
Giluwe, Mt. 14,330	5S 144E	158	Guinea-Bissau (country)	12N 15W	157
Glasgow, Scotland (city)	56N 6W	153	Guyana (country)	6N 57W	151
Gobi Desert	48N 105E	112	Gydan Range	62N 155E	112
Godavari (riv., Asia)	18N 82E	112	Haiti (country)	18N 72W	147
Godwin-Austen (K2), Mt. 28,250	30N 70E	112	Hakodate, Japan (city)	42N 140E	113
Goiania, Goias (city, st. cap., Braz.)	17S 49W	151	Halifax Bay	18S 146E	158
Goias (st., Brazil)	15S 50W	151	Halifax, Nova Scotia (city, prov. cap., Can.)	45N 64W	147
Gongga Shan 24,790	26N 102E	112	Halmahera (island)	1N 128E	112 inset
Good Hope, Cape of	33S 18E	156	Hamburg, Germany (city)	54N 10E	153
Goteborg, Sweden (city)	58N 12E	153	Hammersley Range	23S 116W	158
Gotland (island)	57N 20E	152	Hann, Mt. 2,800	15S 127E	158

Geographic Index

Name/Description	Latitude & Longitude	Page	Name/Description	Latitude & Longitude	Page
Hanoi, Vietnam (city, nat. cap.)	21N 106E	113	Illimani, Mt. 20,741	16S 67W	150
Hanover Island	52S 74W	150	Illinois (riv., N.Am.)	40N 90W	146
Harare, Zimbabwe (city, nat. cap.)	18S 31E	157	Illinois (st., US)	44N 90W	147
Harbin, China (city)	46N 126E	113	India (country)	23N 80E	113
Harer, Ethiopia (city)	10N 42E	157	Indiana (st., US)	46N 88W	147
Hargeysa, Somalia (city)	9N 44E	157	Indianapolis, Indiana (city, st. cap., US)	40N 86W	147
Harrisburg, Pennsylvania (city, st. cap., US)	40N 77W	147	Indigirka (riv., Asia)	70N 145E	112
Hartford, Connecticut (city, st. cap., US)	42N 73W	147	Indonesia (country)	2S 120E	113
Hatteras, Cape	32N 73W	146	Indus (riv., Asia)	25N 70E	112
Havana, Cuba (city, nat. cap.)	23N 82W	147	Ionian Sea	38N 19E	152
Hawaii (st., US)	21N 156W	146 inset	Iowa (st., US)	43N 95W	147
Hebrides (island)	58N 8W	152	Iquitos, Peru (city)	4S 74W	151
Helena, Montana (city, st. cap., US)	47N 112W	147	Iran (country)	30N 55E	113
Helsinki, Finland (city, nat. cap.)	60N 25E	153	Iraq (country)	30N 50E	113
Herat, Afghanistan (city)	34N 62E	113	Ireland (country)	54N 8W	153
Hermosillo, Sonora (city, st. cap., Mex.)	29N 111W	147	Irish Sea	54N 5W	153
Hidalgo (st., Mex.)	20N 98W	147	Irkutsk, Russia (city)	52N 104E	113
Himalayas	26N 80E	112	Irrawaddy (riv., Asia)	25N 95E	112
Hindu Kush	30N 70E	112	Irtysh (riv., Asia)	50N 70E	112
Ho Chi Minh City, Vietnam (city)	11N 107E	113	Ishim (riv., Asia)	48N 70E	112
Hobart, Tasmania (city, st. cap., Aust.)	43S 147E	159	Isla de los Estados (island)	55S 60W	150
Hokkaido (island)	43N 142E	112	Islamabad, Pakistan (city, nat. cap.)	34N 73E	113
Honduras (country)	16N 87W	147	Isles of Scilly	50N 8W	152
Honduras, Gulf of	15N 88W	146	Israel (country)	31N 36E	153
Honiara, Solomon Islands (city, nat. cap.)	9S 160E	159	Istanbul, Turkey (city)	41N 29E	153
Honolulu, Hawaii (city, st. cap., US)	21N 158W	147 inset	Italy (country)	42N 12E	153
Honshu (island)	38N 140E	112	Jabal Marrah, 10,131	10N 23E	156
Hormuz, Strait of	25N 58E	112	Jackson, Mississippi (city, st. cap., US)	32N 84W	147
Horn, Cape	55S 70W	150	Jacksonville, FL (city)	30N 82W	147
Houston, TX (city)	30N 95W	147	Jakarta, Indonesia (city, nat. cap.)	6S 107E	113 inset
Howe, Cape	37S 150E	158	Jalisco (st., Mex.)	20N 105W	147
Huambo, Angola (city)	13S 16E	157	Jamaica (country)	18N 78W	147
Huang (riv., Asia)	30N 105E	112	James Bay	54N 81W	146
Huascaran, Mt. 22,133	8N 79W	150	Japan (country)	35N 138E	113
Hudson (riv., N.Am.)	42N 76W	147	Japan, Sea of	40N 135E	112
Hudson Bay	60N 90W	146	Japura, Rio (riv., S.Am.)	3S 65W	150
Hudson Strait	63N 70W	146	Java (island)	6N 110E	112 inset
Hue, Vietnam (city)	15N 110E	113	Jaya Peak 16,503	4S 136W	158
Hughes, Aust. (city)	30S 130E	159	Jayapura, New Guinea (Indon.) (city)	3S 141E	113 inset
Hungary (country)	48N 20E	153	Jebel Toubkal 13,665	31N 8W	156
Huron (lake, N.Am.)	45N 85W	146	Jefferson City, Missouri (city, st. cap., US)	39N 92W	147
Hyderabad, India (city)	17N 79E	113	Jerusalem, Israel (city, nat. cap.)	32N 35E	153
Ibadan, Nigeria (city)	7N 4E	157	Joao Pessoa, Paraiba (city, st. cap., Braz.)	7S 35W	151
Iceland (country)	64N 20W	153	Johannesburg, South Africa (city)	26S 27E	157
Idaho (st., US)	43N 113W	147	Jordan (country)	32N 36E	153
Iguassu Falls	25S 55W	150	Juan Fernandez (island)	33S 80W	150

Geographic Index

Name/Description	Latitude & Longitude	Page
Jubba (riv., Africa)	3N 43E	156
Jujuy (st., Argentina)	23S 67W	151
Jujuy, Jujuy (city, st. cap., Argen.)	23S 66W	151
Juneau, Alaska (city, st. cap., US)	58N 134W	147
Jura Mountains	46N 5E	152
Jurua, Rio (riv., S.Am.)	6S 70W	150
Kabul, Afghanistan (city, nat. cap.)	35N 69E	113
Kalahari Desert	25S 20E	156
Kalgourie-Boulder, Australia (city)	31S 121E	159
Kaliningrad, Russia (city)	55N 21E	153
Kamchatka Range	55N 159E	112
Kampala, Uganda (city, nat. cap.)	0 33E	157
Kanchenjunga, Mt. 28,208	30N 83E	112
Kano, Nigeria (city)	12N 9E	157
Kanpur, India (city)	27N 80E	113
Kansas (st., US)	40N 98W	147
Kansas City, MO (city)	39N 95W	147
Kara Sea	69N 65E	112
Karachi, Pakistan (city)	25N 66E	113
Karakorum Range	32N 78E	112
Karakum Desert	42N 52E	152
Kasai (riv., Africa)	5S 18E	156
Kashi, China (city)	39N 76E	113
Katherine, Aust. (city)	14S 132E	159
Kathmandu, Nepal (city, nat. cap.)	28N 85E	113
Katowice, Poland (city)	50N 19E	153
Kattegat, Strait of	57N 11E	152
Kazakhstan (country)	50N 70E	113
Kentucky (st., US)	37N 88W	147
Kenya (country)	0 35E	157
Kenya, Mt. 17, 058	0 37E	156
Khabarovsk, Russia (city)	48N 135E	113
Khambhat, Gulf of	20N 73E	112
Kharkiv, Ukraine (city)	50N 36E	153
Khartoum, Sudan (city, nat. cap.)	16N 33E	157
Kiev, Ukraine (city, nat. cap.)	50N 31E	153
Kigali, Rwanda (city, nat. cap.)	2S 30E	157
Kilimanjaro, Mt. 19,340	4N 35E	156
Kimberly, South Africa (city)	29S 25E	157
King Leopold Ranges	16S 125E	158
Kingston, Jamaica (city, nat. cap.)	18N 77W	147
Kinshasa, Congo Republic (city, nat. cap.)	4S 15E	157
Kirghiz Steppe	40N 65E	112
Kisangani, Congo Republic (city)	1N 25E	157
Kitayushu, Japan (city)	34N 130E	113
Klyuchevskaya, Mt. 15,584	56N 160E	112
Kobe, Japan (city)	34N 135E	113
Kodiak Island	58N 152W	146 inset
Kolyma (riv., Asia)	70N 160E	112
Kommunizma, Mt. 24,590	40N 70E	112
Komsomolsk, Russia (city)	51N 137E	113
Korea, North (country)	40N 128E	113
Korea, South (country)	3S 130W	113
Korea Strait	32N 130W	112
Kosciusko, Mt. 7,310	36S 148E	158
Krasnoyarsk, Russia (city)	56N 93E	113
Krishna (riv., Asia)	15N 76E	112
Kuala Lumpur, Malaysia (city, nat. cap.)	3N 107E	113
Kunlun Shan	36N 90E	112
Kunming, China (city)	25N 103E	113
Kuril Islands	46N 147E	112
Kutch, Gulf of	23N 70E	112
Kuwait (country)	29N 48E	153
Kuwait, Kuwait (city, nat. cap.)	29N 48E	153
Kyoto, Japan (city)	35N 136E	113
Kyrgyzstan (country)	40N 75E	113
Kyushu (island)	30N 130W	112
La Pampa (st., Argentina)	36S 70W	151
La Paz, Baja California Sur (city, st. cap., Mex.)	24N 110W	147
La Paz, Bolivia (city, nat. cap.)	17S 68W	151
La Plata, Argentina (city)	35S 58W	151
Laptev Sea	73N 120E	112
La Rioja (st., Argentina)	30S 70W	151
La Rioja, La Rioja (city, st. cap., Argen.)	29S 67W	151
Labrador Peninsula	52N 60W	151
Lachlan (riv., Australasia)	34S 145E	158
Ladoga, Lake	61N 31E	152
Lagos, Nigeria (city, nat. cap.)	7N 3E	157
Lahore, Pakistan (city)	34N 74E	113
Lake of the Woods	50N 92W	146
Lands End	50N 5W	152
Lansing, Michigan (city, st. cap., US)	43N 85W	147
Lanzhou, China (city)	36N 104E	113
Laos (country)	20N 105E	113
Las Vegas, NV (city)	36N 115W	147
Latvia (country)	56N 24E	153
Laurentian Highlands	48N 72W	146
Lebanon (country)	34N 35E	153
Leeds, UK (city)	54N 2W	153
Le Havre, France (city)	50N 0	153
Lena (riv., Asia)	70N 125E	112
Lesotho (country)	30S 27E	157
Leveque, Cape	16S 123E	158
Leyte (island)	12N 130E	112

Geographic Index

Name/Description	Latitude & Longitude	Page	Name/Description	Latitude & Longitude	Page
Lhasa, Tibet (China) (city)	30N 91E	113	Malabo, Equatorial Guinea (city, nat. cap.)	4N 9E	157
Liberia (country)	6N 10W	157	Malacca, Strait of	3N 100E	113
Libreville, Gabon (city, nat. cap.)	0 9E	157	Malawi (country)	13S 35E	157
Libya (country)	27N 17E	157	Malaysia (country)	3N 110E	113
Libyan Desert	27N 25E	156	Malekula (island)	16S 166E	158
Lille, France (city)	51N 3E	153	Mali (country)	17N 5W	157
Lilongwe, Malawi (city, nat. cap.)	14S 33E	157	Malpelo Island	8N 84W	146
Lima, Peru (city, nat. cap.)	12S 77W	151	Malta (island)	36N 16E	152
Limpopo (riv., Africa)	22S 30E	156	Mamore, Rio (riv., S.Am.)	15S 65W	150
Lincoln, Nebraska (city, st. cap., US)	41N 97W	147	Managua, Nicaragua (city, nat. cap.)	12N 86W	147
Lisbon, Portugal (city, nat. cap.)	39N 9W	153	Manaus, Amazonas (city, st. cap., Braz.)	3S 60W	151
Lithuania (country)	56N 24E	153	Manchester, UK (city)	53N 2W	153
Little Rock, Arkansas (city, st. cap., US)	35N 92W	147	Mandalay, Myanmar (city)	22N 96E	113
Liverpool, UK (city)	53N 3W	153	Manila, Philippines (city, nat. cap.)	115N 121E	113
Ljubljana, Slovenia (city, nat. cap.)	46N 14E	153	Manitoba (prov., Can.)	52N 93W	147
Llanos	33N 103W	150	Mannar, Gulf of	9N 79E	112
Logan, Mt. 18,551	62N 139W	146	Maoke Mountains	5S 138E	158
Logone (riv., Africa)	10N 14E	156	Maputo, Mozambique (city, nat. cap.)	26S 33E	157
Lome, Togo (city, nat. cap.)	6N 1E	157	Maracaibo, Lake	10N 72W	151
London, United Kingdom (city, nat. cap.)	51N 0	153	Maracaibo, Venezuela (city)	11N 72W	151
Londonderry, Cape	14S 125E	158	Maracapa, Amapa (city, st. cap., Braz.)	0 51W	151
Lopez, Cape	1S 8E	156	Maranhao (st., Brazil)	4S 45W	151
Los Angeles, CA (city)	34N 118W	147	Maranon, Rio (riv., S.Am.)	5S 75W	150
Los Chonos Archipelago	45S 74W	150	Marseille, France (city)	43N 5E	153
Louisiana (st., US)	30N 90W	147	Maryland (st., US)	37N 76W	147
Lower Hutt, New Zealand (city)	45S 175E	159	Masai Steppe	5S 35E	156
Luanda, Angola (city, nat. cap.)	9S 13E	157	Maseru, Lesotho (city, nat. cap.)	29S 27E	157
Lubumbashi, Congo Republic (city)	12S 28E	157	Mashad, Iran (city)	36N 59E	113
Lusaka, Zambia (city, nat. cap.)	15S 28E	157	Massachusetts (st., US)	42N 70W	147
Luxembourg (country)	50N 6E	153	Massif Central	45N 3E	152
Luxembourg, Luxembourg (city, nat. cap.)	50N 6E	153	Mato Grosso	16S 52W	150
Luzon (island)	17N 121E	112	Mato Grosso (st., Brazil)	15S 55W	151
Luzon Strait	20N 121E	112	Mato Grosso do Sul (st., Brazil)	20S 55W	151
Lyon, France (city)	46N 5E	153	Mauritania (country)	20N 10W	157
Lyon, Gulf of	42N 4E	152	Mbandaka, Congo Republic (city)	0 18E	157
Maccio, Alagoas (city, st. cap., Braz.)	10S 36W	151	McKinley, Mt. 20,320	62N 150W	146 inset
Macdonnell Ranges	23S 135E	158	Medellin, Colombia (city)	6N 76W	151
Macedonia (country)	41N 21E	153	Mediterranean Sea	36N 16E	152
Mackenzie (riv., N.Am.)	68N 130W	146	Mekong (riv., Asia)	15N 108E	112
Macquarie (riv., Australasia)	33S 146E	158	Melbourne, Victoria (city, st. cap., Aust.)	38S 145E	159
Madagascar (country)	20S 46E	157	Melville, Cape	15S 145E	158
Madeira, Rio (riv., S.Am.)	5S 60W	150	Memphis, TN (city)	35N 90W	147
Madison, Wisconsin (city, st. cap., US)	43N 89W	147	Mendoza (st., Argentina)	35S 70W	151
Madras, (Chennai) India (city)	13N 80E	113	Mendoza, Mendoza (city, st. cap., Argen.)	33S 69W	151
Madrid, Spain (city, nat. cap.)	40N 4W	153	Merida, Yucatan (city, st. cap. Mex.)	21N 90W	147
Magdalena, Rio (riv., S.Am.)	8N 74W	150	Merauke, New Guinea (Indon.) (city)	9S 140E	159
Magellan, Strait of	54S 68W	150	Mexicali, Baja California (city, st. cap., Mex.)	32N 115W	147
Maine (st., US)	46N 70W	147	Mexico (country)	30N 110W	147

Geographic Index

Name/Description	Latitude & Longitude	Page	Name/Description	Latitude & Longitude	Page
Mexico (st., Mex.)	18N 100W	147	Musgrave Ranges	28S 135E	158
Mexico City, Mexico (city, nat. cap.)	19N 99W	147	Myanmar (Burma) (country)	20N 95E	113
Mexico, Gulf of	26N 90W	146	Nairobi, Kenya (city, nat. cap.)	1S 37E	157
Miami, FL (city)	26N 80W	147	Namibe, Angola (city)	16S 13E	157
Michigan (st., US)	45N 82W	147	Namibia (country)	20S 16E	157
Michigan (lake, N.Am.)	45N 90W	146	Namoi (riv., Australasia)	31S 150E	158
Michoacan (st., Mex.)	17N 107W	147	Nan Ling Mountains	25N 110E	112
Milan, Italy (city)	45N 9E	153	Nanda Devi, Mt. 25,645	30N 80E	112
Milwaukee, WI (city)	43N 88W	147	Nanjing, China (city)	32N 119E	113
Minas Gerais (st., Brazil)	17S 45W	151	Nansei Shoto (island)	27N 125E	112
Mindoro (island)	13N 120E	113	Naples, Italy (city)	41N 14E	153
Minneapolis, MN (city)	45N 93W	147	Nashville, Tennessee (city, st. cap., US)	36N 87W	147
Minnesota (st., US)	45N 90W	147	Nasser, Lake	22N 32E	156
Minsk, Belarus (city, nat. cap.)	54N 28E	153	Natal, Rio Grande do Norte (city, st. cap., Braz.)	6S 5W	151
Misiones (st., Argentina)	25S 55W	151	Naturaliste, Cape	35S 115E	158
Mississippi (riv., N.Am.)	28N 90W	146	Nayarit (st., Mex.)	22N 106W	147
Mississippi (st., US)	30N 90W	147	N'Djamena, Chad (city, nat. cap.)	12N 15E	157
Missouri (riv., N.Am.)	41N 96W	146	Nebraska (st., US)	42N 100W	147
Missouri (st., US)	35N 92W	147	Negro, Rio (Argentina) (riv., S.Am.)	40S 70W	150
Misti, Mt. 19,101	15S 73W	150	Negro, Rio (Brazil) (riv., S.Am.)	0 65W	150
Mitchell (riv., Australasia)	16S 143E	158	Negros (island)	10N 125E	112
Mobile, AL (city)	31N 88W	147	Nelson (riv., N.Am.)	56N 90W	146
Mocambique, Mozambique (city)	15S 40E	157	Nepal (country)	29N 85E	113
Mogadishu, Somalia (city, nat. cap.)	2N 45E	157	Netherlands (country)	54N 6E	153
Moldova (country)	49N 28E	153	Neuquen (st., Argentina)	38S 68W	151
Mombasa, Kenya (city)	4S 40E	157	Neuquen, Neuquen (city, st. cap., Argen.)	39S 68W	151
Monaco, Monaco (city)	44N 8E	153	Nevada (st., US)	37N 117W	147
Mongolia (country)	45N 100E	113	New Britain (island)	5S 152E	158
Monrovia, Liberia (city, nat. cap.)	6N 11W	157	New Brunswick (prov., Can.)	47N 67W	147
Montana (st., US)	50N 110W	147	New Caledonia (island)	21S 165E	158
Monterrey, Nuevo Leon (city, st. cap., Mex.)	26N 100W	147	New Delhi, India (city, nat. cap.)	29N 77E	113
Montevideo, Uruguay (city, nat. cap.)	35S 56W	151	New Georgia (island)	8S 157E	158
Montgomery, Alabama (city, st. cap., US)	32N 86W	147	New Guinea (island)	5S 142E	158
Montpelier, Vermont (city, st. cap., US)	44N 73W	147	New Hampshire (st., US)	45N 70W	147
Montreal, Canada (city)	45N 74W	147	New Hanover (island)	3S 153E	158
Morelin, Michoacan (city, st. cap., Mex.)	20N 100W	147	New Hebrides (island)	15S 165E	158
Morocco (country)	34N 10W	157	New Ireland (island)	4S 154E	158
Moroni, Comoros (city, nat. cap.)	12S 42E	157	New Jersey (st., US)	40N 75W	147
Moscow, Russia (city, nat. cap.)	56N 38E	153	New Mexico (st., US)	30N 108W	147
Mountain Nile (riv., Africa)	5N 30E	156	New Orleans, LA (city)	30N 90W	147
Mozambique (country)	19N 35E	157	New Siberian Islands	74N 140E	112
Mozambique Channel	19N 42E	156	New South Wales (st., Aust.)	35S 145E	159
Munich, Germany (city)	48N 12E	153	New York (city)	41N 74W	147
Murchison (riv., Australasia)	26S 115E	158	New York (st., US)	45N 75W	147
Murmansk, Russia (city)	69N 33E	153	New Zealand (country)	40S 170E	159
Murray (riv., Australasia)	36S 143E	158	Newcastle, Aust. (city)	33S 152E	159
Murrumbidgee (riv., Australasia)	35S 146E	158	Newcastle, UK (city)	55N 2W	153
Muscat, Oman (city, nat. cap.)	23N 58E	113	Newfoundland (prov., Can.)	53N 60W	147

Geographic Index

Name/Description	Latitude & Longitude	Page	Name/Description	Latitude & Longitude	Page
Nicaragua (country)	10N 90W	147	Omsk, Russia (city)	55N 73E	113
Niamey, Niger (city, nat. cap.)	14N 2E	157	Onega, Lake	62N 35E	152
Nicobar Islands	5N 93E	112	Ontario (lake, N.Am.)	45N 77W	146
Niger (country)	10N 8E	157	Ontario (prov., Can.)	50N 90W	147
Niger (riv., Africa)	12N 0	156	Oodnadatta, Aust. (city)	28S 135E	159
Nigeria (country)	8N 5E	157	Oran, Algeria (city)	36N 1W	157
Nile (riv., Africa)	25N 31E	156	Oregon (st., US)	46N 120W	147
Nipigon (lake, N.Am.)	50N 87W	146	Orinoco, Rio (riv., S.Am.)	8N 65W	150
Nizhny-Novgorod, Russia (city)	56N 44E	153	Orizaba Peak 18,406	19N 97W	146
Norfolk, VA (city)	37N 76W	147	Orkney Islands	60N 0	152
North Cape (NZ)	36N 174W	158	Osaka, Japan (city)	35N 135E	113
North Carolina (st., US)	30N 78W	147	Oslo, Norway (city, nat. cap.)	60N 11W	153
North Channel	56N 5W	152	Ossa, Mt. 5,305 (Tasm.)	43S 145E	158
North Dakota (st., US)	49N 100W	147	Ottawa, Canada (city, nat. cap.)	45N 76W	147
North Island (NZ)	37S 175W	158	Otway, Cape	40S 142W	158
North Saskatchewan (riv., N.Am.)	55N 110W	146	Ougadougou, Burkina Faso (city, nat. cap.)	12N 2W	157
North Sea	56N 3E	152	Owen Stanley Range	9S 148E	158
North West Cape	22S 115W	158	Pachuca, Hidalgo (city, st. cap., Mex.)	20N 99W	147
Northern Territory (st., Aust.)	20S 134W	158	Pacific Ocean	20N 115W	146
Northwest Territories (prov., Can.)	65N 125W	147	Pakistan (country)	25N 72E	113
Norway (country)	62N 8E	153	Palawan (island)	10N 119E	112
Nouakchott, Mauritania (city, nat. cap.)	18N 16W	157	Palmas, Cape	8N 8W	156
Noumea, New Caledonia (city)	22S 167E	159	Palmas, Tocantins (city, st. cap., Braz.)	10S 49W	151
Nova Scotia (prov., Can.)	46N 67W	147	Pamirs	32N 70E	112
Novaya Zemlya (island)	72N 55E	112	Pampas	36S 73W	150
Novosibirsk, Russia (city)	55N 83E	113	Panama (country)	10N 80W	150
Nubian Desert	20N 30E	156	Panama, Gulf of	10N 80W	147
Nuevo Leon (st., Mex.)	25N 100W	147	Panama, Panama (city, nat. cap.)	9N 80W	147
Nullarbor Plain	34S 125W	158	Papua, Gulf of	8S 144E	158
Nyasa, Lake	10S 35E	156	Papua New Guinea (country)	6S 144E	158
Oakland, CA (city)	38N 122W	147	Para (st., Brazil)	4S 54W	151
Oaxaca (st., Mex.)	17N 97W	147	Paraguay (country)	23S 60W	151
Oaxaca, Oaxaca (city, st. cap., Mex.)	17N 97W	147	Paraguay, Rio (riv., S.Am.)	17S 60W	150
Ob (riv., Asia)	60N 78E	112	Paraiba (st., Brazil)	6S 35W	151
Ohio (riv., N.Am.)	38N 85W	146	Paramaribo, Suriname (city, nat. cap.)	5N 55W	151
Ohio (st., US)	42N 85W	147	Parana (st., Brazil)	25S 55W	151
Okavongo (riv., Africa)	18S 18E	156	Parana, Entre Rios (city, st. cap., Argen.)	32S 60W	151
Okavango Swamp	21S 23E	156	Parana, Rio (riv., S.Am.)	20S 50W	150
Okeechobee (lake, N.Am.)	28N 82W	146	Paris, France (city, nat. cap.)	49N 2E	153
Okhotsk, Russia (city)	59N 140E	113	Pasadas, Misiones (city, st. cap., Argen.)	27S 56W	151
Okhotsk, Sea of	57N 150E	112	Patagonia	43S 70W	150
Oklahoma (st., US)	36N 95W	147	Paulo Afonso Falls	10S 40W	150
Oklahoma City, Oklahoma (city, st. cap., US)	35N 98W	147	Peace (riv., N.Am.)	55N 120W	146
Oland (island)	57N 17E	152	Pennsylvania (st., US)	43N 80W	147
Olympia, Washington (city, st. cap., US)	47N 123W	150	Pernambuco (st., Brazil)	7S 36W	151
Omaha, NE (city)	41N 96W	147	Persian Gulf	28N 50E	112
Oman (country)	20N 55E	113	Perth, W. Australia (city, st. cap., Aust.)	32S 116E	159
Oman, Gulf of	23N 55E	112	Peru (country)	10S 75W	151
Omdurman, Sudan (city)	16N 32E	157	Peshawar, Pakistan (city)	34N 72E	113

Geographic Index

Name/Description	Latitude & Longitude	Page	Name/Description	Latitude & Longitude	Page
Philadelphia, PA (city)	40N 75W	147	Pyrenees Mountains	43N 2E	152
Philippine Sea	15N 125E	112	Qingdao, China (city)	36N 120E	113
Philippines (country)	15N 120E	113	Quebec (prov., Can.)	52N 70W	147
Phnom Penh, Cambodia (city, nat. cap.)	12N 105E	113	Quebec, Quebec (city, prov. cap., Can.)	47N 71W	147
Phoenix, Arizona (city, st. cap., US)	33N 112W	147	Queen Charlotte Islands	50N 130W	146
Phou Bia 9,249	24N 102E	112	Queen Elizabeth Islands	75N 110W	146
Piaui (st., Brazil)	7S 44W	151	Queensland (st., Aust.)	24S 145E	159
Piaui Range	10S 45W	150	Queretaro (st., Mex.)	22N 96W	147
Pic Touside 10,712	20N 12E	156	Queretaro, Queretaro (city, st. cap., Mex.)	21N 100W	147
Pierre, South Dakota (city, st. cap., US)	44N 100W	147	Quintana Roo (st., Mex.)	18N 88W	147
Pietermaritzburg, South Africa (city)	30S 30E	157	Quito, Ecuador (city, nat. cap.)	0 79W	151
Pike's Peak 14,110	36N 110W	146	Rabat, Morocco (city, nat. cap.)	34N 7W	157
Pilcomayo, Rio (riv., S.Am.)	23S 60W	150	Race, Cape	46N 52W	146
Pittsburgh, PA (city)	40N 80W	147	Rainier, Mt. 14,410	48N 120W	146
Plateau of Iran	26N 60E	112	Raleigh, North Carolina (city, st. cap., US)	36N 79W	147
Plateau of Tibet	26N 85E	112	Rangoon, Myanmar (Burma) (city, nat. cap.)	17N 96E	113
Platte (riv., N.Am.)	41N 105W	146	Rapid City, SD (city)	44N 103W	147
Po (riv., Europe)	45N 12E	152	Rawalpindi, India (city)	34N 73E	113
Point Barrow	70N 156W	146 inset	Rawson, Chubuy (city, st. cap., Argen.)	43S 65W	151
Poland (country)	54N 20E	153	Recife, Pernambuco (city, st. cap., Braz.)	8S 35W	151
Poopo, Lake	16S 67W	150	Red (of the North) (riv., N.Am.)	50N 98W	151
Popocatepetl 17,887	17N 100W	146	Red (riv., N.Am.)	42N 96W	151
Port Elizabeth, South Africa (city)	34S 26E	157	Red Sea	20N 35E	156
Port Lincoln, Aust. (city)	35S 135E	159	Regina, Canada (city)	51N 104W	147
Port Moresby, Papua N. G. (city, nat. cap.)	10S 147E	159	Reindeer (lake, N.Am.)	57N 100W	146
Port Vila, Vanuatu (city, nat. cap.)	17S 169E	159	Repulse Bay	22S 147E	158
Port-au-Prince, Haiti (city, nat. cap.)	19N 72W	147	Resistencia, Chaco (city, st. cap., Argen.)	27S 59W	151
Portland, OR (city)	46N 123W	147	Revillagigedo Island	18N 110W	146
Porto Alegre, R. Gr. do Sul (city, st. cap., Braz.)	30S 51W	151	Reykjavik, Iceland (city, nat. cap.)	64N 22W	153
Porto Novo, Benin (city, nat. cap.)	7N 3E	157	Rhine (riv., Europe)	50N 10E	152
Porto Velho, Rondonia (city, st. cap., Braz.)	9S 64W	151	Rhode Island (st., US)	42N 70W	147
Portugal (country)	38N 8W	153	Rhone (riv., Europe)	42N 8E	152
Potomac (riv., N.Am.)	35N 75W	146	Richmond, Virginia (city, st. cap., US)	38N 77W	147
Potosi, Bolivia (city)	20S 66W	151	Riga, Gulf of	58N 24E	152
Prague, Czech Republic (city, nat. cap.)	50N 14E	153	Riga, Latvia (city, nat. cap.)	57N 24E	153
Pretoria, South Africa (city, nat. cap.)	26S 28E	157	Rio Branco, Acre (city, st. cap., Braz.)	10S 68W	151
Pribilof Islands	56N 170W	146 inset	Rio de Janeiro (st., Brazil)	22S 45W	151
Prince Edward Island (prov., Can.)	50N 67W	147	Rio de Janeiro, R. de Jan. (city, st. cap., Braz.)	23S 43W	151
Pripyat Marshes	54N 24E	152	Rio de la Plata	35S 55W	150
Providence, Rhode Island (city, st. cap., US)	42N 71W	147	Rio Gallegos, Santa Cruz (city, st. cap., Argen.)	52S 68W	151
Puebla (st., Mex.)	18N 96W	147	Rio Grande (riv., N.Am.)	30N 100W	146
Puebla, Puebla (city, st. cap., Mex.)	19N 98W	147	Rio Grande do Norte (st., Brazil)	5S 35W	151
Puerto Monte, Chile (city)	42S 74W	151	Rio Grande do Sul (st., Brazil)	30S 55W	151
Purus, Rio (riv., S.Am.)	5S 68W	150	Rio Negro (st., Argentina)	40S 70W	151
Putumayo, Rio (riv., S.Am.)	3S 74W	150	Riyadh, Saudi Arabia (city, nat. cap.)	25N 47E	153
Pyongyang, Korea, North (city, nat. cap.)	39N 126E	113	Roanoke (riv., N.Am.)	34N 75W	146

Part VIII *(Continued)*

Geographic Index

Name/Description	Latitude & Longitude	Page	Name/Description	Latitude & Longitude	Page
Roberts, Mt. 4,495	28S 154E	158	San Jose, Costa Rica (city, nat. cap.)	10N 84W	147
Rockhampton, Aust. (city)	23S 150E	159	San Juan (st., Argentina)	30S 70W	151
Rocky Mountains	50N 108W	146	San Juan, San Juan (city, st. cap., Argen.)	18N 66W	147
Roebuck Bay	18S 125E	158	San Lucas, Cape	23N 110W	146
Romania (country)	46N 24E	153	San Luis Potosi (st., Mex.)	22N 101W	147
Rome, Italy (city, nat. cap.)	42N 13E	153	San Luis Potosi, S. Luis P. (city, st. cap., Mex.)	22N 101W	147
Rondonia (st., Brazil)	12S 65W	151	San Matias, Gulf of	43S 65W	150
Roosevelt, Rio (riv., S.Am.)	10S 60W	150	San Salvador, El Salvador (city, nat. cap.)	14N 89W	147
Roper (riv., Australasia)	15S 135W	158	Sanaa, Yemen (city)	16N 44E	157
Roraima (st., Brazil)	2N 62W	151	Santa Catarina (st., Brazil)	28S 50W	151
Ros Dashen Terrara 15,158	12N 40E	156	Santa Cruz (st., Argentina)	50S 70W	151
Rosario, Santa Fe (city, st. cap., Argen.)	33S 61W	151	Santa Cruz Islands	8S 168E	158
Rostov, Russia (city)	47N 40E	153	Santa Fe (st., Argentina)	30S 62W	151
Rotterdam, Netherlands (city)	52N 4E	153	Santa Fe de Bogota, Colombia (city, nat. cap.)	5N 74W	151
Ruapehu, Mt. 9,177	39S 176W	158	Santa Fe, New Mexico (city, st. cap., US)	35N 106W	147
Rub al Khali	20N 50E	112	Santa Rosa, La Pampa (city, st. cap., Argen.)	37S 64W	151
Rudolph, Lake	3N 34E	156	Santiago, Chile (city, nat. cap.)	33S 71W	151
Russia (country)	58N 56E	153	Santiago del Estero (st., Argentina)	25S 65W	151
Ruvuma (riv., Africa)	12S 38E	156	Santiago, Sant. del Estero (city, st. cap., Argen.)	28S 64W	151
Ruwenzori Mountains	0 30E	156	Santo Domingo, Dominican Rep. (city, nat. cap.)	18N 70W	147
Rwanda (country)	3S 30E	157	Santos, Brazil (city)	24S 46W	151
Rybinsk, Lake	58N 38E	152	Sao Luis, Maranhao (city, st. cap., Braz.)	3S 43W	151
S. Saskatchewan (riv., N.Am.)	50N 110W	146	Sao Paulo (st., Brazil)	22S 50W	151
Sable, Cape	45N 70W	146	Sao Paulo, Sao Paulo (city, st. cap., Braz.)	24S 47W	151
Sacramento (riv., N.Am.)	40N 122W	146	Sarajevo, Bosnia-Herz. (city, nat. cap.)	43N 18E	153
Sacramento, California (city, st. cap., US)	39 121W	147	Sardinia (island)	40N 10E	152
Sahara	18N 10E	156	Sarmiento, Mt. 8,100	55S 72W	150
Sakhalin Island	50N 143E	112	Saskatchewan (riv., N.Am.)	52N 108W	146
Salado, Rio (riv., S.Am.)	35S 70W	150	Saudi Arabia (country)	25N 50E	113
Salem, Oregon (city, st. cap., US)	45N 123W	147	Savannah (riv., N.Am.)	33N 82W	146
Salt Lake City, Utah (city, st. cap., US)	41N 112W	147	Savannah, GA (city)	32N 81W	147
Salta (st., Argentina)	25S 70W	151	Sayan Range	45N 90E	112
Salta, Salta (city, st. cap., Argen.)	25S 65W	151	Seattle, WA (city)	48N 122W	147
Saltillo, Coahuila (city, st. cap., Mex.)	26N 101W	147	Seine (riv., Europe)	49N 3E	152
Salvador, Bahia (city, st. cap., Braz.)	13S 38W	151	Senegal (country)	15N 15W	157
Salween (riv., Asia)	18N 98E	112	Senegal (riv., Africa)	15N 15W	156
Samar (island)	12N 124E	112	Seoul, Korea, South (city, nat. cap.)	38N 127E	113
Samara, Russia (city)	53N 50E	153	Sepik (riv., Australasia)	4S 142E	158
Samarkand, Uzbekistan (city)	40N 67E	153	Sergipe (st., Brazil)	12S 36W	151
San Antonio, TX (city)	29N 98W	147	Sev Dvina (riv., Asia)	60N 50E	112
San Cristobal (island)	12S 162E	158	Severnaya Zemlya (island)	80N 88E	112
San Diego, CA (city)	33N 117W	147	Shanghai, China (city)	31N 121E	113
San Francisco, CA (city)	38N 122W	147	Shasta, Mt. 14,162	42N 120W	146
San Francisco, Rio (riv., S.Am.)	10S 40W	150	Shenyang, China (city)	42N 123E	113
San Joaquin (riv., N.Am.)	37N 121W	146	Shetland Islands	60N 5W	152
San Jorge, Gulf of	45S 68W	150	Shikoku (island)	34N 130E	112

Geographic Index

Name/Description	Latitude & Longitude	Page	Name/Description	Latitude & Longitude	Page
Shiraz, Iran (city)	30N 52E	113	St. Marie, Cape	25S 45E	157
Sicily (island)	38N 14E	153	St. Paul, Minnesota (city, st. cap., US)	45N 93W	147
Sierra Leone (country)	6N 14W	157	St. Petersburg, Russia (city)	60N 30E	153
Sierra Madre Occidental	27N 108W	146	St. Vincente, Cape of	37N 10W	152
Sierra Madre Oriental	27N 100W	146	Stanovoy Range	55N 125E	112
Sierra Nevada	38N 120W	146	Stavanger, Norway (city)	59N 6E	153
Sikhote Alin	45N 135E	112	Steep Point	25S 115E	158
Simpson Desert	25S 136E	158	Stockholm, Sweden (city, nat. cap.)	59N 18E	153
Sinai Peninsula	28N 33E	156	Stuart Range	32S 135E	158
Sinaloa (st., Mex.)	25N 110W	147	Stuttgart, Germany (city)	49N 9E	153
Singapore (city, nat. cap.)	1N 104E	113	Sucre, Bolivia (city)	19S 65W	151
Sitka Island	57N 125W	146	Sudan (country)	10N 30E	157
Skagerrak, Strait of	58N 8E	152	Sulaiman Range	28N 70E	112
Skopje, Macedonia (city, nat. cap.)	42N 21E	153	Sulu Islands	8N 120E	113
Slovakia (country)	50N 20E	153	Sulu Sea	10N 120E	113
Slovenia (country)	47N 14E	153	Sumatra (island)	0 100E	112 inset
Snake (riv., N.Am.)	45N 110W	146	Sumba (island)	10S 120E	158
Snowy Mountains	37S 148E	158	Sumbawa (island)	8S 116E	158
Sofia, Bulgaria (city, nat. cap.)	43N 23E	150	Sunda Islands	12S 118E	158
Solimoes, Rio (riv., S.Am.)	3S 65W	150	Superior (lake, N.Am.)	50N 90W	146
Solomon Islands (country)	7S 160E	158	Surabaya, Java (Indonesia) (city)	7S 113E	113 inset
Somalia (country)	5N 45E	157	Suriname (country)	5N 55W	151
Sonora (st., Mex.)	30N 110W	147	Svalbard Islands	75N 20E	112
South Africa (country)	30S 25E	157	Swan (riv., Australasia)	34S 115E	158
South Australia (st., Aust.)	30S 125E	159	Sweden (country)	62N 16E	153
South Cape, New Guinea	8S 150E	158	Sydney, N.S.Wales (city, st. cap., Aust.)	34S 151E	159
South Carolina (st., US)	33N 79W	147	Syr Darya (riv., Asia)	36N 65E	112
South China Sea	15N 115E	158	Syria (country)	37N 36E	153
South Dakota (st., US)	45N 100W	147	Tabasco (st., Mex.)	16N 90W	147
South Georgia (island)	55S 40W	150	Tabriz, Iran (city)	38N 46E	113
South Island (NZ)	45S 170E	158	Tahat, Mt. 9,541	23N 8E	156
Southampton Island	68N 86W	146	Taipei, Taiwan (city, nat. cap.)	25N 121E	113
Southern Alps (NZ)	45S 170E	158	Taiwan (country)	25N 122E	113
Southwest Cape (NZ)	47S 167E	158	Taiwan Strait	25N 120E	112
Spain (country)	38N 4W	153	Tajikistan (country)	35N 75E	113
Spokane, WA (city)	48N 117W	147	Takla Makan	37N 90E	112
Springfield, Illinois (city, st. cap., US)	40N 90W	147	Tallahassee, Florida (city, st. cap., US)	30N 84W	147
Sri Lanka (country)	8N 80E	113	Tallinn, Estonia (city, nat. cap.)	59N 25E	153
Srinagar, India (city)	34N 75E	113	Tamaulipas (st., Mex.)	25N 95W	147
St. Elias, Mt. 18,008	61N 139W	146	Tampico, Mexico (city)	22N 98W	147
St. George's Channel	53N 5W	152	Tanganyika, Lake	5S 30E	156
St. Helena (island)	16S 5W	157	Tanzania (country)	8S 35E	157
St. John's, Nwfndlnd (city, prov. cap., Can.)	48N 53W	147	Tapajos, Rio (riv., S.Am.)	5S 55W	150
St. Louis, MO (city)	39N 90W	147	Tarim Basin	37N 85E	112
St. Lawrence (island)	65N 170W	146 inset	Tashkent, Uzbekistan (city, nat. cap.)	41N 69E	113
St. Lawrence (riv., N.Am.)	50N 65W	146	Tasman Sea	38S 160E	158
St. Lawrence, Gulf of	50N 65W	146	Tasmania (st., Aust.)	42S 145E	159

Part VIII *(Continued)*

Geographic Index

Name/Description	Latitude & Longitude	Page
Tatar Strait	50N 142E	112
Tbilisi, Georgia (city, nat. cap.)	42N 45E	153
Teguicigalpa, Honduras (city, nat. cap.)	14N 87W	147
Tehran, Iran (city, nat. cap.)	36N 51E	113
Tel Aviv, Israel (city)	32N 35E	153
Tennant Creek, Aust. (city)	19S 134E	159
Tennessee (st., US)	37N 88W	147
Tennessee (riv., N.Am.)	32N 88W	146
Tepic, Nayarit (city, st. cap., Mex.)	22N 105W	147
Teresina, Piaui (city, st. cap., Braz.)	5S 43W	151
Texas (st., US)	30N 95W	147
Thailand (country)	15N 105E	113
Thailand, Gulf of	10N 105E	112
Thames (riv., Europe)	52N 4W	152
The Hague, Netherlands (city, nat. cap.)	52N 4E	153
The Round Mountain 5,300	29S 152E	158
Thimphu, Bhutan (city, nat. cap.)	28N 90E	113
Tianjin, China (city)	39N 117E	113
Tien Shan	40N 80E	112
Tierra del Fuego	54S 68W	150
Tierra del Fuego (st., Argentina)	54S 68W	151
Tigris (riv., Asia)	37N 40E	152
Timor (island)	7S 126E	112
Timor Sea	11S 125E	159
Tirane, Albania (city, nat. cap.)	41N 20E	153
Titicaca, Lake	15S 70W	150
Tlaxcala (st., Mex.)	20N 96W	147
Tlaxcala, Tlaxcala (city, st. cap., Mex.)	19N 98W	147
Toamasino, Madagascar (city)	18S 49E	157
Tocantins (st., Brazil)	12S 50W	151
Tocantins, Rio (riv., S.Am.)	5S 50W	150
Togo (country)	8N 1E	157
Tokyo, Japan (city, nat. cap.)	36N 140E	113
Toliara, Madagascar (city)	23S 44E	157
Tolima, Mt. 17,110	5N 75W	150
Toluca, Mexico (city, st. cap., Mex.)	19N 100W	147
Tombouctou, Mali (city)	24N 3W	157
Tomsk, Russia (city)	56N 85E	113
Tonkin, Gulf of	20N 108E	112
Topeka, Kansas (city, st. cap., US)	39N 96W	147
Toronto, Ontario (city, prov. cap., Can.)	44N 79W	147
Toros Mountains	37N 45E	112
Torrens, Lake	33S 136W	158
Torres Strait	10S 142E	158
Townsville, Aust. (city)	19S 146E	159
Transylvanian Alps	46N 20E	152
Trenton, New Jersey (city, st. cap., US)	40N 75W	147
Tricara Peak 15,584	4S 137E	158

Name/Description	Latitude & Longitude	Page
Trinidad and Tobago (island)	9N 60W	150
Tripoli, Libya (city, nat. cap.)	33N 13E	157
Trujillo, Peru (city)	8S 79W	151
Tucson, AZ (city)	32N 111W	147
Tucuman (st., Argentina)	25S 65W	151
Tucuman, Tucuman (city, st. cap., Argen.)	27S 65W	151
Tunis, Tunisia (city, nat. cap.)	37N 10E	157
Tunisia (country)	34N 9E	157
Turin, Italy (city)	45N 8E	153
Turkey (country)	39N 32E	153
Turkmenistan (country)	39N 56E	153
Turku, Finland (city)	60N 22E	153
Tuxtla Gutierrez, Chiapas (city, st. cap., Mex.)	17N 93W	147
Tyrrhenian Sea	40N 12E	152
Ubangi (riv., Africa)	0 20E	156
Ucayali, Rio (riv., S.Am.)	7S 75W	150
Uele (riv., Africa)	3N 25E	156
Uganda (country)	3N 30E	157
Ujungpandang, Celebes (Indon.) (city)	5S 119E	113 inset
Ukraine (country)	53N 32E	153
Ulan Bator, Mongolia (city, nat. cap.)	47N 107E	113
Uliastay, Mongolia (city)	48N 97E	113
Ungava Peninsula	60N 72W	146
United Arab Emirates (country)	25N 55E	113
United Kingdom (country)	54N 4W	153
United States (country)	40N 100W	147
Uppsala, Sweden (city)	60N 18E	153
Ural (riv., Asia)	45N 55E	112
Ural Mountains	50N 60E	112
Uruguay (country)	37S 67W	151
Uruguay, Rio (riv., S.Am.)	30S 57W	150
Urumqui, China (city)	44N 87E	113
Utah (st., US)	38N 110W	147
Uzbekistan (country)	42N 58E	153
Vaal (riv., Africa)	27S 27E	156
Valdivia, Chile (city)	40S 73W	151
Valencia, Spain (city)	39N 0	153
Valencia, Venezuela (city)	10N 68W	151
Valparaiso, Chile (city)	33S 72W	151
van Diemen, Cape	11S 130E	158
van Rees Mountains	4S 140E	158
Vanuatu (country)	15S 167E	158
Vancouver, Canada (city)	49N 123W	147
Vancouver Island	50N 130W	146
Vanern, Lake	60N 12E	152
Vattern, Lake	56N 12E	152
Venezuela (country)	5N 65W	151
Venezuela, Gulf of	12N 72W	150

Part VIII *(Continued)*

Geographic Index

Name/Description	Latitude & Longitude	Page	Name/Description	Latitude & Longitude	Page
Venice, Italy (city)	45N 12E	153	Windhoek, Namibia (city, nat. cap.)	22S 17E	157
Vera Cruz (st., Mex.)	20N 97W	147	Winnipeg (lake, N.Am.)	50N 100W	146
Vera Cruz, Mexico (city)	19N 96W	147	Winnipeg, Manitoba (city, prov. cap., Can.)	53N 98W	147
Verkhoyanskiy Range	65N 130E	112	Wisconsin (st., US)	50N 90W	147
Vermont (st., US)	45N 73W	147	Wollongong, Aust. (city)	34S 151E	159
Vert, Cape	15N 17W	156	Woodroffe, Mt. 4,724	26S 133W	158
Vestfjord	68N 14E	152	Woomera, Aust. (city)	32S 137E	159
Viangchan, Laos (city, nat. cap.)	18N 103E	113	Wrangell (island)	72N 180E	112
Victoria (riv., Australasia)	15S 130E	158	Wuhan, China (city)	30N 114E	113
Victoria (st., Aust.)	37S 145W	159	Wyndham, Australia (city)	16S 129E	159
Victoria, B.C. (city, prov. cap., Can.)	48N 123W	147	Wyoming (st., US)	45N 110W	147
Victoria, Lake	3S 35E	156	Xalapa, Vera Cruz (city, st. cap., Mex.)	20N 97W	147
Victoria, Mt. 13,238	9S 137E	158	Xingu, Rio (riv., S.Am.)	5S 54W	150
Victoria Riv. Downs, Aust. (city)	17S 131E	159	Yablonovyy Range	50N 100E	112
Viedma, Rio Negro (city, st. cap., Argen.)	41S 63W	151	Yakutsk, Russia (city)	62N 130E	113
Vienna, Austria (city, nat. cap.)	48N 16E	153	Yamoussoukio, Cote d'Ivoire (city)	7N 4W	157
Vietnam (country)	10N 110E	113	Yangtze (Chang Jiang) (riv., Asia)	30N 108W	112
Villahermosa, Tabasco (city, st. cap., Mex.)	18N 93W	147	Yaounde, Cameroon (city, nat. cap.)	4N 12E	157
Vilnius, Lithuania (city, nat. cap.)	55N 25E	153	Yekaterinburg, Russia (city)	57N 61E	153
Virginia (st., US)	35N 78W	147	Yellowknife, N.W.T. (city, prov. cap., Can.)	62N 115W	147
Viscount Melville Sound	72N 110W	146	Yellowstone (riv., N.Am.)	46N 110W	146
Vitoria, Espiritu Santo (city, st. cap., Braz.)	20S 40W	151	Yemen (country)	15N 50E	113
Vladivostok, Russia (city)	43N 132E	113	Yenisey (riv., Asia)	68N 85E	112
Volga (riv., Europe)	46N 46E	152	Yerevan, Armenia (city, nat. cap.)	40N 44E	153
Volgograd, Russia (city)	54N 44E	153	Yokohama, Japan (city)	36N 140E	113
Volta (riv., Africa)	10N 15E	156	York, Cape	75N 65W	146
Volta, Lake	8N 2W	156	Yucatan (st., Mex.)	20N 88W	147
Vosges Mountains	48N 7E	152	Yucatan Channel	22N 88W	146
Wabash (riv., N.Am.)	43N 90W	146	Yucatan Peninsula	20N 88W	146
Walvis Bay, Namibia (city)	23S 14E	157	Yugoslavia (country)	44N 20E	153
Warsaw, Poland (city, nat. cap.)	52N 21E	153	Yukon (riv., N.Am.)	63N 150W	146 inset
Washington (st., US)	48N 122W	147	Zacatecas (st., Mex.)	23N 103W	147
Washington, D.C., United States (city, nat. cap.)	39N 77W	147	Zacatecas, Zacatecas (city, st. cap., Mex.)	23N 103W	147
Wellington Island	48S 74W	150	Zagreb, Croatia (city, nat. cap.)	46N 16E	153
Wellington, New Zealand (city, nat. cap.)	41S 175E	159	Zagros Mountains	27N 52E	112
Weser (riv., Europe)	54N 8E	152	Zambezi (riv., Africa)	18S 30E	156
West Cape Howe	36S 115E	158	Zambia (country)	15S 25E	157
West Indies	18N 75W	146	Zanzibar (island)	5S 39E	156
West Siberian Lowland	60N 80E	112	Zemlya Frantsa Josifa (island)	80N 40E	112
West Virginia (st., US)	38N 80W	147	Ziel, Mt. 4,955	23S 134E	158
Western Australia (st., Aust.)	25S 122W	159	Zimbabwe (country)	20S 30E	157
Western Ghats	15N 72E	112			
Western Sahara (country)	25N 13W	157			
White Nile (riv., Africa)	13N 30E	156			
White Sea	64N 36E	152			
Whitney, Mt. 14,494	33N 118W	146			
Wichita, KS (city)	38N 97W	147			
Wilhelm, Mt. 14,793	4S 145E	158			

Sources

After the storm. (1991, August). *National Geographic,* 180.

Alaska's big spill. (1990, January). *National Geographic,* 177.

Amazonia [map]. (1994). *National Geographic,* 186.

An atmosphere of uncertainty. (1987, April). *National Geographic,* 171.

Bahn, P. G. (1998). *The Cambridge illustrated history of prehistoric art*. New York: Cambridge University Press.

Barraclough, G. (ed.). (1978). *The Times atlas of world history*. London: Times Books.

Beals, K. L., Smith, C. L., Dodd, S. M. (1984). "Brain size, cranial morphology, climate and time machines." *Current Anthropology* 25:301–330.

Bodley, J. (2000). *Cultural anthropology: tribes, states, and the global system* (3rd ed.). Mountain View, CA: Mayfield.

Campbell, J. (1983). *The way of the animal powers* (vol.1). San Francisco, CA: Harper & Row.

Conservation International. (2002). *Global hotspots of diversity*. Washington, DC.

Crabb, C. (1993, January). Soiling the planet. *Discover, 14*(1), 74–75.

DeBlij, H. J., & Muller, P. (1998). *Geography: Realms, regions and concepts* (8th ed., revised). New York: John Wiley & Sons.

Department of Geography, Pennsylvania State University. (1996). Unpublished computer model output. State College, PA: Pennsylvania State University.

Domke, K. (1988). *War and the changing global system.* New Haven, CT: Yale University Press.

Driver, H. E. (1969). *Indians of North America* (2nd ed., rev.). Chicago, IL: University of Chicago Press.

Driver, H. E., and Massey, W. C. (1957) *Comparative studies of North American Indians*. (New Series, vol. 47, part 2). Philadelphia, PA: The American Philosophical Society.

Eastern Europe's dark dawn. (1991, June). *National Geographic,* 179.

Economic consequences of the accident at Chernobyl nuclear plant. (1987). PlanEcon Reports, 3.

Environmental Protection Agency. (1996). Unpublished data [Online]. Available: http:// www.epa.gov.

Eveleth, L. B., and J. M. Tanner. (1990). *World Wide Evolution in Human Growth* (2nd ed.). New York: Cambridge University Press.

Fagan, B. M. (1998). *People of the earth* (9th ed.). New York: Longman.

Fagan, B. (2000). *Ancient North America: the archaeology of a continent*. (3rd ed.). London: Thames & Hudson.

Fagan, Brian M. (1995). *People of the earth: an introduction to world prehistory* (8th ed.). New York: Harper-Collins.

Falk, D. (2000). *Primate diversity*. New York: W.W. Norton.

Fellman, J., Getis, A., & Getis, J. (1995). *Human geography: Landscapes of human activities* (4th ed.). Dubuque, IA: Wm. C. Brown Publishers.

Fleagle, J. G. (1988). *Primate adaptation and evolution*. San Diego, CA: Academic Press.

Fuller, Harold. (Ed.). (1971). *World patterns: The Aldine college atlas.* Chicago: Aldine Publishing Co.

Harris, M. (1980). *Culture, people, nature: an introduction to general anthropology* (3rd ed.). New York: Harper & Row.

Haviland, W. A. (1983). *Cultural anthropology* (4th ed.). New York: Holt, Rinehart & Winston.

Hoebel, E. A. (1966.) *Anthropology: the study of man* (3rd ed.). New York: McGraw-Hill.

Holm, J. (1989). *Pidgins and creoles* (vol. II, Reference Survey). New York: Cambridge University Press.

Hymes, D. (1971). *Pidginization and creolization of languages*. New York: Cambridge University Press.

Johnson, D. (1977). *Population, society, and desertification.* New York: United Nations Conference on Desertification, United Nations Environment Programme.

Jordan-Blychkov, T. G. (1990) *The human mosaic* (5th ed.). New York: W.H. Freeman.

Jurmain, R., Kilgore, L., Trevathan, W., and Nelson. H. (2003). *Introduction to physical anthropology* (9th ed.). Belmont, CA: Wadsworth/Thomson Learning.

Köppen, W., & Geiger, R. (1954). *Klima der erde* [Climate of the earth]. Darmstadt, Germany: Justus Perthes.

Kuchler, A. W. (1949). Natural vegetation. *Annals of the Association of American Geographers,* 39.

Lindeman, M. (1990). *The United States and the Soviet Union: Choices for the 21st century.* Guilford, CT: McGraw-Hill/Dushkin.

Linguasphere (2003). "The Linguasphere table of the world's major languages," The Linguasphere Observatory. Online at www.linguasphere.org.

Mather, J. R. (1974). *Climatology: Fundamentals and applications.* New York: McGraw-Hill.

Miller, G. T. (1992). *Living in the environment* (7th ed.). Belmont, CA: Wadsworth.

Molnar, Stephen. (2002). *Human variation: races, types, ethnic groups* (5th ed.). Upper Saddle River, NJ: Prentice-Hall.

Murdock, G.P. (1949). *Social structure*. New York: The Free Press.

Murphy, R. E. (1968). Landforms of the world [Map supplement No. 91]. *Annals of the Association of American Geographers, 58*(1), 198–200.

National Aeronautics and Space Administration. (1999–2001). Unpublished data and images [Online]. Available: http://www.nasa.gov.

National Geographic Society. (1999). *Atlas of the world,* 7th edition. Washington, DC: National Geographic Society.

National Oceanic and Atmospheric Administration. (2001). Unpublished data [Online]. Available: http:// www.noaa.gov.

The Oglalla Aquifer. (1993, March). *National Geographic,* 183.

Park, M. A. (2002). *Biological anthropology* (3rd ed.). New York: McGraw-Hill.

Peoples, J., and Bailey, G., (1991). *Humanity: an introduction to cultural anthropology* (2nd ed.). St.

Paul, MN: West Publishing.

Phillipson, David W. (1993). *African archaeology* (2nd ed.). Cambridge, UK: Cambridge University Press.

Population Reference Bureau. (2001). *2001 world population data sheet.* New York: Population Reference Bureau.

Rand McNally. (1996). *Goode's world atlas* (19th ed.). Chicago: Rand McNally and Co.

Rand McNally answer atlas. (1996). Chicago: Rand McNally and Co.

Rondonia: Brazil's imperiled rainforest. (1988, December). *National Geographic,* 174.

Ross, P. E., "Trends in linguistics: hard words." *Scientific American*, April 1991.

Rourke, J. T. (2003). *International politics on the world stage* (9th ed). Guilford, CT: McGraw-Hill/Dushkin.

Scarre, C., and Fagan B. M. (1997). *Ancient civilizations.* New York: Longman.

Scarre, C. (ed.) (1997). *Past worlds: HarperCollins atlas of archaeology.* London: Borders Group.

Scupin, R., and Decorse, C. R. (2001). *Anthropology a global perspective* (4th ed.). Upper Saddle River, NJ: Prentice Hall.

Sebastian, L. (1997). *The Chaco Anasazi.* Cambridge, UK: Cambridge University Press.

Shelley, F., & Clarke, A. (1994). *Human and cultural geography: A global perspective,* Dubuque, IA: Wm. C. Brown Publishers.

SIL International, (2003). "Ethnologue: languages of the world." Online at www.ethnologue.com/web.asp.

Smith, Dan. (1997). *The state of war and peace atlas,* (3rd ed.). Penguin Books: New York.

Soiling the planet. (1993, January). *Discover,* 14.

Spector, L. S., & Smith, J. R. (1990). *Nuclear ambitions: The spread of nuclear weapons.* Boulder, CO: Westview Press.

Spencer, R. F., and Johnson, E. (1968). *Atlas for anthropology* (2nd ed.). Dubuque, IA: Wm. C. Brown.

Tanton, J. H. (1995). "End of the migration epoch," reprinted by *The Social Contract*, vol. IV(3) and vol. V(1). Online at www.desip.igc.org/.

This fragile earth [map]. (1988, December). *National Geographic,* 174.

Thornthwaite, C. W., & Mather, J. R. (1955). *The water balance* [Publications in Climatology No. 8]. Centerton, NJ: Drexel Institute of Technology, Laboratory of Climatology.

Times atlas of world history. (1978). Maplewood, NJ: Hammond.

United Nations Food and Agriculture Organization (FAO). (1995). *Forest resources assessment 1990: Global synthesis* [FAO Forestry Paper No. 124]. Rome: FAO.

United Nations Population Fund. (2001). *The state of the world's population.* New York: United Nations Population Fund.

United Nations Population Reference Bureau. (2001). *2001 world population data sheet.* New York: Oxford University Press.

United Nations Population Reference Bureau. (1999). *World development report.* New York: Oxford University Press.

U.S. Census Bureau. (1998). *World population profile.* Washington, DC: U.S. Government Printing Office.

U.S. Central Intelligence Agency. (2001). *World factbook 2001.* Washington, DC: Brassey.

U.S. Central Intelligence Agency. (2001). *World factbook 2001.* Available: http://www.odci.gov/cia/publications/factbook/index.html.

U.S. Central Intelligence Agency. (1999). Unpublished data [Online]. Available: http://www.odci. gov/cia/publications.

U.S. Committee for Refugees. *World refugee survey* (Washington, DC, 2002).

U.S. Department of Energy. (1996). *U.S.-Canada memorandum of intent on transboundary air pollution.* Washington, DC: U.S. Government Printing Office.

U.S. Department of State. (2000). *Statesman's year-book, 2000.* Washington, DC: U.S. Goverment Printing Office.

U.S. Soil Conservation Service [now the U.S. Natural Resources Conservation Service]. (1996). *World soils.* Washington, DC: U.S. Soil Conservation Service.

USDA Forest Service. (1989). *Ecoregions of the continents.* Washington, DC: U.S. Government Printing Office.

Vivian, R. G. (1997). *The Chacoan prehistory of the San Juan basin.* Vol. 264 (4), pp. 139–147. San Diego, CA: The Academic Press.

Waldman, C. (2000). *Atlas of the North American Indian* (rev. ed.). New York: Checkmark Books.

Whitehouse, D., and Whitehouse R. (1971). *Archaeological atlas of the world.* San Francisco, CA: W.H. Freeman.

The world almanac and book of facts 2002 (2003). Mahwah, NJ: World Almanac Books.

The World Bank. (1995). *World development report 1995.* Geneva: World Bank.

The World Bank. (1998). *1998 world development indicators.* (Washington, World Bank).

The World Bank. (2002). *Entering the 21st century: World development report 2000/2001.* New York: Oxford University Press.

World Conservation Monitoring Centre. (1996). Unpublished data. Cambridge, England: World Conservation Monitoring Centre.

World Health Organization. (2000). *World health statistics annual.* Geneva: World Health Organization.

World Resources Institute. *World resources 2000–2001: A guide to the global environment.* New York: Oxford University Press.

Worldwatch Institute. (1987). *Reassessing nuclear power: The fallout from Chernobyl* [Worldwatch paper no. 75]. New York: Worldwatch Institute.

Wright, John W. (Ed.). (2002). *The New York Times 2002 Almanac.* New York: Penguin Reference Books.